He IS Real

Other Books by Millie Stamm

Beside Still Waters: Meditation Moments on the Psalms
Be Still and Know
Meditation Moments

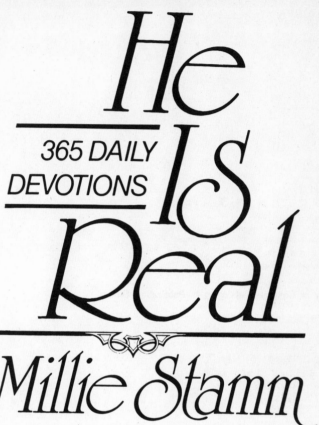

He Is Real

365 DAILY DEVOTIONS

Millie Stamm

ZondervanPublishingHouse

Grand Rapids, Michigan

A Division of HarperCollinsPublishers

HE IS REAL
Copyright © 1991 by Millie Stamm

Requests for information should be addressed to:
Zondervan Publishing House
Grand Rapids, Michigan 49530

Library of Congress Cataloging-in-Publication Data

Stamm, Millie.
　He is real : 365 devotions / Millie Stamm.
　　p.　cm.
　ISBN 0-310-33701-1 (pbk.)
　1. Devotional calendars. I. Title.
BV4811.B79　1991
242'.2—dc20

91–21875
CIP

Edited by Joyce Ellis
Interior design by Kim Koning
Cover design by Art Jacobs

Printed in the United States of America

00　01　02　/DC/　11　10　9　8

*This book is lovingly dedicated
to
the entire
Stonecroft Missionary Family
for their love, dedication, inspiration,
and faithful prayer support.*

FOREWORD

"Come with me by yourselves to a quiet place and get some rest."

This is what Jesus told his disciples who had just returned from a very exciting evangelism experience (Mark 6:31 NIV). Why did He suggest that His followers come away with Him? Because He recognized the stress of life. All of us experience stress in three areas:

(1) the stress of people
(2) the stress of place
(3) the stress of personal inadequacy.

The "stress of people" includes our loving physical family and the family of God. We are often torn apart by all the demands everyone makes upon us (Mark 6:29–30).

The "stress of place" is the sense that nothing will ever happen where we are and that we have not been blessed with all the provisions that others have. We are like the majority members of the fact-finding committee that Moses sent to check out the Promised Land. They came back with the most luscious fruit that they had ever seen, but they had problems with the giants. We, too, have problems with giants.

The "stress of personal inadequacy" is the sudden realization that we can't be all things to all people. Do any of us feel adequate for all situations at all times?

This is the reality of our daily walk. We cannot manage stress on our own. So, in Mark 6:37 when the people are hungry, the Lord turns to His own and says, "You feed them." This is a threat to all of us, and we say, "Lord, how do I do this?"

This daily devotional book can help us manage all three major areas of stress in our lives. We all desperately need that "come apart time" with the Lord (to paraphrase the King James Version) so that we don't come apart physically and emotionally.

Millie Stamm has given us the materials for that "come apart time" so we can manage our stress.

—Millie Dienert
Prayer Chairman
International Ministry
of Billy Graham

PREFACE

Quiet moments! How few of them we seem to have in our hectic, hurried, daily schedules. Sometimes we forget what an awesome privilege is ours to have a personal audience or conversation with the King of Kings!

In her newest book, *He Is Real,* Millie Stamm presents 365 Scripture portions and daily devotional readings that lift our thoughts and hearts into the very presence of God. These devotionals will provide spiritual refreshment and will prepare you to meet the tensions of life that you encounter day by day. Again and again, Mrs. Stamm points us to Scriptures that make God real to us.

Spending time daily with someone you know and love is never a chore but a pleasure. When Jesus Christ is a Living Reality to you, time spent with Him is never wasted. Through the pages of this book, we come to realize in a new way His majesty, His greatness, His love—just who He really is. This is a devotional book you will read again and again, finding new inspiration with each reading.

Millie's easy-to-read style and pertinent illustrations make this book a "must" for your daily appointment with God.

—Helen A. Nichols
Stonecroft Ministries

ACKNOWLEDGMENTS

First of all, I want to thank the Lord for the deepening of the reality of His presence in my life as I have spent time in His Word and in prayer for the writing of this book.

I thank the Lord for the many illustrations, stories, and Scriptures He has given me as I prayed for them for special devotionals.

I thank my family, friends, and the staff of the Stonecroft Ministries, who have faithfully prayed for me.

I appreciate and thank Allayne Spayed and Anne Conrad, who have so graciously typed my manuscript.

I am thankful for the Zondervan Publishing Company, whose editors have been so understanding and encouraging to me. I appreciate their concern that Jesus become real to people as they read this book.

INTRODUCTION

We've probably all heard the comment, "He is for real" or "She is for real." Today people are searching for something genuine and real, right down where they are living. Someone has said, "The trouble with life is that it is so daily."

We have a Guidebook, the Word of God, that tells how we can, in reality, cope with the pressures of today. The life that is real and genuine is wrapped up in the Person of Jesus Christ. In Him we find all we need. In Colossians 3:11 we read, "Christ is all, and in all."

As you use this book this year, my desire is that Jesus become more real to you each day and that you may find in Him fulfillment for each need.

Here are some suggestions to make your daily quiet time more meaningful, to bring the reality of Jesus Christ to your daily walk:

1. Keep a daily journal or notebook to record your learning experiences during the year.
2. Record new biblical truth you have learned.
3. Apply that truth to a specific area of your life right now.
4. Claim a promise that applies to your life.
5. Make a change in some area of your life based on the Scripture you have read.
6. If God spoke to you about something in particular, do something about it.

JANUARY 1

Behold, I will do a new thing; now it shall spring forth; shall ye not know it? I will even make a way in the wilderness, and rivers in the desert (Isa. 43:19).

 new year! A new thing! Suppose God would say, "I will do a new thing for you this year," what would you ask for? Some might ask for a new home, or a new car, a husband, a job. Some would ask for a solution to their problems, healing for their broken hearts, restored family relationships.

Some might even answer, "My life is empty. I have no real purpose for living. I need something to fill the vacuum in my life, something real to give me a reason for living."

A *new thing* brought another dimension into the apostle Paul's life. Those who knew Paul may have assumed that he had it all together. He was proud of his racial heritage, his education, and his religious life. Zealous to please God, he spent much of his time searching for Christians to imprison.

But one day he discovered a reality that changed his life. He had a personal encounter with Jesus Christ. As he committed his life to Him, he discovered that Jesus Christ was "for real."

Paul described the transformation in 2 Corinthians 5:17. "When someone becomes a Christian he becomes a brand new person inside. He is not the same any more. A new life has begun!" (LB).

The indwelling presence of Jesus Christ made his life genuine. "For to me to live is Christ," he said (Phil. 1:21). He had a purpose for living: "Just as you trusted Christ to save you, trust him, too, for each day's problems; live in vital union with him" (Col. 2:6 LB).

God is ready to do a new thing for us this year, but He has to have our cooperation. God says, "I know every day of your next year. I know the joys and storms ahead, and I will lead you safely through them. I know the steep mountains you will have to climb, and I will climb with you. I know the fire necessary to purify your life, and I will regulate the heat Myself."

As we walk with Him through this next year, may we learn in a deeper way the reality of the person of Jesus Christ in each day's living. "Jesus Christ the same yesterday, and today, and for ever" (Heb. 13:8).

Jesus Christ is for real!

And ye shall seek me, and find me, when ye shall search for me with all your heart (Jer. 29:13).

n confusion, the children of Israel wondered what had happened to them. Their land had been invaded. They had been taken captive by Babylon. Had God forgotten them? Did He not care?

God sent them a message through Jeremiah the prophet, "For I know the plans I have for you . . . plans to prosper you and not to harm you, plans to give you hope and a future" (v. 11 NIV). In verse thirteen God continues, "You will seek me and find me." God put them in a situation where they had to seek Him. More than deliverance *from* their captivity they needed to seek Him *in the midst* of it.

Today we feel that we are in captivity, perhaps to loneliness, self-pity, discouragement, disappointment, wrong attitudes, or circumstances beyond our control. We may feel that God has forsaken us.

God says, "Seek Me." Our answer does not come from people, books, tapes, or seminars, although they have a place. He is our answer.

We are to seek Him, and only Him. Paul wrote, "But Christ is all, and in all" (Col. 3:11). We are not to seek people, feelings, or experiences but Him. "For in Christ there is all of God in a human body; so you have everything when you have Christ, and you are filled with God through your union with Christ" (Col. 2:9–10 LB).

But our search for Him must be a wholehearted search—with *all* our heart. Seek nothing less than the Lord Jesus Himself.

In our service for the Lord, it is possible to rush from one project to another and miss Him altogether. While seeking the latest methods, plans, or programs, we can easily become frustrated and exhausted because we aren't seeking Him. God isn't interested in our service. He wants our lives.

Feelings diminish, experiences fade, circumstances overwhelm, but when we seek and find Him, He truly satisfies.

The psalmist wrote, "He [not material things, methods, programs, not even service] satisfieth the longing soul" (Ps. 107:9).

Are you seeking Him? Seeking hearts will find Him and be satisfied.

JANUARY 3

For in Christ there is all of God in a human body; so you have every-thing when you have Christ, and you are filled with God through your union with Christ (Col. 2:9–10 LB).

omeone has said, "What I have to do tomorrow has made a wreck of me today." Many times we rush through today's pressure-packed schedule only to find that tomorrow's is even more hectic. We come to the place where we want to say, "Stop, world. Let me off."

Perhaps we have failed to recognize that Jesus Christ is sufficient for every circumstance we face. Could this explain much of the failure, discouragement, and burnout God's people experience today? Jesus Christ does not *have* the answer. *He is* our answer.

The fullness of God dwells in the Lord Jesus. He is the depository of all God is. "In Christ there is all of God in a human body." The King James translation reads, "For in him dwelleth all the fullness of the Godhead bodily" (v. 9). All the fullness of God has been embodied in Jesus Christ. What God is, Christ is. All that makes God God is in Jesus Christ.

God came to earth in the person of Jesus Christ to reveal Himself to us. The Bible says that "[Christ] is the image of the invisible God, the firstborn of every creature" (Col. 1:15). Wuest's Greek translation reads, "In Him there is continuously and permanently at home all the fullness of the Godhead in bodily form."

And since Christ is all of God in a human body, we are filled with God through our union with Christ! Exclusive of His deity we have the characteristics of Christ Himself. The King James translation reads, "Ye are complete in him" (v. 10).

There is much discussion today concerning personal fulfillment. People are seeking fulfillment in such things as careers, hobbies, and pleasures. Yet we will never find fulfillment in these areas of life. Real fulfillment can only come from Jesus Christ. The Bible says, "you may be filled (through all your being) unto all the fullness of God—[that is] may have the richest measure of the divine Presence, and become a body wholly filled and flooded with God Himself" (Eph. 3:19 AMPLIFIED). What more could we want?

JANUARY 4

You have everything when you have Christ, and you are filled with God through your union with Christ" (Col. 2:10 LB).

onsumed by feelings of inadequacy and low self-esteem, many people spend a great deal of time and money searching for fulfillment.

Our fulfillment is in the person of Jesus Christ. Paul wrote, "Ye are complete in Him" (v. 10). There is nothing to be added. We possess everything in Him.

Being filled with His fullness gives our life potential. It is deposited to our life-account for our use. This potential then becomes our life-power. Paul said, "For to me to live is Christ" (Phil. 1:21).

His completeness now becomes our completeness. We are sufficient in His All-sufficiency. It has been said that all of God is available to those who make themselves available to all there is of God. It is available, but we must appropriate it for our needs.

When I am filled with the fullness of Christ, I am filled with the fullness of His love. This gives me the power to love the unlovely, those whom I cannot possibly love on my own.

I remember a woman I could not love. She had an intense hatred for me. One day I asked God to give me His love for her, and He did. It was such a special relationship. My love for her was so real. She recognized that I loved her even though she didn't deserve it. One day when I called on her she said to her husband, "Millie really does love me." Is there someone you can't love? God can give you His love for that person.

When we are filled with the fullness of Christ we are filled with the fullness of His patience. I am an impatient person and often have to draw on His patience. One time I was traveling in Nova Scotia, speaking in different cities. Three times, one right after another, my luggage didn't arrive. One person who met me at the airport told someone later, "Millie didn't even get upset. I wondered if I should get upset for her."

When we are filled with the fullness of Christ we are filled with the fullness of His strength, His peace, His all. "Christ is all, and in all" (Col. 3:11). Nothing can be added to *all*. Nothing can be added to the completeness or fullness we have in Him.

The fullness of Christ in me! Incredible! But true!

JANUARY 5

As for God, his way is perfect . . . and [he] maketh my way perfect
(Ps. 18:30, 32).

e have just entered a new year. Looking back on the one just
past, we may remember disappointments and failures or joys and
successes. God wants us to forget our past, both failures and
successes. Deuteronomy 17:16 says, "Ye shall henceforth
return no more that way." We must leave the past with God.

God has placed before us *His way* for the new year. "This is the way,
walk ye in it" (Isa. 30:21).

It is His **particular** way, unknown to us but known to Him. "Ye have
not passed this way heretofore" (Josh. 3:4). As He has guided in the past, He
will guide us this year. His way is custom-designed for us.

Not only does He know our way for this whole year, He knows our
present way. Today may be dark, blocked by obstacles, or clouded with
sorrows. Our life direction may have completely changed. We may not know
which way to turn.

But as we commit our present way to Him, He will make it His **perfect**
way for us. When Job was experiencing great suffering in his life, he said, "He
knoweth [this present moment] the way that I take: when he hath tried me, I
shall come forth as gold" (Job 23:10). Job realized that his suffering was a
refining process God was using to accomplish His purpose for him. God uses our
present way to refine us like gold.

God's way is **personal.** Moses said, "If I have found grace in thy sight,
shew me now thy way" (Ex. 33:13). God is so ready to show us His way. "I
will instruct thee and teach thee in the way which thou shalt go: I will guide
thee with mine eye" (Ps. 32:8). He reveals His way to us through His Word,
through prayer, and through circumstances.

God's way is also **perpetual.** The psalmist says, "Lead me in the way
everlasting" (Ps. 139:24). We will continue on His way with Him throughout
all eternity.

As we look back, we can leave the past with Him. As we look ahead, we
can rejoice that He has a perfect way for us this year. And He will *make* our
way perfect as we commit each day to Him.

JANUARY 6

Call unto me, and I will answer thee, and shew thee great and mighty things, which thou knowest not" (Jer. 33:3).

ecause there is a mysterious quality about prayer, we may miss the simplicity of it. Prayer is described in such simple words as *call, ask,* and *cry.* Jeremiah had been imprisoned for preaching God's message of judgment. How he must have been reassured by God's invitation to come to Him in prayer! The Lord said, "Call unto me." Calling implies a need, a request for help.

"Call unto me"— **simple request.** Some television ads say that if we call a special telephone number by a certain time, we will receive an additional gift or a special price for the merchandise. The condition for receiving is to call. So God invites us to call on Him. He is always waiting at the other end of the line. The Bible says, "Ask, and it shall be given you" (Matt. 7:7).

What is your need today? Is it financial? physical? personal? God says, "Call unto Me." Sometimes we turn to people for help, but often they are unable to do so. God says, "Call Me. I can help you whatever your need may be."

God gave Jeremiah and us His promise of a **sure reply.** He doesn't say, "I may answer," or "I'll try to answer. He says, "I *will* answer."

The answer may not always come when expected. God's promises are like certificates of deposit, but they don't always mature in ninety days.

Years ago, three mothers covenanted to meet every week to pray for their children until each became a Christian. They had fourteen children between them. One by one, the children became Christians. The last one, a young man, was nineteen when he received Christ, and he became a preacher.

God can do the impossible. The Bible says, "God . . . is able to do far more than we would ever dare to ask or even dream of—infinitely beyond our highest prayers, desires, thoughts, or hopes" (Eph. 3:20 LB).

The answer may not come in the way we expect, but if we trust God enough to bring our requests to Him, surely we can trust Him enough to accept His answer. He knows our need better than we do.

We are only a call away from God.

JANUARY 7

Look carefully then how you walk! Live purposefully and worthily and accurately . . . making the very most of the time—buying up each opportunity—because the days are evil (Eph. 5:15–16 AM-PLIFIED).

ime has been defined as a stretch of direction in which things happen. It is a fragment of eternity. Someone has said that time is a clock nibbling at eternity. This precious commodity is a gift from God. To think of time in the light of eternity puts greater importance on it.

Perhaps you've heard this bit of verse:

> I have just a minute
>   only sixty seconds in it.
> Forced upon me
>   can't refuse it.
> Didn't seek it, didn't choose it,
>   but it's up to me to use it.
> I must suffer if I lose it,
>   give account if I abuse it.
> Just a tiny little minute,
>   but eternity is in it."

> *Anonymous*

Suppose a bank would credit your account each morning with $86,400 to spend that day. Any balance left at the end of the day could not be added to the next day's amount but would be canceled. What would you do? Of course, you would make every effort to spend the entire amount each day.

Each of us has a time account in the Bank of Heaven. Each morning God deposits 86,400 seconds in it. They are ours to invest for Him that day. When the day ends, that day's allotment of time is completely gone.

Our daily walk is made up of these choice seconds given to us by God. The important question is not the amount of time we have but how we spend it. We must make a wise investment of it. Every day is ours to use or lose.

Someone has said that the way we use what God has given us will determine the value of our contribution to our generation.

Our allotment of time is short. Yesterday is gone, tomorrow has not yet come. Today is the only time we have to invest for God. Lost opportunities can never be regained.

The Bible says, "Teach us to number our days and recognize how few they are; help us to spend them as we should" (Ps. 90:12 LB).

What are you doing now that will live on throughout eternity?

JANUARY 8

Peace I leave with you, my peace I give unto you: not as the world giveth, give I unto you. Let not your heart be troubled, neither let it be afraid (John 14:27).

As a well-known television personality was being interviewed on a talk show, the host posed this question, "How would you define happiness?" The interviewee hesitated, then said, "I believe I would define it as inner peace."

As Jesus came to the close of His earthly ministry, He knew that through the centuries to come many people would have trouble-filled hearts. He knew that today we would experience times of fear and anxiety. Problems would need solutions, discouragements would come, lives would fall apart.

Many people become emotionally disturbed, tense, burned out, on the verge of a nervous breakdown. They turn to tranquilizers, vacations, golf, exercise—all in an effort to find relief. But none of these remedies alone bring the peace they are searching for.

Inner peace comes from a Person, the Lord Jesus Christ. Jesus told His disciples that He was leaving a will, and in it was something they would need. "I am leaving you with a gift—peace of mind and heart!" (v. 27 LB).

We, too, are included in the will Jesus left. The peace He left them He left for us, too. "I give you my own peace and my gift is nothing like the peace of this world. You must not be distressed and you must not be daunted" (v. 27 PHILLIPS).

The peace that He gives is not the fragile peace the world gives. It comes from Jesus. In effect Jesus is saying, "Don't be troubled. Don't be anxious. My peace will calm and quiet your troubled heart. My peace soothes frayed nerves. My peace eases your heart and mind."

At the center of a hurricane is an eye, a place of perfect calm. In the hurricane of our lives, in the very center, is a place of perfect peace, His peace, "for he [Jesus Himself] is our peace" (Eph. 2:14).

The psalmist said, "The LORD will give strength unto his people; the LORD will bless his people with peace" (Ps. 29:11).

JANUARY 9

A land which the LORD thy God careth for: the eyes of the LORD thy God are always upon it, from the beginning of the year even unto the end of the year" (Deut. 11:12).

 n the midst of the uncertainty of life, assurance and strength come as we realize that God sees not only the beginning of our year, but He sees down the year to the very end. "A land that the Lord your God personally cares for! His eyes are always upon it, day after day throughout the year!" (LB).

God assured the children of Israel that His eyes would be upon them every single day of the year. In preparation for their trek through the wilderness the Lord revealed Himself to Moses, their leader, in a three-fold way.

He is the God of the **past.** "I am the God of thy father, the God of Abraham, the God of Isaac, and the God of Jacob" (Ex. 3:6). God assured Moses that as He had led Abraham, Isaac, and Jacob, so would He lead Moses.

As we look into our past, we can remember the faithfulness of God in meeting our needs. From thankful hearts we can say with the psalmist, "The Lord hath done great things for us; whereof we are glad" (Ps. 126:3).

But the God of the past is also the God of the **present.** "I *am* come down to deliver them" (Ex. 3:8). He is ready to deliver His children in time of need—today. "God is our refuge and strength . . . a very present and well-proved help in trouble" (Ps. 46:1 AMPLIFIED). He is the God of our present circumstances. "Is any thing too hard for the LORD?" (Gen. 18:14).

And this same God who is present with us today will be with us through all our tomorrows. He is the God of the **future.** "Come now therefore, and I will send thee" (Ex. 3:10). As we look into the future, not knowing what it holds for us, fear sometimes creeps into our hearts.

Sometimes we fear that He will send us as missionaries to some other country. He does that with some people, but most of us are sent into our own communities—to our families, neighbors, and co-workers. We can enter each tomorrow with quietness and peace, knowing that wherever He sends us, whatever He gives us to do, He will be there to guide and direct.

We can relax in our God of the past, present, and future—God of yesterday, today, and tomorrow.

JANUARY 10

But my God shall supply all your need according to his riches in glory by Christ Jesus" (Phil. 4:19).

he Philippians had often provided Paul's temporal needs. He could never repay them, but he had a God who could. He said, "Your generosity is like a lovely fragrance, a sacrifice that pleases the very heart of God" (v. 18 PHILLIPS). Paul assured them that because of their generosity, God would provide their needs.

This same God will provide for our needs. "My God will supply all that you need from his glorious resources in Christ Jesus" (v. 19 PHILLIPS). What a wonderful promise this is for us as we have entered a new year!

God is the **source** of our provisions. Where could we find a greater supply? The God of the Universe, the God who made heaven and earth, can provide every need.

We can be **certain** of His provisions. He promises that He "shall supply" all our needs. This indicates certainty. He is a faithful God. He stands behind His promises.

The **sufficiency** of His provisions is also clear. He supplies *all* your needs, not most of them or some of them, but all. This includes your needs today.

The **measure** of his provision is "according to His riches." This is our heavenly deposit. Can you begin to estimate His riches? They are all available to you. No request is too great to be filled from His limitless supplies.

The **channel** of His provision is through Jesus Christ. All of God's riches are ours in Christ. "You have everything when you have Christ, and you are filled with God through your union with Christ" (Col. 2:10 LB).

One time a man of God was in great need for a trip he had to make. His banker came to see him and slipped a folded paper into his hand. When the man looked at it he saw a check with no amount filled in. "Are you giving me a blank check?" he asked. "Yes," said his banker. "Fill it in for whatever your needs may be." All the resources of his banker were at his disposal.

How often we draw on our own limited resources when we could draw on God's glorious resources in Christ Jesus.

"Because the Lord is my Shepherd, I have everything I need!" (Ps. 23:1 LB).

And [Martha] had a sister called Mary, which also sat at Jesus' feet, and heard his word (Luke 10:39).

ntertaining is my hobby, so I can relate to the excitement in the home of Martha and Mary when Jesus stopped by for a visit. They welcomed him into their home, and soon Martha was busy preparing a meal for Him. However, before long Mary was sitting at Jesus' feet, giving rapt attention to His every word.

Martha became frustrated and distraught because she had to prepare the meal alone. Finally she stormed over to Jesus to complain. "Lord, don't you care that my sister has left me to do the work by myself? Tell her to help me!" (v. 40 NIV). Sound familiar?

Jesus appreciated Martha's concern for His well-being, but I wonder if He wouldn't have preferred that she prepare something more simple. Then she, too, could have sat at His feet and listened. I believe Jesus had stopped by that day to have fellowship with them. He would soon be facing crucifixion. He knew they loved Him, and He felt the special need of their love that day.

Jesus gently but firmly rebuked Martha, not because of her service, but because her spirit had become critical. "Martha, Martha," the Lord answered, "you are worried and upset about many things, but only one thing is needed. Mary has chosen what is better, and it will not be taken away from her" (v. 41 NIV).

Mary had been drawn to sit at the feet of Jesus. His words touched her heart. She was hungry, not for the food Martha was preparing, but for the spiritual food Jesus was sharing. She didn't want to miss one of His words. Some day I hope I can ask Mary what Jesus talked about that day. Perhaps He shared something about the crucifixion and resurrection. It must have been very special.

You and I cannot sit at Jesus' feet in person as Mary did. But each day we can have a quiet time, sitting at His feet and eagerly listening to Him as we read His Word and talking to Him as we pray.

Jesus is always there waiting for us when we come. The psalmist said, "The one thing I want from God, the thing I seek most of all, is the privilege of . . . living in his presence every day of my life, delighting in his incomparable perfections and glory" (Ps. 27:4 LB).

JANUARY 12

But his delight is in the law of the LORD; and in his law doth he meditate day and night (Ps. 1:2).

his psalm is called the Psalm of the Blessed Person, the happy person—the contented, fulfilled person. This person's happiness results from a relationship. It comes from the Lord.

Because of the reality of the relationship with the Lord, the happy person takes pleasure in His Word. Jeremiah said, "Thy word was unto me the joy and rejoicing of mine heart" (Jer. 15:16). Happiness is an attitude of the *heart*.

How we look forward to receiving a letter from someone dear to us! We read it again and again until we know every word. The Bible is a special letter to us from God—the One who loves us more than anyone else in the world. No wonder our hearts are delighted as we read it.

We need to meditate on it until it becomes a part of us. This takes more than an occasional reading. We need to be in God's Word daily. We won't find time to read it unless we *make* time. Meditation is an attitude of the *mind*.

The life of the happy person is regulated by God's Word. He does not read it from a sense of duty but carefully considers each word. It is his guidebook from God—his special book of directives, revealing God's will to him.

We all have our own way of reading and meditating on it. As I read the Scriptures, I make notes of new thoughts God has given me. I check on any instructions I need to put into practice. I note promises that apply to me. Then I use the Scripture in my prayer. For example, as I meditate on the above verse, I would probably ask God to help me delight more and more in His Word and let my life be regulated by it. In this way, the Holy Spirit makes the Scripture more real to me. I am sure you have your special way of meditating on it.

May we make it a habit to spend time in God's Word regularly. As we do, we will not only delight in God's Word, but we will delight in the God who has given it to us.

JANUARY 13

And he shall be like a tree planted by the rivers of water, that bringeth forth his fruit in his season; his leaf also shall not wither; and whatsoever he doeth shall prosper (Ps. 1:3).

appiness is not the feeling that everything is going my way. Real happiness can occur when nothing seems to be going my way. The happy person can be content no matter what the circumstances.

The contented, joyful person is like a tree that has not only been planted, but has been firmly planted. The word, *planted,* indicates that it was carefully set in a specific place. We can be content knowing that God has planted us in the place of His choosing. It may not be our choice, but it is His.

The contented person is like a tree planted by the rivers of water. A strong root system provides its strength and nourishment from God. Such a tree, well-rooted in God, cannot be moved or uprooted. It has stability.

Not long ago I saw a large tree which had been uprooted during a severe windstorm. As I looked at it, I observed that it had a shallow root system.

But with roots going down deep into the river of God, the contented person will not be affected by circumstances, however catastrophic. His strength is adequate for any emergency.

The contented person is like a tree that produces an abundant harvest of fruit in its season. God controls the production of the fruit for the right season. "Even so every good tree bringeth forth good fruit" (Matt. 7:17). Fruit pickers look for fruit. So does our Master.

The contented person is like a tree whose leaf never withers. Spiritual vitality will characterize his inner person even though the years take their toll. The Bible says, "For which cause we faint not; but though our outward man perish, yet the inward man is renewed day by day" (2 Cor. 4:16).

The contented person will prosper spiritually. When we are rooted in Christ, drawing on His resources, our lives will glorify the Lord.

Is your life spiritually prosperous? Have you reached your spiritual potential? When you are planted in the place of God's choosing and nourished by His Word, you will have a fruitful harvest in season. Your life will have spiritual vitality and complete fulfillment that comes only from being in constant touch with God.

JANUARY 14

But as many as received him, to them gave he power to become the sons of God, even to them that believe on his name (John 1:12).

ne of the excitements of my life is to receive a gift. I am always so fascinated with the package that I hesitate to open it. But my curiosity finally overrules, and I begin to tear off the wrappings to see what my gift is.

Two people are involved in a gift exchange, the giver and the receiver. The giver purchases or makes the gift for the receiver, but the exchange is not complete until the receiver has accepted it.

God is the greatest Giver this world has ever known. He has a gift for every person who will ever live. It is His love-gift to us. "For God so loved the world, that he gave his only begotten Son, that whosoever believeth in him should not perish, but have everlasting life" (John 3:16). What more wonderful gift could anyone receive than the gift of everlasting life!

With this gift comes the indwelling Presence of the Lord Jesus Christ and a reservation for heaven. We have the assurance that we will go to live in heaven when our time on earth is over. But also the life we receive from Him is a special quality of life. The power of the resurrection life of Jesus Christ helps us live today.

Have you ever received a beautifully wrapped gift containing other smaller packages to be opened, one each day? This is an illustration of the many additional gifts that become ours when we receive Christ into our lives.

One of the gifts we receive in Christ is His peace. "Peace I leave with you, my peace I give unto you" (John 14:27). Another is His strength. "The Lord will give strength unto his people" (Ps. 29:11). He also gives us inner satisfaction. "For he satisfieth the longing soul, and filleth the hungry soul with goodness" (Ps. 107:9). He gives us His love as well, "and his love is perfected in us" (1 John 4:12). As we read His Word we find many gifts which are ours when Christ indwells us.

But more wonderful than these gifts is the Giver of the gifts, God Himself. More wonderful than the joy of receiving a present, more exciting than opening packages is the reality of the Presence of Christ. "Christ in you, the hope of glory" (Col. 1:27).

JANUARY 15

Rejoice in the Lord always: and again I say, Rejoice (Phil. 4:4).

With the name *Lemon-Fresh Joy*™ the dishwashing soap manufacturer suggests that there can be joy in the humdrum work of washing dishes.

The apostle Paul encourages us to be joyful. Phillips's paraphrase reads, "Delight yourselves in the Lord; yes, find your joy in Him at all times." Do you know where Paul was when he wrote that? He was in prison.

Some equate happiness with joy. But Paul wasn't talking about happiness. Happiness is dependent on circumstances, people, or possessions. This is not the joy Paul is talking about. Joy is more than happiness. The source of real joy is the Lord. Jesus said, "These things have I spoken unto you, that my joy might remain in you, and that your joy might be full (John 15:11). God's people are to be joyful. We can rejoice in who He is.

Perhaps you are saying, "But you don't know what I am going through. You don't know the pressures I have or the heartaches. Joy? In my circumstances?"

James gives us an answer. He says, "Dear brothers, is your life full of difficulties and temptations? Then be happy, for when the way is rough, your patience has a chance to grow. So let it grow, and don't try to squirm out of your problems. For when your patience is finally in full bloom, then you will be ready for anything, strong in character, full and complete" (James 1:2–4 LB).

Not only does Paul say we are to rejoice, but we are to rejoice *always*. The secret of continuous joy comes from companionship with the Lord.

The great composer Haydn was once asked why all of his sacred compositions had such a joyful sound. He replied, "I cannot compose any other way. I translate into music the state of my heart. When I think of the grace of God in Jesus Christ, my heart is so full of joy that the music fairly dances and leaps from my pen."

Our state of heart is usually reflected in our daily living. What is the state of your heart today—sorrowful or joyful? Whatever it is, may the Lord give you a song of joy in the midst of it.

JANUARY 16

He got up, rebuked the wind and said to the waves, "Quiet! Be still!" Then the wind died down and it was completely calm (Mark 4:39 NIV).

ow often we hear an announcement such as, "Due to circumstances beyond our control . . . the power will be off for several hours" or "the program has been changed" or "the flight has been canceled."

What do you do when circumstances are beyond your control? Where do you turn? To whom do you go when there is nothing more you can do?

The Bible tells of a group of Jesus' disciples who were caught in that situation out on the Sea of Galilee with Jesus. Suddenly, terrifying winds tossed their boat around on the turbulent sea. The disciples were frightened! They were in a storm beyond their control.

Couldn't they trust Jesus to take them to the other side, even through a fierce storm? Didn't they have faith that He could control the tumult at sea?

Hurriedly awakening Jesus, they cried, "Teacher, don't you care if we drown?" Of course Jesus cared. He looked at the storm and said, "Peace, be still." Instantly the wind ceased and the sea was calm. Then Jesus said, "Why are you so afraid? Do you still have no faith?" (v. 40 NIV). Wasn't He in control?

Who is in control when the storms rage in your life? You have access to the "Top Controller" Himself. He draws near and says, "Peace, be still," offering immediate inner calm. He whispers, "Where is your faith? Just trust me. I am in control."

I used to approach God with the attitude that He was my last resort. There was nothing else I could do. Now I have learned to face my storms with confidence in Him, knowing that His love for me is so deep I cannot fathom it. He whispers, "Remember, I am in control, preparing you to live with me throughout eternity. This storm is part of your preparation."

Then I can experience His inner peace. I hear Him say, "Let not your heart be troubled. You are trusting God, now trust in me . . . I am leaving you with a gift—peace of mind and heart! And the peace I give isn't fragile like the peace the world gives. So don't be troubled or afraid" (John 14:1, 27 LB)!

What is beyond *your* control is in *His* control!

JANUARY 17

These things have I written unto you that believe on the name of the Son of God; that ye may know that ye have eternal life, and that ye may believe on the name of the Son of God (1 John 5:13).

In my travels around the world I engage in conversation with people, often asking if they are Christians.

Sometimes the answer is, "I hope so" or "I'm doing my best." The Bible says we don't have to live with that kind of uncertainty: "I write this to you who believe in (adhere to, trust in, and rely on) the name of the Son of God . . . so that you may **know** (with settled and absolute knowledge) that you [already] have life, yes, eternal life" (1 John 5:13 AMPLIFIED).

Eternal life is a gift. It comes wrapped up in the Person of Jesus Christ. "God hath given to us eternal life, and this life is in his Son" (v. 11). Jesus said, "I came that they may have and enjoy life" (John 10:10 AMPLIFIED).

When I married, I was certain about it. If asked, I would say, "Yes, I am." I didn't say, "I think I am," or "I hope I am." I was sure. Why? Because during the wedding ceremony when the minister asked me if I would take Clarke for my lawfully wedded husband, I replied with no hesitation, "I will." My husband made the same vow. Then we were pronounced husband and wife. We can be just as certain of our relationship with Christ.

Suppose God asked, "Do you believe my Son, Jesus Christ died for your sins and rose from the dead to give you eternal life?"

You reply, "Yes, I do."

"Will you take Jesus to be your personal Saviour?"

"Yes, I will."

Then the moment you ask Him into your life, you receive God's gift: "The gift of God is eternal life through Jesus Christ our Lord" (Rom. 6:23). From then on, you can know you are a Christian. The word *know* is a strong one. "I have written like this to you who already believe in the name of God's Son so that you may be quite sure that, here and now, you possess eternal life" (1 John 5:13 PHILLIPS).

We can be *confident* that through our personal relationship with Jesus Christ we *have* eternal life *today*.

We have life with a purpose! Life that is full! Life that is real!

JANUARY 18

*In the year that King Uzziah died I saw also the Lord sitting upon a
throne, high and lifted up, and his train filled the temple (Isa. 6:1).*

s you enter this new year, you bring into it some unsettled
matters from last year, such as decisions you have to make,
problems that need to be solved, a heart that is hurting, a habit
that controls you.

You may have become so engrossed with your problem that you have
lost your perspective. Your greatest need may be a new vision of the reality of
God and who He is. God wants to do a new thing for you, putting your needs
in perspective and giving you a fresh look at Himself.

At the time of today's Scripture, King Uzziah had died. Changes in
leadership often bring uncertainty, concern, and confusion. Isaiah felt the king's
death keenly, for not only was Uzziah his king, he was a dear friend.

Isaiah went to the temple, and there he was transformed! God knew that
what Isaiah needed at this time of crisis was a new focus, a fresh vision of the
Lord. There in the temple Isaiah saw the Lord in all His glory, perhaps a
manifestation of the pre-incarnate Christ.

As he gazed in rapt worship, the glory of God was revealed to him. He
saw the Lord on His throne, reigning in all His majesty and power. There was
no need to fear the future, for God was still on His throne. He was in control.
The occupant of the earthly throne had changed; but God's throne is eternal,
occupied by the One who said, "I am the Lord, I change not" (Mal. 3:6).
Earthly events do not change God.

After Isaiah's perspective changed, he was never the same again. Our
need, too, may be to shift our focus from people, possessions, and problems to a
fresh vision of the Lord.

A Sunday school teacher passed around a picture of Jesus and His disciples
to her class. When it came back to her, she asked if everyone had seen the
picture. "I didn't," one little boy said. He pointed to the figure of Jesus. "I
didn't see the picture. I only saw Him."

What are your eyes focusing on? What is filling your vision? Your life
with its failures and disappointments—or Him? Isaiah saw the *Lord*. May *our*
vision be filled with Him in all His beauty, majesty, and power. He is still on the
throne.

JANUARY 19

And one cried unto another, and said, Holy, holy, holy, is the L<small>ORD</small> of hosts: the whole earth is full of his glory (Isa. 6:3).

esterday we considered Isaiah's life-changing experience. His vision of the Lord was a vision of God's holiness, majesty, and glory. Seraphim flew around the throne, exalting and worshiping God as they chanted, "Holy, holy, holy, is the L<small>ORD</small> of hosts." The word *holy* is derived from the word *whole*. To be holy is to be pure, blameless, complete, perfect, whole.

In light of the holiness of God, Isaiah saw himself as God saw him, and faced with his sinful condition, he fell on his face before God. All he could say was, "Woe is me! for I am undone; because I am a man of unclean lips, and I dwell in the midst of a people of unclean lips: for mine eyes have seen the King, the L<small>ORD</small> of hosts" (v. 5).

Then one of the seraphim flew to the altar. With a pair of tongs he picked up a burning coal and touched Isaiah's lips with it, touching Isaiah in the area of his need. The seraph said, "You are pronounced 'Not guilty' because this coal has touched your lips. Your sins are all forgiven" (v. 6 LB).

From time to time, we need to take a fresh look at ourselves in the light of God's holiness. With today's tendency to view sin too casually, we need to see our sin as God sees it. Then we, too, can only cry out, "Woe is me! I am undone!" Our sin may be unclean lips, or it may be criticalness or gossip. It may include wrong attitudes, indifference, busyness, an unforgiving spirit, bitterness, egotism, lack of compassion, or materialism.

How can a holy God look upon our sin? Because He is a God of love, He has provided a way for our lives to be cleansed and made acceptable to Him. We are to confess our sin as soon as we are aware of it. The Bible says, "If we confess our sins, he is faithful and just to forgive us our sins, and to cleanse us from all unrighteousness" (1 John 1:9).

As we enter His presence, cleansed and forgiven, we can lift our voices in worship, singing, "Holy, holy, holy, is the L<small>ORD</small> of hosts." The Bible says, "Give unto the L<small>ORD</small> the glory due unto his name; worship the L<small>ORD</small> in the beauty of holiness" (Ps. 29:2).

JANUARY 20

Also I heard the voice of the Lord, saying, Whom shall I send, and who will go for us? Then said I, Here am I; send me (Isa. 6:8).

orship is our heart response to God. It is the overflow of a heart filled with adoration and love for the Lord. What a privilege is ours! We can kneel in the presence of the holy, loving God and worship Him. Out of a heart filled with love for the Lord comes our response for service.

God had a message for His people but He needed a messenger. It would not be an easy assignment for they were a disobedient and rebellious people. When God called for someone to go as His representative, Isaiah was ready. Filled with a vision of the holiness of God, his life cleansed, Isaiah heard God's call. He answered, "Here am I; send me."

Today God is calling for representatives to go into the world with His message. He doesn't draft us but waits for us to volunteer.

Often we become so filled with our plans, programs, schedules, and appointments that we become burned out with pressured activity and are ready to quit. We get so busy planning what we want to do for God that we miss what He wants to do through us. We may have become indifferent to those on their way to a Christless eternity.

We need to come into His presence and let Him fill our vision with Himself. How? The Bible says, "For God, who commanded the light to shine out of darkness, hath shined in our hearts, to give the light of the knowledge of the glory of God in the face of Jesus Christ" (2 Cor. 4:6). God reveals Himself to us in the person of Jesus Christ. Our focus must be on Him.

Then we are ready for God's call to put us where He wants us. We are available to Him. He will show us His agenda.

When we are filled with His love, He can love the world through us. We will see the world through His eyes and seek His plans for reaching the world. We will begin to pray that "the Lord of the harvest . . . will send forth labourers into his harvest" (Matt. 9:38).

As we see the world as He sees it and pray for it through His heart of love, our response will be, "Here am I; send me."

JANUARY 21

And the LORD went before them by day in a pillar of a cloud, to lead them the way: and by night in a pillar of fire, to give them light; to go by day and night (Ex. 13:21).

fter years of bondage in Egypt, the children of Israel knew freedom! Under God's guidance, Moses had brought the Israelites out of Egypt, and now they would begin their journey across the desert. It was an uncharted way for them, but every step had been planned by God.

He provided a visible guide, an ever-present guide—a cloud by day and a pillar of fire by night. Always in their view, this visible evidence of God's Presence gave twenty-four-hour-a-day direction. They didn't know what each day would hold, but they trusted the One who controlled the cloud and fire.

With no highway signs to direct them, they had to depend on God to guide them. They were to follow the movement of the cloud. When it moved, they were to move; when it stopped, they must stop. Regardless of how tired they were, they must move forward when the cloud did. No matter now impatient they were to continue, they must wait for the cloud to move.

It was a walk of faith—putting their faith in God into action.

Today we are traveling an unknown way. We may be perplexed and confused. We may not understand what God is doing. We do not travel by map but are led by the trustworthy Guide. Even though we can't see ahead, we can trust Him. God has promised, "I will instruct thee and teach thee in the way which thou shalt go: I will guide thee with mine eye" (Ps. 32:8).

He promises to lead us, to go before us and make our crooked ways straight and our rough places smooth. At times, we move forward; other times we have to wait. He knows where the dangers are and will lead us around them or go through them with us. No emergency will take Him unawares.

God doesn't always lead us the shortest way. There may even be some detours, but He will lead us the best way. It may be longer but safer. He is not in a hurry. He never makes a wrong move.

The Bible says that when Jesus "putteth forth his own sheep, he goeth before them, and the sheep follow him: for they know his voice" (John 10:4).

Following God is better than following a well-known path.

JANUARY 22

*And the Lord went before them . . . to lead . . . the way
(Ex. 13:21).*

hile driving through a rural area on the way to speak for a women's luncheon, we came to a red traffic light. When we stopped, our car quit running. My driver asked God to start the car and turn every traffic light green the rest of the way. The car started, but the next traffic light was red. Again the motor died. The driver of a large transport truck stopped, checked the engine, and told us the transmission had gone out. He promised to send someone from a nearby garage to tow it in.

I rode to the garage to telephone someone to come and take me to the luncheon. I asked the young man in the office for a phone. However, before I could make the call, the car was towed in, and we decided to rent another automobile and drive on.

That evening we stopped back at the garage just as the young man was leaving. He asked if I had gotten to the meeting in time to speak, and I assured him I had.

"What did you talk about?" he asked.

"Many people are searching for the answer to life," I replied, "and I have that answer, so I share it with them."

He said, "I am searching too." Then I knew why the traffic light had been red that morning. I talked with him for an hour about the real answer to life—Jesus Christ.

Later I thought of the *traffic lights* God uses in our lives for guidance. Our traffic light may be red at a circumstance we do not like. We ask God to turn it green and move us on, but it stays red. Or we may be content at a red light, then it turns green, and we are moved out of our comfort zone. Our traffic light may be yellow. We wait patiently for it to change, but we are kept waiting.

God has a reason for our traffic lights. As we trust His control, He will use them to accomplish His purposes.

The Bible says, "Trust in the LORD with all thine heart; and lean not unto thine own understanding. In all thy ways [at red, green, and yellow lights] acknowledge him, and he shall direct thy paths" (Prov. 3:5–6).

JANUARY 23

Launch out into the deep, and let down your nets for a draught (Luke 5:4).

t was morning, and already people were crowding around Jesus, listening to Him. As the crowd pushed closer, He stepped into Peter's fishing boat and preached from there. Afterward, He said to Peter, "Now go out where it is deeper and let down your nets and you will catch a lot of fish!" (Luke 5:4 LB).

Didn't Jesus know the best time to fish was at night? Peter said to the Lord, "Master, we have toiled all the night, and have taken nothing: nevertheless at thy word I will let down the net (v. 5). Obediently, Peter moved out to deeper water. When he let down his net, immediately it filled with so many fish that it began to break, and he had to call for help.

Today many people are floundering in the deep waters of despair and unbelief, and the Lord asks us to launch out into our deep places and let down our nets.

Our *net* is whatever God has given us to use for Him: the ability to speak, a beautiful singing voice, a typewriter, personal sharing of the Gospel. Our *deep place* may be our family, friends, neighbors, those we work with, our community, or the world at large. God will guide us.

One day a friend and I went into a coffee shop in a lovely hotel for a cup of coffee. A darling young girl took care of our order. As we left, I went to her, gave her a little booklet, and said, "This tells how to get to heaven."

"Oh, I really need that," she replied.

"You read it, do what it says, and you can know you are ready for heaven," I told her.

Again she said, "Oh, I really need that."

God had given me a *deep place* to let down my net that day.

But we won't catch fish if we fail to let down our nets. Are you missing fish because of excuses: I'm too busy, I'm burned out, I deserve time for myself, I'm not capable?

God needs "fishers of souls" today. Let Him show you your deep place. Hear Him say, "Follow me, and I will make *you* [a fisher] of men" (Matt. 4:19, emphasis mine).

And Caleb stilled the people before Moses, and said, Let us go up at once, and possess it; for we are well able to overcome it (Num. 13:30).

he Israelites had reached the Promised Land. But before they entered, Moses sent twelve spies in to survey the area. What were the people like? Were their cities well fortified? Was it a fruitful land?

When they returned, the spies reported that the land was fruitful but the cities were well fortified and the enemy was strong. Hebron, a mountainous area, was filled with giants. "We were in our own sight as grasshoppers, and so we were in their sight" most of the spies said (Num. 13:33).

Then Caleb and Joshua gave their report. They agreed it was a mountainous country filled with giants, but they believed that God would do what He had said He would do—give them the land. In His power they could conquer it.

Caleb and Joshua were out-voted ten to two. The ten spies had matched their strength against *giant strength.* Caleb and Joshua matched their strength against *God's strength.* Because of the Israelites' unbelief, they were not allowed to enter the Promised Land but wandered in the wilderness for forty years.

Caleb and Joshua must have been disappointed not to enter the land at that time. But God promised that in His timing He would take them in to possess the land.

Has God given you a mountain to possess? Perhaps you desire a deeper walk with Him. It may be a more effective prayer life. You may want Christ to become more real to you. Your mountain may be a physical, financial, or material need in your own life or in the life of a loved one or friend.

We can expect giants with our mountains. Our giants may be lack of faith, feelings of inadequacy, a wrong attitude, a wrong motive. Your course of action depends on your focus. Are you focusing on your giant or on the God who will give you the mountain? A grasshopper concept focuses on the giants. A God concept focuses on God. Are you controlled by your giant or God? Our God is greater and more powerful than any giant.

"For whatsoever is born of God overcometh the world: and this is the victory that overcometh the world, even our faith. Who is he that overcometh the world, but he that believeth that Jesus is the Son of God?" (1 John 5:4–5).

JANUARY 25

And Joshua blessed him, and gave unto Caleb . . . Hebron for an inheritance . . . because that he wholly followed the LORD God of Israel (Josh. 14:13–14).

ive me this mountain!"

When the Israelites were ready to enter the Promised Land, Caleb went to Joshua, the new leader, and requested Mount Hebron as his portion of the land. God had promised it to him forty-five years earlier.

Through the forty long years of wandering in the wilderness, Caleb never forgot God's promise. He treasured it, knowing that a day would come when God would keep His word.

Now the day had come. Caleb could go in and possess his mountain. Mount Hebron was the most difficult part of the land, for it was giant country, the stronghold of one of the most warlike tribes. Caleb could have said, "I am eighty-five. Give me an easy place to possess. I want to go in and enjoy myself. At my age I don't want much to do. I want to play golf and swim."

But not Caleb! He told Joshua, "As yet I am as strong this day as I was in the day that Moses sent me. . . . Now therefore give me this mountain, whereof the LORD spake in that day; if . . . the LORD will be with me, then I shall be able to drive them out, as the LORD said" (v. 11–12).

What a warrior! A man of invincible spirit, Caleb's strong faith in God never wavered. He learned that delay does not mean denial. Delay didn't keep him from receiving what God had promised. His secret? He wholly followed the Lord. He was willing to walk by faith. He wanted what God wanted for him.

Are you waiting to possess Mount Hebron? Hebron means fellowship. It is the place of God's blessing. Whatever your mountain may be, God wants it to become your Hebron, your place of blessing.

In Hebron, you will experience the reality of a sweet, close fellowship with the Lord Jesus. In Hebron you will come to know Jesus in a more intimate way. In Hebron you will walk by faith, obedience, and commitment. In Hebron you learn to wholly follow Him.

Paul sums up the secret of wholly following the Lord in 2 Corinthians 2:14. "But thanks be to God, who always leads us in triumphal procession in Christ and through us spreads everywhere the fragrance of the knowledge of him" (NIV).

JANUARY 26

You are God's garden (1 Cor. 3:9 LB).

s we walk in a garden filled with flowers in bloom, we are aware of the lovely perfume they give forth. In other gardens— orchards—the trees are loaded with luscious fruit for our enjoyment.

Our life garden should be a combination of fragrance and fruit. It is filled with the fragrance of the life of Christ. The Bible says, "As far as God is concerned there is a sweet, wholesome fragrance in our lives. It is the fragrance of Christ within us, an aroma to both the saved and the unsaved all around us" (2 Cor. 2:15 LB).

Fragrance is the result of a process. In the making of perfume, the petals of the flowers have to be crushed. It has been discovered that sometimes the petals of the flowers picked in the dark hours just before dawn produce the sweetest fragrance. Are you experiencing a time of darkness in your life? Are you in the crushing process? Out of this experience the Lord can produce the sweet fragrance of the life of Jesus within—if you let Him.

One day a group of factory workers went into a restaurant for lunch. After they left, someone said that he noticed a special fragrance while they were there. "They work in a perfume factory nearby," someone else explained.

We need time in *God's Perfume Factory* that we might carry His fragrance wherever we go.

Not only is our life garden to give forth the *fragrance* of His life but also the *fruit* of His life.

We cannot produce this fruit ourselves. It is the work of the Holy Spirit. "But when the Holy Spirit controls our lives he will produce this kind of fruit in us: love, joy, peace, patience, kindness, goodness, faithfulness, gentleness and self-control" (Gal. 5:22–23 LB).

In John 15 Jesus speaks of degrees of fruitbearing: fruit, more fruit, much fruit. To produce an abundant harvest requires pruning. If you are feeling the pruning knife, remember: It is necessary if we are to increase our harvest.

How is your garden growing? Is it filled with the *fragrance* of Christ? Is the *fruit* of His life being produced in you? In the days of the early Christians, others "took knowledge of them, that they had been with Jesus" (Acts 4:13).

JANUARY 27

Whereas ye know not what shall be on the morrow. For what is your life? It is even a vapour, that appeareth for a little time, and then vanisheth away (James 4:14).

ne morning a special news report interrupted the television program I was watching. The newscaster announced that a few hours earlier a gunman had entered a bank in a small town nearby and killed the bank employees.

As I pondered what had happened, I thought about the uncertainty of life. Little did those people realize that that would be their last day on earth.

Life is uncertain. The Living Bible paraphrases the above verse this way: "How do you know what is going to happen tomorrow? For the length of your lives is as uncertain as the morning fog—now you see it; soon it is gone." We do not know what might happen in the next moment that could radically change our lives.

The Bible says, "What you ought to say is, 'If the Lord wants us to, we shall live and do this or that.' Otherwise you will be bragging about your own plans, and such self-confidence never pleases God" (v. 15–16 LB). "If the Lord wills" is not a trite saying. It recognizes that God is in control and we accept what He sends or allows. Only when we are in His will can we be confident of tomorrow, for our tomorrows are in His hand.

A number of years ago I walked into my surgeon's office, knowing that I was facing surgery, but I didn't know how serious it was. He said, "I have to be honest with you. There is a big possibility that you won't come through." During the month I had to wait for the operation, I knew that my life on earth might soon be over. What should I do, rush about seeing how much I could do in that short time? No! I simply committed my time and life to the Lord and went on with my regular schedule of what God had given me to do.

The Bible says, "Don't be anxious about tomorrow. God will take care of your tomorrow too. Live one day at a time." (Matt. 6:34 LB).

May we not just *spend* our years; may we *invest* them for eternity. "But lay up for yourselves treasures in heaven, where neither moth nor rust doth corrupt, and where thieves do not break through nor steal" (Matt. 6:20).

JANUARY 28

Thou art my portion, O LORD: I have said that I would keep thy words (Ps. 119:57).

oday worldly success is measured by accumulation of possessions, achievement in business, or fame through entertainment, sports, or society.

The psalmist had learned a very important truth. He realized that the One who filled his life with blessings was more important to him than the blessings themselves. He told God, *"Thou* art my portion."

This Scripture could be translated literally, "Thou art all I need, O Lord." We sing a chorus that says, "He is all I need." This was very real to the psalmist.

Portion is defined as an allotment to a person, a share. It may be part of an inheritance received by an heir. The Lord Jesus Christ is our portion. In Him all the riches of heaven are available to us. Romans 8:17 says, "If we are children, then we are heirs—heirs of God and co-heirs with Christ" (NIV). In Him we have everything necessary for our daily living. David told God, "You are my refuge, my portion in the land of the living" (Ps. 142:5 NIV).

Most of us have a bank account and use a checkbook to draw on our account for our needs. As Christians we also have an account in the Bank of Heaven. Whatever our need may be—peace, rest, strength, patience—we "write a check" for that need, drawing upon our resources in the Bank of Heaven. As we receive what we need, the Lord Jesus Himself becomes our portion.

Jesus is ready, but we have to make the choice. We may choose as our portion possessions, achievement, education, high fashion, self-pity when forsaken by family and friends; however, these do not bring peace and quietness, satisfaction and fulfillment to a troubled, distraught heart.

What is your portion? your possessions? family? home? position? hobby? Or can you say, "Thou art my portion, O LORD." None can compare with Him. Colossians 3:11 says, "Christ is all, and in all."

When He becomes all you need, He *is* all your need.

JANUARY 29

When thou passest through the waters, I will be with thee; and through the rivers, they shall not overflow thee: when thou walkest through the fire, thou shalt not be burned; neither shall the flame kindle upon thee (Isa. 43:2).

hen I became a Christian, I thought my troubles were over. But I soon learned that this was not true. We need not be surprised when floods sweep over our lives nor when we find ourselves in the deep waters of trouble or in the heat of the fire. Isaiah said, *when* you pass through the waters . . . and *when* you walk through the fire . . . not *if*.

Jesus said to His disciples, "Ye shall have tribulation: but be of good cheer; I have overcome the world" (John 16:33).

Remember that storm on the Sea of Galilee when huge waves dashed over the boat with such fury that the disciples thought they would drown? Above the roar of the storm Jesus called, "Peace, be still," and immediately the storm ceased and the sea was calm.

In the book of Daniel we read of three Hebrew men who were sentenced to death in a fiery furnace for their loyalty to God. As the king watched, he said, "Did not we cast three men bound into the midst of the fire? . . . Lo, I see four men loose . . . and the form of the fourth is like the Son of God" (Dan. 3:24–25).

Today we may be in the floodwaters or in a furnace of affliction, but there is someone with us—the Lord Jesus, the Son of God. He controls the waters' depth and adjusts the temperature of the fire to achieve His purpose. He is carefully watching the blueprint of our lives, and when He sees His purpose accomplished, He lifts us out of the waters or turns off the heat. He doesn't send help before needed, but when we encounter trouble He is already there to do what is needed.

No, our troubles are not over when we become Christians, but God promises His presence and protection in the flood and fire experiences of our lives. He says, "Don't be afraid, for I am with you. . . . I am the Lord, who opens a way through the waters, making a path right through the sea" (Isa. 43:5, 16 LB). A living faith in the Living God will take us through. "I will trust, and not be afraid" (Isa. 12:2).

JANUARY 30

Are not two sparrows sold for a farthing? and one of them shall not
fall on the ground without your Father. (Matt. 10:29). Are not five
sparrows sold for two farthings, and not one of them is forgotten be-
fore God? (Luke 12:6).

ave you ever hit a bird while you were driving down the
highway? The Bible tells us that not one little bird falls to the
ground without the knowledge of the Heavenly Father.
        When Jesus lived on earth sparrows were of little value.
The very poor used them for food. Sparrows provided an apt illustration when
Jesus wanted to teach His disciples an important lesson on God's loving care for
His children.

Both Matthew and Luke included Jesus' illustration about the insignificant
sparrow. Matthew said the price of two little sparrows was a farthing, which is
comparable to a penny. But Luke said that for two farthings, the price of four
sparrows, a fifth bird was thrown in without charge.

God's love and care is so great for these little sparrows that not one could
fall without His knowledge. Even the fifth little sparrow "thrown in" is never
forgotten by God.

Today you may feel that no one cares for you. Your heart may be
breaking. You may be ready to give up. Remember, if God cares for the little
sparrow, He must care infinitely more for you and me. Jesus said, "Never fear,
you are far more valuable to [God] than a whole flock of sparrows" (Luke
12:7 LB). To God no one is insignificant.

Regardless of what your troubles may be, He has not forgotten you. The
smallest detail of your life is under His loving care. The Bible advises, "Casting
the whole of your care—all your anxieties, all your worries, all your concerns,
once and for all—on Him; for He cares for you affectionately, and cares about
you watchfully" (1 Peter 5:7 AMPLIFIED).

One day Sir Michael Costa was directing a rehearsal of his orchestra. In
one piece of music the piccolo player had only one note to play. Deciding that it
was not important, when it was his time to play his one note, the piccolo player
remained silent. Suddenly the conductor held up his hand. "Where is the
piccolo?" he asked. The maestro had quickly detected the missing note. It *was*
important.

You may think you are insignificant to God. But in His eyes you are
special, you are valuable, you are important. His eye is on you. His ear is open
to your cry. *He cares.*

I have set the LORD always before me: because he is at my right
hand, I shall not be moved (Ps. 16:8).

rother Lawrence is known for the small book he wrote called
Practicing the Presence of God. This is what the psalmist is
talking about in Psalm 16. It is a psalm of trust written from the
heart of one who lived close to God.

Throughout the psalm David reveals his deep faith in God. His desire was
for God to control his life. He faced many impossible situations. Heartaches
often filled his life. He was lonely. Yet he always seemed to live on a plane of
victory and praise. Why? Because his *sight* was focused on the Lord. "I have
set the LORD always before me."

When we set the Lord before us, He becomes our personal Guide. We
take Him into account in all our ways. He charts our course and we follow
Him. We practice His presence in the course of our daily living.

The River Jordan follows a very crooked course. If it ran in a straight line,
it would cover only sixty-five miles, but actually, the meandering river measures
two hundred miles. Rivers always take the line of least resistance.

What about our lives? Have we carved out a crooked course because we
have taken the line of least resistance? Often we give in to people or
circumstances instead of keeping our eyes on the Lord and following His course.

We need to set the Lord before us as our pattern for daily living in the
decisions we have to make and in the temptations we have to resist.

With the Lord at our right hand we will know the security of His
presence. When the buffeting storms of life come, we will not be moved. David
said, "He only is my rock and my salvation; he is my defense; I shall not be
greatly moved" (Ps. 62:2).

King Jehoshaphat knew the importance of focusing on the Lord. As a
strong enemy was advancing upon his nation, he went to the Lord and prayed,
"Neither know we what to do: but our eyes are upon thee" (2 Chron.
20:12). He won the victory.

What have you set before you today? Problems? Temptations? Pleasures?
Possessions? Earthly security? Who or what are you focusing on? Have you set
the Lord before you?

David said, "Mine eyes are ever toward the LORD" (Ps. 25:15).

FEBRUARY 1

*When the priests who are carrying the Ark touch the water with
their feet, the river will stop flowing as though held back by a dam,
and will pile up as though against an invisible wall! (Josh. 3:13 LB).*

his verse has special meaning for me. One morning, my husband
showed me a large lump that had popped out on his neck
overnight. I promised to call the doctor for an appointment.

As he left for work, I remembered that the staff at the
Stonecroft Ministries Headquarters would be meeting for prayer in a few
minutes. Soon I had Mrs. Baugh, the founder of the Ministries, on the
telephone, and she assured me of their prayer for us. A few minutes later, Miss
Clark, her partner, called. "Millie," she said, "you have written devotionals
telling women what God will do in time of trouble. He will do the same for you
if you let Him."

That day we learned that my husband had Hodgkin's disease, and I faced
a crisis in my life. Could I trust God as I had told others to do?

I had been writing a devotional on the above verse the night before. My
last sentences read, "The rivers of trouble may be flowing before you today. As
you place your foot down on the river of your trouble, God will begin to work
for you." That had been easy to write at midnight when my river was a quiet,
flowing stream. Now a flood had swept in with such fury that I felt myself
sinking. Could I trust God in the midst of *my* flood? I had told others *they*
could. Could I trust my loved one to Him? If I couldn't, I could never write
another devotional.

I spent most of the day on my knees in prayer and in searching His Word.
By the close of the day, I had committed my husband and myself to God with
the assurance that I did trust Him. From my innermost being, I could say with
Paul, "I know whom I have believed, and am persuaded that he is able to keep
that which I have committed unto him against that day" (2 Tim. 1:12).

Someone has said that God doesn't want us to try to *understand* Him so
that we'll know His reasons; He wants us to *believe* Him so that He remains
God.

FEBRUARY 2

Then the LORD said to Moses, "I will rain down bread from heaven for you" (Ex. 16:4 NIV).

efore the Israelites lay the wide expanse of the hot, dusty desert they were to travel over. For the first time its desolation stared them in the face. Only Moses' faith in God gave him the courage to lead over two million people on such a long, hazardous journey. Only daily miracles from God could accomplish it.

Soon the people became dissatisfied. Forgetting the harshness of their captivity, they longed to be back in Egypt. Instead of being thankful for God's guidance and provision for them, they complained about the lack of water to drink, and they complained about their food. How human they were!

In spite of their grumbling spirit, God promised to send bread from heaven. Each person would receive a certain portion. Each morning they were to gather a fresh supply for that day. God faithfully provided this heavenly bread, called manna, every day during their forty-year journey.

During our journey here on earth we need not only food for our bodies but food for our souls. God has provided a balanced diet of spiritual food for us in His Word. Jeremiah said, "Your words are what sustain me; they are food to my hungry soul" (Jer. 15:16 LB).

If we are to maintain a strong spiritual life, we must gather a fresh supply each day. We should daily set aside time with the Lord—time reading the Bible and time in prayer.

As we regularly feed on His Word, our faith is strengthened to face life day by day. "So then faith cometh by hearing, and hearing by the word of God" (Rom. 10:17).

The manna was a picture of the Bread of Heaven, the Lord Jesus Christ. The written Word—the Bible—reveals the reality of the Living Word—Jesus Christ. Jesus Himself said, "I am the bread of life: he that cometh to me shall never hunger; and he that believeth on me shall never thirst" (John 6:35).

As we fellowship with Him through His Word, not only are we strengthened spiritually, but we have His close companionship on our journey through our life's desert. Are you keeping your daily appointment with Him?

FEBRUARY 3

In quietness and in confidence shall be your strength: and ye would not (Isa. 30:15).

 he last four words of this verse came home to me during one of the most difficult times of my life. My husband and I had made a trip to the east coast, and one evening I was alone for a time in the home where we were staying. Desperate for help with a problem I was struggling with, I decided to spend time in prayer.

Repeating my request, I reminded God that I was still waiting for Him to answer. Then it seemed God said, "I am doing what you want, but you are rebelling against the way I am doing it." Suddenly I realized that was true. I was telling God how to answer my request. It's common to try to help God out by telling Him the answer along with the request. Because He wasn't working things out the way I was asking Him to, I thought He wasn't answering.

That night I committed my burden completely to Him, holding nothing back. As I released it into His hand, my heart overflowed with a greater peace than I had ever experienced.

For a time my situation became worse, but I knew God was in control. I could trust Him. He did answer later, but it was in His own way and in His own time, not mine.

After I totally released my problem to Him, I had new spiritual strength. I learned to let God be God in my life, the Lord of each day, the Lord of each need. The Bible says, "For the LORD shall be thy confidence" (Prov. 3:26).

In Psalm 37:5 the psalmist wrote, "Commit thy way unto the LORD; trust also in him; and he shall bring it to pass" (Ps. 37:5). Total commitment gives us confidence to trust Him for the answer.

The Bible says, "Then they cried out to the LORD in their trouble, and he brought them out of their distress. He stilled the storm to a whisper; the waves of the sea were hushed. They were glad when it grew calm, and he guided them to their desired haven. Let them give thanks to the LORD for his unfailing love and his wonderful deeds for men" (Ps. 107:28–31 NIV).

Are you standing in the way of His answers today?

FEBRUARY 4

But Jesus the Son of God is our great High Priest who has gone to heaven itself to help us; therefore let us never stop trusting him (Heb. 4:14 LB).

ne day we decided to go on a roller coaster ride at Long Beach, a wild ride, going out over the water. Our only safety device was a steel bar in front of us. "Do not let go of that bar," the attendant warned us. Halfway through the ride, I was sure I couldn't hold on any longer. In panic I promised the Lord that if He would take me safely to the end of the ride, I would never take another such ride. And I haven't!

Early in my Christian life I learned that I could not make it on my own. I could never hold on to the end. But I made a wonderful discovery. The Lord Jesus became my great High Priest to hold me securely throughout my entire life. I could trust my life to Him.

In the Old Testament, the high priest represented the people before God. He entered into the Holy of Holies once a year to make atonement for the sins of the people. This was a picture of the Lord Jesus who later become our *great* High Priest, a once-for-all sacrifice for our sins.

Jesus is both God and man. He came to represent God on earth, and now He has returned to heaven to represent us before God. He "has gone into heaven itself to help us."

Scripture says, "We *have* a great High Priest." The word *have* indicates possession or ownership. We say, "I have a family (or a home or a car)." But more wonderful than earthly possessions is the reality of having a great High Priest representing us personally before our Heavenly Father. When we say, "I have a great High Priest," it means that we have all His resources to meet our needs. All His resurrection power is available to hold us steadfast and secure.

As we speed along the roller coaster of life, we can experience the reality of our great High Priest's strength and power. His hand will never let go of us.

The Bible says, "Fear thou not . . . for I am thy God: I will strengthen thee; yea, I will help thee; yea, I will uphold thee with the right hand of my righteousness" (Isa. 41:10). No wonder the author of Hebrews says, "Let us never stop trusting him" (Heb. 4:14 LB).

FEBRUARY 5

This High Priest of ours understands our weaknesses, since he had the same temptations we do, though he never once gave way to them and sinned (Heb. 4:15 LB).

ne day I was visiting with a woman whose husband had recently died. Several others were trying to comfort her, also, but suddenly she looked at me and said, "You understand. You know what I'm feeling. You have gone through it, too."

Yes, I had gone through it. I did understand. So I could share some of the lessons I had learned.

A king of long ago wanted to understand his people better, so he disguised himself as a peasant and went throughout his country living among his people, walking with them, working with them. In this way he gained insight into how to be a better king to them. This is what the Lord Jesus did for us.

He came to earth as Jesus, the Son of God. The name *Jesus* speaks of His humanity. "Thou shalt call his name JESUS: for he shall save his people from their sins" (Matt. 1:21). But also He came that He might live life as we live it. Because of His experiences He can enter every area of our lives with real understanding. "For we have not an high priest which cannot be touched with the feeling of our infirmities" (Heb. 4:15). He feels with us in our need. He suffers with us.

He enters into our joys with us—our joy over a new job, a new home, a new grandchild. He enters into our hurts with us—our hurts over rejection, disillusionment, disappointment. He feels our heartaches, loneliness, frustrations, hate, anger, bitterness. He knows what it is to be hungry, thirsty, and weary. When we hurt, He hurts. When we rejoice, He rejoices. Whatever touches us, touches Him.

Are you in need of love, sympathy, and understanding? Do you feel defeated and discouraged? He understands what you are going through. He is right there going through it with you as no one else can.

As we bring each need to Him, Jesus, our great High Priest, lovingly says, "I am with you. I am going through it and feeling it with you. I understand. I care." The Bible says, "Let him have all your worries and cares, for he is always thinking about you and watching everything that concerns you" (1 Peter 5:7 LB).

FEBRUARY 6

Let us come boldly to the very throne of God and stay there to receive his mercy and to find grace to help us in our times of need (Heb. 4:16 LB).

 hat a privilege it is to receive an invitation to visit a well-known personality. Occasionally I have had such a privilege. Yet I am overwhelmed as I realize the greater privilege that is mine—a personal audience with the King of kings.

After completing His work of redemption on earth, Jesus, the Son of God, returned to His home in heaven. There He sits at the right hand of God as our great High Priest, interceding in our behalf. "He ever liveth to make intercession for [us]" (Heb. 7:25). Jesus spent only thirty years on earth, but He has been intervening for us in heaven for nearly two thousand years.

Jesus Christ, our great High Priest, is our only way into God's presence. He said, "I am the way, the truth, and the life: no man cometh unto the Father, but by me" (John 14:6). We can come boldly to the throne of grace confident that the Lord is able to meet *all* our needs. "Let us then fearlessly and confidently and boldly draw near to the throne of . . . God's unmerited favor [to us sinners]" (AMPLIFIED).

He has invited us to come that we may receive mercy. Because He is a merciful God, He does not give us what we deserve. Regardless of our failures and mistakes, He loves us and cares for us.

We are also invited to the throne of God to find grace to help us in our time of need—*help* in the nick of time. God told Paul, "My grace is sufficient for thee" (2 Cor. 12:9). We receive His grace for living in our family world, our business world, our school world, our leisure world, our community world. Our great High Priest is bigger than any and all of our problems. He is always accessible.

His invitation is to come. "Let us come boldly to the very throne of God and stay there to receive his mercy and to find grace to help us in our times of need" (Heb. 4:16 LB).

What is your need today? Because Jesus became man, He understands you and your needs as no one else can. Because He is God, He can act for you. What confidence to know that we have such a great High Priest in heaven today interceding for us!

FEBRUARY 7

He first findeth his own brother Simon, and . . . brought him to
Jesus (John 1:41–42).

ecause of my extensive travels, I am often introduced to people. Someone will want me to meet her husband, mother, sister, or friend. This is always a joy for I have a deep interest in people.

But I find greater joy in the privilege of introducing my dearest Friend, Jesus Christ, to others. I enjoy sharing how He became real to me and what He is doing for me each day.

The Bible tells of a man who had a caring heart for the spiritual needs of others. Andrew cared enough for his brother to introduce him to Jesus. The Bible doesn't tell us much about Andrew, but often he is bringing someone to the Lord.

Andrew had spent time with the Lord, and he was so excited that he hurried to find his brother Peter to bring him to Jesus. He didn't enter into a theological discussion but simply shared his personal experience. Peter went back with him, and as a result, Peter committed his life to Christ.

The greatest work Christians can do is sharing their faith with others.

Bishop Teylor Smith had a passion for souls. Not long before his death, he became ill and was taken to the hospital. Two of his friends went to see him one evening. When they opened the door to his room, his hands were resting on the head of a nurse as he prayed earnestly for her. Not wanting to intrude on this sacred moment, they waited outside. Later, the nurse came out with tears in her eyes. "That dear man," she said. "I am the third nurse he has led to Christ today."

When I married, I moved from my hometown and soon afterward became a Christian. One day a dear friend from home came to visit me. As we talked late at night she said, "Since you left something has happened to you. I don't know what it is, but I want what you have." At two o'clock in the morning we knelt together, and she invited Christ into her life.

After you received Christ as Savior weren't you excited about sharing Him with others? Do you still have that excitement? I believe one of the joys of eternity will be hearing someone say, "I am here in heaven because of you."

FEBRUARY 8

One thing have I desired of the LORD, that will I seek after; that I may dwell in the house of the LORD all the days of my life, to behold the beauty of the LORD, and to inquire in his temple (Ps. 27:4).

f each of us were asked what the greatest desire of our heart is, what would our answer be? It might be a new home, success in business, a new position, a larger bank account, a happy family life. Yet we would discover that acquiring such things alone does not bring inner satisfaction.

In this psalm David spoke of his one desire: "One thing have I desired of the Lord, that will I seek after." David had a one-track mind. He made this desire his life goal.

His goal was threefold. First, his desire was to "dwell in the house of the Lord [in His presence] all the days of my life" (AMPLIFIED). David would not settle for anything less than a close companionship with the Lord. He wanted to feel at home with the Lord, and he wanted the Lord to feel comfortable living in his life.

Next, his desire was to behold the beauty of the Lord. Symbolically, Song of Solomon 5:16 describes the person and character of the Lord Jesus Christ this way: "He is altogether lovely." David wanted "to behold and gaze upon the beauty [the sweet attractiveness and the delightful loveliness] of the Lord" (Ps. 27:4 AMPLIFIED). As we behold Him, He transfers His beauty to us. Our physical beauty fades, but His beauty in us never changes.

Finally, his desire was to "meditate, consider and inquire in His temple" (AMPLIFIED). David needed answers for his life that only God could give. He was an eager inquirer, seeking God's Word, discovering His will and plan for his life.

What is the desire of your heart? Is it to know Him more intimately? To love Him more deeply? To spend more time worshiping and adoring Him?

Once I was visiting a missionary family whose little girl had just been released from the hospital. That evening I stayed with her while her family went to church. As I rocked her, we chatted about many things. Finally she said, "You and I are going to play together in heaven—and Jesus is going to play with us, too," she added.

Later, as I thought about how real Jesus was to her, I prayed that He would always be that real to me.

FEBRUARY 9

What a wonderful God we have—he is the Father of our Lord Jesus Christ, the source of every mercy, and the one who so wonderfully comforts and strengthens us in our hardships and trials. And why does he do this? So that when others are troubled, needing our sympathy and encouragement, we can pass on to them this same help and comfort God has given us (2 Cor. 1:3–4 LB).

 hat do you do when trouble strikes? when you receive a call that your child has been in an accident? when you return home and find a note that your mate has moved out? when you are all alone? Where do you go for comfort?

We have a Comforter who is an unfailing source of consolation. God's comfort surpasses all other. Comfort is defined as someone coming alongside to help, to encourage, to strengthen. In times of trouble God comes alongside. His loving arms uphold us. He comforts as no one else can.

There have been times when I have said, "Father, I can't take any more." Then I can hear His loving whisper, "Yes, you can. I am with you to comfort you. I'll carry your load. If it gets too heavy, don't worry. I will carry you." At times I have sensed Him lifting me up in His arms and carrying me.

Not only does *He* come alongside to comfort us, but He puts other people along our way to be our comforters. One time a member of my family was going through a deep tragedy, and she was afraid I would not be able to come to her. When I arrived on the next plane and she saw me coming up the sidewalk, she said, "Everything will be all right now. Millie is here."

Perhaps God will use you as a comforter to someone else. God doesn't *send* trouble, but He often *allows* it. One reason is to prepare us to comfort others. How can we comfort other people if we can't understand or feel what they are going through?

Out of my own sorrow, heartache, physical pain, and tragedy has come a ministry of comforting others I could never have had otherwise. I can say to people, "I have been there. I understand." And I know how to pray for them.

The greatest comfort I have received from others has not been in words. It has been the tears of my comforters (tears of their heart if not of their eyes). It has been the comfort of their hand holding mine or a hug.

When you need comfort, turn to God first. He who made our hearts knows how to comfort them.

FEBRUARY 10

*The people living in darkness have seen a great light; on those
living in the land of the shadow of death a light has dawned
(Matt. 4:16 NIV).*

ur world is filled with darkness. The darkness of immorality,
materialism, and compromise runs rampant. The Bible says, "If
your eye is evil, your whole body will be full of darkness. If all
the light you have is darkness, it is dark indeed" (Matt. 6:23
PHILLIPS).

Centuries ago, the prophet Isaiah spoke of the Messiah who would one
day come into the world: "You will open the eyes of the blind, and release
those who sit in prison darkness and despair" (Isa. 42:7 LB).

In God's perfect time the Messiah came in human flesh in the person of
Jesus Christ to bring eternal light into this world of darkness. "In him was life;
and the life was the light of men. And the light shineth in darkness; and the
darkness comprehended it not" (John 1:4–5).

Jesus came to bring light not only into this darkened *world,* but into our
darkened *lives.* "[God] hath delivered us from the power of darkness, and hath
translated us into the kingdom of his dear Son" (Col. 1:13).

Jesus said, "I am the Light of the world. So if you follow me, you won't
be stumbling through the darkness, for living light will flood your path" (John
8:12 LB), He was saying, "When you follow me, I will bring My light into the
darkness of your path each day, into the darkness of your uncertain decisions,
into the darkness of your sorrows and heartaches."

Along with our gift of light, comes the responsibility of sharing that light.
We become "light containers" for Him. "For though once your heart was full
of darkness, now it is full of light from the Lord, and your behavior should show
it!" (Eph. 5:8 LB).

In His Sermon on the Mount, Jesus reminded His disciples that they were
to be light for Him in our dark world. "Let your light so shine before men, that
they may see your good works, and glorify your Father which is in heaven"
(Matt. 5:16).

In his boyhood days, Robert Louis Stevenson would see the lamplighters
making their rounds in the evening, lighting the street lamps. One evening, he
said to his nurse, "Look! There is a man punching holes in the dark."

How many holes have you punched in the dark?

And he blessed him, and said, "Blessed be Abram of the most high God, possessor of heaven and earth: And blessed be the most high God, which hath delivered thine enemies into thy hand" (Gen. 14:19—20).

he Hebrew word for *God* in the above Scripture is *El Elyon*. *El* means the Strong One. *Elyon* means to go up, to ascend, or supremacy. As *El Elyon*, God is the Exalted One, the Supreme Being. There is no one higher or mightier than *El Elyon*. This name for God indicates His authority not only in the heavenly realm, but also in the earthly realm. "That men may know that thou, whose name alone is JEHOVAH, art the most high over all the earth" (Ps. 83:18).

There was a time in Abraham's life when he began a new relationship with God as the Most High God. One day he received word that Sodom had been invaded, and his nephew, Lot, had been taken captive. Immediately, he mustered his servants into an army and led them against Lot's captors. With this small army Abraham was able to rescue Lot—not because of his power, but because the Most High God had fought and won the battle for him.

On his way home from battle, Melchizedek, priest of the Most High God, appeared to Abraham, blessing him and reminding him that the Most High God, the Possessor of heaven and earth, had given him the victory.

Abraham learned in a new way who God was. As the Most High God, He could be and do for Abraham what no one else could.

Today you may be in the midst of a battle, under an attack of the enemy. You may not know which way to turn. You have access to *El Elyon*, the Most High God. There is no one higher or more powerful to whom you can go. God says that He is our Most High God. He is in control. No battle is too much for Him. He hasn't lost one yet.

He will hide you in the secret place of the Most High. The Bible says, "He that dwelleth in the secret place of the most High shall abide under the shadow of the Almighty. I will say of the LORD, He is my refuge and my fortress: my God; in him will I trust" (Ps. 91:1—2).

FEBRUARY 12

See then that ye walk circumspectly, not as fools, but as wise (Eph. 5:15).

alking is a part of our lifestyle today. Many people walk for their physical well-being.

Paul suggests a profitable kind of walk for us—a wisdom walk. The word for *walk* here means the way we live. We are to be wise in our daily conduct.

We do not have sufficient wisdom to cope with the needs of life day by day. We face problems we do not have the wisdom to solve. Decisions have to be made and our wisdom is not sufficient. We need a wisdom beyond our own. God has promised to give us wisdom for each need. But we must ask for it. "If you want to know what God wants you to do, ask him, and he will gladly tell you, for he is always ready to give a bountiful supply of wisdom to all who ask him" (James 1:5 LB).

Not only can we receive wisdom by asking for it in prayer, but we receive it through His Word also. "Remember what Christ taught and let his words enrich your lives and make you wise" (Col. 3:16 LB).

Our wisdom comes to us through Jesus Christ, for He is the wisdom of God. The Bible says, "But of him are ye in Christ Jesus, who of God is made unto us wisdom, and righteousness" (1 Cor. 1:30). The New International Version puts it this way: "It is because of him [God] that you are in Christ Jesus, who has become for us wisdom from God."

Paul prayed for wisdom for the Colossians: "Ever since we first heard about you we have kept on praying and asking God to help you understand what he wants you to do; asking him to make you wise about spiritual things; and asking that the way you live will always please the Lord and honor him, so that you will always be doing good, kind things for others, while all the time you are learning to know God better and better" (Col. 1:9–10 LB).

May our walk be a walk of wisdom, revealing Jesus Christ, so that those around us will desire to walk with Him, too.

FEBRUARY 13

But thou, when thou prayest, enter into thy closet, and when thou hast shut thy door, pray to thy Father which is in secret; and thy Father which seeth in secret shall reward thee openly (Matt. 6:6).

he city of Memphis, Tennessee, is very special to me. Little did I realize as I attended a banquet in that city one evening that the direction of my life would be changed.

As the soloist began to sing, the Spirit of God spoke to my heart in a way that would change my life. The soloist sang the song, "Teach me to Pray." As I listened to the words, tears began to flow down my cheeks. I whispered, "God, will You teach me to pray, to *really* pray?"

Prayer and God's Word had always had top priority in my life, but this was different. God was calling me to a ministry of prayer.

I decided that if my ministry were to change in this way, I would learn everything I could about the subject. I bought every book on prayer I could find. However, as I began to read them, I became confused. One would tell me to pray one way, another would suggest a different way. Soon I put the books away. (Later I could read them and take from them what God wanted me to have.)

I knelt down and asked God if *He* would teach me to pray the way He wanted me to pray. I began my own personalized prayer course—the Lord as teacher and I as His student. Lovingly and patiently, my heavenly Father taught me step by step not just *how* to pray but *to pray*.

What helpful lessons He taught me! I have always been afraid to pray aloud, but God taught me to pray aloud when alone. As I became used to hearing my voice, it helped me to phrase my prayers. Another lesson I learned was to pray my own way in words I was used to. God didn't want me to pray like everyone else. As a result, this gave me freedom to pray aloud with others.

Through my own special prayer course I have learned that prayer is not giving God a news report. He knows already. It isn't demanding my rights from Him. It is not giving Him ideas on how to handle my life and the lives of others. There have been times when I have tried to help Him out.

Prayer is entering into fellowship with God. It is being in partnership with Him. It is praying for our families as God would; for our neighbors as God would; for our friends, our state, our country, our world as He would.

"Lord, teach us to pray" (Luke 11:1).

FEBRUARY 14

I have loved you with an everlasting love; I have drawn you with loving-kindness (Jer. 31:3 NIV).

uring the first World War, three Christian soldiers were stationed in London. On their way to downtown London on Christmas Eve, they passed Queen Anne's Orphanage and decided to stop and help in the children's Christmas celebration. Discovering that the children had no Christmas tree, decorations, or packages, they shared what few things they had, such as pocket knives, pens, and other small articles.

One of the soldiers spotted a little boy sitting in a corner by himself. Walking over to the boy, he asked, "What do you want for Christmas?"

The boy answered quickly, "All I want is to be loved."

In today's world, people all about us are searching for love. The universal cry is, "I want someone to love me."

God answered that cry. He said, "I, Myself, have loved you." He cannot do anything less. "God is love" (1 John 4:8).

It is a **personal** love. Because God is love, He needed an object on which to pour out His love. Through Jesus Christ, we became the recipients. Perhaps you are saying, "He couldn't love me. I am unlovable. I am unworthy." But He *does* love you. He says He does, and we can believe Him.

It is a **permanent** love. It is unchangeable, everlasting. His love does not vary according to who we are, what we do, or how we feel. It is steadfast. "Having loved his own . . . he loved them unto the end" (John 13:1).

Paul says, "For I am convinced that nothing can ever separate us from his love. Death can't, and life can't. The angels won't, and all the powers of hell itself cannot keep God's love away. Our fears for today, our worries about tomorrow, or where we are—high above the sky, or in the deepest ocean—nothing will ever be able to separate us from the love of God demonstrated by our Lord Jesus Christ when he died for us" (Rom. 8:38–39 LB).

God's love is also a **pulling** love. He says, "I have drawn you." Reaching out to us from His loving heart, He pulls us to Himself by cords of love.

Rest and revel in the reality of His love for you. His love is for real, for He is for real!

I can do all things through Christ which strengtheneth me
(Phil. 4:13).

aul is a "Can-Do" Christian. He learned the secret of a strength that can do anything. This does not mean, however, that his life was easy. He was persecuted, beaten, stoned, imprisoned. Many of us would have thrown up our hands and said, "I'm through." But not Paul. He said, "I can . . . " When we say "I can't," we limit the ability of God to work in our lives.

Paul had discovered that his source of strength was "through Christ." He possessed all the resources of God for facing life and its situations, but his access to these resources was through Christ.

No circumstances could defeat Paul, for he knew that nothing was beyond the power of God. He considered his obstacles stepping-stones, not stumbling blocks. He recognized that each difficulty was an opportunity for God to demonstrate His power.

Because the source of his strength was Christ, he was secure in the fact that he could accomplish *all things* God wanted to do through him. "I have strength for all things in Christ Who empowers me—I am ready for anything and equal to anything through Him Who infuses inner strength into me; [that is, I am self-sufficient in Christ's sufficiency]" (AMPLIFIED).

We can say with Paul, "I can do all things through Christ, which strengtheneth me." Christ is our Enabler, our Power. The power of Christ living in us causes us to rise above our circumstances as we trust them to Him. He will not require anything of us that He will not enable us to do. I can be what God wants me to be, do what He wants me to do, go where He wants to send me, and say what He wants me to say, not in my power but His.

More than Christ *giving* us strength, He *is* our strength. *Strengthen* in this verse is the Greek present tense which emphasizes continuous action. His strengthening comes moment by moment and day by day.

How often, I wonder, do we try to serve God limited by our incompetence rather than in His limitless omnipotence? When we stand before Him, we will have no excuses.

Are you missing out on something God wants to do in your life because you are saying, "I can't do it?"

FEBRUARY 16

[God] is able to keep you from falling, and to present you faultless before the presence of his glory with exceeding joy (Jude 24).

ccasionally, we watch little babies taking their first steps. Everything goes fine as long as someone holds their hand. However, as soon as the hand is withdrawn, down they go. When the person helps them up, the babies continue their walking experience.

We begin our Christian walk with faltering steps, too. We encounter obstacles that cause us to stumble. Burdens become so heavy, we almost go down under their weight. Our paths are often rough and our enemy strong. We need help.

We have a Guide who is able to keep us from falling. A key word in this verse is *keep*. It means to protect, guide, watch over. The Bible says, "For I the LORD thy God will hold thy right hand, saying unto thee, Fear not; I will help thee" (Isa. 41:13). We can be thankful that He holds our hand. If we had to hold onto His, we might lose our grip and fall.

At times, our paths may take us up rocky mountains. Mountain climbers often rope themselves together, so that if an inexperienced climber should slip, the skilled climber could hold him steady and break his fall. In our Christian climb, we are *tied* to our Guide, the One who never misses a step. With Him, we can scale the dangerous mountain cliffs before us in safety.

The Bible says, "He makes my feet like hinds' feet [able to stand firmly or make progress on the dangerous heights of testing and trouble]; He sets me securely upon my high places" (Ps. 18:33 AMPLIFIED).

If we stumble or fall, He is there to lift us up and put us back on our feet. "The Lord lifts the fallen and those bent beneath their loads" (Ps. 145:14 LB).

And one day Christ will present us *faultless* to His Heavenly Father. Paul wrote of this presentation day: "That he might sanctify and cleanse [us] with the washing of water by the word, that he might present [us] to himself a glorious church, not having spot, or wrinkle, or any such thing; but that [we] should be holy and without blemish" (Eph. 5:26–27). Through our position in Christ, we can stand before Him perfect and complete. What a day!

FEBRUARY 17

O Israel, can't I do to you as this potter has done to his clay? As the clay is in the potter's hand, so are you in my hand (Jer. 18:6 LB).

od sent Jeremiah the prophet to the potter's house and there gave him this message: "As the clay is in the potter's hand, so are you in my hand."

God is in the business of molding lives for His glory. He has a plan and purpose for each of us. Whether He can accomplish His purpose depends on our response to His touch upon our lives.

One time, I watched a potter working on his potter's wheel. He had a particular pattern in mind for the vase and selected the right clay for that particular vessel. As I watched him put it on the wheel, the wheel began to turn, and he applied the right amount of pressure in the right place to form the vase according to his pattern. Out of his labor evolved a lovely vessel reflecting his workmanship.

The Master Potter selects a certain lump of clay, clay having no particular value or beauty, for each vessel. He plans to mold something lovely out of it, a vessel of special beauty. From the beginning he can see the image of Jesus Christ in that formless lump of clay.

Then He puts the clay on the Wheel of Life and begins His work. We do not have anything to say about it, for we might spoil His beautiful design. As God works, perhaps He is thinking, "If only this lump of clay would submit to my hand . . ."

It is not easy to submit. We begin to ask, "Why?" or "Does it have to be done this way?" The Bible says, "O man, who art thou that repliest against God? Shall the thing formed say to him that formed it, Why hast thou made me thus? Hath not the potter power over the clay, of the same lump to make one vessel unto honour, and another unto dishonour?" (Rom. 9:20–21).

When it is finished, the vessel is an expression of the very heart and will of God in our lives. He leaves something of Himself in us. We can say, "We are the clay, and thou our potter; and we all are the work of thy hand" (Isa. 64:8).

It is amazing what a blob of clay can become in the hands of God.

O Israel, can't I do to you as this potter has done to his clay? As the clay is in the potter's hand, so are you in my hand (Jer. 18:6 LB).

od had a special purpose for the apostle Paul's life. He said, "He is a chosen vessel unto me, to bear my name before the Gentiles, and kings, and the children of Israel" (Acts 9:15).

We, too, are chosen vessels to bear the Name of Jesus in the world today. His name represents who He is, His character. We have been molded into vessels to share Jesus Christ with our families, neighbors, schools, and communities.

Our Master Potter has a custom-designed plan for our lives to fulfill His particular purpose for each of us. We are to become His custom-designed vessels for His custom-designed purpose.

As He works with us, He knows where and how much pressure to apply to bring out the beauty of the vessel. For each of us He uses special custom-designed pressures, such as sorrow, fear, uncertainty, sickness, broken hearts, and pain.

Suddenly, we begin to rebel. We don't like what is happening. We question His process. We ask Him why. We begin to argue with Him. Sometimes, we even become bitter. We shift our focus from the Potter to what is happening on the wheel and we cry, "Stop!" We must learn that His part is to work; our part is to submit.

The Bible says, "Woe to the man who fights with his Creator. Does the pot argue with its maker? Does the clay dispute with him who forms it, saying, 'Stop, you're doing it wrong?'" (Isa. 45:9 LB). The Master Potter gives His answer. "Jehovah, the Holy One of Israel, Israel's Creator, says: What right have you to question what I do? Who are you to command me concerning the work of my hands?" (Isa. 45:11 LB).

None of His work is wasted. He uses each turn of the wheel, each degree of pressure from His hand to fashion a vessel to reflect His glory.

The apostle Paul says, "We are his workmanship, created in Christ Jesus unto good works, which God hath before ordained that we should walk in them" (Eph. 2:10).

What skill the Master Potter displays to bring value and purpose to the shapeless lump of clay!

FEBRUARY 19

O Lord . . . we are the clay, and thou our potter; and we all are the work of thy hand (Isa. 64:8).

ou are special to God! Because His individual design for your life is unique, He doesn't trust the work to anyone but Himself.

The day I watched the potter, I saw one of the vessels crumble in his hand. A bubble or hard bit had spoiled the clay. He tossed it away.

Not so with our loving Potter. As He works on our lives, hard bits or bubbles may cause our vessel to break. There may be bits of self-will, demanding our rights, a critical spirit, stubbornness, or personal ambition. Bubbles of envy, jealousy, pride, or self-centeredness may appear. Right there in the hand of the Potter our vessel is marred. "So he made it again another vessel, as seemed good to the potter to make it" (Jer. 18:4).

Our Potter doesn't scold or rebuke us. He doesn't toss us aside. He holds us in His loving hands and begins to restore our marred lives as we submit to Him. He continues with the work of making us more Christlike. Never does His patience run out. He isn't in a hurry. He has our lifetime to complete His work.

Today you may feel your life is useless, a failure, of no value. You may feel discouraged, as though life isn't worthwhile. But you are in the Master Potter's hand, and He can remake your life into one of beauty to reflect Jesus Christ.

One day as Paganini, the great violinist, attended an auction, he noticed a violin that no one seemed interested in. Paganini picked it up and started to play. Everyone became quiet as they heard the exquisite music of the instrument.

When he finished playing, the crowd stood silent in almost reverential awe. Then everyone clamored to bid. The violin had become an instrument of great value. Why? The master's touch.

God deeply desires us to be molded into the image of Jesus Christ. The important thing is not what we have been, or what we are, but what we are becoming through the touch of the Master's hand on our lives.

And let the beauty of the LORD our God be upon us: and establish thou the work of our hands upon us; yea, the work of our hands establish thou it" (Ps. 90:17).

For there stood by me this night the angel of God, whose I am, and whom I serve (Acts 27:23).

aul was a champion survivor. On the way to Rome as a prisoner, he experienced a storm so severe that all hope vanished. But Paul had three stabilizers that carried him through. His first stabilizer was his true **identity,** "whose I am." He discovered that neither his cultural nor religious background was sufficient. His personal relationship with Jesus gave him his identity. He said, "I consider everything a loss compared to the surpassing greatness of knowing Christ Jesus my Lord" (Phil. 3:8 NIV).

His identification with Christ brought reality and genuineness into his life. We find our real identity, too, in our relationship with Jesus. "For in him we live and move and have our being" (Acts 17:28 NIV).

His next stabilizer was his **trust in the Lord.** He said, "I know whom I have believed" (2 Tim. 1:12). His belief was not in some*thing* but in some*one*. It is easy to believe God when everything is going smoothly, but we can trust the Lord when hope is gone. We can say, "I believe God, that it shall be even as it was told me" (Acts 27:25).

The third stabilizer in his life was his **involvement,** "whom I serve." Serving the Lord brought purpose into his life. He said, "this one thing I do, forgetting those things which are behind, and reaching forth unto those things which are before, I press toward the mark for the prize of the high calling of God in Christ Jesus" (Phil. 3:13–14).

When we're going through a storm, it's easy to feel sorry for ourselves. But when we become involved in serving Christ, we have to leave our pity party and focus our attention on others.

What do you do when a storm hits? What stabilizes your life? With our spiritual stabilizers at work, nothing can move us. Our stabilizers are: I am *His*! I believe *Him*! I serve *Him*! Nothing can move us for our anchor in Jesus Christ stabilizes our lives.

The psalmist said, "O God, be merciful unto me: for my soul trusteth in thee: yea, in the shadow of thy wings will I make my refuge, until these calamities be overpast" (Ps. 57:1).

FEBRUARY 21

Elijah was as completely human as we are (James 5:17 LB).

e often assume that people from the Bible lived on a high spiritual level, free from problems. Yet, as we study their lives, we discover they were ordinary people like you and me who became extraordinary because they let God work in their lives. This was true of Elijah. He was one of God's giants, yet he was as human as we are.

Elijah lived in one of the most evil times of Israel's history. He was an ordinary person from an obscure town, but he was God's man of the hour to take a message of impending judgment to King Ahab. God wanted to demonstrate through Elijah that Jehovah was the true and living God.

One day, Elijah strode into the palace of King Ahab and said, "As the LORD God of Israel liveth, before whom I stand, there shall not be dew nor rain these years, but according to my word" (1 Kings 17:1).

What gave this rugged individualist his boldness and courage? The meaning of his name gives some indication. It means *my God is Jehovah*. His life proved it. To Elijah God was "for real." Elijah had an intimate relationship with Him. He could courageously stand before the king because he had first stood in the presence of the One greater than the king. He could say, in effect, "I represent the living God. You may not know it, King Ahab, but God is still alive and in control."

Elijah's confidence was also the result of his prayer life. The Bible says, "he prayed earnestly" (James 5:17). His life revealed the power of God working in a person humble enough to believe God. Elijah at God's disposal was all God needed.

In our day, when morals have declined and wickedness prevails, the most effective way to convince the world of the reality of Jesus Christ is not by our words alone, but by the way we live—living the reality that only God can produce. People are watching to see our reactions to the circumstances in our lives.

God is still looking for Elijahs. Can people see the reality of the Lord in you? What is happening in the world because you are praying?

Someone has said that God often shows *His* power through "nobodies."

FEBRUARY 22

Then the Lord said to Elijah, "Go to the east, and hide by Cherith Brook . . . where it enters the Jordan River" (1 Kings 17:3 LB).

lijah had been sent on a special mission to warn King Ahab that his nation was to be punished for its wickedness. No rain would fall for three-and-a-half years. This angered the king, and Elijah had to flee for safety.

God told Elijah to go to Cherith Brook to hide. This would be the ideal time for God to prepare Elijah for future missions God had scheduled. Elijah would learn to know God in a more intimate way and to completely depend on Him.

There were no restaurants in Elijah's desert hideaway, no grocery stores. God sent food by special delivery. "Thou shalt drink of the brook; and I have commanded the ravens to feed thee there" (v. 4). In effect, God was saying, "I have told you to go there. I have a purpose for your being there. And I will provide for you there." *There* is any place God sends us.

By the brook Elijah had priority time with God. God enrolled him in His School of Solitude. Elijah's major was Communion with God. Included in his curriculum were such subjects as worship, praise, prayer, trust, and obedience. During this time alone with God, his faith deepened. God became more real to him. Out of this preparation and training developed a man God could use.

Today God may have hidden you by a brook in a desert place. Your brook may be sickness, bereavement, a family situation. Take priority time with Him. In His School of Solitude, major in Communion with God. The Bible says, "Be still, and know that I am God" (Ps. 46:10). Study the subjects Elijah took—worship, praise, prayer, trust, and obedience. You may need to reevaluate your motives, change your attitudes, rearrange your priorities, commit certain areas of your life to God.

Perhaps you have become so busy you have not been giving Him that quality time He desires. So many voices have clamored for your attention that you have missed His voice.

At your brook, you will have time to commune with God. At your brook, you will have time to learn to trust Him. At your brook, you will be strengthened and encouraged for whatever mission God has ahead.

The Bible says, "In quietness and in confidence shall be your strength" (Isa. 30:15).

FEBRUARY 23

And it came to pass after a while, that the brook dried up, because there had been no rain in the land (1 Kings 17:7).

hen I was in school, it was easy for me to learn from the textbooks. I could quote them perfectly. But in an examination if I had to apply what I had learned to some problem, that was not as easy. God gives us examinations occasionally to see how well we have learned His lessons. He did this with Elijah.

One morning Elijah noticed that the water level at the brook was lower than usual. There had been no rain for some time, and it was affecting his water supply. Perhaps he thought, "Surely this brook won't fail. Am I not here at God's command?"

But the brook did dry up. God wanted to teach Elijah not to trust in the brook but in Him. When resources are exhausted, God remains. Elijah could have wondered if God had forgotten him, but he knew he must not move until God moved him. He must wait by the dried-up brook until God directed his next step. God knew where Elijah was, and in His time He revealed the next move.

Perhaps you are sitting by a dried-up brook—a broken home, a move, financial reverses, failing health. Maybe something you have been trusting in is gone. You may be perplexed, bitter, even blaming God.

At our dried-up brooks we realize that we are not able to cope with our problems. God is the only One who is sufficient. There is nothing like a dried-up brook to bring us to our knees.

At our dried-up brook our faith can be developed and strengthened. The Bible speaks of, "Faith which is that leaning of the whole human personality on God in absolute trust and confidence in His power, wisdom, and goodness" (2 Thess. 1:11 AMPLIFIED).

At our dried-up brook we learn whether we love God for what He gives us or for who He is. It has been said that life looks much the same from a dried-up brook as from a brook full of water if we are looking at God and not at the brook. "Acquaint now thyself with him, and be at peace: thereby good shall come unto thee" (Job 22:21).

When nothing is left except God, we find that He is all we need.

FEBRUARY 24

And the barrel of meal wasted not, neither did the cruse of oil fail,
according to the word of the LORD, which he spake by Elijah
(1 Kings 17:16).

lijah's brook had dried up, but God had not forgotten him. One day He told Elijah to go to Zarephath. Obediently Elijah went.

Zarephath means a smelting furnace, a crucible, a refining process. Someday Elijah would stand against the prophets of Baal and the people of Israel. He would challenge God's people to turn from their false gods to the living God. It would not be an easy assignment. He must be totally committed to God. Every bit of Elijah had to be purged from Elijah.

When the prophet arrived in Zarephath, he discovered that his hostess had only enough meal and oil left for one cake for her son and herself. Then they faced starvation. What were her resources? A little meal! A little oil! God had sent Elijah to a poverty-stricken widow so that his faith would have to be in God, no one else.

Elijah told the widow to make a cake for him first, then God would provide for her and her son. In faith she obeyed. Perhaps this was an answer to her prayer for provisions.

Because of her obedience, she had an inexhaustible supply. Every day there was enough left for their next meal. The widow and her son learned to trust God. Elijah learned that the God he trusted was a miracle-working God, a God who could do the impossible.

God may move us to a Zarephath, a refining plant in our lives. He wants us to learn to put our trust completely in Him, no matter what. He may see traits such as self-reliance, self-pity, and self-sufficiency, that need to be removed so that we may learn to trust our God who can do the impossible.

Our great Refiner puts us in the crucible and turns on the heat, knowing the exact degree of heat necessary for our refining. Lovingly, He watches over the melting process. As the dross rises to the surface, He removes it. Pure metal remains. When the refining is accomplished, He turns off the heat.

Is the heat turned on in your life? Are you in the refining process? God is lovingly removing all of self so that your dependence will be completely in Him. "When he hath tried me, I shall come forth as gold" (Job 23:10).

FEBRUARY 25

Then pray to your god, and I will pray to the Lord; and the god who answers by sending fire to light the wood is the true God! And all the people agreed to this test (1 Kings 18:24 LB).

 ow was God's time for a contest between Jehovah and Baal, between the Living God and the false gods. God sent Elijah back to King Ahab, requesting that he call together the children of Israel and the prophets of Baal.

At Mount Carmel Elijah stood before the two groups with the courage and power of one who trusts God in every circumstance.

Elijah challenged the people to make a choice—either worship the true God or Baal. "How long halt ye between two opinions? if the LORD be God, follow him: but if Baal, then follow him. And the people answered him not a word" (v. 21).

First, the prophets of Baal were to sacrifice a bullock on the altar and call on their gods. Then Elijah would do the same thing. Whichever one answered by fire was God. The prophets began calling on their gods. In a state of frenzy they shouted and leaped about, cutting themselves until blood flowed. There was no response. Eventually, they had to give up in defeat.

Now it was Elijah's turn. After the altar was repaired, the sacrifice and wood were arranged, then saturated with water. Elijah prayed: "LORD God of Abraham, Isaac, and of Israel, let it be known this day that thou art God in Israel, and that I am thy servant, and . . . that thou art the LORD God, and that thou hast turned their heart back again" (v. 36–37). His prayer was brief, specific, and concerned only for God's glory.

Suddenly, the fire fell. God had heard and answered Elijah's prayer. "And when all the people saw it, they fell on their faces: and they said, The LORD, he is the God; the LORD, he is the God" (v. 39).

The fire fell because one man prayed. The people acknowledged the true God because one man was in touch with Him.

God is looking for modern-day Elijahs—people whose prayers can turn a world back to the living God.

What is happening in the world today because of your prayers? The Bible says, "I sought for a man among them, that should make up the hedge, and stand in the gap before me for the land, that I should not destroy it: but I found none" (Ezek. 22:30).

Are you available?

There is a sound of abundance of rain (1 Kings 18:41).

 great spiritual awakening came to Israel when the fire fell on Mount Carmel. But even though God's promise to send rain had not yet been fulfilled, Elijah told Ahab, "There is a sound of abundance of rain." At that time, there was no sign of a cloud in the sky. Yet with Elijah's ears of faith, he could hear the rain. God had promised, and he believed God.

Elijah went to the top of the mountain to pray. He humbled himself before God, recognizing his sole dependence on Him. James 5:17 says, "He prayed earnestly." It delights God when we come in simple faith with all the earnestness of our heart.

Elijah then sent his servant to look for a rain cloud. When the servant returned, saying, "There is nothing" (1 Kings 18:43), Elijah continued praying, looking, and expecting. If he had depended on what he could see, he would have been discouraged and quit. But he knew God's delays are not denials.

Persistent, Elijah sent his servant back seven times. And it was not until the seventh time that his servant said, "Behold, there ariseth a little cloud out of the sea, like a man's hand" (v. 44). He told his servant to hurry and tell Ahab that the rain was coming. And soon it came.

God didn't answer Elijah's prayer because he was a prophet or because he lived on a special spiritual level. The Bible says that "Elijah was as completely human as we are, and yet when he prayed earnestly that no rain would fall, none fell for the next three and one half years! Then he prayed again, this time that it *would* rain, and down it poured" (James 5:17 LB). Prayer made the difference in Elijah's life. He simply believed God. "And the hand of the LORD was on Elijah" (1 Kings 18:46).

Are you looking for a raincloud of relief from some drought in your life? Are you discouraged because you can't see even a sign of a cloud? If Elijah's God is your God, He is with you today. Elijah's God will answer prayer for you, too.

FEBRUARY 27

And after the fire a still small voice (1 Kings 19:12).

After a great victory, we often experience a letdown, a time of depression. After Elijah's victory at Mount Carmel, Jezebel warned that she would have him killed. Terrified, Elijah fled for his life.

Finally, he sat under a juniper tree. Filled with self-pity, he prayed, "I've had enough . . . Take away my life" (v. 4 LB). He was probably thinking, "Lord, I've been faithful to you, but this is too much. I give up."

He was physically and emotionally exhausted. The Lord knew he needed rest and food. After he was physically refreshed, he continued on his way until he came to a cave, where he retreated. It became a cave of self-pity with an invisible sign over it: Out of Service.

God asked, "What are you doing here, Elijah?" God didn't rebuke or scold him. He loved him just as he was and where he was. But Elijah had his eyes on Jezebel, his circumstances, and himself instead of the Lord. He needed a fresh revelation of the Lord and who He was.

God said, "Go forth, and stand upon the mount before the LORD" (v. 11). God sent the wind, the earthquake, and the fire, but the Lord was not in them. They were a mighty demonstration of the power of God, but they didn't reveal the person of God.

Finally Elijah heard the still, small voice. It was God's voice of gentle stillness, a whisper of love for Elijah.

I believe that as Elijah stood in God's presence, all the bitterness and self-pity poured out of his heart. Cleansed of self and refreshed by God's Spirit, he gave the control of his life back to God. He was ready for service again. Now he could hang out a new sign: Back in Service.

Today are you in a cave of disappointment? self-pity? failure? heartache? Have you said, "I'm through"? Have you hung up an Out-of-Service sign? God cannot use you hidden in a cave. He says, "Come out of your cave and stand before me."

Listen to Him lovingly speaking to you in the still small voice of His Word. As you listen, you, too, are cleansed, refreshed, and ready for service again. Then you can hang out a new sign: Back in Service.

I being in the way, the LORD led me (Gen. 24:27).

n Abraham's culture, the father selected his son's bride. Abraham sent Eliezer, his faithful servant, back to the homeland to select Isaac's bride. Eliezer had confidence that God would lead him on this mission.

Approaching his destination, Eliezer stopped by a well, a gathering place for women as they drew water. Sensitive to his mission, he committed the result of his errand to God: "O LORD . . . give me success today, and show kindness to my master Abraham" (v. 12 NIV). It was a simple prayer, and specific. He went on to ask that the girl of God's choice would not only give Eliezer a drink but would offer to water his camels also.

God answered his prayer. Rebekah, the right girl, took him home to meet her family. When Eliezer told why he had come, Rebekah accepted the proposal and her family agreed to let her become Isaac's bride. Eliezer could then say, "I being in the way, the LORD led me" (v. 27). Mission accomplished!

The same God who led Eliezer is ready to lead us. The psalmist said, "You chart the path ahead of me" (Ps. 139:3 LB). He knows each step of our way, each insurmountable obstacle, each unknown area. He commits Himself to be our Guide.

My husband and I needed a guide the first time we went to New York City. The huge metropolis was frightening. How would we be able to find our way around and see the many things that interested us?

A friend introduced us to someone who lived there, and he became our guide. In two days we saw more than we would have in several days on our own.

The psalmist said, "Order my steps in thy word" (Ps. 119:133). God guides those who walk in obedience, those "in His way." *Being in the way* means being in His will. So we must spend time in His Word, for His will is always in agreement with His Word.

Our Guide has never given wrong directions. The Lord perfectly charts each day of our lives. As we follow Him, we can say, "I being in the way, the LORD led me."

It has been said that God-yielded people will have God-planned lives.

MARCH 1

*Pray ye therefore the Lord of the harvest, that he will send forth la-
bourers into his harvest (Matt. 9:38).*

verywhere Jesus went crowds followed Him. Some needed a
healing touch from Him. Some were curious. Others wanted to
hear every word He spoke, for no one else spoke as He did.
He saw people, not as a mass of humanity, but as
individuals whom He loved. Many of them had a form of religion but did not
know the reality of God Himself in their lives. His heart was moved with
compassion for them.

The Greek word used here for *compassion* means an intense yearning for,
feeling from the depths of His innermost being. The Bible says, "And what pity
he felt for the crowds that came, because their problems were so great and they
didn't know what to do or where to go for help. They were like sheep without a
shepherd" (v. 36 LB).

Take a sightseeing tour today, looking at people through the eyes of Jesus:
in airports, shops, banks, restaurants, neighborhoods, on the street, everywhere.
What a difference it makes when we see them through His eyes. When He saw
them, He was moved with compassion.

What moves us? We are moved with excitement at a ball game. We are
moved with appreciation at a concert. We are moved with tears or laughter
during a television program.

Are we moved with compassion for the lost? Can we hear the crying of
millions and millions of souls in the darkness of despair because their hearts are
broken and their lives are filled with hurts, disappointments, and failures? Are
we afraid to see the multitudes as Jesus did, to be disturbed in our comfortable
lives?

As Jesus looked on people, He saw their potential: "the harvest truly is
plenteous" (v. 37). Their future destiny was at stake. His heart must have
ached as He had to say "but the labourers are few" (v. 38).

Then He gives the key to recruiting workers. He says, "Pray ye."
Methods alone won't reach them. Plans won't. Programs won't. The secret to
recruiting workers is **prayer.** *"Pray ye. ..the Lord of the harvest, that he* will
send forth labourers into his harvest" (v. 38, emphasis mine).

But remember, as you begin to pray for workers to go into the harvest
fields, *you* may be God's answer to your own prayer.

MARCH 2

When they walk through the Valley of Weeping it will become a place of springs where pools of blessing and refreshment collect after rains!" (Ps. 84:6 LB).

The Valley of Weeping has been described as the longest valley in the world, heavily populated with turmoil, fear, perplexity, suffering, uncertainty, bitterness, rejection, and pain.

The Lord knows that sometime we will go through this valley. But the psalmist says we will walk *through* it. This implies an exit.

And in the valley He is our strength. "As thy days, so shall thy strength be" (Deut. 33:25).

As thy day —the kind of a day such as one Thanksgiving when my husband's family was coming for dinner. First I spilled grease on the stove. Then I spilled something on the tablecloth and had to wash it and iron it. Finally, I knocked a pan of sweet sauce onto the floor. By that time it was a joke.

As thy day —the kind of a day when I received an early phone call that my mother was dying, and she was gone before I arrived.

"They go from strength to strength" (Ps. 84:7). Normally, we go from strength to exhaustion. But in this valley we go, not from fear to fear or struggle to struggle, but from strength to strength.

His strength is sufficient for each day as it comes, whatever it holds. His strength is made perfect for each day. The Lord told Paul, "My strength is made perfect in weakness" (2 Cor. 12:9).

Another resource is our commitment to God's way. "Above all else to follow your steps" (Ps. 84:5 LB). Sometimes we want to go our way, the easy way, or the way someone else is going. But when we go God's way, He accompanies us, holds our hand, and leads us through it.

What will we let God do in our lives in the valley? The psalmist said, "It will become a place of springs where pools of blessing and refreshment collect after rains." God can transform our tears into pools of blessing for the benefit of others.

Best of all, in the valley we have a dear Companion. "Each of them is invited to meet with the Lord in Zion" (v. 7 LB).

As we go from strength to strength, following Him, may we create pools of blessing that will help others find Jesus Christ.

MARCH 3

Blessed are the undefiled in the way, who walk in the law of the LORD (Ps. 119:1).

any people today are searching for that elusive thing called happiness. The real source of happiness is God. The word *blessed* in Scripture is often translated *happy*. "Happy are all who perfectly follow the laws of God" (v. 1 LB).

Happy are those who are "in the way," God's way as revealed in His Word. "As for God, his way is perfect: the word of the LORD is tried: he is a buckler to all those that trust in him" (Ps. 18:30). God's perfect way is manifest in the person of His Son, Jesus Christ. Jesus said, "I am the way, the truth, and the life" (John 14:6).

Many equate happiness with pleasure, position, and prosperity, but real happiness comes from living according to the principles in God's Word. "Who walk—that is, order their conduct and conversation—in [the whole of God's revealed will]" (Ps. 119:1 AMPLIFIED).

God's Word is a map to guide us on life's journey. "The whole Bible was given to us by inspiration from God and is useful to teach us what is true and to make us realize what is wrong in our lives; it straightens us out and helps us to do what is right. It is God's way of making us well prepared at every point, fully equipped to do good to everyone" (2 Tim. 3:16–17 LB).

But knowing God's Word is not enough. We must also obey it. "How blessed are those who observe His testimonies, who seek Him with all their heart" (v. 2 NASB). It is not a half-hearted obedience but a desire to do that which will please God.

His laws are not options that we choose either to follow or ignore. They are directives from Him to be kept diligently. The psalmist said, "You have given us your laws to obey—oh, how I want to follow them consistently" (v. 4–5 LB). When we are walking God's way in obedience to His Word, we will seek *Him* with all our heart.

Is your heart's desire to know the reality of Jesus Christ more than anything else?

LORD, thou hast been our dwelling place in all generations . . . from everlasting to everlasting (Ps. 90:1–2).

Those who have to travel regularly in their work have a particular appreciation for home.

Moses did not know the certainty of a permanent home. He spent only a few years with his parents, some years in the pharaoh's palace, then the rest of his life in the desert. In Psalm 90 Moses says that he has another home, more real than any earthly dwelling. In essence he wrote, "Lord, you are my home."

Moses knew God as the God of eternity. "Before the mountains were brought forth . . . thou art God" (v. 2). He existed before anything else existed. He was **the God of eternity past.**

On one of my trips to Switzerland, I had a lovely view of the lofty Alps from my bedroom window. As I gazed at the towering heights of those majestic peaks, they looked ageless. Yet Moses wrote that even before the mountains were, "thou art God." Our God is unchanging. He has always been and always will be.

No wonder Moses was able to lead the children on their trackless march through the wilderness. His trust was in the God who made the mountains, who was from everlasting to everlasting.

Our homes are our earthly dwelling places. In our homes we are fed, we rest, we are protected, and we have fellowship with our family.

But we have another dwelling place, an eternal one, the Lord Himself. The Lord provides nourishment for our inner being, rest, and fellowship. In the Lord, our eternal dwelling place, we find perfect satisfaction.

God is also **the God of eternity future.** Before returning to heaven, Jesus said to His disciples, "In my Father's house are many mansions . . . I go to prepare a place for you . . . I will come again, and receive you unto myself; that where I am, there ye may be also" (John 14:2–3). One day He will return for us, His children, and our eternity future will begin.

Not only is He the God of eternity past and future, He is **the God of today.** "Thou art God." Need we fear when He is the solid foundation of our lives? No matter what we face today, we have this confidence, "My God is the rock of my refuge" (Ps. 94:22). I am safe at home with Him.

But God's correction is always right and for our best good, that we may share his holiness. Being punished isn't enjoyable while it is happening—it hurts! But afterwards we can see the result, a quiet growth in grace and character (Heb. 12:10–11 LB).

t has been said that the heavenly Father has no spoiled children. He loves them too much to allow it.

Good parents accept the responsibility of guiding their children's lives. Part of the training includes discipline. No child welcomes it, and at times it may seem unjust. But for the good of the child it must be administered.

We often think of the Lord's chastening as punishment. But the word used for *chastening* does not mean punishment. It means the discipline of child training, that which is needed to bring a person to maturity.

God's chastening process proves His love for us. An earthly father may act in anger, but not our heavenly Father. He disciplines not because He is angry, but because Hé loves us. He never chastens because His patience is exhausted, but rather because it is necessary. The writer of Hebrews says, "Regard not lightly the chastening of the Lord" (v. 5 PHILLIPS).

God's chastening also proves our sonship. God only disciplines His own children. "My son, don't be angry when the Lord punishes you. Don't be discouraged when he has to show you where you are wrong. For when he punishes you, it proves that he loves you. When he whips you, it proves you are really his child" (v. 5–6 LB).

Finally, He disciplines us so that we may partake of His holiness. "But God corrects us all our days for our own benefit, to teach us his holiness" (v. 10 PHILLIPS). As we face such testing, instead of being angry and questioning God, we need to yield to His will that we may learn His lessons for us.. Someone has said that God educates His children to be a credit to Him.

God's motives are always pure. He disciplines for our good. Our earthly father disciplines us for our temporal welfare, but our heavenly Father disciplines us for our eternal welfare also. This is part of the process of perfecting His ultimate purpose for our lives. Take time to thank Him that He loves you enough to involve Himself in your life, to make you more like Himself in the image of His holy Son.

MARCH 6

*Now no chastening for the present seemeth to be joyous, but griev-
ous; nevertheless afterward it yieldeth the peaceable fruit of righteousness unto them which are exercised thereby (Heb. 12:11).*

ow quickly you and I would agree with the author of Hebrews
that chastening is not joyous. We don't like it. Yet what we may
consider punishment may be God's method of molding and
making us into the person He wants us to be.

When God chastens, it is important how we react to it. We can accept it
from the loving hands of God and mature spiritually, or we can rebel and miss
God's intended purpose. We may not like the process, but it can result in
spiritual maturity.

When we are going through discipline, we long to be out of it. We
cannot understand what God is doing. But the Lord promises that there will be
an *afterward*. "Being punished isn't enjoyable while it is happening—it hurts!
But afterwards, we can see the result, a quiet growth in grace and character"
(v. 11 LB). The King James version reads, "Afterward it yieldeth the peaceable
fruit of righteousness unto them which are exercised thereby."

If we accept discipline from God in the right attitude, we will mature and
grow in righteousness—the righteousness of being right and doing right. Phillips
paraphrases verse eleven: "Yet when it is all over we can see that it has quietly
produced the fruit of real goodness in the characters of those who have accepted
it in the right spirit."

One day as a bystander observed a silversmith heating silver in his
crucible, he asked, "Why do you watch the silver so closely? What are you
looking for?"

"I am looking for my face," the silversmith replied. "When I see my
own image in the silver, then I stop. The work is done."

Why was the fire lighted under the silver? To purify and perfect it. Has the
fire been burning in your life? It is God's method of purifying your life until He
can see in you the face of His Son.

The Bible says, "For the time being no discipline brings joy but seems
grievous and painful; but afterwards it yields a peaceable fruit of righteousness
. . . [that is, in conformity to God's will in purpose, thought, and action,
resulting in right living and right standing with God]" (v. 11 AMPLIFIED).

Ask, and it shall be given you; seek, and ye shall find; knock, and it shall be opened unto you (Matt. 7:7).

sking is God's appointed way for us to receive. When we ask, we acknowledge our complete dependence on Him. God delights to have us come to Him and ask so He can give us what we need.

Prayer has a very important place in the Bible. There are many Scriptures covering the various aspects of prayer. Sometimes we base our understanding on one or two verses, but they do not give us a complete picture of prayer. Certain conditions need to be met in order to expect God to answer. Certain hindrances may prevent an answer.

God says that when we ask we receive. But you say, "I did ask and God didn't answer. I did not receive."

As we consider the above Scripture verses we often stop with the seventh and eighth verses. Read on. Jesus says, "Or what man is there of you, whom if his son ask bread, will he give him a stone? Or if he ask a fish, will he give him a serpent? If ye, then . . . know how to give good gifts unto your children, how much more shall your Father which is in heaven give good things to them that ask him?" (v. 9–11).

We usually say God is good when He answers our prayers our way. Is He any less good when He doesn't? When we bring our requests to Him, we may not know what is good for us, but He does. We can trust God to give us His best, for He never makes a mistake.

Sometimes our prayers are not answered because we ask selfishly, for our own interests, or with the wrong motive. The Bible says, "You don't get what you want because you don't ask God for it. And when you do ask he doesn't give it to you, for you ask in quite the wrong spirit" (James 4:2–3 PHILLIPS). The Living Bible adds, "Your whole aim is wrong—you want only what will give *you* pleasure" (v. 3).

No request is too great for His power to handle, and no request too small for His loving concern. He is delighted and pleased to have us ask so that He can open to us His limitless resources.

Delight thyself also in the LORD; and he shall give thee the desires of thine heart (Ps. 37:4).

esterday we considered the privilege of having a direct line to the Throne Room of heaven where we can ask and receive. Today I want to share another aspect of asking and receiving.

The psalmist assures us that we can have the desires of our heart. God wants us to have them. However, there is a secret to receiving them—the secret lies in what we desire. He doesn't promise to give us our wants or even our desires. He promises us the desires of our *heart.*

The question is, "How can I have the right desires in my heart?" The answer is revealed in the first part of the verse. The right desires in our heart come from delighting ourselves in the Lord.

Some people delight in things, possessions, position, fame, money; yet none of these things bring lasting joy. Only the heart delighting in Him finds joy, peace, and contentment.

If we are delighting in Him, we spend time in God's Word, for He reveals Himself to us in it. In His Word we learn of Him: Who is He? What is He like? What are His interests? What pleases Him?

As we learn about Him and develop a friendship with Him, His interests become our interests. Are they? His thoughts become our thoughts. Are they? His will becomes our will. Is it? His desires become our desires. Are they? As we get to know Him, delighting in Him becomes a way of life.

This affects our prayer life, too. We make our requests with Him in mind. Are our requests the ones He would pray for? Will our requests please Him? Will they glorify Him?

A story is told of a young girl who prayed for snow. She asked God to send snow because the farmers needed it. After her prayer she said, "I fooled God that time. I really wanted snow so I could play with my new sled." We can't fool God. He knows.

As we give Him priority time, as we delight in Him, we will be surprised how it will affect our prayer requests and amazed at the answers to them. Ask and ye shall receive.

MARCH 9

Thy name is as ointment poured forth (Song 1:3).

ne of the delights of Hawaii is the profusion of beautiful flowers. I never get over the breathtaking color of the exotic island flowers and exquisite fragrance that permeates the air. However, I have discovered that it is not always the spectacular, colorful flowers that exude the most fragrant perfume.

One day as we were sightseeing, I could smell a delightful fragrance coming from a hedge. The small white flower was almost hidden from view, yet it filled the atmosphere with its sweet scent.

Today's Scripture speaks of a fragrant name. The Amplified Bible reads, "The odor of your ointments is fragrant; your name is like perfume poured out." This is symbolic of the Lord Jesus. Throughout the Bible, He is called by such names as the *Lily of the Valley* and the *Rose of Sharon.* These names represent the beauty of His holiness and loveliness. Who He is gives fragrance to what He does.

The fragrance of His Name was poured forth when He came to earth. "And thou shalt call his name JESUS: for he shall save his people from their sins" (Matt. 1:21).

The fragrance of His Name was poured forth as He died on the cross. "While we were yet sinners, Christ died for us" (Rom. 5:8).

The fragrance of His Name was poured forth at His resurrection. "He is not here: for he is risen" (Matt. 28:6).

When Jesus returned to His heavenly Father, He left us the privilege of being ointment poured out for Him. Our lives are perfume bottles to carry the fragrance of His presence wherever we go.

"Thanks be to God who leads us, wherever we are, on Christ's triumphant way and makes our knowledge of him spread throughout the world like a lovely perfume! We Christians have the unmistakable 'scent' of Christ, discernible alike to those who are being saved and to those who are heading for death. To the latter it seems like the deathly smell of doom; to the former it has the refreshing fragrance of life itself. Who could think himself adequate for a responsibility like this? Only the man who . . . speaks . . . in the name of God (2 Cor. 2:14–17 PHILLIPS).

Our privilege! Perfume bottles to carry the fragrance of Christ!

MARCH 10

Boast not thyself of tomorrow; for thou knowest not what a day may bring forth (Prov. 27:1).

 ife is uncertain. We cannot predict what will happen. Neither can we control our circumstances. The only time we are sure of is the present moment. We do not know what message the next letter or phone call will bring.

The Bible says, "Look here, you people who say, 'Today or tomorrow we are going to such and such a town, stay there a year, and open up a profitable business.' How do you know what is going to happen tomorrow? For the length of your lives is as uncertain as the morning fog—now you see it; soon it is gone" (James 4:13–14 LB).

Our days come to us one by one as a sacred trust from God. He metes them out second by second. It is awesome to consider that as a second enters and leaves our life, it will never return.

The Bible says, "Thou art my God. My times are in thy hand" (Ps. 31:14–15). His desire is that we live them to the full, making each day count for Him. Because we see our days from our narrow, immediate viewpoint, we do not have the wisdom to invest them for the greatest spiritual profit. We need direction from the Lord.

The Bible says, "Teach us to number our days and recognize how few they are; help us to spend them as we should" (Ps. 90:12 LB). God can teach us to spend them according to His will.

As we look ahead, it is easy to become fearful and begin to worry. Too often we are carrying all of tomorrow's burdens, plus next month's and next year's along with today's, and it is too heavy. The Bible says, "Don't be anxious about tomorrow. God will take care of your tomorrow, too. Live one day at a time" (Matt. 6:34 LB). God expects us to plan ahead, mindful of our dependence on Him.

It has been said that today is the tomorrow we worried about yesterday. We must remember that each day is God-given. There will never be another day like today. Make it count for Him. If we live one moment at a time, God will take care of the long years ahead.

MARCH 11

And when the LORD saw that he turned aside to see, God called unto him out of the midst of the bush, and said, Moses, Moses. And he said, Here am I (Ex. 3:4).

ave you ever started out for a drive and suddenly decided to turn off the beaten path, taking an intriguing side road, wondering what you might find? Suddenly you come to a shady nook among the trees or a gorgeous view of the mountains. How delighted you were that you took time to turn aside.

One day Moses had a breathtaking experience when he turned aside from his beaten path. While he was taking his flock out to the desert, "the angel of the LORD appeared unto him in a flame of fire out of the midst of a bush: and he looked, and, behold, the bush burned with fire, and the bush was not consumed. And Moses said, I will now turn aside, and see this great sight, why the bush is not burnt" (v. 2−3).

As far as Moses was concerned, it was an ordinary day, but as he watched the burning bush, to his amazement, it did not burn up. Then unexpectedly he had a personal visit from the Lord. God spoke to him from the bush, revealing Himself in a special way. That day Moses stood on holy ground.

God also desires to have a personal visit with us. But in our busy world we become so entangled with our full schedules that we fail to turn aside. We neglect our daily quiet time with Him.

Then some ordinary day God may put a burning bush in our life to get our attention. Suddenly, we know we are in the presence of God. In the quietness we bow in worship and adoration. In joy over the reality of being in His presence we whisper, "My Lord and my God."

As we turn aside, He may have some special message for us from His Word. He may place a burden on our heart to pray for someone with a need. He may reveal His will to us regarding a decision we must make. He may give a word of comfort or His healing balm for a hurt deep within.

Most of all, he wants to draw us closer to His heart of love and care. "Whom having not seen, ye love" (1 Peter 1:8). May we always take time to turn aside for our special visit each day with our wonderful Lord.

MARCH 12

If God be for us, who can be against us? (Rom. 8:31).

 hen trouble comes, we may question whether God really is for us. When our bodies are racked with pain, we say, "He has forgotten me." When we lose our earthly possessions, we ask, "Does He really care?" When difficulties arise in the home, we wonder if He is aware of what is happening. But God *does* care. Of that we may be sure. The word *if* in the above Scripture can be translated *since*. Since God is for us, who or what can be against us?

God has a perfect plan to fulfill in our lives. "And we know that all that happens to us is working for our good if we love God and are fitting into his plans" (Rom. 8:28 LB). When life is going smoothly, it is easy to say we love God. The test is how much we love Him when the going is rough, when life is falling apart. Do we recognize then that He is for us?

At such times, instead of being filled with self-pity, discouragement and frustration, we must remember that God is for us. He will take all our disturbing circumstances, our environment, our abilities and even our inabilities, failures, and mistakes and fit them into His perfect plan to make us the person He wants us to be.

God is always for us. When we hurt, He is for us. When we fail, He is for us. When we are misunderstood, He is for us. There is never a time when He is not for us. The important thing is not *who* is *against* us but *who* is *for* us.

Through the years, I have suffered excruciating pain in the trigeminal nerve in my face. Even massive doses of medication often failed to control it. When tears streamed down my cheeks from the intensity of the pain, it was not easy to remind myself that He was for me. At times, I have even asked Him if He really cared. Yet in my heart, I knew He did.

What greater proof do we need that He is for us than His love demonstrated in the person of Jesus Christ, "who loved me, and gave himself for me" (Gal. 2:20)?

MARCH 13

If God be for us, who can be against us? (Rom. 8:31).

There was a time when I thought if I was not worrying, I was overlooking something. Then I discovered the reality of God being *for* me. I had nothing to fear.

Since God is for us, Paul asks, "Who shall bring any charge against God's elect [when it is] God Who justifies—Who puts us in right relation to Himself?" (v. 33 AMPLIFIED). Satan may accuse us, others may accuse us, we may accuse ourselves, but God will not. Because Jesus paid the penalty for our sins, we are secure and at peace in Him.

Paul asks, "Who then will condemn us? Will Christ? *No!* For he is the one who died for us and came back to life again for us and is sitting at the place of highest honor next to God, pleading for us there in heaven" (v. 34 LB). Christ is now our intercessor in heaven.

Again Paul asks, "Who shall separate us from the love of Christ?" (v. 35). Nothing! No matter what happens, He never stops loving us.

However, this does not exempt us from trouble. God knows what we need in the continual refining process of our lives. "When we have trouble or calamity, when we are hunted down or destroyed, is it because he doesn't love us anymore? And if we are hungry, or penniless, or in danger, or threatened with death, has God deserted us?" (v. 35 LB).

Our troubles are not the same as Paul's, but we are promised the same victory through Jesus. "Despite all this, overwhelming victory is ours through Christ who loved us enough to die for us" (v. 37 LB).

When we realize the depth of His love for us, how can we help but love Him with our whole heart? "We love him, because he first loved us" (1 John 4:19). And we show our love through obedience. Jesus said, "If ye love me, keep my commandments" (John 14:15). Knowing the reality of His love, how can we do less than walk in close fellowship with Him? "Whom having not seen, ye love" (1 Peter 1:8).

MARCH 14

But when the Holy Spirit controls our lives he will produce this kind of fruit in us: . . . peace (Gal. 5:22 LB).

Peace is a state of our inner being, not the result of our circumstances. It is the work the Holy Spirit produces within when we have given Him the control of our lives.

The angels brought the message of peace the night Jesus was born. "Suddenly a great company of the heavenly host appeared with the angel, praising God and saying, "Glory to God in the highest, and on earth peace to men on whom his favor rests" (Luke 2:13–14).

Ephesians 2:14 says, "For [Christ] is our peace." Through our relationship with Jesus, He becomes our peace, making it real in our life situations.

But we have to take time to listen and to be close enough to hear His messages of peace to us. "I will listen to what God the LORD will say; he promises peace to his people, his saints" (Ps. 85:8 NIV).

This peace comes from prayer. "Don't worry about anything; instead, pray about everything; tell God your needs and don't forget to thank him for his answers. If you do this you will experience God's peace, which is far more wonderful than the human mind can understand. His peace will keep your thoughts and your hearts quiet and at rest as you trust in Christ Jesus" (Phil. 4:6–7 LB)

We experience peace as we trust God. "You will keep in perfect peace him whose mind is steadfast, because he trusts in you. Trust in the LORD forever, for the LORD, the LORD, is the Rock eternal" (Isa. 26:3–4 NIV).

This peace is complete; it leaves no place for worry. It has been said that a steadfast mind is one who stops at God. When you stop at God you exchange all your cares, your worries, your frustrations, for His perfect peace.

In my own nature I am a fearful person. I have learned that when I bring my fears to Him, He removes them and gives me His peace. I have experienced the reality of this Scripture—"The LORD gives strength to his people; the LORD blesses his people with peace" (Ps. 29:11 NIV).

But I trusted in thee, O LORD: I said, Thou art my God. My times are in thy hand (Ps. 31:14–15).

ne day I was to fly from Victoria, British Columbia to Seattle in a small commuter plane. A blizzard had been raging and our flight was delayed. At last the airline decided it was safe to go. As an employee helped me out to the plane, he said, "When we get to the end of this building, we will turn the corner. The wind will be very strong." He was right. It was so strong I couldn't move. He had to lead me the rest of the way.

David experienced many storms in his life. They often beat on him with such fury that he couldn't make it without help. He enumerates some of the overwhelming storms he faced. He says, "I am in trouble" (v. 9); "my life is spent with grief" (v. 10); "I have heard the slander of many; fear was on every side . . . they devised to take away my life" (v. 13).

Yet as he looked back on all his trouble he could say, "But I trusted in thee, O LORD" (v. 14). He survived his storms, for he trusted the trustworthy One, God Himself.

As he looked ahead, he could say, "My times are in thy hand." He knew that He could trust his future to the all-powerful hand of God. Even though David's enemies were strong, he could say, "I trust in thee." He was not in their hands but in God's.

Is a storm of hurricane proportions beating upon your life today? Is it so strong you cannot move? Your heavenly Father will hide you in His all-powerful hand. As the storm rages, nothing can touch you. "How he loves his people—His holy ones are in his hands" (Deut. 33:3 LB).

Secure in His care, you can say, "My problem is in His hand"; "My decision is in His hand"; "My heartache is in His hand."

Dan Crowford, missionary to Africa, said that if we were to quote, "My times are in your hand" to a national in his area, it would be translated, "All my life's whys, whens, wheres, and wherefores are in God's hand."

Where better could they be?

MARCH 16

*That he would grant you, according to the riches of his glory, to be
strengthened with might by his Spirit in the inner man (Eph. 3:16).*

 s Paul prayed for the early Christians, he asked God to give them
spiritual strength. This strength comes from the Holy Spirit's
work within. Paul wrote, "That out of his glorious, unlimited
resources he will give you the mighty inner strengthening of his
Holy Spirit" (Eph. 3:16 LB). Before Jesus left earth, He promised us the power
of the Holy Spirit. He said, "Ye shall receive power, after that the Holy Ghost is
come upon you" (Acts 1:8).

The inner person is the *real you*. It includes intellect, emotions, and will.
It is there that we need strength; it is there that we face such weaknesses as
frustration, discouragement, failure, self-pity.

When the Holy Spirit controls our life, His might fortifies our inner
person. The power of the Spirit keeps us going when the way gets rough.
Through the Holy Spirit we can forgive, we can love, we can continue when
life falls apart.

Several years ago, a young woman brought a puppet to a luncheon,
where the puppet was to sing. As I looked at the puppet lying on the table, I
thought, *If I asked the puppet to sing now, it couldn't sing a note.* However,
when the puppet was introduced, the young woman picked it up, slipped her
hand into it, and the puppet sang beautifully. That puppet could do nothing
without the power of the hand inside it.

So it is in our lives. The Holy Spirit, released within, empowers and
enables us to face life each day. It gives us the power to stand firm when storms
strike. What *we* cannot do, the Holy Spirit can.

The Bible says, "May your strength match the length of your days!"
(Deut. 33:25 LB). There is no power shortage in the spiritual realm. God
provides a continual source of power for our daily walk.

It is important that the inflow matches the outflow. Paul wrote, "We are
persecuted, but we never have to stand it alone: we may be knocked down but
we are never knocked out! . . . This is the reason why we never collapse. The
outward man does indeed suffer wear and tear, but every day the inward man
receives fresh strength" (2 Cor. 4:9, 16 PHILLIPS).

MARCH 17

That Christ may dwell in your hearts by faith (Eph. 3:17).

vividly recall the day I moved from Denver to Kansas City. It was difficult to leave my home in Denver and move into a small room on the third floor of a large home.

I went to my room alone. Stacks of boxes towered everywhere. In tears I asked the Lord if He were sure He knew what He was doing. Yet I knew deep in my heart that the move was in His will.

Friends came to help me unpack, and as we placed my furniture around the room, hung pictures, and put knickknacks and mementos around the room, it began to feel like home. I was comfortable in it.

The above Scripture says that Christ wants to dwell in our hearts by faith. Your heart is your personality. The Greek word for *dwell* means to be at home, to settle down. The Lord wants to settle down and be at home in our lives.

However, when He first enters as Savior, He sees many things with which He is not comfortable. The Holy Spirit has God's blueprint and knows what changes have to be made to build a life that pleases Him. He begins to work in us, making our lives a place where Christ can feel at home.

As we commit our lives to Him, the Holy Spirit begins this work of conforming us to Jesus Christ.

First, the Holy Spirit removes the things that are not like Jesus in our lives. Some things will have to be moved to a less conspicuous place. Other things need to be added.

Certain habits will have to be eliminated, others established. We may have to make some changes in our circle of friends. Attitudes may have to be adjusted. Areas of our conduct will need changing. All of this is necessary if the Lord Jesus is to be at home in us.

When Christ settles down and lives in our lives, He desires to control what we do and where we go. He wants to control our actions, our reactions, our conversations, our thoughts, our emotions.

Is the Lord Jesus comfortable with your friends, your reading, your entertainment, your habits? Are there changes still to be made? Is Christ at home in every area of your life?

MARCH 18

Being rooted and grounded in love . . . and to know the love of Christ, which passeth knowledge (Eph. 3:17–19).

s roots reach down into the soil of the earth, believers are rooted in the love of Christ. As a building is built on a firm foundation, our lives are built on the love of Christ. The very atmosphere in which we live is God's love.

Being rooted and grounded in God's love gives stability in our lives. "May your roots go down deep into the soil of God's marvelous love" (v. 17 LB). With Christ as our foundation we have a stability that cannot be shaken, "founded securely on love" (v. 17 AMPLIFIED).

Only as we are rooted and grounded in His love, can we begin to comprehend the measure of it. Paul wrote of the four-dimensional love of God. His love is *long* enough to stretch from eternity to eternity, *wide* enough to reach the whole world, *deep* enough to lift people from the depths of sin, and *high* enough to place us in the heavens with Christ.

The greatest illustration of this is in John 3:16: "For God so loved [its length] the world [its width], that he gave his only begotten Son [its depth], that whosoever believeth in him should not perish but have everlasting life [its height]."

When that love permeates our lives, we will be concerned for others. We will love those He loves, even the unlovely. We may not be able to love them by ourselves, but God in us can love them.

A pastor tells of visiting a prison. One of the prisoners said, "Do you remember me?" When the pastor said no, the prisoner said, "You got me out of the ghetto and sent me to a mission where I found shelter. You gave me clothes. You dressed me, for I was shivering with delirium tremens. You even shined my shoes. I wasn't interested in what you said about Christ then, but I never forgot that you shined my shoes. Now I am ready to know Christ."

"We . . . know how dearly God loves us, and we feel this warm love everywhere within us because God has given us the Holy Spirit to fill our hearts with his love" (Rom. 5:5 LB). Is your life controlled by God's love?

MARCH 19

That ye might be filled with all the fullness of God (Eph. 3:19).

hat a prayer! Paul prayed that the Holy Spirit would strengthen the Ephesians in their innermost being, that Christ would be at home in every part of their lives, and that they might comprehend more fully the measure of God's love. Now he prays for their spiritual depth.

As I meditate on this Scripture, I am overwhelmed with the magnitude of this thought. Filled! Filled with God! Filled with the fullness of God! Filled with all the fullness of God!

The fullness of God is all that God is, excluding His deity. It includes His attributes and characteristics—all that makes Him God. We may wonder how the finite can be filled with the infinite. Yet God's Word tells us it is possible. God desires to impart Himself in His fullness to us.

Our hearts are always filled with something, and it is important to know what fills our hearts. We are controlled by what we are filled with. To be filled with fear is to be controlled by fear. To be filled with bitterness is to be controlled by bitterness. To be filled with the Lord Jesus is to be controlled by Him.

Through our relationship with Jesus we are filled with the fullness of God. The Bible says, "For in Christ there is all of God in a human body; so you have everything when you have Christ, and you are filled with God through your union with Christ" (Col. 2:9–10 LB). All the fullness of God is resident in Jesus Christ. When we have Christ we have all of God.

When indwelt by Christ, we have in Him all of God's attributes and characteristics available for our use. This includes His strength, wisdom, peace, joy. As we need them in our everyday life the Holy Spirit puts them into operation for our needs.

To be filled with the fullness of God means that every area of our lives is committed to Him. Our hearts are filled with His love; our minds are filled with His thoughts; our will is controlled by His Spirit.

It has been said that 100 percent fullness requires 100 percent yieldedness.

MARCH 20

Now unto him that is able to do exceeding abundantly above all that we can ask or think, according to the power that worketh in us, unto him be glory in the church by Christ Jesus throughout all ages, world without end (Eph. 3:20–21).

hink of the greatness and majesty of God! He is able to do all that we ask—exceedingly abundantly above all that we ask or even think. The Greek could be rendered, God is all of that and then some.

What confidence this gives us in prayer. Our petitions can never exceed His ability to answer. God is able to do superabundantly above all that we can ask. What a God! There is no limit to what God can do. Paul said, "I pray that you will begin to understand how incredibly great his power is to help those who believe him. It is that same mighty power that raised Christ from the dead and seated him in the place of honor at God's right hand in heaven" (Eph. 1:19–20 LB).

The greatest thing we can do for God or others is to pray. More is accomplished by our prayers than by our works. Prayer is omnipotent; it can do anything God can do. When we pray, God works.

His unlimited power works in and through us "according to the power that is working in us." There is no lack with God, but we may limit His power in us if we don't believe it or don't avail ourselves of it. The Spirit of God can only do what we allow Him to do.

No wonder Paul writes, "Unto him be glory in the church by Christ Jesus throughout all ages, world without end" (3:21).

Beginning in the sixteenth verse of this chapter there is progression: As we are strengthened within by the Holy Spirit, we have stability. As God's love permeates our lives, we are filled with Christ's presence and controlled by Him. As our lives become a channel of His power, we can make a great impact on our world.

We will pray for our families as God would; we will pray for friends and neighbors as God would; we will pray for the world as God would. When God answers our prayers, the answers will bring glory to Him.

How are you praying today? For what and for whom are you praying? Are you expecting God to do exceeding abundantly above what you ask or think?

May the supernatural become the natural in our lives.

MARCH 21

Walk in wisdom toward them that are without, redeeming the time
(Col. 4:5).

ho has made a great impression on your life, especially before you became a Christian? Was there some Christian whose life you watched? In this Scripture Paul speaks of the influence we can have on those outside of God's family.

People are watching us. Many will not read the Bible, but they are reading its translation in the way we live.

Paul writes that we are to walk in wisdom. This means that we must not do anything that would hinder anyone from receiving Christ. We must live above reproach. Of the early Christians it was said that others, "took knowledge of them, that they had been with Jesus" (Acts 4:13). The apostle Paul encourages us to "walk honestly toward them that are without" (1 Thess. 4:12).

Our family and neighbors may be watching us much closer than we realize. Those who work with us may be more influenced by what they see in our lives than by what we say. The words we speak will only have meaning when we live the truth of them daily.

Day by day we walk among those who do not know Christ personally. To redeem the time is to go into the marketplace and buy up the opportunities God gives us to share Jesus Christ.

After I had foot surgery, I had to use a wheelchair in the airports. One day a lovely young lady who worked for the airline pushed me in the wheelchair to the entrance and brought my luggage as well. Along with a tip, I gave her a booklet, *Choose Your Future*. I said, "It is so important to choose the right future, to choose the way to heaven." When she told me she didn't know how to get there, I told her the booklet would tell her how to get to heaven, and I shared a few verses from the Bible with her.

She said, "I have a Bible, but I didn't know it said things like that."

God gave me an opportunity to redeem the time, sharing Jesus Christ with someone outside His family. Are you redeeming the time in the marketplace, sharing the Gospel with your God-given opportunities?

We know how dearly God loves us, and we feel this warm love everywhere within us because God has given us the Holy Spirit to fill our hearts with his love (Rom. 5:5 LB).

t has been said that we can't define love; it has to be experienced and demonstrated.

Today, right from the heart of God, comes His special message to each of us, "I love you." His love is real for He Himself is love.

We are the object of God's love. "For God so loved the world that he gave his only begotten Son, that whosoever believeth in him, should not perish but have everlasting life" (John 3:16). This includes each of us. God revealed His love to us through Jesus Christ. "But God showed his great love for us by sending Christ to die for us while we were still sinners" (Rom. 5:8 LB).

I found the following aspects of God's love written in one of my notebooks. I don't know where they came from, but they enlarge our concept of His love.

The love of Christ is **permanent.** "Having loved his own which were in the world, he loved them unto the end" (John 13:1). The love of Christ is **personal.** "I live by the faith in the Son of God, who loved me, and gave himself for me" (Gal. 2:20 NIV). His love is **powerful.** "Who shall separate us from the love of Christ? . . . In all these things we are more than conquerors through him that loved us" (Rom. 8:35, 37).

The love of Christ **passeth knowledge.** "[That you may really come] to know—practically, through experience for yourselves—the love of Christ, which far surpasses mere knowledge (without experience)" (Eph. 3:19 AMPLIFIED). The love of Christ is our **pattern.** "Walk in love, as Christ also hath loved us, and hath given himself for us" (Eph. 5:2).

The love of Christ is **propelling.** "For the love of Christ controls and urges and impels us" (2 Cor. 5:14 AMPLIFIED). Christ's love is always **present.** "To Him Who ever loves us" (Rev. 1:5 AMPLIFIED).

As the message of His love becomes real in our hearts, it will overflow to others. "Be full of love for others, following the example of Christ who loved you and gave himself to God as sacrifice to take away your sins" (Eph. 5:2 LB).

Let His love overflow!

Thou art my hiding place; thou shalt preserve me from trouble; thou shalt compass me about with songs of deliverance. Selah (Ps. 32:7).

 once had the privilege of visiting Holland's Haarlem and seeing the watch shop and home of the ten Boom family. As I stood looking at the building, the name *ten Boom* on the window deeply stirred my heart. I thought of the many who had found a hiding place there in time of danger. I reflected on this dear family's faith in God, which had given them an eternal Hiding Place, for their faith was in the person of Jesus Christ.

Today many are seeking hiding places. They try to hide from their circumstances, from people, from problems, and from themselves. Yet they fail to find security for they are hiding in the wrong places.

When troubles rage around us, we need a hiding place where we can be safe. The psalmist says that the Lord is that Hiding Place. In our time of desperation and despair, we can run into our Hiding Place, and He becomes our place of refuge. David said, "You are my hiding place from every storm of life" (v. 7 LB).

The prophet Daniel experienced the security of the right hiding place. Because of his faithfulness to God, Daniel was cast into a den of lions, but that place of danger became a special hiding place because the Lord protected him. God closed the mouths of the lions so they could not harm him.

Sometimes we try to be our own hiding place. We hide in self-pity, self-pride, self-satisfaction, loneliness, and discouragement. We close the door and there we stay, feeling sorry for ourselves but finding no real peace or satisfaction.

Only one hiding place brings safety, security, and satisfaction—Jesus Christ. The Bible says, "Your life is hid with Christ in God" (Col. 3:3). We are secure in Him.

God has provided this refuge, but we have to avail ourselves of it. "Deliver me, O LORD, from mine enemies: I flee unto thee to hide me" (Ps. 143:9).

Someone has said that nothing can harm us until God's omnipotence is exhausted.

Looking unto Jesus the author and finisher of our faith (Heb. 12:2).

Life is a race, and God has chosen you and me to be runners. Each of us has our own personal race with our own unique, God-given racetrack.

Someone has said that the reason many of us don't get anywhere is that we weren't going any place when we started. It is important for us to know where we are going if we are to successfully run the race. Not only must we have a goal for our life race, but it must be the right goal.

A number of years ago a great crowd of spectators watched a football player run for a touchdown—in the wrong direction. They yelled at him, but to no avail. As he crossed the goal, he discovered that, although he had made a spectacular run, it was in the wrong direction. He made the touchdown but across the opponent's goal. How sad it would be if at the end of our life's race, we find we have run to the wrong finish line.

Our goal is the Lord Jesus, "the author and finisher of our faith."

Jesus was the goal of Paul's life. Jesus Christ was his priority. "For to me to live is Christ" (Phil. 1:21). Jesus was not just *top* priority in Paul's life; He was *the* priority of his life. He must be *the* priority in our lives, too, if we are to run His race. There is no room for detours.

Early one morning my host in a home where I was staying took me for a walk through the woods as the sun was coming up. His little dog romped along behind us. When we returned after an hour's walk, the dog was exhausted. It stretched out, panting for breath.

I said, "Do you know what is wrong with your dog? It is exhausted from all the detours it took. It was off the trail more than on."

Some of our exhaustion and frustration may be the result of our detours. Things we do that are not in God's schedule detour us from our goal and cause burnout.

Run the race straight to the goal!

MARCH 25

Wherefore seeing we also are compassed about with so great a
cloud of witnesses, let us lay aside every weight, and the sin which
doth so easily beset us, and let us run with patience the race that is
set before us, looking unto Jesus the author and finisher of our faith
(Heb. 12:1–2).

 ur race in life is a daily one. It is not easy, but the Lord never
promised it would be. We need discipline, for a racer must run
light in the race. The Bible says, "let us strip off anything that
slows us down or holds us back, and especially those sins that
wrap themselves so tightly around our feet and trip us up" (v. 1 LB).

The weights and sin that slow us down are things that dull our spiritual
hunger. They may be ambitions, hobbies, careers. They may not be harmful,
but if they impede our race, they must be cast aside. We have to choose
between the good and the best. Are you carrying excess weight that needs to be
cast aside?

We must persevere to the end of the race. It will take determination to
reach the goal. We may be tempted to give up. We may become so weary that
we can hardly take the next step. At times we will say, "I'm through. I can't go
on." Then we need to take a fresh look at the Lord Jesus and hear His
encouraging words, "You can make it. I am with you. I will help you."

A "great cloud of witnesses" encourages us to continue. These are the
people enrolled in God's Hall of Fame in the previous chapter.

What an encouragement these witnesses have been to me as I have run
my race. I have learned how they persevered through their difficulties, failures,
and heartaches; how they made it through dark valleys and hazardous
mountains; how through joys and sorrows they made it to the end.

But our greatest encouragement comes from the Lord Jesus Himself. He
was with us as we began our race and will be with us as we complete it. He
supplies all the resources we need. Keeping our eyes fixed on Him, we can say
with Paul, "I run straight to the goal with purpose in every step" (1 Cor. 9:26
LB).

When we cross the finish line, the Lord will greet us, and it will be worth
it all. When we look into His face, we will fall on our knees at His feet and
praise and worship Him.

MARCH 26

And the LORD said unto Moses, Wherefore criest thou unto me?
speak unto the children of Israel, that they go forward (Ex. 14:15).

t last Moses and the Israelites were on their way out of Egypt to the Promised Land. After several days of traveling, God directed them to a mountainous area of the wilderness. By this time, Pharaoh regretted his decision to let them go, and he and his army were in hot pursuit.

The Israelites quickly forgot God's promise to deliver them. They became frightened. Surrounded by mountains, desert, and the Red Sea, they could see no way of escape. There was no way around, no way back. What could they do? They couldn't move the mountains or dry up the sea.

Moses said, "Do not be afraid. Stand firm and you will see the deliverance the LORD will bring you today. The Egyptians you see today you will never see again. The LORD will fight for you; you need only to be still" (v. 13–14 NIV).

Then God said to move forward. It was time for action. Only one way remained for them—through. With bated breath they watched as Moses held out his rod, the symbol of God's power. Then, as they moved forward step by step, God opened a path before them, and they walked through on dry ground. When they reached the other side, Moses again stretched out his rod. The water rushed over the Egyptians who had followed them into the sea, and they all drowned. God had led them safely through, and they began their walk of faith to the Promised Land.

We may be hemmed in by insurmountable problems. In such hopeless situations we find that our one sure refuge is our God of Hope, our God of the Impossible. God allows us to be put in a hemmed-in place so that we will look up.

He says to us in effect, "Don't be afraid. Trust Me. Stand still, and see what I will do." Faith enables us to stand still and let God work. He can do for us what we cannot do for ourselves.

Then He says, "Go forward, take the next step. Don't be afraid. I am with you."

Someone has said that faith expects from God what is beyond all expectation.

MARCH 27

That I may know him, and the power of his resurrection, and the fellowship of his sufferings, being made conformable unto his death (Phil. 3:10).

 ust before Easter one year I had the joy of spending two weeks in Israel. One morning at the Garden Tomb I sat alone, meditating. I thought of the great price the Savior had paid for our salvation. I thought of the agony He endured, taking the punishment for our sin—a punishment He didn't deserve. "Christ died for our sins according to the scriptures" (1 Cor. 15:3).

Years before, God had revealed to me that Jesus' death was for *me,* for all *my* sin. I confessed that I believed He died for me, asked His forgiveness, and invited Him into my life. Then I had the assurance that I was a member of His family. Before that I had known *about* Him. Afterward I *knew* Him.

Sitting by the Garden Tomb, I said, "Thank you, Jesus, for the gift of eternal life I received years ago."

When I walked into the tomb, a sense of awe and worship swept over me. I thought about the Resurrection. What power! The power of God is so great that it brought Jesus forth from the dead, a living Savior! As I turned to leave, over the entrance I saw the words, *He is risen.* All I could say was, "Hallelujah! What a Savior!"

Often we sing, "Because He lives I can face tomorrow." I remember when I could hardly face today. It seemed I was on an elevator—some days up, some days down.

Then I discovered that because of my relationship with the Lord Jesus Christ, the same resurrection power that raised Him from the dead is available to me. Jesus told His disciples that "all power is given unto me in heaven and in earth" (Matt. 28:18).

The Resurrection has become a vital truth in my life. No matter what my circumstances are or what problems arise, I can face each day, not in my human weakness but in His resurrection power.

God told Paul, "My power shows up best in weak people." Paul replied, "I am glad to be a living demonstration of Christ's power" (2 Cor. 12:9 LB).

MARCH 28

Lift up now thine eyes, and look from the place where thou art northward, and southward, and eastward, and westward: for all the land which thou seest, to thee will I give it, and to thy seed for ever (Gen. 13:14–15).

braham and Lot had become wealthy, having so many cattle and sheep there was insufficient pastureland. Recognizing they must separate, Abraham gave Lot first choice. Lot looked at the well-watered pastureland and selfishly selected that portion.

After Lot left, the Lord told Abraham to lift up his eyes and look in every direction—north, south, east, and west. Previously God had promised the land to Abraham and his seed. Now He says, "Arise, walk through the land in the length of it and in the breadth of it; for I will give it unto thee" (v. 17). In other words, "Even now you can possess it by faith."

Today there is a land for us to possess for Jesus Christ. Millions do not know Him personally. Jesus said, "Do you think the work of harvesting will not begin until the summer ends four months from now? Look around you! Vast fields of human souls are ripening all around us, and are ready now for reaping" (John 4:35 LB).

A man riding through wheat country with a farmer asked, "Why is the wheat so white? I thought wheat was a golden color."

"It is when it is ripe," replied the farmer, "but when it is overripe, it turns white."

God wants us to *lift* our eyes on the overripe fields and *look,* because "where there is no vision, the people perish" (Prov. 29:18).

This call is *personal.* God says, "Look around *you.* I need laborers in my fields." But you may say, "What can I do? How can I go? I have a family. I have responsibilities." God told Abraham, "Look from the *place where thou art."* There are God-given opportunities to share the Gospel all around us, with neighbors, friends, co-workers. God has chosen a place of service for each of us. We are to walk through *our* land, harvesting it for Him.

Someone has calculated that every time we take a breath four people go out of this life without Jesus Christ. Today, lift up your eyes where you are and see the overripe fields of souls. Walk through them and possess them for Him.

MARCH 29

While we wait for the blessed hope—the glorious appearing of our great God and Savior, Jesus Christ, who gave himself for us to redeem us from all wickedness and to purify for himself a people that are his very own, eager to do what is good (Titus 2:13 NIV).

n a world on the brink of collapse, gripped by hate, and filled with despair, Easter has a powerful message. It brings a message of hope, for it is a message of life beyond our earthly span.

Hope is defined as anticipation, desire, fulfillment, that in which we place our confidence.

Paul speaks of "that blessed hope." After the death and resurrection of Christ, as His earthly ministry was coming to a close, Jesus' disciples were promised that He would return. "While they looked stedfastly toward heaven as [Jesus] went up, behold, two men stood by them in white apparel; which also said, Ye men of Galilee, why stand ye gazing up into heaven? this same Jesus, which is taken up from you into heaven, shall so come in like manner as ye have see him go into heaven" (Acts 1:10−11).

Jesus, our blessed hope, will return one of these days, and we live in expectation of that promise. We do not know when He will return, but we look up in anticipation.

Not only is His return our living hope, it also affects the way we live. When we are expecting company, we make preparation for their arrival. We clean our homes and set everything in order. As we await Christ's return, we need some inner preparation. Our lives must be put in order and kept clean. "And every man that hath this hope in him purifieth himself, even as he is pure" (1 John 3:3).

The return of Jesus Christ is our hope for the future. But what about our hope for today? As believers, our hope for today is the person of Jesus Christ. He is the One in whom we have placed our confidence. He is the object of our hope. "Christ in you, the hope of glory" (Col. 1:27).

Waiting for our blessed hope means to look for, to expect. "Our citizenship is in heaven. And we eagerly await a Savior from there, the Lord Jesus Christ" (Phil. 3:20 NIV). Are you eager for His return? Is that your blessed hope? Are you living in the light of His return?

MARCH 30

But thanks be to God, Who in Christ always leads us in triumph—
as trophies of Christ's victory—and through us spreads and makes
evident the fragrance of the knowledge of God everywhere
(2 Cor. 2:14 AMPLIFIED).

I love the beautiful Easter hymn, "Christ Arose." The chorus begins, "Up from the grave He arose, with a mighty *triumph* o'er His foes" (emphasis mine).

Suppose we had been among the crowd at the crucifixion of Jesus. We would have watched the lifeless form of Jesus being taken down from the cross and placed in the tomb. Imagine our amazement three days later to hear that Jesus was alive. What unbelievable joy it would have brought to our hearts. That actually took place! After three days in the tomb, Christ arose from the dead. What a triumph! What a victory!

He became the Victor. The glorious news for us is that through Him and His victory over death, we, too, can experience a life of resurrection victory. "Thanks be to God, which giveth us the victory through our Lord Jesus Christ" (1 Cor. 15:57).

In Paul's time when a victor returned home from battle, the conquering general took the lead, followed by the army in their chariots. As the procession made its way along the street, crowds of people shouted their acclaim to the victors. The prisoners, trophies of battle, were chained to the chariots and dragged behind.

This is a picture of the triumphant procession led by our Commander, the Lord Jesus Christ. "In this way God took away Satan's power to accuse you of sin, and God openly displayed to the whole world Christ's triumph at the cross where your sins were all taken away" (Col. 2:15 LB).

As we submit to Him as Lord and Savior, we will follow in His triumphant procession of victory, not as trophies bound with iron chains, but as trophies of His grace bound to Him with cords of love. "But thanks be to God, Who in Christ always *leads* us in triumph" (2 Cor. 2:14 AMPLIFIED).

In Him we are victorious wherever we are, whatever happens. He leads us in victory. Through disappointment there is victory. Through loneliness there is victory. Through failure there is victory. Through heartache there is victory.

With God leading, we can *always* triumph. The victory is His.

*Now thanks be unto God, which always causeth us to triumph in
Christ, and maketh manifest the savour of his knowledge by us in
every place (2 Cor. 2:14).*

omeone has said that God fashions trumpets of triumph out of
the brass of trials. Perhaps you say, "I have the trials but not the
trumpets."

The above Scripture assures us that we can triumph
consistently. We can always triumph, not *from* our circumstances, but *in* them.
Victory is available for you and me personally. God causes *us* to triumph.
Regardless of our trials, wherever we are, victory is for us.

Our trials can become triumphs because our source of victory is Jesus
Christ. He leads us in His triumph. He has made no provision for defeat, only
victory. The victory is His, not ours.

Not only will we live a triumphant life in Him, but a fragrant life as well.
As He communicates the fragrance of His resurrection life to us, we will manifest
it wherever we go. "God . . . maketh manifest the savour of his knowledge by
us in every place" (2 Cor. 2:14).

As we share the Gospel, manifesting the knowledge of Him wherever we
go, it will be like the fragrant perfume of His presence. "Through us spreads and
makes evident the fragrance of the knowledge of God everywhere, for we are
the sweet fragrance of Christ [which exhales] unto God, [discernible alike]
among those who are being saved and among those who are perishing" (vv.
14−15 AMPLIFIED).

As we let Him always lead us in triumph, wherever we go, we will leave
the fragrance of His presence—the aroma of God manifesting Himself through
us.

In the Phillips paraphrase we read, "Thanks be to God who leads us,
wherever we are, on Christ's triumphant way and makes our knowledge of him
spread throughout the world like a lovely perfume! We Christians have the
unmistakable 'scent' of Christ, discernible alike to those who are being saved
and to those who are heading for death" (vv. 14−15).

He delights in using us to spread the knowledge of Him in every place we
go. How wonderful it is that every time we speak a word for Him or tell what
He has done for us, we are a sweet fragrance of Christ.

APRIL 1

As the rain and snow come down from heaven and stay upon the ground to water the earth, and cause the grain to grow and to produce seed for the farmer and bread for the hungry, so also is my Word. I send it out and it always produces fruit. It shall accomplish all I want it to, and prosper everywhere I send it (Isa. 55:10–11 LB).

hen we read the Bible, unlike any other book, the author is always present while we read. God's heart of love desires that we might know Him and what He has planned for us. So He has given us His special message in the Bible.

The above Scripture assures us of the faithfulness of God in accomplishing His purpose through His Word as it goes forth. As the rain and snow falling on the earth results in the growth of the seed, so the Word of God will accomplish God's purposes. Whether we see the results immediately or not, He promises they will come. We can wait for them patiently.

God has a purpose He wants to accomplish in our lives as we read His Word each day. I do not read His Word hurriedly. I take time to reflect on what I have read. What should it accomplish in my life? How will it help to answer a problem I face? What does it show me that I need to confess? How will it help me grow? If I pay attention, His Word accomplishes His purpose in my life.

One day as I was reading about the fruit of the Spirit, I stopped at the word *gentle* and said, "Lord, I am not gentle. Will you please give me a large portion of Your gentleness?" Several months later someone said, "Millie, you are such a gentle person." Silently I said, "Thank you, Lord. You did it."

God's Word has also produced results when I have used it with other people. When a high school teacher talked with me about her philosophy of life, I replied with a quotation from Scripture. Again she commented on her belief. Again I answered with the same verse of Scripture. Suddenly a light came over her face. She said, "I see what you mean. I never saw that before." Quietly she bowed her head and invited Jesus Christ into her life. His Word had accomplished His work.

What is God speaking to you about from His Word? Is it accomplishing His purpose in your life? What is it accomplishing as you use it with others? We have His promise: It will accomplish His purpose.

APRIL 2

And he hath put a new song in my mouth, even praise unto our
God: many shall see it, and fear, and shall trust in the LORD
(Ps. 40:3).

 hat an effect music can have on people. Often, when we are depressed or discouraged, music can lift our spirits and chase away feelings of despair. God, the Master Musician, gives songs an important place in our Christian experience.

God filled David's life with song. David had a "singing heart." The Book of Psalms is filled with his songs and praises to God. David didn't have an easy life. He experienced much trouble and persecution. King Saul tried to kill him. Some of his family and close friends became his enemies. Yet in spite of his heartaches, he could say, "I will bless the LORD at all times: his praise shall continually be in my mouth" (Ps. 34:1).

He could sing in the midst of trouble for his security was in God, the Source of his song. He wrote, "You are my hiding place from every storm of life" (Ps. 32:7 LB).

Although David was often protected *in* storms, at times he was even protected *from* them. "Thou shalt preserve me from trouble," he told God (Ps. 32:7). No wonder David could sing. "You surround me with songs of victory" (v. 7 LB). Encompassed with deliverance songs, why shouldn't he sing?

Do you have a singing heart today? Regardless of your present circumstances you can have a song—a song of deliverance. A singing heart is one of our lines of defense. C. H. Spurgeon said, "Any fool can sing in the day. It is easy to sing when we can read the notes by daylight; but the skillful singer is he who can sing when there is not a ray of light to read by."

Remember how Paul and Silas sang in the prison dungeon at midnight? When we pause to think of the Lord, Who He is, and all He has done for us, how can our hearts help but burst forth in praise! He has provided salvation through our relationship with Jesus Christ, empowered us through His Spirit, and guided us through His Word.

David said, "Every day will I bless thee; and I will bless thy name for ever and ever. Great is the LORD, and greatly to be praised; and his greatness is unsearchable" (Ps. 145:2–3).

I live by the faith of the Son of God, who loved me, and gave himself for me (Gal. 2:20).

ave you ever wondered what your reaction would have been if you had been at the tomb that first Easter morning? How would you have responded to the angel's message, "He is not here: for he is risen, as he said" (Matt. 28:6).

What amazing news! Jesus was alive! The One who loved them and had died for them (the one who loved *me* and died for *me*) had risen from the dead. The wonder of such love! It is pure. It never changes. It is all-inclusive, for it takes in the entire world. It is God's love and God *is* love.

He proved His love for us through His death and resurrection. "But God showed his great love for us by sending Christ to die for us while we were still sinners" (Rom. 5:8 LB).

The price He paid for our redemption was not small. It meant leaving the glories of heaven to come to earth. It meant enduring excruciating, lingering death by crucifixion. It meant taking on Himself the penalty for our sins.

But through His death and resurrection we are cleansed from sin and receive eternal life. What love!

Through Him all the resources of God are now available for us. "He that spared not his own Son, but delivered him up for us all, how shall he not with him also freely give us all things?" (Rom. 8:32).

His love is sacrificial. Paul beautifully describes Christ's role as a servant when he says, "Who, being in the form of God, thought it not robbery to be equal with God: but made himself of no reputation, and took upon him the form of a servant, and was made in the likeness of men: and being found in fashion as a man, he humbled himself, and became obedient unto death, even the death of the cross" (Phil. 2:6−8).

The story is told of someone who asked Jesus how much He loved him. Jesus stretched out His arms and said, "This much," and then died.

As I read these Scriptures, my heart is overwhelmed in praise and worship for the One who did all of this for me. Isn't yours?

APRIL 4

But I tell you: Love your enemies and pray for those who persecute you (Matt. 5:44 NIV).

esus said, "Love your enemies." How that statement startled those who heard it. The Old Testament commanded, "Love your neighbor." The rabbis had added, "and hate your enemies." Now Jesus was saying that they were to love their enemies and pray for those who persecuted them.

Human nature loves only those who are lovable. It is easy to love your friends, but Jesus said that we are to love even our enemies. Our natural reaction is to retaliate toward someone who has wronged us, but that contradicts Jesus' teaching.

Jesus' love will "bless them that curse you, do good to them that hate you, and pray for them which despitefully use you, and persecute you" (v. 44).

You may say, "But I can't love my enemies." Maybe not, but Jesus' love can go beyond your ability to love.

Jesus said, "If you love those who love you, what reward will you get?" (v. 46 NIV). How different are we if we only love the lovable? The Holy Spirit can help us love those we don't love. "The love of God is shed abroad in our hearts by the Holy Ghost which is given unto us" (Rom. 5:5).

The story is told of a Christian girl from Armenia whose brother had been killed by a Turkish soldier during a massacre. The girl escaped and later became a nurse.

One day a wounded Turkish soldier was brought into the hospital where she worked. He was near death. Immediately she recognized him as the soldier who had killed her brother. With a little negligence he would die, but she could not yield to this temptation. She gave him the best of care.

When the soldier regained consciousness and recognized her, he asked why she had nursed him so carefully when she knew he had killed her brother. She replied that the love of Christ in her life had enabled her to do it.

Is there someone in your life you have not been able to love? Have you let the Holy Spirit fill your heart with the love of Christ for that person? If not, let the Holy Spirit accomplish that work in your life today.

APRIL 5

I know that my redeemer liveth, and that he shall stand at the latter day upon the earth (Job 19:25).

ob's life was filled with uncertainty and confusion. Although he did not understand what God was doing, suddenly his declaration of truth came like a light in the dark tunnel of his life. He said, "I know that my redeemer liveth."

Many things had happened that he couldn't understand. Doubts filled his mind. Heartbreaking calamities robbed him of peace and joy. Yet his solid confidence in God carried him through the turbulence of his life. His assurance was a present reality. "I know that my redeemer liveth." And it gave him hope for the future. "He shall stand at the latter day on the earth. . . . In my flesh shall I see God" (vv. 25–26).

We can have this same confidence today. Jesus said, "Because I live, ye shall live also" (John 14:19). His crucifixion and burial left His disciples seemingly without hope. But He came forth a living Savior—victor over death and the grave.

The angel said to the women who came to the tomb, "Fear not ye: for I know that ye seek Jesus, which was crucified. He is not here: for he is risen, as he said. Come, see the place where the Lord lay" (Matt. 28:5–6). The resurrection message dispels fear. It brings hope. He is risen! He is alive!

Victory, joy, peace, and praise characterize our Christian faith because Jesus came forth triumphant over death: "I am he that liveth, and was dead; and, behold, I am alive for evermore" (Rev. 1:18).

At a rehearsal of Handel's oratorio, *Messiah*, the soprano soloist began to sing the aria, "I Know that My Redeemer Liveth." Her technique was perfect, but something was lacking. The conductor asked, "Do you really believe that your Redeemer lives?"

She looked surprised. "Of course I believe it."

"Then sing as if you believed it," said the conductor.

Again she sang of the resurrected Redeemer, this time from her innermost being. All who listened were moved to tears. When she finished, the auditorium was quiet. Finally the conductor said, "Yes, you do believe it."

Jesus Christ is alive! Are you singing today from the depth of your innermost being, "I know that *my* Redeemer liveth?" Do people know you believe it?"

APRIL 6

Now therefore thus saith the LORD of hosts; Consider your ways (Hag. 1:5).

 onsider your ways! This was the admonition of the prophet Haggai to the Jews who had returned from captivity to rebuild the temple at Jerusalem. When opposition came, their enthusiasm had waned. They became discouraged and quit.

Becoming indifferent to their work, they postponed it. They excused themselves by saying it was not the right time to rebuild the temple. Putting their own interests first, they built comfortable houses. After they took care of themselves, then they would consider God's work.

They became so preoccupied with their own plans they had no time for the work of God. They didn't want to be inconvenienced. How often this is true of us. We will do something for God if it doesn't interfere with our plans.

God sent a message to them through Haggai. He reminded them that their efforts were failing. Their lack of concern and neglect of God's work was the underlying cause of their economic problems.

God's message was, "Consider your ways." They needed to re-evaluate their lives and rearrange their priorities. Then God commanded, "Go up to the mountain, and bring wood, and build the house; and I will take pleasure in it" (v. 8). In obedience, they began to rebuild the temple. Eventually it was completed and the glory of God filled it.

This same message is relevant for us today. We become so preoccupied, accumulating money and possessions, that we neglect God's work. We are not saying no to God's work; we just postpone it.

God says, "Consider your ways." Most of us would confess our schedules are too full. We need to evaluate our activities and put our priorities in God's sequence. Sometimes the good keeps us from the best.

When we put God first, He will arrange our priorities and adjust our schedules to fit His plan for us. When we put Him first, He will take care of our families, our business, our activities, every area of our lives.

Where does He fit into your life today? Jesus said, "Seek ye first the kingdom of God, and his righteousness; and all these things shall be added unto you" (Matt. 6:33).

Consider your ways! Consider His ways! Consider Him!

APRIL 7

O Lord, you have examined my heart and know everything about me (Ps. 139:1 LB).

od is omniscient, an All-knowing God. The psalmist David was aware that God knew all about him. What a staggering thought! "You know me, God!" It is a scary thought but a comforting one, too.

Sometimes we wish God didn't know all about us. Yet it is a comfort that He knows when we are lonely, discouraged, or disappointed. He knows when we have come to the end of ourselves. He knows us better than we do.

David said, "You know when I sit or stand" (v. 2 LB). He knows our daily routine—when we get up, what we do at home, when we go to work, when we sit down to rest. He knows our activities, our hobbies, our pleasures.

Our every thought is known to Him (v. 2). He knows the thoughts of love and understanding we have for others. He also knows the critical, unloving thoughts that come into our mind.

He knows where we are every minute. "You chart the path ahead of me, and tell me where to stop and rest. Every moment, you know where I am" (v. 3 LB).

I recall a weekend I spent alone in a motel. It had been raining for weeks, and all the rivers were overflowing their banks. Tornados had touched down in several areas. Television news bulletins kept reporting flooding and potential tornados. Finally I said, "Lord, just remember I am here." Late that evening I learned that a tornado had almost touched down one-half mile from my motel.

Our very words are known to him. "You know what I am going to say before I even say it" (v. 4 LB). Then I say, "Lord, why didn't you keep me from saying it?"

What security to know that we are completely surrounded by God! "You both precede and follow me, and place your hand of blessing on my head" (v. 5 LB).

How wonderful! He knows all about each one of us all of the time, and His knowledge is more than information. He knows us in an intimate, loving relationship. Believing that God is an All-knowing God gives us a sense of well-being and security. We can join the psalmist in a majestic symphony of praise: "This is too glorious, too wonderful to believe!" (v. 6 LB).

APRIL 8

I can never be lost to your Spirit! I can never get away from my God!
(Ps. 139:7 LB).

he second attribute of God that David focused on in Psalm 139 was the omnipresence of God. God is everywhere! Wherever David went, he knew God was already there.

There is no place we can go to get away from God. Any place we go on the vertical plane God is there waiting for us. "If I go up to heaven, you are there; if I go down to the place of the dead, you are there" (v. 8 LB). Anywhere we go on the horizontal plane we will find God there, too. "If I ride the morning winds to the farthest oceans, even there your hand will guide me, your strength will support me" (vv. 7–8 LB).

In Genesis 21 we discover someone who experienced the comfort of the omnipresent God. When Sarah and Hagar couldn't get along in the home, Abraham sent Hagar and her son, Ishmael, away.

They wandered in the desert until they were exhausted and their water supply was gone. Then, placing Ishmael under a bush to die, Hagar began to cry. God heard and an angel of God said, "Hagar, what's wrong? Don't be afraid! For God has heard the lad's cries as he is lying there" (v. 17 LB). God opened Hagar's eyes, and to her amazement, she saw a well. She was able to give her son water. God spared their lives.

You may be in a desert situation. You try to use the wings of the morning to fly away from your problem. It may be a difficult work situation, overloaded home responsibilities, a breaking heart over a hurtful situation. Running away doesn't solve the problem. The only One who can help is the omnipresent God. He is with you where you are, and He has prepared a special well in your desert situation. All you have to do is drink.

Paul says, "I am convinced that nothing can ever separate us from his love. . . . Our fears for today, our worries about tomorrow, or where we are . . . nothing will ever be able to separate us from the love of God" (Rom. 8:38–39 LB).

Oh the greatness and yet the personalness of a God who is with *all* of us at *all* times!

*You saw me before I was born and scheduled each day of my life
before I began to breathe. Every day was recorded in your Book!
(Ps. 139:16 LB).*

ho could take a course in human anatomy and not say with the
psalmist, "I will praise thee; for I am fearfully and wonderfully
made: marvellous are thy works; and that my soul knoweth
right well" (v. 14)? Only the skilled handiwork of an
Omnipotent God could accomplish it.

In Psalm 119:73 we read, "Thy hands have made me and fashioned
me." We are not just a chance product. God fashioned us with a special
purpose in mind. This gives us a self-image of purpose and importance because
God has taken time to plan for each of us individually.

We are not cookie-cutter Christians, all made from the same mold. We
have our own unique God-given personality of His design. When we become a
part of God's family, He enters our personality to make us individually like Jesus
Christ. What a challenge it is to let our great Designer fashion us according to
His design.

Perhaps you are dissatisfied with your appearance or personality. You are
tall but want to be short. You are a blond but wish you were a brunette. You
are an introvert but wish you were an extrovert. Whatever your personality,
God plans to show the world the likeness of Jesus Christ expressed by your
individual personality.

Whether you are a child, teenager, young person, man, or woman, God
will fashion you according to His purpose.

In a recent winter Olympics one of the gold-medal winners was a
beautiful girl physically. Yet there was a hardness that detracted from her
beauty. There was never a smile on her face, nor any warmth of personality.

The girl who won the silver medal was not as attractive physically, yet she
seemed more beautiful. Why? She radiated the warmth of her personality.

The Bible says, "Your beauty should not come from outward adornment,
such as braided hair and the wearing of gold jewelry and fine clothes. Instead, it
should be that of your inner self, the unfading beauty of a gentle and quiet spirit,
which is of great worth in God's sight" (1 Peter 3:3–4 NIV).

God wants to make you into the wonderful person He has planned. Are
you letting Him? You are special to God!

Hear my cry, O God; attend unto my prayer (Ps. 61:1).

hrough the centuries, David's psalms have been God's "comforters" in times of need. Because David's life was filled with trouble we can relate to him. He always expressed his feelings honestly, for he didn't always understand what God was doing. Yet God was always his source of help.

David had learned that no matter where he was, near or far, no matter what his trouble was, God was always there, undertaking for him. "Wherever I am, though far away at the ends of the earth, I will cry to you for help" (v. 2 LB). God didn't always take David out of his trouble, but He taught David through difficulties.

In our times of trial we can be comforted knowing that God is only a cry away from our hurting heart. He knows what we need, and He knows how to accomplish it in our lives.

Most of us know what it's like to come to the end of ourselves. David cried, "When my heart is faint and overwhelmed, lead me to the mighty, towering Rock of safety" (v. 2 LB). When we let God lead us, we won't get lost. We will reach the Rock of safety and security.

First Corinthians 10:4 says that Rock is Christ Jesus. Secure in Him, our strong Rock, we will never be moved. When sorrow and fear overwhelm us, we can securely rest on our solid Rock.

David had confidence that God would keep him in the midst of his present trouble, for he had learned the security of trusting the Lord. "You are my refuge, a high tower where my enemies can never reach me" (Ps. 61:3 LB). His place of security was in God Himself. Surrounded by the All-powerful God, nothing touches our lives that He doesn't allow.

In Psalm 71:3 we read, "Be thou my strong habitation, whereunto I may continually resort . . . for thou art my rock and my fortress." This refuge is not a last resort but a continual resort. It is not an emergency shelter but a constant dwelling place, a permanent home. "I shall live forever in your tabernacle" (Ps. 61:4 LB).

Someone has said that safety isn't the absence of danger but the presence of Christ.

APRIL 11

My voice shalt thou hear in the morning, O LORD; in the morning will I direct my prayer unto thee, and will look up (Ps. 5:3).

avid experienced the reality of trouble in his life. But greater to him was the reality of the One to whom he could bring his troubles. Prayer was his place of refuge. "Give ear to my words, O LORD, consider my meditation. Hearken unto the voice of my cry" (v. 1–2).

But David didn't wait until he was in trouble to pray. There was regularity in his prayer time. Prayer had priority in his daily schedule. "In the morning, O LORD, you hear my voice; in the morning I lay my requests before you and wait in expectation" (v. 3 NIV).

David said he would *direct* his prayer unto God. In Hebrew, the word *direct* in this verse is a word used to describe laying sacrificial wood in order. "Each morning I will . . . lay my requests before you, praying earnestly" (v. 3 LB). David wasn't satisfied to hurry into God's presence with his requests and hurry out again. He took time to be aware of God's presence as he came with his needs.

If prayer is to be our place of refuge in times of trouble, we must give it priority in our busy schedules each day. We will never find time to pray. We will have to make time.

To prepare our hearts for prayer, we can begin by reading His Word. As God begins to speak to us, our hearts and minds are prepared to commit our requests to Him. Then we can look expectantly for His answer.

Your schedule may make it difficult for you to begin your day with prayer. It has been said that the sunrise of the day may come later for some. The early morning time is good, but more important than the time is the regularity of it.

In some African countries, when people become Christians, they select a place out in the bush for prayer each day. As they go there daily, they beat a path to it. Because the grass grows rapidly, missing a day at prayer becomes obvious. They say you can gauge the spiritual life of the native Christians by the condition of their prayer path.

What is the condition of your prayer path?

Who knoweth whether thou art come to the kingdom for such a time as this? (Est. 4:14).

The Miss Persia Beauty Contest had been held to select the most beautiful woman to be the new queen. Esther won the contest, becoming the queen of King Xerxes.

One day Mordecai, Esther's cousin, learned that a decree had been issued to kill all Jewish people in the kingdom. Mordecai sent a message to the queen, asking her to plead with the king in their behalf.

But Queen Esther was hesitant to commit herself to such an assignment. She knew that if anyone approached the king without an invitation, it could mean death. Only if the king held out his golden scepter could anyone enter his presence.

Mordecai knew that Esther was their only hope. He sent another message, reminding her that though she was queen, she would suffer the same fate, for she, too, was one of God's people. Mordecai challenged her: "Who knoweth whether thou art come to the kingdom for such a time as this?"

Knowing it meant total commitment, Esther accepted the challenge. She asked all her people to join her in fasting and prayer for three days. Then she was willing to go to the king on their behalf, even if it meant her death. She said, "If I perish, I perish" (v. 16). Her people were more important to her than her desires, her interests, or even her danger.

After a time of prayer and fasting, she approached the king. Would he hold out the golden scepter, giving her permission to approach, or would she be led to her death? With bated breath she watched him lift his scepter, giving her permission to approach. Through a God-given plan she spared God's people from death.

This same challenge comes today. God has a mission for you in His kingdom. What is your response to His challenge? Is it total commitment to God, whatever your mission is?

When you write a letter, you put it in an envelope, address it, stamp it, and take it to the mailbox. But it is not committed to the postal department to deliver until you drop it into the mailbox.

Have you dropped your life into God's mailbox in total commitment to His plan for your life? "Who knoweth whether thou art come to the kingdom for such a time as this?" Have you accepted the challenge?

APRIL 13

Surely God is good to Israel, to those who are pure in heart (Ps. 73:1 NIV).

ometimes we question the goodness of God. We wonder why he is allowing some of the things that come into our lives. Too often we think of God as good only when He gives us what we ask for.

This had happened to Asaph. As he looked about, the ungodly seemed to be prospering. They weren't experiencing the trouble he was. Asaph couldn't understand what God was doing. He tried to live a life that was pleasing to God, but all he had was trouble.

Asaph expressed his feelings honestly: "As for me, I came so close to the edge of the cliff! My feet were slipping and I was almost gone . . . All I get out of it is trouble and woe—every day and all day long!" (vv. 2, 14 LB). This was a natural reaction. God understood that. Asaph said, "When I tried to understand all this, it was oppressive to me till I entered the sanctuary of God; then I understood their final destiny" (vv. 16–17 NIV).

In the sanctuary he began to understand. In the presence of God everything became clear. He discovered he had been looking at the problem from his viewpoint. He was seeing the problem from the immediate. God was looking at it from the ultimate. God knew what was going on, but He wasn't through with the evildoers yet.

Asaph's eyes had been focusing on people and circumstances instead of the Lord. He had left God out of his thinking. As God began to deal with him, Asaph recognized that God was good.

Does everything seem to be falling apart today? Are you trying to please God, yet everything is going wrong? You may be having financial reverses, your children may have broken your heart, the promotion you expected may have been given to someone less qualified. It doesn't seem fair that the ungodly have an easier life than you.

Into the sanctuary of God's presence we can bring our perplexities, questions, even our rebellion. Frustration comes when we focus on what we see. In the sanctuary we can commit our problems to God and learn to trust Him when we can't understand. "For we walk by faith, not by sight" (2 Cor. 5:7). As we look at our problems with His perspective, we can say, "Surely God is good to me."

APRIL 14

*My flesh and my heart faileth; but God is the strength of my heart
(Ps. 73:26).*

ven when Asaph was questioning, he wanted to believe. And in the sanctuary, God helped him understand. What a relief and joy to find God waiting for him. God hadn't turned from Asaph because of his doubts.

In spite of Asaph's wrong thoughts and attitudes, God still accepted him. He had been waiting for Asaph to turn back to Him. Not only was there joy in Asaph's heart, but I believe joy welled up in God's heart, too.

Asaph reached a deeper position of faith in God now. He realized that not only was God in control of the evildoers, but He was working in his life as well. When he focused his eyes on the Lord, his attitude changed completely. He had a new awareness of Who God was and what He wanted to do for Asaph. Today, we too, can experience the reality of Jesus Christ living with us in our daily walk.

Asaph told God, "I am continually with thee" (v. 23). This is also true for us. We have the presence of Jesus with us day by day. He said, "I am with you alway, even unto the end of the world" (Matt. 28:20).

Asaph said, "You are holding my right hand" (v. 23 LB). What a comfort to know that since Jesus holds my hand, He can keep me from falling. Asaph continued, "You will keep on guiding me all my life with your wisdom and counsel" (v. 24 LB).

Your heart may be failing. With your eyes fixed on Jesus your whole outlook can change. Friends may forsake, troubles may come, but God never fails or forsakes.

Today, look beyond yourself and your needs to God Himself. In Him you will find your answers. Someone has said that while we are looking for *the blessed thing,* we may miss *the Blessed Person,* the Lord Jesus Christ. He is our portion forever.

Asaph finished the psalm with, "But as for me, I get as close to him as I can! I have chosen him and I will tell everyone about the wonderful ways he rescues me" (v. 28 LB).

Blessed are the meek: for they shall inherit the earth (Matt. 5:5).

e usually think of a meek person as having a weak, timid, mousy personality. But this is not so. A meek person is not weak. Moses was a meek person. The Bible says, "Now the man Moses was very meek, above all the men which were upon the face of the earth" (Num. 12:3). Yet Moses could not be considered weak. He was one of the strongest leaders the world has known.

Various characteristics describe a meek person. He is humble, submissive, gentle, and patient. He does not assert his rights. He does not retaliate. He refrains from condemning others. He does not judge the actions or motives of another. He does not criticize, murmur, or complain but accepts injury without resentment. He is not easily offended.

Jesus is the perfect example of a meek person. He said, "Take my yoke upon you, and learn of me; for I am meek and lowly in heart: and ye shall find rest unto your souls" (Matt. 11:29). We learn meekness as we are yoked together with Christ. His yoke does not break our spirit but supplies the gentleness of the Lord in our lives. Being yoked together with Christ gives us a gentle power. As we wait on the Lord the Holy Spirit produces this inner gentleness in our lives. Our inner power will be equal to our outer stress.

Those who are meek will not argue with God but will be submissive to His will and obedient to His Word. They will radiate a peace and joy of spirit independent of circumstances. They will need no pretense or shame because they know the genuine reality of God's presence.

To be meek is to be aware of our littleness in the light of God's greatness, to rely on God for everything, let God *be* everything in our lives. The meek inherit the earth as they claim their resources. They walk quietly with God.

Are you wearing the yoke of tension and pressure today? Is your life hectic outwardly? You can release it and take upon yourself the yoke of Christ. Yoked to His meekness you will find that gentle inner power sufficient for your daily needs.

Find happiness through meekness!

APRIL 16

By faith Moses' parents hid him for three months after he was born, because they saw he was no ordinary child, and they were not afraid of the king's edict (Heb. 11:23 NIV).

he eleventh chapter of Hebrews is sometimes called God's Hall of Faith, and Moses' parents, Jochebed and Amram, are included in the roster.

The Israelites were enslaved in Egypt, and the pharaoh had declared that all Hebrew baby boys were to be killed. During this crisis, Moses was born to Jochebed and Amram. Although the baby's life was in danger, his parents had faith that God would save him. As people of faith, they recognized their helplessness and dependence upon God.

Their faith was so strong that "they were not afraid of the king's commandment" (Heb. 11:23). Someone has said that a dangerous place becomes a place of safety when God has given it a divine purpose. Jochebed and Amram did all they could to ensure Moses' safety, then committed him to God's protection.

They hid him in their home for three months. Then when they could keep him quiet no longer, they placed him in a basket on the Nile River, expecting God to protect him. Their faith was in God, not in a basket on the river.

God intervened in an unusual way. Miriam, Moses' sister, stayed close by to watch. Soon Pharaoh's daughter found the baby, asked Miriam if she knew a wet nurse, and gave the baby back to his own mother to nurse for her. The princess even paid her for it! God had a plan for Moses' life that even the mighty pharaoh could not thwart.

Today, you may be in a crisis. You don't know which way to turn. Even though you can see no way out, by faith you can trust God. The Bible says that "your faith should not stand in the wisdom of men, but in the power of God" (1 Cor. 2:5).

To strengthen our faith, we need to read and meditate on God's Word consistently. "So then faith cometh by hearing, and hearing by the word of God" (Rom. 10:17). Then we need to apply God's Word to our daily needs.

Faith is the capacity of the human heart for God. People of faith are God-filled, God-motivated, and God-possessed. The work accomplished through them is God's work, not theirs. "For we walk by faith, not by sight" (2 Cor. 5:7). Do you qualify as one who walks by faith?

APRIL 17

The Israelites groaned in their slavery and cried out, and their cry for help because of their slavery went up to God (Ex. 2:23 NIV).

ave you ever had the feeling that no one really cared about you, that even God had forgotten you? God does care! He is not indifferent to your cry.

The Israelites were slaves in Egypt. For years, they had been cruelly mistreated by their taskmasters. Finally, in desperation they cried for help, and God was waiting.

He was already preparing a deliverer for them. Moses was the one chosen by God to eventually lead them out of Egypt.

As soon as they cried, God *heard*. God hears the weakest cry of one of His children. God *remembered* His promise that He would bring His people out of Egypt. God *saw* their oppression, and his heart went out to them. More than that, "God . . . was concerned about them" (Ex. 2:25 NIV).

Today He knows the burden of our hearts. Silent though He may seem, He is not indifferent. The Lord is as concerned for us as He was for the Israelites. He is a *prayer-hearing* God. He is a *promise-keeping* God. He is an *all-seeing* God. He is an *all-caring* God. He feels our every burden and heartache with us.

There are times when our hearts are so heavy we can't put our prayer into words. But God hears the prayers of our hearts. "The eyes of the Lord are over the righteous, and his ears are open unto their prayers" (1 Peter 3:12). He sees our need and knows it even better than we do. He assures us of His help. "He healeth the broken in heart, and bindeth up their wounds" (Ps. 147:3). Someone has said that tears have a voice and God interprets them.

He knows what He wants to accomplish in our difficulties. When it is time, He will provide a deliverer. It may be a person or a circumstance. It may be a change of attitude or motive. He may deliver us from our circumstances or in the midst of them. "Call upon me in the day of trouble:" He says, "I will deliver thee, and thou shalt glorify me" (Ps. 50:15).

It is as easy for God to do a difficult thing as an easy one.

APRIL 18

*It was by faith that Moses, when he grew up, refused to be treated as
the grandson of the king, but chose to share ill-treatment with God's
people instead of enjoying the fleeting pleasures of sin. He thought
that it was better to suffer for the promised Christ than to own all the
treasures of Egypt, for he was looking forward to the great reward
that God would give him (Heb. 11:24–26 LB).*

The day came when Moses' mother took him to live in the
palace. How her heart must have ached. But she committed him
to God, not Pharaoh's daughter.

He enjoyed great opportunities in the royal family. "Moses
was learned in all the the wisdom of the Egyptians, and was mighty in words
and in deeds" (Acts 7:22). He likely became one of the best-educated young
men of that time.

But Moses, aware of the Israelites' condition, longed to help them.
Finally, he had to make a choice: identify himself with his people and suffer
with them or remain comfortable in the palace. Earthly reward or eternal
reward? By faith he turned his back on the palace and identified with his people.
By faith he chose God's plan.

Years ago in a family of wealthy linen merchants in Ireland, one of the
sons, Walter, was being trained to manage the business. One Sunday evening,
as Walter was reading a sermon, he realized that although he went to church
regularly, he was not a Christian. He invited Christ into his life and soon knew
that God wanted him in full-time Christian service. Upset at the news, his father
offered to support two missionaries in his place. "It is not your *money* God
wants," Walter replied, "but my *life.*"

Disinherited by his family, Walter later came to America and became a
pastor. Reverend Walter Duff, Sr. was the father of Mrs. Helen Duff Baugh, the
founder of the Stonecroft Ministries. Although Walter Duff's choice meant giving
up his family, he had to be obedient to God. What a reward he will have!

We, too, have to make choices. They may cost dearly, but the rewards
will surpass the cost. Jesus said, "If any man will come after me, let him deny
himself, and take up his cross daily, and follow me" (Luke 9:23).

Some choices lead to earthly rewards, others to eternal rewards. Life on
earth is short; eternity is forever. Jesus said, "Seek ye first the kingdom of God,
and his righteousness; and all these things shall be added unto you" (Matt.
6:33).

Are you making your choices in faith, in the light of eternity?

APRIL 19

When Moses was grown . . . he went out unto his brethren, and
looked on their burdens (Ex. 2:11).

oses chose to leave the palace and become involved in his people's affairs. One day when Moses went to visit them, he saw an Egyptian beating one of the Israelites. After looking this way and that (instead of looking up), he killed the Eyptian and hid his body. Perhaps he felt justified in trying to defend the Israelites. But to his surprise, instead of appreciating him, they misjudged his motive and rejected his help. Didn't they understand that he had come to help them?

Then Pharaoh threatened to kill him, so he fled to the desert. He arrived in the desert alone, discouraged, a failure. What had happened? Wasn't he to be their deliverer? God had called him, but Moses' actions were premature. This was God's work, not his. Moses was too strong for God to use. God's work must be done God's way. Moses had committed himself to the task instead of committing himself to the God who gave the task.

When he came to the desert, he sat down by a well. Only then did he become quiet enough to listen to God. Only then could God begin the removal of Moses' self-life and prepare him for His use. Moses had to learn that *being* must have priority over *doing*.

Perhaps you are in a desert, discouraged and distressed. Your plans have failed. One of the processes God uses is failure. Perhaps you have tried to do God's work in your way. You, too, must learn that your way won't work.

In your desert, God has a well. There, by your well, God begins the process of removing your self-sufficiency and making you into the instrument He can use. There you will discover a new dimension of power. Commit yourself to God. Then He can do His work in His way. Someone has said that we can't fail when God does it and we can't be successful when we do it.

"Not that we are sufficient of ourselves to think any thing as of ourselves; but our sufficiency is of God" (2 Cor. 3:5).

Are you operating under self-sufficiency or God-sufficiency?

APRIL 20

And he said, Draw not nigh hither: put off thy shoes from off thy feet, for the place whereon thou standest is holy ground (Ex. 3:5).

Although Moses thought he had failed, God wasn't through with him. Moses was still God's chosen leader.

God had another lesson to teach His servant before He could use him. Moses needed to learn who God was and what He could do for him because his own wisdom, power, and strength would not be sufficient for the stupendous task of leading God's people out of Egypt. God would be his sufficiency.

To move two million people out of their present home and take them across the desert into a new land seemed impossible. Moses would have to let God use him for God's glory, not his.

One morning when Moses was out on the desert caring for his sheep, he saw a strange sight—a bush on fire but not being consumed. Fire in the Bible is a symbol of the presence of God. This ordinary bush became extraordinary, for in it God revealed His presence to Moses.

When Moses turned aside to see it, God called, "Moses, Moses!" Suppose Moses had been too busy to turn aside. He would have missed God's visit and God's call. When Moses replied, "Here am I," God said, "Take off your shoes for in my presence you are on holy ground." There in his regular everyday round of duties, Moses came face to face with God, and he hid his face in humble worship.

Sometimes in the midst of our activity and busyness, God has to put a burning bush in our lives to get our attention. We, too, need to turn aside and take time to commune with God. We must recognize His holiness, His greatness, and His majesty.

Too often we quickly voice our needs to God and rush away without realizing that we have been in the holy presence of God. We do not take time to worship and adore Him.

Wherever our burning bush is, when we turn aside, we are on holy ground. We can have a heart-to-heart meeting with our Holy God. "Give unto the LORD the glory due unto his name. Worship the LORD in the beauty of holiness" (Ps. 29:2).

Do we take time to turn aside in God's presence and worship Him? He is waiting for us.

APRIL 21

I am come down to deliver them out of the hand of the Egyptians
. . . Come now therefore, and I will send thee unto Pharaoh, that
thou mayest bring forth my people (Ex. 3:8, 10)

oving time had come! In effect God said, "I am coming down to deliver my people, Moses, and I am going to do it through you."

By now Moses had lost his self-confidence. All feeling of self-worth was gone. He felt unqualified for the task. "Who am I, that I should go unto Pharaoh?" (v. 11). Moses *was* an unlikely prospect—eighty years of age, out of touch with people, only a shepherd from the desert. He queried, "Why should God use me? I'm a nobody." While there is danger in thinking too highly of ourselves, there is also danger in belittling ourselves. It is not important whether we are somebody or nobody, but it is important who God is.

God replied, "Certainly [without a doubt], I will be with thee" (v. 12). It was as if God were saying, "Moses, just trust me."

Moses still wasn't sure. He asked what he should say when the Israelites asked him who sent him. Moses knew he didn't have all the answers. God said, "Say . . . I AM hath sent me unto you" (v. 14). Then God gave him a new revelation of Himself. He wanted Moses to know Him in a more real way. He wanted Moses to know He could depend on Him for every need on their daily walk through the desert.

All of Israel knew that the name of God was Jehovah, *Yahweh*. This name of God reveals His character. God was saying "I am all you will need. I have the answers." Beginning his great journey across the desert, what greater assurance could Moses have than that God would be with him, becoming to him all that he would need.

As we face each day, what assurance we have, knowing that God is our great I AM. He is ready to become all we need. In God's vocabulary there is no past or future but the I AM of the present moment. It is not important who we are or what we can or cannot do. God is the great I AM of right now.

The Bible promises, "But my God shall supply all your need according to his riches in glory by Christ Jesus" (Phil. 4:19).

And Moses said unto the LORD . . . I am not eloquent . . . but I am slow of speech, and of a slow tongue (Ex. 4:10).

oses said, "They will not believe me" (v.1). It was as if he were saying, "I don't have their respect. They rejected me before. Won't they reject me again?"

God gave Moses three miraculous signs to prove that He merely wanted an instrument for a special mission. God was not concerned about Moses' ability or inability. He wanted someone through whom He could do the supernatural—that which could only be explained because of God.

Moses continued his excuses. "O Lord, I have never been eloquent . . . I am slow of speech and tongue" (v. 10 NIV). God answered, "Who gave man his mouth? . . . Now go; I will help you speak and will teach you what to say" (vv. 11–12 NIV). God is not dependent on human eloquence. No task is beyond His resources. All He needed was an obedient messenger.

In one final attempt to get out of it, Moses asked God to send someone else. God became angry, not because Moses was insecure, not because he felt incapable, but because he was not willing. Yet how gracious God was. He didn't give up on Moses. He sent Aaron, Moses' brother, with him. But gradually Moses took over the leadership and became one of the greatest leaders of the world.

When I was asked to assume responsibility of the Prayer Ministry for the Stonecroft Ministries, I was told it would also include writing devotional material. I gave God all my excuses. I reminded God that I couldn't pray aloud and had *no* ability to write. My English teachers gave up on me.

As I prayed, however, I knew God was calling me to this ministry. Even now I do not pray aloud easily. I still cannot write, but it has been exciting to be a pen in the hand of God as He has written through me.

I couldn't do it, but God could and did!

Is God asking you to do something? Are you telling Him you can't? That may be your best recommendation. He uses natural ability committed to Him, but He is not hindered by our inability. All He wants is our availability.

Do not let your hearts be troubled. Trust in God; trust also in me (John 14:1 NIV).

As we read the newspapers and listen to newscasts, our hearts may become fearful. We worry about business, the stock market, world conditions, families, health, the uncertainty of the future. God's Word predicted this. Luke 21:26 speaks of "Men's hearts failing them for fear." More people are seeking help from psychologists and psychiatrists than ever before. Books on peace make the best-seller lists. People are seeking everywhere for inner peace.

In Jesus' day the world was in turmoil. There was much greed and oppression. Jesus' disciples were confused and disappointed. They had expected Jesus to set up a kingdom on earth. Instead, they learned that He would leave them soon and return to His heavenly Father. Fear gripped their hearts. What would they do without Him?

How comforting it must have been to hear Jesus say, "Do not let your hearts be troubled." Jesus promised a remedy for anxious, troubled hearts, for the pressures and stress of living. He said, "Peace I leave with you; my peace I give you. I do not give to you as the world gives. Do not let your hearts be troubled and do not be afraid" (v. 27 NIV).

This same remedy works for us today. Jesus didn't say that we would be free from difficulties. We can expect troublesome, stressful times. But Jesus tells why we need not worry. He gives the secret of an untroubled heart. He says, "Trust in God; trust also in me." If we have troubled hearts it is because we are not trusting the Lord.

Fear is a natural reaction when trouble strikes. Jesus tells us not to be troubled, fearful, or disturbed but to bring our fears to Him. Paul said, "Don't worry about anything; instead, pray about everything; tell God your needs and don't forget to thank him for his answers" (Phil. 4:6 LB).

Exchange your troubled heart for an untroubled one. "If you do this you will experience God's peace, which is far more wonderful than the human mind can understand. His peace will keep your thoughts and your hearts quiet and at rest as you trust in Christ Jesus" (v. 7 LB).

A peaceful life comes from trusting the future completely to our Father's hands.

O Lord, I know that the way of man is not in himself: it is not in man that walketh to direct his steps (Jer. 10:23).

 ften all we see before us is a maze of confusion. There are many roads ahead, and we are uncertain which one to take. There are decisions to be made, and we do not know which one is best. Bewildered, we ask, "What is the right thing to do?"

How true was Jeremiah's statement, "O Lord, I know it is not within the power of man to map his life and plan his course" (LB). Is there anyone who can give us the right direction?

Think of God as our Great Master Controller at the Control Center of Life. "The steps of a good man are ordered by the LORD" (Ps. 37:23). David said, "You chart the path ahead of me, and tell me when to stop and rest" (Ps. 139:3 LB).

God's love and concern for us is so great that He doesn't leave the direction to us. He knows the mistakes and failures we would make.

But we can be assured of a life of *directed steps.* "The steps of a [good] man are directed and established of the Lord, when He delights in his way, [and He busies Himself with his every step]" (Ps. 37:23 AMPLIFIED). God promises that He will involve Himself with every step we take. He "busies Himself" with our lives *when* He (God) delights in (our) way.

Yet sometimes we try to direct our own lives. One time while driving from Denver to Albuquerque, I told my husband I knew a short cut. When we came to a junction in the highway, without consulting a map, I told him which way to turn. My husband was apprehensive, but I insisted I knew. Much to my chagrin, we soon discovered we were on a narrow, gravel road winding through the mountains, which took us hours longer.

Often I have directed my own steps, taking a short cut to avoid a road I did not want to take, or taking a road I thought was the right one without consulting God, and I've ended up on the wrong road.

God says, "I, the Lord, will instruct you and teach you in the way you should go; I will counsel you with My eye upon you" (Ps. 32:8 AMPLIFIED).

APRIL 25

I will bless the LORD at all times: his praise shall continually be in my mouth (Ps. 34:1).

avid wrote this psalm at a time when his life was in danger. Because Saul had threatened to kill him, he had gone into hiding in a cave. He was discouraged, disappointed, and lonely. With him was a motley, loyal group of men who had been in trouble and needed to be in hiding, too.

As in many of David's psalms, he begins with a joyful note of praise. He knew the One to whom praise is due. Then he relates the trouble he is going through and closes the psalm, again praising God for what He has done.

He begins, "I will bless the LORD at all times." *I will* indicates this is an act of his will. He may not feel like blessing the Lord but he does anyhow. He will bless the Lord *at all times.* In his easy situations and his difficult ones! Praising the Lord at all times will be his lifelong habit. God deserves to be praised continually, even when adversity comes. What an effect it has on others when they see us blessing the Lord in the midst of our trials.

From his heart overflowing with praise, he continues, "O magnify the LORD with me and let us exalt his name together" (v. 3). To magnify means to make something appear larger. John the Baptist said, "He must increase, but I must decrease" (John 3:30).

My husband, an amateur photographer, and I often spent our Saturdays in the mountains above timberline hunting for small mountain flowers to photograph. At that altitude many were no larger than the head of a pin. Using his high-powered lens, he would take pictures of them.

When we returned home, he would develop the film, and the flowers I could hardly see with my naked eye would fill the photograph. I could see minute details and delicate shadings that I had not seen before.

In Luke 1, Mary sings the magnificent Magnificat. Her heart was so filled with love for the Lord that it overflowed in praise and worship. "My soul doth magnify the Lord" (v. 46). Mary wanted to magnify Him, to declare Him great.

May our hearts' song be "O magnify the LORD with me!"

I sought the LORD, and he heard me, and delivered me from all my fears (Ps. 34:4).

ecause David's life was in danger, he was hiding in a cave. His future was uncertain. In the midst of his trouble, he sought the Lord. What a refuge for him in his fear-filled life. The Lord heard him and delivered him from *all* his fears—every one of them. The Lord became his "Fear Remover."

The secret of his deliverance? He sought the Lord. David had learned that when he was at the end of himself, he had a wonderful source of help. Not knowing what the future held, not knowing where to go next, his only sure source of help was the Lord. David wrote, "The LORD is my light and my salvation; whom shall I fear? the LORD is the strength of my life; of whom shall I be afraid?" (Ps. 27:1).

No wonder David could say, "I will bless the LORD at all times; his praise shall continually be in my mouth" (34:1) The Lord heard him. The Lord delivered him.

David had reason to say, "O taste and see that the LORD is good" (v. 8). In effect, he says, "Try Him! Test Him! See how He has delivered me? Trust Him and He will do the same for you."

What do you do when you are filled with fear? To whom do you go? Perhaps you are hiding in a cave of fear today. Have you sought the Lord to deliver you from it?

God says, "Fear not, for I am with you. Do not be dismayed. I am your God. I will strengthen you; I will help you; I will uphold you with my victorious right hand" (Isa. 41:10 LB).

Perhaps the cave you're hiding in is not fear. It may be disillusionment, misunderstanding, false accusation, financial disaster, disease. Whatever your need, the Lord has promised deliverance. David says, "The righteous cry, and the LORD heareth, and delivereth them out of all their troubles" (v. 17).

As you *release* your trouble to Him, you can *relax* in the Lord. The Bible says, "Rest in the Lord, and wait patiently for him" (Ps. 37:7). Then you can *rejoice* in Him. "Rejoice in the Lord alway: and again I say, Rejoice." (Phil. 4:4).

Release! Relax! Rejoice!

APRIL 27

You saw me before I was born and scheduled each day of my life
before I began to breathe. Every day was recorded in your Book!
(Ps. 139:16 LB).

 n the old television program, "This Is Your Life," host Ralph Edwards brought back memories of people and events in his subject's lives. God has a "This is Your Life" scrapbook for each of us, put together by "Jesus, the author and finisher of our faith" (Heb. 12:2). God is keeping a record of our spiritual history, page by page, day by day, from our first breath till our last.

We can think of our life story in terms of chapters. Each chapter represents some area of growth and development, maturing into the person God wants us to be.

The first chapter records God's purpose and plan for our lives—to conform us to the image of Jesus Christ. In this chapter He records day by day the progress we make toward reaching this goal.

Also included in our life book are chapters covering other areas of our lives—our prayer life, Bible reading, fruit of the Spirit, Christian growth, behavior, handling of life's situations, and sharing the Gospel.

Our Author records how He sees us living our lives. He is always honest in evaluating and recording it. For instance, what we do on one day may seem like failure to us. But He records the right motive He saw behind it. Another day He may observe that we didn't make the best use of our time, that we were not willing to be involved for Him. He enters this as well. God is fair and understanding as He makes each entry.

There may be things we wish we could erase from the record, and it is wonderful to know that God has an "eraser" that removes these things when we confess them. "The blood of Jesus Christ his Son cleanseth us from all sin" (1 John 1:7).

In all of this Paul reminds us to keep moving forward. "Forgetting those things which are behind, and reaching forth unto those things which are before, I press toward the mark for the prize of the high calling of God in Christ Jesus" (Phil. 3:13–14).

And he said unto them, Let us go into the next towns, that I may preach there also: for therefore came I forth (Mark 1:38).

fter a schedule-packed day, what do you want to do? Relax? Get some extra sleep? It is interesting to note what Jesus did after such a busy day. Weary from ministering to the crowds all day, did He take an extra hour of sleep? Not Jesus. The Bible says, "Rising up a great while before day, he went out, and departed into a solitary place, and there prayed" (Mark 1:35).

As the crowds began to gather, the disciples went to find Him. They knew where He was, and when they found Him, they said, "Everyone is looking for you!" (v. 37 NIV). But this didn't deter Him from the work His Father had sent Him to do.

Instead of returning, Jesus said, "Let us go into the next towns." There were people in other areas with great spiritual needs, and Jesus' heart was filled with compassion for them. He had come to preach to them, too. He must go.

Thousands of people since then have been concerned for reaching the people in their *next towns*. Hudson Taylor told of praying one day about China. As he prayed, the Holy Spirit seemed to be saying that He, (the Holy Spirit), was going to walk through China and if Hudson Taylor cared to, he could walk with Him. And he did.

Today, we live in a world of needy people. Our *next towns* are filled with them—family, friends, neighbors, even people we don't know. We, too, need to go to them, sharing God's love.

Today, when many people are walking for their health, perhaps you would consider converting your daily walk into a prayer walk? If you are not a walker, you may wish to start this way.

In your prayer walk, you can pray for the people in homes, apartments, schools, or businesses you pass. Occasionally you may want to walk through a different neighborhood or a new subdivision. Another effective way of reaching many in *your next towns* is to pray for missionaries you know or people in the news. Prayer walks can enlarge your outreach for the Lord Jesus. You may never know the results until you get to heaven.

Prayer walks can take you around the globe. Prayer walks can change the world. Prayer walks can count throughout all eternity.

APRIL 29

Fret not thyself because of evildoers (Ps. 37:1).

Fret is defined as worry, irritability, or inner disturbance. Are you a member of the Fretful Club? I have a secret formula called, "The Formula to Take the Fret out of Life."

Fear can cause us to fret. Some members of the Fretful Club are fearful by nature. I used to be such a member, for I was a fretful worrier. If I wasn't worrying about something, I knew I must be overlooking something. David said, "Fret not." Paul wrote, "Don't worry about anything" (Phil. 4:6 LB). Fear not only affects our physical life, but our spiritual life as well.

One day while sitting in a train station, I watched a woman who was apparently having trouble. Finally as she came and sat by me, she began telling me all that had gone wrong. Then she said, "Can you think of anything else I should be worrying about?"

Another problem for some members of the Fretful Club is frustration. Frustration can come from an overloaded schedule. We cannot possibly accomplish everything in the time allotted. And the many things that go wrong complicate it.

A third problem area for a Fretful Club member is futility. What is life all about? What are we living for? Life seems to have no purpose for us.

There is a remedy. Instead of fear we can have *peace*. Jesus said, "My peace I give unto you" (John 14:27). In place of frustration we can have *rest*. "Come unto me . . . and I will give you rest" (Matt. 11:28). Replacing futility we can find *purpose*. "I am come that they might have life" (John 10:10).

"My peace." "Come unto *Me." "I* am come." These three ingredients are centered in a person—the person of Jesus Christ—"My, Me, I."

Many stores have a special department to exchange unsatisfactory articles. God's Exchange Department is open to you today. You can exchange your fear for His peace, your frustration for His rest, your futility for His purpose.

Paul wrote, "Everything else is worthless when compared with the priceless gain of knowing Christ Jesus my Lord. I have put aside all else, counting it worth less than nothing, in order that I can have Christ" (Phil. 3:8 LB).

APRIL 30

Is any thing too hard for the LORD? (Gen. 18:14).

od asked Abraham this question. He had promised Abraham and Sarah that they would have a son. But they had passed the age of childbearing, and the promise had not yet been fulfilled.
Even though it was humanly impossible, God assured Abraham that He would keep His promise. He said, "Is anything too hard for God? Next year, *just as I told you,* I will certainly see to it that Sarah has a son" (v. 11 LB, emphasis mine).

Could Abraham and Sarah believe God for this miracle? The Bible says that Abraham "staggered not at the promise of God through unbelief; but was strong in faith, giving glory to God; and being fully persuaded that, what he had promised, he was able also to perform" (Rom. 4:20–21).

Of Sarah we read, "Sarah, too, had faith, and because of this she was able to become a mother in spite of her old age, for she realized that God, who gave her his promise, would certainly do what he said" (Heb. 11:11 LB).

The next year God gave them a son just as He promised!

We read of others in the Bible who faced impossible circumstances. When Jeremiah was in the midst of an insurmountable situation, he said, "Ah Lord GOD! behold, thou hast made the heaven and the earth by thy great power and stretched out arm, and there is [present tense] nothing too hard for thee" (Jer. 32:17).

Maybe there is something in your life today that you think is impossible. You are confused, not knowing what to do or where to go. Listen as God whispers to you, "Is anything too hard for Me?"

You reply, "No, Lord."

Then He says, "Trust your present need to Me. It is not too hard for Me. I can do the impossible."

Our difficulty may lie in focusing on our need instead of the God of the impossible. Sometimes we say, "It will take a miracle to work this out." It may, but God is in the miracle-working business. You can trust Him.

Nothing is too hard for God.

MAY 1

Enoch walked [in habitual fellowship] with God (Gen. 5:24 AMPLIFIED).

hat more wonderful thing could be said of you than that you walk with God. Today many people walk for their physical well-being, but the Bible says the goal of Enoch's walk was his spiritual well-being. Enoch lived during a time of great wickedness on earth. In Genesis 6:5, we read that people's thoughts were evil continually. Yet Enoch made it a habit to walk with God.

How did Enoch maintain a walk of faith in evil surroundings? "Even before he was taken to heaven he received testimony [still on record] that he had pleased and been satisfactory to God. . . . For whoever would come near to God must (necessarily) believe that God exists and that He is the Rewarder of those who earnestly and diligently seek Him (out)" (Heb. 11:5–6 AMPLIFIED).

What wonderful times they had as walking companions. The presence of God was real to Enoch. The Living Bible says that Enoch was in constant touch with God (Gen. 5:24). He pleased God because he went in God's direction. He kept in step with God. He didn't run ahead or lag behind.

Enoch and God must have been in agreement on interests and purposes. The prophet Amos asked, "Can two walk together, except they be agreed?" (3:3).

Enoch was not a man who lived in isolation. Neither did he live in a perfect environment. He was a family man with responsibilities. He faced problems just as we do but sought God's counsel in solving them.

You may say, "If only I were in different surroundings or circumstances, I could walk with God." However, our walk is not dependent on circumstances but on God and our faith in Him.

A walk of faith must be a consistent walk—everywhere, in every situation. We must walk with God on Monday morning when breakfast is late and everyone is cross and the telephone is ringing. We must walk with God when our children fight with the neighbor's children. We must walk with God when the refrigerator repairman fails to come. We must walk with God when we lose a valuable business account. Our daily walk in our every day round of duties is what counts.

Are you pleasing God with a walk of faith with Him daily?

MAY 2

You search the Scriptures, because you think that in them you have eternal life; and it is these that bear witness of Me (John 5:39 NASB).

 omeone has said that we must know the Word of God to know the God of the Word. Jesus says that we become acquainted with Him through the Word. It is not enough just to know the Scriptures; we must see and know the One revealed in them.

The Jewish leaders knew the Scriptures. They knew the very letter of the law, and they thought that was sufficient. But people do not receive eternal life by merely knowing the Scriptures. We receive eternal life through Christ. "The gift of God is eternal life through Jesus Christ our Lord" (Rom. 6:23).

We may say, "How blind they were." Yet what does the Word of God mean to us? Why do we read it? Has it revealed to us the One who died on the cross and rose from the dead the Living Savior? Is He personal and real to us?

We need to search the Bible each day for a fresh revelation of Jesus Christ. In today's verse, the word *search* means diligently seeking a precious treasure such as gold. As we search the Word more and more, we see Him in all His beauty and come to know Him in a deeper way.

Just as the silkworm becomes similar in color to the leaves on which it feeds, Christians become what our souls consume. As we feed on the Word of God, not only do we see Him more perfectly and know Him more intimately, but we become more like Him.

A beggar drifted into a mission hall one cold night and was converted. He began reading the Bible and wore out three copies in three years.

A newspaper editor came to the beggar's attic room one day to interview him. Finding the beggar on his knees with his Bible open before him, the editor said, "Would you read your Bible to me?" As the beggar read, tears flowed down his cheeks.

Impressed, the editor said, "Tell me the secret of your power."

The beggar closed his Bible, hesitated, and then replied, "I have seen Jesus."

Oh, that we might search the Bible until our eyes behold the beauty and loveliness of the Lord Jesus. "Thine eyes shall see the king in his beauty" (Isa. 33:17). May we see *Him!*

MAY 3

But I give myself unto prayer (Ps. 109:4).

any people limit their prayer to petitions, assuming that prayer is asking God to supply our needs. But prayer is more than that.

One of the fundamental reasons for our quiet time is to get to know God better. The psalmist said, "Be still, and know that I am God" (Ps. 46:10).

This means spending time with Him daily. God told Jeremiah, "Ye shall seek me, and find me, when ye shall search for me with all your heart" (Jer. 29:13).

Our quiet time needs to have priority in our lives just as Mary of Bethany gave priority to time with Jesus. Mary chose to sit at Jesus' feet and listen in order to know Him better.

As we spend time with Him, we will become more like Him. We will begin to think His thoughts and do what He wants. Someone has suggested that we lean our arms on the windowsill of heaven, gaze into Jesus' face, and then go out and tell what He has said.

When I first became a Christian, I had a daily quiet time because someone told me I should. I was told that if I would read five chapters a day, I would finish reading the Bible in about a year. As I did this each day, I would put my Bible down, feeling I had done my duty.

However, the more time I spent with Him, the better acquainted I became with Him. More important to me than the number of chapters I read, were the new things I learned about Jesus. He became more real to me and our friendship deepened. Psalm 27:8 took on special meaning for me: "When thou saidst, Seek ye my face; my heart said unto thee, Thy face, LORD, will I seek." Getting to know Jesus better takes priority in my quiet time.

There are times, of course, when I question Him, when I don't understand what He is doing, and I tell Him so. Then we work through it together.

But because I have spent time with Him, I have learned to trust Him. I have a deep, settled confidence in Him that has carried me through the storms of my life.

An effective prayer life is Person-centered, not petition-centered. With the Lord in His rightful place, our petitions will be in their rightful place.

MAY 4

Lord, teach us to pray (Luke 11:1).

well remember the day I asked the Lord to teach me to pray aloud. As a new Christian I prayed at home alone, but not in front of people.

I had agreed to teach a Sunday school class, and when I attended the first teachers' meeting, the superintendent asked me to pray. I didn't think I could, but I struggled through a prayer.

After that meeting, I asked God to teach me to pray aloud. I needed to be prepared. He taught me in several ways.

First, I began praying aloud at home to become used to hearing my voice and phrasing my prayers. But I was still afraid to pray before people. I couldn't pray as they prayed. God taught me that He wanted me to pray my own way, the way in which I was most comfortable. All he wanted was to hear the prayer of my heart. It need not be beautifully worded. Others weren't listening to the words of my prayer, anyway. They were silently praying with me. God wasn't grading me on the length of my prayers, either. Even a brief prayer can please Him.

I usually begin with worship and praise, but sometimes I have a burden so great that I pray about it first. Then I can worship and praise as I commit my problem to Him. Sometimes my prayer is all intercession.

I can bring every request to Him, regardless of how small it is. When I was in Germany, my hostess realized I had been in an area where the usual breakfast was bread and cheese. She asked if I would like hot cereal such as oatmeal or cream of wheat but didn't ask me which one I would like. I prayed, "Lord, you know I don't like oatmeal." Guess what she served. Cream of wheat.

Prayer is a two-way conversation. Instead of hurriedly voicing my requests and rushing out, I've learned to spend time listening to Him.

I am not bound to a set prayer pattern. I don't want technique to keep me from the freshness and joy of my visit with Jesus, my dearest friend. The Bible says, "In thy presence is fulness of joy; at thy right hand there are pleasures for evermore" (Ps. 16:11).

MAY 5

For this cause we also, since the day we heard it, do not cease to pray for you, and to desire that ye might be filled with the knowledge of his will in all wisdom and spiritual understanding; that ye might walk worthy of the Lord unto all pleasing (Col. 1:9–10).

 will never forget the night I sat at the bedside of my dear mother-in-law, expecting her to slip away to be with the Lord any minute. As she lay there with her hand in mine, it was my privilege to hear her pray for the various members of the family. I will always cherish that experience.

In the above Scripture, we are privileged to hear Paul's prayer for the Colossians. He was concerned that they might know God's will and be committed to it. The word used for *filled* has the idea of being filled full—to have a full knowledge of God's will.

He prayed that they might have all the wisdom of God and spiritual understanding needed to discern His will and to make right decisions in the light of it.

Knowledge refers to knowing God's will while *wisdom* and *spiritual understanding* refer to putting it into practice. Our knowledge of His will grows as our knowledge of His Word grows.

When we know God's will, we can walk *worthy* of Him. "So that you may lead lives worthy of the Lord to His full satisfaction" (v. 10 WILLIAMS). God's will and our walk must not be separated. "We also pray that your outward lives, which men see, may bring credit to your master's name" (v. 10 PHILLIPS). A worthy walk means that we will live Christ in all we do and say.

A worthy walk will please God. We will please Him in our actions, habits, pleasures, conversation, motives, attitudes—everything. "Finally then, brethren, we request and exhort you in the Lord Jesus that, as you received from us instruction as to how you ought to walk and please God (just as you actually do walk), that you may excel still more" (1 Thess. 4:1 NASB).

A worthy walk will attract others to Christ. There was a Chinese Christian who had the joy of reaching many Chinese for Christ. His friends said of him, "There is no difference between him and *The Book.*"

Is your ambition to please Him in everything? Is your walk worthy of Him because you are walking in His will? Is your life attracting others to Him?

MAY 6

Being fruitful in every good work, and increasing in the knowledge of God (Col. 1:10).

 love to walk through the fruit department of the grocery store. What a colorful array! I want a sample immediately.

One of the colorful areas of our life is our *fruit department*. A life that pleases God will be characterized by a beautiful, fruitful life.

We have been selected to be fruit bearers for Jesus. Jesus said, "I have chosen you—I have appointed you, I have planted you—that you might go and bear fruit and keep on bearing; that your fruit may be lasting (that it may remain, abide)" (John 15:16 AMPLIFIED) The fruit He produces in our lives will radiate from Him.

In the grocery store there is always fruit year round. Our fruit, too, will be continual. The psalmist wrote, "They are like trees along a river bank bearing luscious fruit each season without fail" (Ps. 1:3 LB).

In the store there is a large variety of fruit. So in our lives we will be fruitful in various good works. The Holy Spirit produces the fruit of the Spirit in us: the luscious fruit of love, joy, peace, patience, kindness, goodness, faithfulness, gentleness, self-control. We don't work for Him. He works through us.

He will reproduce the fruit of leading others to Christ. "When the Holy Spirit has come upon you, you will receive power to testify about me with great effect . . . about my death and resurrection" (Acts 1:8 LB).

Not only will there be fruit from our Christian activities but fruit from our everyday living. It may be a gentle spirit reflected in a tense home situation, patience when the car won't start, taking time to speak a kind word. One day as I boarded a plane I smiled at the hostess and said, "How are you today?" She looked at me and replied, "Thank you for caring enough to ask."

What fruit are you bearing in your life? Do people want to sample what they see in your fruit department? "Herein is my Father glorified, that ye bear much fruit" (John 15:8).

Are you a productive fruit bearer?

MAY 7

That at the name of Jesus every knee should bow, in heaven and on earth and under the earth, and every tongue confess that Jesus Christ is Lord, to the glory of God the Father (Phil. 2:10−11 NIV).

Philippians chapter two contains one of the most moving expressions of Jesus' love. Jesus was part of the Godhead, but He willingly relinquished His place in heaven to redeem humanity.

Yet in all His glory and majesty, we find the most perfect example of humility. Paul wrote that "though he was God, [Jesus] did not demand and cling to his rights as God" (v. 6 LB). In His humbleness, He stepped down from heaven to become part of the human race.

He emptied Himself of the glory that belonged to Him as God. He "laid aside his mighty power and glory, taking the disguise of a slave and becoming like men" (v. 7 LB). Laying aside His Sonship, He put on the badge of a servant.

But His humbleness did not stop there. "He humbled himself even further, going so far as actually to die a criminal's death on a cross" (v. 8 LB). Being nailed to the cross in our place was a shameful death! Someone has said that He paid a debt he didn't owe because we owed a debt we couldn't pay. The Bible says, "You know the grace of our Lord Jesus Christ, that though he was rich, yet for your sakes he became poor, so that you through his poverty might become rich" (2 Cor. 8:9 NIV).

Because Jesus humbled himself to the lowest depths, "God raised him up to the heights of heaven and gave him a name which is above every other name" (v. 9 LB). One day everyone will bow at the name of Jesus and confess that He is Lord. But even now we can kneel before Him and confess Him as Lord of our lives.

David wrote, "Thine, O LORD, is the greatness, and the power, and the glory, and the victory, and the majesty . . . thou art exalted as head above all. . . . thou reignest over all; and in thine hand is power and might; and in thine hand it is to make great, and to give strength unto all. Now therefore, our God, we thank thee, and praise thy glorious name" (1 Chron. 29:11−13).

As we bow in worship and adoration, we can sing, "All hail the power of Jesus' name . . . and crown him Lord of all."

Whoever wants to become great among you must be your servant (Matt. 20:26 NIV).

he mother of James and John came to Jesus, requesting that her two sons might sit at His right and left hand in His kingdom. Jesus reminded her that He was unable to assign positions in the kingdom of God. This was the right of His Father, not Him.

Then Jesus explained the measure of true greatness. Those who would be great do not seek a place of prominence but are willing to serve. Jesus said, "Whosoever wishes to be great among you must be a servant." How often we see a power play instead of a spirit of humbleness. The standard of greatness in God's sight is servanthood.

True servants are those who put the interests of others above their own, those who seek to help others, those who yield their own rights. The Bible says, "Let nothing be done through strife or vainglory; but in lowliness of mind, let each esteem other better than themselves. Look not every man on his own things, but every man also on the things of others" (Phil. 2:3–4).

Millie Dienert, a well-known speaker around the world, was invited to the House of the Dying in India, a place which ministers to poor people off the street. Many of them have only a short time to live.

What Millie saw was almost more than she could take. She watched as the nurses ministered to these people with loving care. One nurse in particular had a sweet smile for each person as she tried to make them all comfortable.

Finally, Millie asked her how she could do it. The nurse looked at a picture of Jesus hanging on the wall with the words, *My Lord and my God* underneath. Her face radiated joy. "I do it for Him," she said. "He is my Lord and my God. My hands are His hands. My feet are His feet. My smile is His smile."

Jesus came to minister to needy people. He said, "I am among you as he that serveth" (Luke 22:27). He ministers to them today through you and me. He has no other hands today but our hands; no other feet, eyes, ears, or lips but ours. Are we available for Him to use however, wherever, and whenever He desires? May each of us wear His badge of servanthood.

MAY 9

The LORD will perfect that which concerneth me: thy mercy, O
LORD, endureth for ever: forsake not the works of thine own hands
(Ps. 138:8).

 ave you ever said, "No one cares about me"?
The Lord cares about everything that concerns His
children. "You can throw the whole weight of your anxieties
upon him, for you are his personal concern" (1 Peter 5:7
PHILLIPS).

David said, "The Lord will work out his plans for my life—for your
lovingkindness, Lord, continues forever. Don't abandon me—for you made
me" (Ps. 138:8 LB). Often God uses trouble in His perfecting process.
"Though I am surrounded by troubles, you will bring me safely through them"
(v. 7 LB). David didn't say that his faith was great enough. He said he was
depending on the Lord to bring him through. He was satisfied to leave the work
to God.

David didn't say, "The Lord *can* perfect. . . ." He said, "The Lord *will*
perfect. . . ." God knows what is necessary to fulfill His purpose in the lives of
His children.

Sometimes we question God's purposes, but we can be confident that He
makes no mistakes. He will only allow the circumstances needed to develop and
complete His plan.

Job knew the importance of God's working in his life. He said, "He
knows the way that I take; when he has tested me, I will come forth as gold"
(Job 23:10 NIV). The things He is doing in our lives will bring forth pure gold.
"For he performeth the thing that is appointed for me" (v. 14).

God will complete the plan He has for us according to His specifications.
Paul wrote, "I am convinced and sure of this very thing, that He Who began a
good work in you will continue until the day of Jesus Christ—right up to the
time of His return—developing [that good work] and perfecting and bringing it
to full completion in you" (Phil. 1:6 AMPLIFIED).

Is trouble filling your life today? Are you experiencing one calamity after
another? Remember that God is working out His life-plan for you. It will take
your entire lifetime to bring it to perfection.

He wants us to find fulfillment in Jesus Christ. "Moreover we know that
to those who love God, who are called according to his plan, everything that
happens fits into a pattern for good. God, in his foreknowledge, chose them to
bear the family likeness of his Son" (Rom. 8:28–29 PHILLIPS).

If my people, which are called by my name, shall humble them-
selves, and pray, and seek my face, and turn from their wicked
ways; then will I hear from heaven, and will forgive their sin, and
will heal their land (2 Chron. 7:14).

ith many forces at work in the world today trying to take away our freedom, our greatest need is a spiritual awakening. God's prescription for such an awakening begins with His own people—you and me.

However, God has outlined some conditions that must be met before He can work. The first condition is to humble ourselves. We recognize our dependence upon God. We put aside our interests and plans in exchange for His. Jesus was the perfect example of One who humbled Himself. "And being found in fashion as a man, he humbled himself, and became obedient unto death, even the death of the cross" (Phil. 2:8). John the Baptist also exhibited a spirit of humility. He said, "He must increase, but I must decrease" (John 3:30).

Prayer is another important condition, for it puts us in touch with the power of God. In prayer we receive God's *work plan* for us. The greatest need in our world today is Christians who will give themselves to the ministry of prayer. David said, "I give myself unto prayer" (Ps. 109:4). Prayer is still a powerful weapon to change the course of world history.

Seeking God's face is another condition that brings us in touch with Him. This means that we seek His glory, we seek His will, we seek His burden for souls. John Knox was seeking God's face when he asked God to give him Scotland or he would die.

What are you seeking? People? Possessions? Or are you seeking His face? To seek His face, we have to turn our eyes from things and people to Him. Even more important than seeking His gifts, is seeking His face.

Finally, we must turn from our wicked ways. We must turn from anything that causes a power failure in our lives. Such things as busyness, indifference, or lack of compassion can cause a short circuit.

How do you rate on these points? Are there hindrances that need removing? Do you need to refocus?

When we meet all the conditions, God has promised to hear our prayers, forgive our sins, and heal our land. What part are you having in world change?

The LORD is nigh unto them that are of a broken heart; and saveth such as be of a contrite spirit (Ps. 34:18).

avid wrote the above Scripture out of his own personal experience. He knew what it was to have a broken heart. But he also knew the comfort of a God who was near at all times.

Most of us have gone through times when our hearts have been completely crushed. No one seemed to understand. Even today, your life may be falling apart. Tears may fill your eyes. The Lord Jesus is our real source of comfort. The psalmist said that the Lord is near the brokenhearted. Isaiah prophesied of Jesus: "The Spirit of the Lord God is upon me . . . he hath sent me to bind up the broken-hearted" (61:1).

When we are grief-stricken, He speaks words of comfort. "Remember, I love you. I am going through this with you. I would spare you if I could, but there is a reason for this experience even though you can't understand. I will not give you more than you can bear. Turn your eyes from your broken heart to Me."

He doesn't promise immunity from heartaches, but He does promise His constant, unfailing Presence. "I will never leave thee, nor forsake thee" (Heb. 13:5).

Where do you turn when your heart is broken? People? Alcohol? Drugs? They will never heal a broken heart. The only source of healing is the Lord Jesus, who said, "Let not your heart be troubled: ye believe in God, believe also in me" (John 14:1). Jesus is the Mender of broken hearts, but He has to have all the pieces.

When Mr. and Mrs. Snead went out on Long Island Sound for a family outing, they heard cries for help from a drowning boy. Mr. Snead tried to save him, but the panicked boy pulled Mr. Snead under and both drowned.

Grief-stricken, Mrs. Snead prayed, "Why, Lord, why?" Suddenly, the words of the hymn, "'Tis so Sweet to Trust in Jesus," came to her mind. A spirit of childlike trust brought peace to her broken heart.

Trials can make us bitter or better. We may never fully understand why our hearts are broken, but we can know the reality of the heart-comforting Presence of the Lord. "He healeth the broken in heart, and bindeth up their wounds" (Ps. 147:3).

MAY 12

Trust in the LORD with all thine heart; and lean not unto thine own understanding (Prov. 3:5).

any of us have become so used to automatic doors that we become irritated if a door does not operate automatically. However, before the door opens we must approach it, trusting that it will open for us.

This is an illustration of trust—*confident trust*. The Bible says, "Lean on, trust, and be confident in the Lord with all your heart and mind, and do not rely on your own insight or understanding" (Prov. 3:5 AMPLIFIED). *Trust* means to lean on even when there is no visible means of support. The object of our trust is God Himself.

Someone has said that faith consists of belief and trust. We believe with our mind, but when it reaches the heart, it becomes trust.

We are not to trust in people, friends, or our own wisdom, ability, feelings, or experiences. We are not to trust in ourselves. The psalmist wrote, "It is better to trust in the Lord than to put confidence in man" (Ps. 118:8).

We can easily trust when all is going well, but we find it harder when we face insurmountable obstacles, disappointments, and frustrations. Yet during such experiences, Job could say, "Though he slay me, yet will I trust in him" (Job 13:15). God never makes a mistake. He never fails. We can count on the faithfulness of God. Sometimes we say, "I trust Him, *but* . . ." Perfect trust eliminates each *but* and leans completely on God.

Not only are we to have a confident trust in the Lord, but a *complete* trust *with all our heart*. How often we try to solve our problems by our own wisdom. We are not to have a partial or a half-hearted trust but a whole-hearted trust—with *all* our heart.

Emphasizing our total reliance upon the Lord, the Scriptures contrast it with trusting in ourselves. "Lean not unto thine own understanding." Our wisdom falls short. God has provided divine wisdom for us in Jesus Christ. "But of him are ye in Christ Jesus, who of God is made unto us wisdom" (1 Cor. 1:30). Trusting in the Lord means recognizing and appropriating His wisdom.

Paul wrote, "Not that we are sufficient of ourselves to think anything as of ourselves; but our sufficiency is of God" (2 Cor. 3:5).

*In all thy ways acknowledge him, and he shall direct thy paths
(Prov. 3:6).*

 esterday we considered *confident* and *complete* trust in the Lord. The above Scripture speaks of a *committed* trust. "Acknowledge him in all thy ways." This speaks of *total* commitment. "In everything you do, put God first, and he will direct you and will crown your efforts with success" (Prov. 3:6 LB).

To acknowledge Him means to recognize His lordship in our lives, to welcome Him into all our experiences. We walk His paths with Him. We take no hidden trails. We release to Him our ambitions, choices, decisions, friendships, habits, everything. We commit our perplexities, pressures, and frustrations to Him.

Someone has said that we should acknowledge Him in the affections of our heart, the contemplations of our mind, the expressions of our lips, and the deportment of our life.

A committed trust leads to a *conducted* trust. David said, "You chart the path ahead of me, and tell me where to stop and rest" (Psalm 139:3 LB). Although God has mapped out our path for us, we sometimes take a shortcut. It doesn't work when we leave God out of our plans.

The Bible tells of many who let God direct their paths. When the children of Israel were to enter the Promised Land, Joshua gave them direction, saying, "That ye may know the way by which ye must go; for ye have not passed this way heretofore" (Josh. 3:4).

The Amplified Bible paraphrases Proverbs 3:5–6: "Lean on, trust, and be confident in the Lord with all your heart and mind, and do not rely on your own insight or understanding. In all your ways know, recognize, and acknowledge Him, and He will direct and make straight and plain your paths."

One day at Sunday school after a little girl heard the story of Jesus' walk to Emmaus, she said, "Sometimes Jesus comes and walks with me anywhere I am—on the sidewalk, at school, in the yard." When the teacher asked what she did when Jesus came to walk with her, the little girl replied, "I just move over and make room for Him to walk close to me."

Are we making room for Jesus to walk with us in our daily activities?

If we acknowledge and trust Him, God will keep His promise to direct all our ways.

MAY 14

He that dwelleth in the secret place of the most High shall abide under the shadow of the Almighty (Ps. 91:1).

 f you were asked where you live, you would probably give your street address and city. But those who are in God's family have another dwelling place—the special secret place of the Most High.

When we become Christians, we begin abiding in the Lord Jesus. Jesus said, "Abide in me, and I in you" (John 15:4). Abiding means living in the reality that Christ is in us and we are in Him. Christ Himself is our abiding place. He illustrates this relationship with the picture of the vine and the branches (John 15). Believers are the branches, who possess a vital union of life with Christ, the Living Vine.

From this union, we receive our spiritual nourishment. "For in him we live, and move, and have our being" (Acts 17:28). As the branch draws its sustenance and strength from the vine, so we draw our needs moment by moment from Him.

The Most High God has a special dwelling place for us near to himself. A beautiful gospel song says, "There is a place of quiet rest, near to the heart of God." In this place of closeness we have heart-to-heart communion with Him. We may share our innermost thoughts and desires with Him and He with us.

In the secret place we worship Him. "O come, let us worship and bow down: let us kneel before the LORD our maker" (Ps. 95:6). In the secret place we learn from His Word. In the secret place we talk to Him in prayer. Close to the heart of God, we find peace, understanding, joy, and strength.

The important thing is not the secret place itself but the One in whose presence we abide—the Most High God. As we live close to Him, we become willing to obey His Word and to commit ourselves to His will. If we stay close, we will hear His every whisper to us.

Are you living on the fringe of your relationship with the Lord, or are you abiding close to His heart? Do you just visit the secret place, or do you live there? Why not move closer? There is always room close to His heart for everyone who desires to move a little closer to Him.

"Draw nigh to God, and he will draw nigh to you" (James 4:8).

MAY 15

The Lord is my shepherd; I shall not want (Ps. 23:1).

 his psalm came out of David's life experiences. Having been a shepherd boy, he could translate the shepherd-sheep relationship into the experiences of his life with God.

Through the years, he had found God all sufficient. The Amplified Bible reads, "The Lord is my shepherd [to feed, guide, and shield me]; I shall not lack."

Because the Lord takes care of my needs, I shall not want for anything. God promises to *be* everything we will ever need, and we can be so contented in His care that we will want nothing more.

As His sheep, I will not want because He is dedicated to providing my needs. "Because the Lord is my Shepherd, I have everything I need!" (LB). I am the personal object of His care. He cares for each one of us as if we were His only child.

I will have no want, for His resources are unlimited. "My God shall supply all your need according to his riches in glory in Christ Jesus" (Phil. 4:19).

When He is our Shepherd, we need not worry. We trust the One who is in control of everything. "So don't be anxious about tomorrow. God will take care of your tomorrow too. Live one day at a time" (Matt. 6:34 LB).

With God's twenty-four-hour answering service He hears our weakest cry and sees our smallest need. If we have strayed from Him, He will spare nothing to seek us and bring us back to Himself. No storm is too fierce, no place too dangerous for Him to come after us.

Centuries after David wrote this psalm, One came to earth who said, "I am the good shepherd, and know my sheep, and am known of mine" (John 10:14). Jesus redeemed us that we might be a sheep in His fold. "I am the good shepherd:" He said, "the good shepherd giveth his life for the sheep" (v. 11).

The little word *my* in Psalm 23:1 indicates David's vital relationship with the Lord. David didn't say that the Lord is *a* shepherd but *my* shepherd.

Can you say, "The Lord is *my* shepherd?" If you have to say no or you are not sure, the page opposite tells how to receive Him as your own personal Savior and Shepherd.

MY RESPONSE

After reading these psalms of David, you may be wondering how you can know the Good Shepherd as your shepherd. If this is your desire, invite Jesus Christ into your life so you, too, can say, "The Lord is *my* shepherd."

My Commitment to Jesus Christ

I *believe* Jesus Christ, the Son of God, gave His life on the cross to free me from the penalty of sin and give me forgiveness. I believe He rose from the dead as the living Savior.

I *invite* Jesus Christ into my life as Savior and Lord.

I *accept* Jesus Christ as God's gift of eternal life.

My Prayer

Dear Lord Jesus:

I confess my need of a Savior. I believe you died on the cross to pay the penalty of my sin. I believe you rose from the dead to give me the gift of eternal life. I invite You into my life as my personal Savior and Lord. Thank You for Your gift of eternal life, which I have just now received.

In Jesus' name I pray, amen.

Signed _____

Date _____

Your signature and today's date will remind you of this moment when you received Christ as Savior. It will indicate your sincerity in this transaction between you and God.

MAY 16

The Lord is my shepherd; I shall not want (Ps. 23:1).

A good shepherd delights in his flourishing, well-nourished flock. He gives himself to their well-being.

Our Good Shepherd, the Lord Jesus, desires to have a spiritually healthy flock. Because we are loved and cared for by such a Shepherd, we can have complete contentment and satisfaction. "He satisfieth the longing soul, and filleth the hungry soul with goodness" (Ps. 107:9).

Contentment is the hallmark of the one who has put himself and his affairs into the hands of the Good Shepherd. Knowing that He does that which is best for His sheep, gives us peace.

Through all the heartaches in his life, David found the Good Shepherd faithful. We, too, can prove the faithfulness of our Good Shepherd. When a test comes, when the heart is burdened, when fear creeps in to trouble us, we have Someone to wipe away the tears, lighten our burden and replace fear with peace. The sheep have all the weaknesses, but the Good Shepherd has all the strength. We prove the Lord's all-sufficiency when we trust our lives to Him. It is only as we let Him *be* our Shepherd in the situations we face day by day, that we can truly say, "I shall not want."

Our Good Shepherd assumes responsibility to supply our every need. All the resources of heaven are at our disposal. The reality of our experience depends on our response to the Shepherd. David had confidence in his Shepherd. As we turn the control of our lives over to Him, we, too, can be confident He will supply all our needs.

One day, a pastor asked a group of children if anyone could repeat the first verse of the Twenty-third Psalm. A little girl waved her hand excitedly. "I can," she said. But as she stood, she became frightened and confused. She recited, "The Lord is my shepherd; He is all I need." This may not be the correct wording of the verse, but there was truth in the way she repeated the verse.

If you can say that the Good Shepherd is *my* Shepherd, then you can also say, "He is all I need."

Rejoice evermore (1 Thess. 5:16).

ejoice evermore'' is a short verse, easy to memorize but not so easy to put into practice. Jesus challenges us to be happy. "These things have I spoken unto you, that my joy might remain in you, and that your joy might be full'' (John 15:11).

Paul echoes that challenge. "Rejoice in the Lord alway: and again I say, Rejoice'' (Phil. 4:4). Rejoicing is an outward expression of joy, a fruit of the Holy Spirit.

Rejoice always? I can be happy and rejoice most of the time. I can rejoice on bright days when everything is fine. I can be joyful when I have no problems. But can I really rejoice always? The Bible says I can.

Paul knew it was possible, for he wrote this while he was in prison. He could have said, "Why is all of this happening to me? Am I not serving God? Has He forgotten me?" However, rejoicing is not dependent on circumstances but on the Lord.

Since God has said that we can rejoice at all times and in all things, it must be possible—not just in pleasant surroundings at times when everything is going smoothly for us, but also in times of discouragement, despair, and doubt.

As a woman was changing trains in a London station an old man spoke to her. "I want to thank you for something," he said. "I used to be a ticket collector, and when you went through the gate you always gave me a smile and said good morning regardless of the weather. I began to wonder where you got your smile. One day when I saw you with a little Bible in your hand, I said to myself, 'Perhaps that is where the smile comes from.' So I bought a Bible and began to read it. I found Christ as my Savior, and now I can smile, too."

A gospel chorus says, "Joy is the flag flown high from the castle of my heart when the King is in residence there."

Rejoicing is not some ecstatic feeling but an inner joy that comes from confidence that God is in control. "Whom having not seen, ye love; in whom, though now ye see him not, yet believing, ye rejoice with joy unspeakable and full of glory" (1 Peter 1:8).

MAY 18

And He led them on safely and in confident trust, so that they feared not (Ps. 78:53 AMPLIFIED)

n this psalm Asaph recounts how God directed the Israelites to leave Egypt for a new home in the Promised Land. "[God] led His own people forth like sheep" (v. 52 AMPLIFIED). The journey was too much for them. The dangers were too great. They were as defenseless as sheep, but they were safe in the care of their Great Shepherd.

God personally conducted their tour. "[He] guided them [with a shepherd's care] like a flock in the wilderness" (v. 52 AMPLIFIED). They didn't know the way, but their Guide knew it well.

While I was waiting in a bus depot one day, I saw a bus line advertisement that read, "What a difference the guide makes." I paused and said, "Thank you, God, that I have learned what a difference it makes in my life with Jesus Christ as my Guide."

God never leads us astray; He always leads us to the right destination. But He often leads us on an unknown path. The uncertainty of it fills our hearts with fear. The Great Shepherd says, "Fear not, I am your own personal Guide every step of your way." We can trust our way to Him, for He leads us on safely. Trust removes fear from our heart.

God's Word is our map, revealing the path of His will to us. This is why it is so important to make His Word a vital part of our daily life.

My young niece takes piano lessons. One time, several piano teachers in her area arranged a combined piano recital. On the way to the recital, my niece felt a little tense. "I am glad my teacher will be there," she said. "I won't be scared."

As we travel down an unknown path we may be afraid, but we can say, "I won't be scared. You are with me, close beside me, holding my hand."

"Fear not [there is nothing to fear] for I am with you; do not look around you in terror and be dismayed, for I am your God. I will strengthen and harden you [to difficulties]; yes, I will help you; yes, I will hold you up and retain you with My victorious right hand of rightness and justice" (Isa. 41:10 AMPLIFIED).

MAY 19

Whatever may be your task, work at it heartily (from the soul), as [something done] for the Lord and not for men (Col. 3:23 AMPLIFIED).

Wherever God places us (business, neighborhood, school), whatever He wants us to do, we are to do our work heartily for Him.

Because I am a sports enthusiast, I get excited as I watch. I participate wholeheartedly. People around me soon know which team I am for because I give that team my full support.

We must be enthusiastic in all we do, having the *right manner.* "Whatever may be your task, work at it heartily." We are to put every part of our being into whatever we are doing.

We must also serve with the *right motive* "as [something done] for the Lord and not for men." Everything is to be done in His Name and for His glory: all that we do—our work at home, in our business, our shopping, our hobbies—should glorify Him.

When I taught about this in Bible school, a young woman came back the next week with a spirit of joy. She said, "I hate to wash dishes, but this week I have done them for Him. It has changed my attitude toward my work at home completely."

One day an army officer serving in India stopped to have his shoes polished by a poor Indian boy. The boy did his work with such vigor that the officer asked why he was so diligent. "Well, sir," replied the boy, "last week I invited Jesus into my heart, and now I belong to Him. Now every time I shine shoes, I keep thinking they are His, so I do my very best." This should be the motive behind our work. Whatever we are doing, we are doing it for the Lord Jesus.

Then we will have the *right reward.* God is keeping the record and will be giving out the rewards. "Knowing (with all certainty) that it is from the Lord [and not from men] that you will receive the inheritance which is your (real) reward. [The One Whom] you are actually serving [is] the Lord Christ the Messiah" (v. 24 AMPLIFIED).

What is your manner of serving? Wholehearted? What is your motive? To please Him? For His glory? "Obey [your masters] willingly because of your love for the Lord and because you want to please him" (v. 22 LB).

Someone has said that real service is the love of Christ in working clothes.

MAY 20

Hear me when I call, O God of my righteousness: thou hast en-
larged me when I was in distress; have mercy upon me, and hear
my prayer (Ps. 4:1).

avid was in deep trouble, but he had learned to turn to God, his
certain source of help. In time of need, he knew he was only a
call away from God.

He remembered, in the past, during times of trouble,
"Thou hast [past tense] enlarged me." *Enlarged* means to set free. The
Amplified reads, "You have freed me when I was hemmed in." The fact that
God had previously undertaken for David, encouraged him to bring his present
needs to God. He could pray, "Have mercy upon me, and hear my prayer."

Once while vacationing in the California Bay Area with my nephew and
his family, our car stalled on the freeway as we were returning to our motel after
church. The children—Jeff, Jon, and Janelle—were frustrated, for they were
eager to get back to the swimming pool at the motel. There was no telephone
nearby, and cars rushed by, their drivers paying no attention to us.

I said, "It is time to pray." Committing our need to God, we thanked
Him that He was in control. As we looked up, a car pulled off the highway and
backed up.

My nephew knew one family in that area. We weren't close to their
home, but the evening before we had enjoyed a picnic with them. Suddenly,
we realized the people in the car were our friends.

God had heard our prayers and sent friends to our aid. I shall never forget
the look on the faces of the children as they realized that God had answered our
call to Him for help.

By that time, another car had stopped. The man in that car took my
nephew to a garage, and our friends took us back to our motel. What a joy to
know that God is concerned for every detail of our lives.

Are you in distress today? Have you sent an SOS to the Throne of the
One who can meet your distress? Your need may be greater than a frustrated
family stranded beside a busy freeway. But if God cared enough to answer our
cry for help, surely He will answer your distress signal!

The Bible says, "Call upon me in the day of trouble: I will deliver thee,
and thou shalt glorify me" (Ps. 50:15)

MAY 21

My help cometh from the LORD, which made heaven and earth (Ps. 121:2).

ne day, after I had spoken to a women's group, a young woman handed me a note and left. When I opened the note, I saw one word: Help! In that word I could read the heart cry of one in desperate need. I prayed that she would turn to the One I had talked about that day—the One who could give her help.

The psalmist knew to whom he could cry for help in time of need. As he lifted his gaze to the majestic mountains about him, he questioned, "From whence cometh my help?" But he knew the mountains weren't the source of his help. He said, "My help cometh from the LORD, which made heaven and earth."

On our journey through life, we often face hopeless situations, not knowing which way to turn, but we can experience the certainty of the Lord's help. We can cry to God as King Asa did in a time of desperate need. "LORD, there is no one like you to help the powerless against the mighty" (2 Chron. 14:11 NIV). Our cry reaches His ear and help is on the way.

We can be secure, knowing that He gives "round-the-clock" help. He never sleeps. He is never off duty.

The psalmist wrote, "He will never let me stumble, slip or fall. For he is always watching, never sleeping. Jehovah himself is caring for you! He is your defender. He protects you day and night. He keeps you from all evil, and preserves your life. He keeps His eye upon you as you come and go, and always guards you" (v. 3-8 LB).

One moonlit night, as a little girl was getting ready for bed, she asked, "Mommy, is the moon God's light?" When her mother assured her it was, the little girl continued, "Will God turn off His light and go to sleep, too?" "No," said her mother. "God's light is always shining. God doesn't go to sleep." "I'm so glad," answered the little girl. "While God is awake, I am not afraid."

There is never a moment, day or night, when the problems and needs of His children are not under God's watchful eye.

"You are my help and my deliverer. O my God, do not tarry!" (Psalm 40:17 AMPLIFIED).

MAY 22

And he said unto them, Come ye yourselves apart into a desert place, and rest awhile" (Mark 6:31).

re you exhausted today? Are you taking pills for energy to get through the day? Or are you on a nervous high and need something to slow you down? Perhaps what your body is really crying for is rest. Is there rest for anyone in this tension-filled world?

As the disciples returned from a missionary journey, they were elated with their success. They gave glowing reports of how God had worked. Jesus was glad to hear their accounts, but He knew they needed physical rest after their arduous journey. He invited them to come rest with Him in a quiet place.

We, too, need to refresh ourselves to maintain physical and spiritual strength. Our schedules are demanding. They drain our physical, mental, emotional, and spiritual life.

God's Holy Spirit gives us strength for His schedule for us. I believe God plans for us to include times of rest and relaxation in our schedule. If the disciples needed rest, so do we.

Our rest times may consist of a vacation where we can rest and relax, a change of environment, or simply a respite right where we are. Time spent with the Lord brings renewal and refreshment. "They that wait upon the LORD shall renew their strength; they shall mount up with wings as eagles; they shall run, and not be weary; and they shall walk, and not faint" (Isa. 40:31).

Jesus invites us to *come* apart with Him, not *go* apart. Regardless of where our resting place may be, our rest is in the Lord. "Rest in the LORD, and wait patiently for him" (Ps. 37:7).

One day a dealer was buying a number of diamonds. Occasionally, he would look from the stones he was selecting to a diamond on his finger, then resume his selection. When questioned, he explained that the diamond in his ring was perfect. After looking at the diamonds on the counter awhile, he needed to look at the perfect diamond to refresh his perspective.

We refresh our perspective by refocusing our spiritual eyes on Jesus, our Rest Giver. The psalmist wrote, "He refreshes and restores my life" (Ps. 23:3 AMPLIFIED).

Jesus invites, "Come unto me, all ye that labour and are heavy laden, and I will give you rest" (Matt. 11:28).

MAY 23

Finally, my brethren, be strong in the Lord, and in the power of his might (Eph. 6:10).

e are in spiritual warfare against a strong enemy. "Our struggle is not against flesh and blood, but against the rulers, against the authorities, against the powers of this dark world and against the spiritual forces of evil in the heavenly realms" (v. 12 NIV).
Satan is the supreme ruler of his kingdom. He uses every tactic he knows to defeat us. He is so subtle we fail to recognize him. He is so sly, we never know from what angle he will strike next. We must constantly be prepared for his attacks.

Satan's greatest tool is discouragement. He says, "You say you are a Christian. Look how weak you are. Look how you fail the Lord. You might as well give up." But in Christ we have victory. "In all these things we are more than conquerors through him who loved us" (Rom. 8:37 NIV).

God wants us victorious. He is the source of our victory. "Your strength must come from the Lord's mighty power within you" (v. 10 LB). All the power of heaven—the same power that raised the Lord Jesus from the dead—is at our disposal. Our strength is not only *from* Him but *in* Him. He fights our battles for us.

Spiritual warfare must be fought with spiritual weapons. Man-made weapons are not strong enough. God has provided a complete armor to protect us from every missile Satan hurls against us. Clad in His armor, we will still be standing at the end of the battle. "So use every piece of God's armor to resist the enemy whenever he attacks, and when it is all over, you will still be standing up" (v. 13 LB).

Romans 13:14 gives the key to the strength of our armor. "Put ye on the Lord Jesus Christ." In the person of Jesus Christ we can stand fast as long as life lasts. It is a moment-by-moment victory.

Are you in the thick of battle? Do you feel you are going down in defeat? Just remember that in His power, equipped with His armor, you will have victory over Satan. "Thanks be to God, which giveth us the victory through our Lord Jesus Christ" (1 Cor. 15:57). In Christ we have His all-sufficient provision for total victory.

MAY 24

Therefore put on the full armor of God, so that when the day of evil comes, you may be able to stand your ground, and after you have done everything, to stand (Eph. 6:13 NIV).

od promises complete armor to protect us in our spiritual warfare against the wiles of the Devil and evil spiritual forces. Our armor enables us to ward off the attacks of the enemy. We can stand firm, holding our ground. Jesus Christ is our armor.

However, if we are to stand firm against our enemy, we must have on every piece of our armor and keep it on during our entire lifetime.

The first piece is the girdle of truth. "Stand therefore—hold your ground—having tightened the belt of truth around your loins" (v. 14 AMPLIFIED).

Truth is defined as honesty, sincerity, conformity to fact, agreement with a standard. Jesus Christ is our girdle of truth. He said, "I am the way, the truth, and the life" (John 14:6). He is the Living truth. Jesus also said, "Ye shall know the truth, and the truth shall make you free" (John 8:32).

Jesus is saying to them, "I am the truth about God. I am what you need to know about God. As the truth, I will set you free from sin." This He did through the atoning work of Christ on the cross. "We see real love, not in the fact that we loved God, but that he loved us, and sent his Son to make personal atonement for our sins" (1 John 4:10 PHILLIPS). Controlled by the truth of God, we are free from Satan's power.

Jesus said, "Thy word is truth" (John 17:17). The Bible gives guidelines for conforming to God's standard. By it we can live a life of honesty, genuineness, and reality.

To have our loins girded about with truth is to have both the Living Word and the written Word controlling our lives. We will be free from deception and lying. We will not only be speaking the truth but living the truth. We will be genuine. We will be real.

Are you wearing your belt of truth? Is your life controlled by the truth of God's Word? The Bible says, "We will lovingly follow the truth at all times— *speaking truly, dealing truly, living truly*" (Eph. 4:15 LB, emphasis mine).

Stand firm then . . . with the breastplate of righteousness in place (Eph. 6:14 NIV).

he second piece of our armor is the breastplate of righteousness. Covering the upper part of the soldier's body, it is an important part of the believer's armor, protecting the heart from the wiles of the devil.

When we receive Christ, we receive His righteousness. He gives us a right standing before God. The Bible says, "But of him are ye in Christ Jesus, who of God is made unto us wisdom, and righteousness" (1 Cor. 1:30). Satan cannot touch the righteousness which Christ has put to our account.

Not only is Christ our righteousness as we stand before God, but also as we stand before the world. "We should live soberly, righteously, and godly, in this present world" (Titus 2:12). Our position in Christ should be reflected in the way we live.

Satan delights to hurl his fiery darts at us to hinder our testimony before the others. But God has provided our breastplate to deflect these fiery darts.

Paul says, "According to my earnest expectation and my hope, that in nothing I shall be ashamed, but that with all boldness, as always, so now also Christ shall be magnified in my body, whether it be by life, or by death. For to me to live is Christ, and to die is gain" (Phil. 1:20–21).

Once while conducting a seminar with a group of women, I talked about the rest we have in Christ. That evening, I was to fly to Seattle for a meeting early the next morning. When I went to the airport, the flight had been canceled because of fog. If the fog lifted, the flight would leave the next morning.

As my hostess took me back to her home, she said, "You are having to take a dose of your own medicine, aren't you?" She was watching me to see if the rest I had been talking about was real in my life.

My mother often said, "What you do speaks so loudly, I cannot hear what you say." Satan is aware that people are watching us to see how real our faith is. With our armor in place, Satan's fiery darts can be deflected.

We could not possibly defeat Satan in our own power. Only in Christ can we come through standing. In our daily walk Christ is our Victor.

MAY 26

And your feet shod with the preparation of the gospel of peace (Eph. 6:15).

Through the various pieces of armor God has provided adequate protection for each part of our body. We may meet our foe and emerge victorious.

Even our feet are protected with armor. Roman soldiers wore a sandal with cleats for firm footing. Our gospel shoes give us a firm foundation. "Having shod your feet in preparation [to face the enemy with the firm-footed stability, the promptness and the readiness produced by the good news] of the Gospel of peace" (AMPLIFIED).

We need not fear our enemy for our shoes give us a firm-footed stability in the gospel of peace, the Gospel of Jesus Christ, "For he is our peace" (Eph. 2:14). Planted firmly in Him, we cannot be moved. We can *stand* against the attacks of the enemy.

No matter what difficulties may come, we can stand in confidence. Nothing can move us. Through it all, we will experience a deep-settled peace as we rest in the One who is our Peace.

Our Gospel shoes not only provide security and stability, but they prepare us for service. The word *preparation* also has the thought of readiness. As a soldier for Jesus Christ, we need to be ready to do the will of God, ready for action, ready to go on God's assignment for us. The Bible says, "Preach the word; be instant in season, out of season" (2 Tim. 4:2).

Not only are we to be ready for action, but we must be prompt to respond to our call. A friend of mine received a telephone call one day from a former high school acquaintance. As they visited, my friend realized the girl was desperate. She said, "I'll be right over. Don't do anything until I get there."

When she arrived, the girl had a dose of poison in a glass ready to take but decided to call her friend first. My friend shared with the girl that Jesus Christ was her answer. Suppose she had said, "I'll come over tomorrow."

In God's sight, our feet are beautiful when they carry the gospel of peace. "How beautiful are the feet of them that preach the gospel of peace, and bring glad tidings of good things!" (Rom. 10:15).

Are your feet prepared and beautiful?

MAY 27

In addition to all this, take up the shield of faith, with which you can extinguish all the flaming arrows of the evil one (Eph. 6:16 NIV).

he shield of faith protects the entire body. Faith is our confidence in the Lord in every situation.

In our spiritual warfare when Satan hurls his fiery arrows at us, the shield of faith—complete trust in the Lord—puts out these darts. One of his arrows is doubt. He tries to cause us to doubt the Lord's love and concern for us. He makes every attempt to destroy our faith in Christ. We can use our shield to ward off these attacks.

More important than faith itself is the object of our faith, Jesus Christ. "Looking unto Jesus the author and finisher of our faith" (Heb. 12:2). We place our faith in Him and live by it. "I live by the faith of the Son of God, who loved me, and gave himself for me" (Gal. 2:20).

Satan will attack from every angle. But using the shield of our Victor, we will come through victorious every time. "Whatever is born of God is victorious over the world; and this is the victory that conquers the world, even our faith" (1 John 5:4 AMPLIFIED).

When the Bible says, "Faith cometh by hearing, and hearing by the word of God" (Rom. 10:17), we realize the importance of our daily quiet time with God and His Word.

Our next weapon is the helmet of salvation. It gives us personal knowledge of salvation through Jesus Christ and the assurance of our salvation. "The gift of God is eternal life through Jesus Christ our Lord" (Rom. 6:23). "These things have I written unto you that believe on the name of the Son of God; that ye may know that ye have eternal life, and that ye may believe on the name of the Son of God" (1 John 5:13).

The helmet of salvation protects us from all that Satan tries to implant in our mind: lies, deception, evil thoughts, criticalness, despair. The Bible says, "Don't always believe everything you hear just because someone says it is a message from God: test it first to see if it really is" (1 John 4:1 LB).

Our spiritual weapons used by faith will defeat the enemy and bring victory, accomplishing God's will. Someone has prayed, "Lord, help me to understand that nothing can happen that you and I can't handle together."

MAY 28

Therefore, my beloved brethren, be ye stedfast, unmoveable, always abounding in the work of the Lord, forasmuch as ye know that your labour is not in vain in the Lord" (1 Cor. 15:58).

ow privileged we are to be partners with the Living God! Our part is to let Him use our lives; His part is to furnish us with all that we need for His work. The above Scripture gives some qualifications for God's workers.

Be steadfast. Steadfastness means to be constant, firmly planted, devoted to a cause, adherent to a person. In our Christian life our adherence, our steadfastness is to the person of the Lord Jesus Christ. Our confidence is in Him. Paul said, "For to me to live is Christ" (Phil. 1:21).

Be unmoveable. This means being grounded and settled so that nothing and no one can dislodge us. Our lives may be shaken by discouragement, disappointment, or pressure. It would be easy to give up or turn our responsibilities over to someone else. Paul said, "None of these things move me" (Acts 20:24). Remembering it is not our work but the Lord's, we remain steadfast in our commitment, unmoveable in our purpose.

Be always abounding. Are we are abounding *always* or just occasionally? From time to time we need to evaluate whether we are doing the work the Lord wants us to do or what we want to do for Him. Faithfulness in the Lord's work yields bountiful results. "Nothing you do for the Lord is ever wasted" (LB).

For our work to abound always does not mean ceaseless activity. We need times of rest. We may become weary *in* His work not *of* His work.

When General Booth of the Salvation Army was asked the secret of his success, he replied, "God has had all there is of me. If there has been anything of success for God in my work, it is because God has had all of the love of my heart, the power of my will and the influence of my life."

Perhaps you wonder if your work has been worthwhile. God is keeping the record. "God is not unfair. How can he forget your hard work for him, or forget the way you used to show your love for him—and still do—by helping his children? And we are anxious that you keep right on loving others as long as life lasts, so that you will get your full reward" (Heb. 6:10–11 LB).

MAY 29

*I am crucified with Christ: nevertheless I live; yet not I, but Christ
liveth in me" (Gal. 2:20).*

Before Michelangelo would carve his masterpieces, such as the
statues of David and Moses, he would envision in his mind the
completed sculptures.

Before you and I were created, God planned for us to be
conformed to the image of His Son, and then "when someone becomes a
Christian he becomes a brand new person inside. He is not the same any more.
A new life has begun!" (2 Cor. 5:17 LB).

Before Christ, self reigns supreme on the throne of our lives. But when
Christ enters, that place belongs to Him. Paul expressed it this way: "I am
crucified with Christ: nevertheless I live." Paul had exchanged his life for the life
of Christ.

Paul's own nature had died with Christ; now his life would be lived by a
new principle. No longer was his life self-centered; it was Christ-centered. He
died, yet he lived. Paul's new life consisted of Jesus Christ living within: "Yet
not I, but Christ liveth in me." He knew the reality of Christ's all-sufficiency. He
experienced Jesus' strength, power, joy, love, and peace in place of his own
weakness and helplessness.

However, self does not abdicate easily. It struggles to retain the throne of
our lives. It tries to get us to do what we want to do, go where we want to
go—self, not Christ. We may try harder or resolve to do better, but even our
best is not good enough.

Jesus illustrated crucifixion when He said, "Except a corn of wheat fall
into the ground and die, it abideth alone: but if it die, it bringeth forth much
fruit" (John 12:24).

A seed planted in the ground dies and springs up again in newness of life.
When we are willing to die to our ambitions, plans, and interests, we will
experience the new life of Christ's plan and purpose for us. It has been said that
the only life rightfully living in us is the risen life of Jesus Christ.

Christ's rightful place is the throne of our lives. As we let Him occupy it
and have control, we will experience the reality of His resurrection life: power,
peace, joy, rest, and victory in our daily walk.

MAY 30

The life which I now life in the flesh I live by the faith of the Son of God, who loved me, and gave himself for me (Gal. 2:20).

oon after becoming a Christian, we realize that it is impossible to live the Christian life in our own strength. Then we learn that God knows we can't, and He has provided His life for us. It is easy to struggle over our problems instead of relying on Him to solve them. We rely on *our* faith, but the only faith equal to our needs is the faith of Jesus Christ. Paul didn't say that he lived by faith *in* the Son of God, but by the faith *of* the Son of God. Paul proved Him sufficient.

As we live by faith, we can face our daily struggles in the strength of Jesus Christ. His power is sufficient when we are sick and the children are impossible, when we are already swamped at the office and the phone keeps ringing, when our business partner fails us, when we are tempted to cheat on our exams, or when we receive a message that a loved one has passed away.

When I became a Christian, I totally commited my life to the Lord. But I discovered that living by faith in Jesus Christ required day-by-day commitments. As I waken each morning, I commit that day and myself to Him. It's like reporting to God for duty. Letting Him become the Lord of that day takes the tension out of my life and makes God responsible for getting me through the day. This is what He wants to do. My old self is dead, and by my daily commitment Christ lives His life in and through me. During the day, I commit each need to Him as it arises.

I have even been learning to commit my interruptions to God. Letting Him be the Lord of my interruptions, eases the pressure. Some of my schedule for the day does not seem as important to God as it does to me.

The Lord Jesus loved us so much that He willingly gave Himself for us that we might live by His faithfulness. We need only release our need to Him and depend on His faithfulness. Jeremiah wrote, ''Great is thy faithfulness'' (Lam. 3:23).

What a difference it makes when we take self off the throne of our lives and let Jesus Christ in His faithfulness control our lives.

MAY 31

The LORD is good, a strong hold in the day of trouble; and he knoweth them that trust in him (Nah. 1:7)

rouble is universal. No one escapes it. You may be experiencing it today. Do not be surprised. Jesus said that we could expect trouble.

But what we do about it? We can worry, panic, be fearful, and feel sorry for ourselves, or we can commit our trouble to the Lord, trusting Him to take us through it.

The prophet Nahum's declaration is reassuring. First, he says, "The LORD is good." He is good for He is God. As God, He has custom-designed a plan for our lives. He works in our trouble so that good will come out of it. He can take each difficulty and weave it into a beautiful pattern. We can't see good in it, for we view it as it is happening. But God sees the finished product.

Not only does He transform trouble into good, but He becomes a stronghold for us in the time of our trouble. He becomes our place of security and safety—a strong refuge. "The name of the LORD is a strong tower: the righteous runneth into it, and is safe" (Prov. 18:10).

God is a stronghold to those who trust Him. He will never fail you, forsake you, or forget you.

One day, tragedy struck my life. I had never faced such trouble and everything looked black around me. The tragedy was not good, but the Lord was good in the midst of it. I ran to my Stronghold, and there I found One who could comfort and uphold me. He poured His healing balm into my crushed heart.

Gradually, the Lord comforted and restored my heart. I felt secure because His presence was upholding me. Only He was sufficient at that time. No human being could have brought the healing He did. I proved the reality of the goodness of the Lord.

Where do you run when trouble comes? Some run to people or seminars, some seek solitude, some turn to alcohol or drugs, and some search for an answer in books. But our strong tower is the Lord, who can bring healing as no one and nothing else can.

"God is our refuge and strength [mighty and impenetrable to temptation] a very present and well-proved help in trouble" (Ps. 46:1 AMPLIFIED). He is "a tested help in times of trouble" (LB).

JUNE 1

And we know that all things work together for good to them that love
God, to them who are the called according to his purpose
(Rom. 8:28).

od is so good! How easy that is to say when things we consider good are happening to us. But someone may say, "God is good? Do you know what is happening to me?" However, isn't God as good in times of trouble as He is when everything is going smoothly?

God's Word says that everything works together for good to those who love Him and follow His purpose. The next verse tells us His purpose: that we "be conformed to the image of his Son" (v. 29). God is so satisfied with His Son that He wants all of His children to be like Him.

God has a plan for shaping us. He keeps the blueprint close by and watches it constantly to check on our progress.

The problems and perplexities of our lives are not good, but because He is in control, he fits each circumstance into His plan. "All that happens to us is working for our good if we love God and are fitting into his plans" (LB).

Unfortunately, we see only the immediate, today. But God sees our difficulties with the ultimate in view. When we stand before Him and see the end result, we will know He worked constantly for His glory and our good and we will be satisfied.

We often overlook an important word in this verse. It says that all things *work* together. If I want to bake a cake, I do not sit down and eat a cup of sugar, then a half cup of butter, three eggs, two cups of flour, and two teaspoons of baking powder. The ingredients separately are not good. But when I mix them into a batter and bake it, the ingredients work together to produce a delicious cake. *All* the ingredients of our circumstances are not good, but they work together for our good.

Michelangelo sculpted his statue of David from a piece of discarded marble. When someone asked how he knew to carve David out of the marble, he said, "I didn't carve it. I saw David and released him."

In God's plan for our lives, He sees the person of Jesus Christ. Day after day, He chisels away to release Him, that He might be revealed to the world through us.

JUNE 2

*And we know that all things work together for good to them that love
God, to them who are the called according to his purpose
(Rom. 8:28).*

 t the time of my husband's death, people would quote the above
Scripture to me, and I almost resented it. His death was not
good. We were happy. I was a timid person. He encouraged me
in everything I did. How could his death be good? I depended
on his love and strength. He was my security.

I cried out to God, "Do you realize what you are doing to me? Did you
have to do this?" I had to leave my security and move from Denver to Kansas
City. I didn't want to move. I didn't feel these things were good. The Lord was
first in my life, but I had to work through this test He was giving me.

I am always honest with God. If I am disturbed I tell Him so. He knows it
anyhow. Then we begin to work through my situation together. In this way, I
learn to trust when I cannot understand. This is what I did about my move. As
we spent time together, I came to the place where I could truthfully say, "If you
want me in Kansas City, that is where I want to be."

I learned the reality of what David meant in the Twenty-third Psalm
when he said, "He restoreth my soul." When we let God touch our lives, His
gentleness and power begin a restoration process. Going through a time of
questioning does not mean you are not spiritual.

My husband could fix anything. No matter what I broke, I always knew
that he could touch it with his expert fingers and restore it. At the time of his
death, I experienced in a new way the touch of my heavenly Father on my life.
The Bible says, "He healeth the broken in heart, and bindeth up their wounds"
(Ps. 147:3). The Lord and my home had been my security. I now discovered
that my security was in God alone. "The name of the LORD is a strong tower:
the righteous runneth into it, and is safe" (Prov. 18:10).

Let God touch your broken heart with His loving fingers and begin His
special work of restoration today.

JUNE 3

Then Nebuchadnezzar said, "Blessed be the God of Shadrach, Meshach, and Abednego, for he sent his angel to deliver his trusting servants when they defied the king's commandment, and were willing to die rather than serve or worship any god except their own" (Dan. 3:28 LB).

 hree young Hebrew men stood in front of an angry king who had decreed that anyone refusing to bow before the golden image he had erected would be thrown into a fiery furnace. These young men had refused.

There was no question about their course of action. They would not worship the golden image. They believed God could save them. "But even if he does not, we want you to know, O king, that we will not serve your gods or worship the image of gold you have set up" (v. 18 NIV). They demonstrated faith totally committed to God.

Their words, "But even if he does not," didn't mean that they doubted God. They had faith that God could deliver them, but their loyalty did not depend on their circumstances. They would obey God at any cost.

The king was furious. He commanded that the furnace be heated seven times hotter than usual. The young Hebrew men were tied up and thrown into the furnace. The fire was so hot that the servants who cast them into the furnace were burned to death.

Suddenly, the king saw something he couldn't believe. Their ropes had burned off, and the men were walking about. Also, a fourth person had joined them. The king was sure it was an angel.

When Nebuchadnezzar ordered the men brought out, they were not singed, and didn't even smell of smoke. Their God had honored their loyalty.

We go through fiery furnace experiences in our lives. You may be going through one now. Our loyalty needs to be refined and tested.

Our world is filled with idols in family situations, business associations, social life. Idols come in the form of habits, pleasure, ease, and indifference. We have to make choices. Will we be true to God, or will we compromise? God is looking for those who will not compromise or bow to idols whatever the cost.

Loyalty to God is not always easy, but God assures us of His constant presence through trials. "When thou walkest through the fire, thou shalt not be burned; neither shall the flame kindle upon thee. For I am the LORD thy God" (Isa. 43:2–3). What choices are you making?

JUNE 4

And when they had lifted up their eyes, they saw no man, save Jesus only (Matt. 17:8).

early everyone in America today has a television. Several factors enter into selecting a set: it must fit the space available; the style and type of wood must fit the room's decor; and most important, it must have a clear picture.

Our lives can be likened to the television set. We come in different types and sizes, but the picture on the screen of our lives is most important. God wants the picture of Jesus to fill our life screen so that others may see Him. The Bible says, "He also destined from the beginning (foreordaining them) to be molded into the image of His Son [and share inwardly His likeness]" (Rom. 8:29 AMPLIFIED).

Sometimes certain adjustments are necessary to get a clear television picture. So, too, with the television set of our lives. We must adjust the vertical hold—keeping a close intimate relationship with God—by consistently spending time with God through Bible reading and prayer. "Continue to learn more and more of the life that pleases God" (1 Thess. 4:1 PHILLIPS).

The horizontal hold—a right relationship with others—must also be adjusted properly. "Practice tenderhearted mercy and kindness to others. . . . Be gentle and ready to forgive; never hold grudges. Remember, the Lord forgave you, so you must forgive others" (Col. 3:12–13 LB).

The brightness has to be adjusted, too. "Let your light so shine before men, that they may see your good works, and glorify your Father which is in heaven" (Matt. 5:16).

A native woman asked to work for a missionary in her village, hoping to learn the secret of her shining face. Soon she became a Christian. One day she said, "It's coming on my face, too." "What do you mean?" asked the missionary. "I became a Christian watching you. Now, my face is beginning to shine."

The focus, too, often needs adjustment. "No one can serve two masters; for either he will hate the one and love the other, or he will stand by and be devoted to the one and despise and be against the other" (Matt. 6:24 AMPLIFIED).

The Bible says, "You are living a brand new kind of life that is continually learning more and more of what is right, and trying constantly to be more and more like Christ who created this new life within you" (Col. 3:10 LB).

JUNE 5

What is faith? It is the confident assurance that something we want is going to happen. It is the certainty that what we hope for is waiting for us, even though we cannot see it up ahead (Heb. 11:1 LB).

 aith is an assurance and a conviction of the reality of things we do not see. Suppose a person I trust promises to give me a book. Because I believe her word implicitly, I consider the book mine even before it is in my possession. I possess it by faith.

Faith gives the hoped-for object reality just as if it were already possessed. "Faith is the substance of things hoped for."

By personal faith in Jesus Christ and His finished work on Calvary, we become members of God's family. "Now we are all children of God through faith in Jesus Christ" (Gal. 3:26 LB). "For by grace are ye saved through faith; and that not of yourselves: it is the gift of God: not of works, lest any man should boast" (Eph. 2:8–9).

But faith doesn't stop with our conversion. It is a continuing life principle. "The just shall *live* by faith" (Rom. 1:17, emphasis mine).

Faith **believes** that God can do what He promises because He has power to do it. Faith **trusts** God to fulfill His promises, knowing God has all the resources of heaven at His disposal. Faith **expects** God to keep His promises. "My soul, wait thou only upon God; for my expectation is from him" (Ps. 62:5). Faith **accepts** God's provision. Faith takes God at His Word, considering already accomplished what he has promised. It may not come in just the way or time frame we expect, but our trust is in God who promised.

James McConkey said, "Faith is dependence upon God; and this God-dependence only begins when self-dependence ends." Are you one of God's own children through your personal acceptance of Jesus? Are you self-dependent or God-dependent?

Someone has said, "Those who put their faith in things beyond the strength of man, await with quiet confidence the working of His plan."

JUNE 6

Casting all your care upon him; for he careth for you (1 Peter 5:7).

ave you ever felt that no one cared for you?

As I travel, I see many care-etched faces. In every strata of society people are crying out for someone who cares. Sometimes we even wonder if God cares. But He does! He cares for *you* personally.

Jesus exemplifies caring. Repeatedly in Scripture we read about Him ministering to the needs of the people, showing His love and concern for them. Never was He too busy. One night Jesus and His disciples were caught in a dangerous storm at sea. The disciples woke Jesus and said, "Master, carest thou not that we perish?" (Mark 4:38). Jesus cared about their fears. He looked out at the turbulent sea and said, "Peace, be still." The storm ceased.

When several thousand people had been listening to Jesus all day, they became hungry. There was no place to get food. Jesus cared about their hunger and miraculously provided a meal for them.

The Bible tells us to cast our cares on Him. To cast can mean to roll. Sometimes our burdens or worries are too heavy to cast, but we can roll them upon Him. "Casting the whole of your care—all your anxieties, all your worries, all your concerns, once and for all—on Him; for He cares for you affectionately, and cares about you watchfully" (AMPLIFIED). To worry is to doubt God's ability to handle our need.

We can trust the Lord with our burdens. Not one is too great for Him. Our heavy circumstances may not disappear, but our Lord will carry the weight of them.

Each day we can expect Him to take care of us. We can turn every care over to Him—the small ones, the big ones, the hard ones, the easy ones.

The Lord's care replaces anxiety and concern with peace, rest, and love. Paul wrote, "Don't worry about anything; instead, pray about everything; tell God your needs and don't forget to thank him for his answers. If you do this you will experience God's peace, which is far more wonderful than the human mind can understand. His peace will keep your thoughts and your hearts quiet and at rest as you trust in Christ Jesus" (Phil. 4:6–7 LB).

It matters to Him about you!

JUNE 7

And the angel of the LORD found her by a fountain of water in the wilderness, by the fountain in the way to Shur (Gen. 16:7).

A braham and Sarah waited a long time for the son God had promised them. As time passed and no son was born, they became impatient. They decided to help God fulfill His promise. According to the custom of their time, a woman could permit her maid to have a child for her. This was the scheme Sarah devised by which she might have a son.

When Hagar knew she was to have a child, she evidently began to gloat over the fact. As a result, Sarah inflicted such harsh treatment on her that Hagar fled to the desert.

Lonely and weary, Hagar sat down by a well in the desert. There was no one to whom she could turn. But God knew she was there and God cared. Hagar might get away from Sarah, but she could not get away from herself or God. There by the well God found her.

"And the angel of the LORD found her by a fountain of water in the wilderness" (v. 7). The angel said, "Whence camest thou? and whither wilt thou go?" (v. 8). He knew all about her, but he wanted her to face herself and her situation. Then the angel told her she must return and submit to Sarah. This would not be easy for her to do.

There by the wall Hagar had an experience with God Himself. "And she called the name of the Lord that spake unto her, Thou God seest me" (v. 13). The name she used for God was El Roi, the God who sees. The first time in the Bible that God revealed Himself as El Roi, the God who sees, was to this unloved, rejected slave girl. She responded, "Thou God seest me." Then she called the well where the revelation took place Beer-lahai-roi, which means, "the well of him that liveth and seest me." In her place of need God brought her the assurance of His love and care.

Are you in the desert today? Are you running away from some situation in your life, perhaps something for which you are not to blame? It may be an unpleasant home situation, a misunderstanding, a disagreeable neighbor, a difficult person at work. Usually the solution does not come from running away from it.

El Roi, the God who sees and cares, draws near to *you* in a special way. There is a well in your desert where you may sit down. It is the well of Him that liveth and seeth. At His well God refreshes, encourages, and strengthens you.

Someone has said, "To such a well many weary and disillusioned wayfarers have come. Trusting the God who sees, knows, and loves, they return ready to face their situation, knowing God will be with them."

JUNE 8

He giveth power to the faint; and to them that have no might he in-creaseth strength (Isa. 40:29).

or several days a man watched a vine as it reached across space, trying to fasten itself to a pine tree. The night after it had successfully attached itself, a storm swept through the area. The next morning the man saw that the vine had been torn from the tree, yet still held to the broken branch. As he looked more closely, he saw that it was not the tree that had caused the vine to fall. The vine had anchored itself to a dead branch that could not hold the vine steady during the storm.

What an important lesson for us. Sometimes we fasten ourselves to things that appear to be strong, but when the storms come, we do not have sufficient support and our lives crash.

Storms come into our lives, bringing us to the point of exhaustion. Storms may be physical, emotional, mental, or spiritual. We say, "I'm through. I can't go on. I am at the end of my strength. I can't cope with this."

But there is One who is an All-powerful support system for us. No one anchored to Him can crash. The Creator of the heavens and the earth says, "Lift up your eyes on high, and behold who hath created these things, that bringeth out their host by number: he calleth them all by names by the greatness of his might . . . he is strong in power; not one faileth" (v. 26).

He continues, "Don't you know by now that the everlasting God, the Creator of the farthest parts of the earth, never grows faint or weary?" (v. 28 LB). God never gets tired.

When we consider His All-powerful support system, it puts everything in perspective. Someone has said that the bigger we see God, the smaller our problems become.

God, the source of power, shares His strength with the weary and gives increased power to those who are weak. God's strength is constant, always available to us.

Perhaps you are completely exhausted today—emotionally, physically, mentally, spiritually. You have reached the end. Help is available. Plug into your strong support system, God Himself, and appropriate His strength for your needs, whatever they are today. His strength is for you. "The LORD *will* give strength unto his people" (Ps. 29:11, emphasis mine).

JUNE 9

But they that wait upon the LORD shall renew their strength; they shall mount up with wings as eagles; they shall run, and not be weary; and they shall walk, and not faint (Isa. 40:31).

ow many times have you said, "Oh, if only I had wings so I could fly away from my problems, if only I had power to rise above them"? You may not be able to get away from problems, yet there is a power that can lift you above them.

The above Scripture not only promises strength but a strength that can be renewed. This comes from waiting on the Lord. *Waiting* in this verse carries the thought of an exchange, of entwining ourselves in our weakness around the Lord in His strength. As we do this, an exchange takes place. We exchange our weakness for His strength.

We can trade all that we have for all that Jesus is. We give Him our weakness and He gives us His strength. We say, "I can't do it." God says, "I can and will do it for you." He gives us the strength to keep going when we say we are through. The Bible says, "As thy days, so shall thy strength be" (Deut. 33:25). We can experience the reality of God's strength step by step in our daily walk.

The secret of renewed strength comes from waiting on the Lord. It means not only to bring Him our need, but to wait to receive something from Him. How often we rush into His presence and out again without taking time to think of the One to whom we are bringing our request.

The psalmist said, "Rest in the Lord, and wait patiently for him" (Ps. 37:7). Our exhaustion may come because we fail to take time in His presence to exchange our weakness for His strength.

As we wait on Him we may also exchange our pressures for His peace and quietness. In His presence there is a restfulness that quiets our hearts and minds. The Bible says, "In quietness and in confidence shall be your strength" (Isa. 30:15).

If we wait on Him, His strength will sustain us in the hectic activities of our day. In His presence we exchange our weakness for His strength, our frustration for His peace, and our weariness for His rest.

Someone has said that when we make the secret place of the Most High our permanent abiding place, we shall always be in touch with the almightiness of God.

JUNE 10

But they that wait upon the LORD shall renew their strength; they
shall mount up with wings as eagles; they shall run, and not be
weary; and they shall walk, and not faint (Isa. 40:31).

y work requires that I fly often, but I am always thrilled as the plane leaves the earth and begins to ascend. I feel that I am leaving the frustrations of earth behind and mounting up closer to God. Looking down, I discover a new perspective of planet earth.

Isaiah says that the result of waiting on the Lord is the ability to "mount up with wings as eagles." The eagle has the power to rise above the storms of earth. The storms may rage, the thunder may roar, but the eagle mounts up on its wing power and soars above.

In our Christian experience we have supernatural wing power by which we can be lifted up into the heavens. "[God] hath raised us up together, and made us sit together in heavenly places in Christ Jesus" (Eph. 2:6).

Using our wing power to gain altitude, we mount up above our storms of disappointments, hurts, misunderstandings, heartaches, worries, and pain. There may not be a way out, but there is a way up. God says, "Ye have seen . . . how I bare you on eagles' wings, and brought you unto myself" (Ex. 19:4).

Paul reminded the early Christians of the importance of living above. "If ye then be risen with Christ, seek those things which are above, where Christ sitteth on the right hand of God" (Col. 3:1). As we rise above our problems, we see life from a different perspective. Altitude widens our vision.

An Indian chief tested the mettle of his braves by making them run up the side of the mountain as fast and high as they could. One day four braves ran the test. One returned with a spruce branch, one with a twig of pine, and the third with an evergreen shrub. The fourth didn't return until after dark. He came in exhausted. "How high did you go?" asked the chief. The brave replied, "I found no spruce or pine or flowers—only rocks and barren land. My feet are bruised and I am exhausted. But," he said with a light in his eyes, "I saw the sea."

Our problems do not seem as big when viewed from the heavens. Seated there, we find a reserve of strength. They that wait upon the Lord shall receive wing power to soar above.

JUNE 11

Adorn the doctrine of God our Saviour in all things (Titus 2:10).

aul was writing here to slaves whose environment was not conducive to Christian living. Their circumstances were far from ideal. Yet he encouraged them to adorn the doctrines of God in every area of their lives. This truth applies to us, too. We can adorn the gospel, whatever our environment, whatever our circumstances.

The word *adorn* means to add beauty. The doctrine of God can be adorned by our character and our conduct. Henry Drummond once said, "The best evidence of Christianity is a Christian." Through the transforming power of God, we can adorn His doctrine in our daily living, giving evidence of the life of Christ within. We can reveal to our world how a Christian lives. The world will not be impressed by what we say about the gospel if we don't consistently live what we speak.

An interior decorator often uses extra little touches to enhance a home's beauty. A vase of flowers makes an inconspicuous table come alive. A picture grouping adds interest to a wall. A chair upholstered in a striking fabric changes the atmosphere of a room. These adornments transform an ordinary-looking room into one of warmth, reflecting the personality of the one living there.

Our lives, too, can reflect the loveliness of the person of Jesus Christ, who lives within us. This is easier on calm and peaceful days, but Paul said we are to do it at all times, even when our hearts are breaking, when we are frustrated, when we feel we have failed, when we are disappointed, when we are lonely. We need to remember to reflect the presence of Christ when the children are crying, the potatoes are boiling over, and the phone is ringing.

A sculptor displayed a replica of a famous cathedral in his studio. It was a remarkable piece of work, but no one noticed it. One day his assistant put a light inside it to examine the windows but forgot to remove the light afterward. Then everyone who came into the studio admired the beauty of the cathedral. What made the difference? A light had been turned on inside it.

"Let the beauty of the LORD our God be upon us: and establish thou the work of our hands upon us; yea, the work of our hands establish thou it" (Ps. 90:17).

JUNE 12

For He will give His angels [especial] charge over you, to accompany and defend and preserve you in all your ways [of obedience and service] (Ps. 91:11 AMPLIFIED).

What a bulwark this psalm has been to God's children through the ages. It was written by one who had found the "secret place of the most High" (v.1).

God's Word promises us the protective care of the angels of the Lord. He has commissioned them to watch over our interests. They accompany us on our way through life, defending and preserving us.

We have a **constant** protection in *all* our ways, not some of our ways but all of them—our daily living, our business, our service, our fears, our discouragements—nothing is excluded.

Not only is His protection constant, but it is also **personal**—in all of *your* ways.

The psalmist wrote that the angels "will steady you with their hands to keep you from stumbling against the rocks on the trail. You can safely meet a lion or step on poisonous snakes, yes, even trample them beneath your feet" (v. 12–13 LB).

We need not fear such dangers, for God sends his angels to protect us. "Are not the angels all (servants) ministering spirits sent out in the service [of God for the assistance] of those who are to inherit salvation?" (Heb. 1:14 AMPLIFIED).

God promises safety in time of danger "because you have made the Lord your refuge, and the Most High your dwelling place" (Ps. 91:9 AMPLIFIED). When we make Him our dwelling place, He promises divine security.

One day as I headed for the store by way of our alley, a garage obstructed my view. I started to step out into the alley but seemed held back momentarily. Just then a truck sped past me. Had I not paused, I would have been struck by the truck. At the speed it was going I could have been seriously injured. I experienced the protection of my special angel.

One day Chiang Kai-shek and his wife were walking arm in arm in a place where many dangers lurked. Someone said, "Look, they don't even have a bodyguard." Another person replied, "They don't need a bodyguard. They have God."

When we make God our refuge and take normal precautions, we can trust God to protect us. "A thousand shall fall at thy side, and ten thousand at thy right hand; but it shall not come nigh thee" (Ps. 91:7).

For I have learned, in whatsoever state I am, therewith to be content (Phil. 4:11).

ow true it is with most of us that the more we have the more we wish we had.

Paul learned well the lesson of contentment. He was in prison when he wrote the book of Philippians. How many of us could have said in such circumstances, "I have learned, in whatsoever state I am, therewith to be content."

Paul learned not to live under his circumstances, but to live peacefully and victoriously in and through them. In spite of his environment and circumstances, he was not defeated, for he had a *contented* heart.

The secret of his contentment is found in verse 9: "The God of peace— of untroubled, undisturbed well-being—will be with you" (Phil. 4:9 AMPLIFIED).

Paul could say, "I know how to be abased and live humbly in straitened circumstances, and I know also how to enjoy plenty and live in abundance. I have learned in any and all circumstances, the secret of facing every situation, whether well-fed or going hungry, having a sufficiency and to spare or going without and being in want" (Phil. 4:12 AMPLIFIED).

Paul had learned contentment through his ability to exchange his insufficiency for Christ's sufficiency. "I am ready for anything through the strength of the one who lives within me" (Phil. 4:13 PHILLIPS). We can face anything and everything through the enabling power of Christ.

His confidence in God was unwavering because He had learned to be content, whatever his lot. He wasn't content with his circumstances, but in them. He didn't say it was natural for him to be content. He was content because of his God-given adjustment to every situation.

As we look about us, we discover the world is filled with many discontented people. They are never satisfied with what they have or where they are. We may ask, "Is it possible to be content in today's troubled world?" Paul experienced the reality of a contented heart through Jesus Christ.

Have you learned the secret of contentment? Are you at peace in your circumstances and environment today? The secret of contentment is satisfaction with what we have, where we are. This contentment does not depend on our possessions or freedom from trouble, but the person of Christ within.

JUNE 14

That the trial of your faith, being much more precious than of gold
that perisheth, though it be tried with fire, might be found unto
praise and honour and glory at the appearing of Jesus Christ
(1 Peter 1:7).

nce, while in Minneapolis, I toured the Pillsbury Kitchens, where they test all of their products before putting them on the market. Testing is something God does, too. He tests us to prove our faith and make us more valuable to Him as He sends us forth in His service.

Though we often try to avoid them, God doesn't promise that becoming a Christian will make us exempt from trials. In fact, some of God's children seem to face one right after another. But we need not be afraid as we go through trials, for Peter wrote that we "are kept by the power of God" (v. 5). He will not let one thing touch our lives that hasn't first come through Him. He is right there to go through it with us. He feels what we feel.

We often ask why our trials come. We can be sure all of them have a purpose, and the Lord longs to become more real to us in them. Confident that God will carry us through, we learn endurance.

Our faith must stand the test of fire. Faith is said to be more precious than gold. Gold is a precious metal, but it is not as precious as our faith. Gold will perish, but not faith; it is eternal.

Gold is purified by fire at a higher heat than some metals. As gold needs to be purified by heat, so does our faith. God tests us by fire to remove the impurities—whatever is not of faith. He puts us in circumstances that will bring us to the end of ourselves, to a place of complete trust in the Lord. Our tested lives will reflect a faith that is pure and genuine.

Our trials have value. "If your faith remains strong after being tried in the test tube of fiery trials, it will bring you much praise and glory and honor on the day of his return" (v. 7 LB).

When asked the secret of his incredible faith, George Mueller replied, "The only way to have strong faith is to endure great trials."

Trials result in love for Christ and a stronger trust in Him. "Whom having not seen, ye love; in whom, though now ye see him not, yet believing, ye rejoice with joy unspeakable and full of glory" (v. 8).

JUNE 15

After this manner therefore pray ye: Our Father which art in heaven (Matt. 6:9).

someone has said that the great people of the world are those who pray. The above Scripture is the beginning of what is known as the Lord's Prayer. It could more correctly be called the Disciples' Prayer. Jesus gave it as a model or pattern for praying effectively.

When the disciples asked Jesus about prayer, He said, "After this manner . . . pray ye." Note the importance of the word *ye.*

The first three requests in this prayer are an *uplook*. We must always remember that first of all prayer is for the glory of God. His glory comes before our needs. True prayer is not trying to get God's will in line with ours but to get our will in line with God's.

We approach God through the Lord Jesus. He said, "I am the way, the truth, and the life: no man cometh unto the Father, but by me" (John 14:6).

God is our Father! "Father" is an intimate name. In Him we find all that we could ever desire in a parent. We come into His presence in a spirit of humbleness and bow before Him, calling Him our Father.

When a Roman emperor returned from a successful battle, he and his army would parade through the streets with their prisoners trailing behind. One time, the empress and her family were watching a triumphant parade. As the emperor came near, his little son dashed out to meet him. One of the soldiers stopped him and said, "Don't you know that's the emperor in that chariot?" The little boy replied, "He may be your emperor but he is my father."

Through the Lord Jesus Christ, we have the privilege of coming to God in all of His majesty and power and calling Him "our Father." He is dedicated to providing for us and protecting us. He knows each of us by name. Incredible! Could we ever question His care?

Someone has said that in Jesus we are as near to God as Jesus is. His love is beyond our understanding but not beyond our ability to experience. His love is for real.

JUNE 16

Hallowed be thy name (Matt. 6:9)

rayer is not primarily for us but for God. Many people think of prayer as a shopping list to present to God. But in Jesus' model prayer, He focuses his disciples' attention upon God rather than their needs: *"Our Father* which art in heaven."

He began with worship and adoration: "Hallowed be thy name." To *hallow* God's name means to keep it holy, to set it apart as special, to reverence it.

When we hallow God's name, we want to keep it holy. We also hallow the person His name represents. We reverence Him for who He is. We acknowledge the worthiness of the One to whom we speak.

When God sent Moses to lead the children of Israel out of Egypt, Moses asked God what he should answer when they asked the name of the one who sent him. "God said unto Moses . . . Thus shalt thou say unto the children of Israel . . . I AM hath sent me unto you" (Ex. 3:14). This name was represented by the letters *YHWH,* later expanded to the name *JEHOVAH.* God was saying, "This is my name, Jehovah."

Jehovah is the name above all God's names. He is the self-existent one. He becomes to His people what they need in order to supply that need. In effect He is saying, "I am your strength, your peace, your patience, your love." When we realize who He is, how can we help but bow in worship as we come to Him in prayer?

We can also reverence His name and keep it holy in the way we live— our conversation, habits, reading material, places we go, even our trials. We can bear His name in such a way that others will see His character expressed in our lives. Carelessness in our speech and conduct can bring reproach to that name.

When we pray, can we sincerely write over our petitions, "Hallowed be thy name in this request"? When our prayer is filled with worship, adoration, and love, a new reverence comes into our prayers, and our lives are filled with the desire to please Him. Then as we leave our prayer time, we will radiate His presence.

"O magnify the LORD with me, and let us exalt his name together" (Ps. 34:3).

JUNE 17

And I will do whatever you ask in my name, so that the Son may bring glory to the Father. You may ask me for anything in my name, and I will do it (John 14:13–14 NIV).

ow vital, how exciting is your prayer life? Is it just a ritual, a habit established because it is expected of you as a Christian? Have you missed the joyous, exciting reality of communicating with God through the person of His Son, Jesus Christ?

Answered prayer doesn't depend on the words we use, our posture, or the tone of our voice. Jesus said, "Whatever you ask, I will do." Do you have a need today? Then you may ask Him for it. Our part is to ask; God's part is to answer.

We are to ask in His Name. This means a great deal more than adding His Name at the end of our prayer. It is not a magical phrase to be tacked on when we're finished. We have no merits on which we can claim an answer to our petitions. We are not worthy. Through His death and resurrection, Jesus provided the only way by which we can come to our Father. Jesus said, "I am the way, the truth, and the life: no man cometh unto the Father, but by me" (John 14:6).

We approach God through the merits of Jesus. His Name gives us the right to voice our requests to the Father. When we pray in His Name we pray according to His will. We are praying as one who is at one with Him, whose mind is at one with His mind, and whose desires and interests are at one with Him. Praying in His Name is praying as Jesus would pray for our requests. The Father recognizes our right and gives us what He would give His Son.

All the wealth of God is behind the Name of Jesus. While we pray in His Name, we are drawing on all that God is and all that God has.

And in effective prayer, bringing glory to the Father should be our motive. One day I was challenged with this thought: Could I write over every one of my prayer requests, "I pray this for your glory, Father?" It changed my prayer life. Prayer is not just a means of receiving our needs from God. It's a means of glorifying Him.

If we were to pray as Jesus would pray for our neighborhood, our community, our city, our world, how would our prayer life change today?

The Spirit helps us in our weakness. We do not know what we
ought to pray for, but the Spirit himself intercedes for us with groans
that words cannot express (Rom. 8:26 NIV).

ometimes I bring my request to the Father, but I am perplexed as to how to pray for it. I want to pray according to God's will, yet I am uncertain what that is. The Holy Spirit knows my deepest heart's desire and helps me formulate my prayer in accordance to the will of God.

We may recognize our helplessness in prayer, but the Holy Spirit enables us to pray. He even motivates us to pray. Paul speaks of "praying always with all prayer and supplication in the Spirit" (Eph. 6:18).

Whenever I am uncertain how to pray, I am thankful that I can trust the Holy Spirit to pray my prayer aright before the heavenly Father.

When my sister was very ill, and I knew she could not recover, I would pray, "Dear Father, I can't give her up. Please heal her." Then I would pray, "Oh, Father, don't listen to that prayer. I want Your will for her, not mine." Other times as I looked at her, I would pray, "Dear Father, please take her. I can't bear to see her this way." Then I would pray, "Dear Father, don't listen to that prayer." My emotions were so mixed up that I couldn't pray rationally. The Holy Spirit understood. He prayed the real desire of my heart, which was for God's will. In His own perfect timing He took her to heaven, and we had real peace.

Praying in His will takes more than our human reasoning. It takes the power of the Holy Spirit. When we pray in our human wisdom and power, we get what they can do. But when we pray in the wisdom and power of the Holy Spirit we get what He can do.

The Living Bible paraphrases it, "By our faith—the Holy Spirit helps us with our daily problems and in our praying. For we don't even know what we should pray for, nor how to pray as we should; but the Holy Spirit prays for us with such feeling that it cannot be expressed in words" (Rom. 8:26).

We can trust the Holy Spirit to help us in our prayers. "He that searcheth the hearts knoweth what is the mind of the Spirit, because he maketh intercession for the saints according to the will of God" (v. 27).

JUNE 19

If ye abide in me, and my words abide in you, ye shall ask what ye will, and it shall be done unto you (John 15:7).

In the above Scripture Jesus gives a promise with a two-fold condition for answered prayer.

The first condition is, "If ye abide in me." The word *abide* means to dwell permanently; to be at home with. To abide in Christ means living in His presence, moment-by-moment fellowship with Him.

The other condition is "and my words abide in you." Someone has said that the Bible is the Christian's Prayer Book. As God's words are at home in us, our lives are sustained and matured. Jesus said, "The words that I speak unto you, they are spirit, and they are life" (John 6:63).

We must meditate regularly on God's Word, letting it shape and control every area of our lives. We must seek to conform our lives to its guidelines and walk in obedience to it.

As His Word dwells in us, His thoughts and desires will become such a part of us that we will think as He thinks. We will react as He reacts. We will be brought into harmony with His will. The Holy Spirit will make us aware of the petitions that are in accordance with the will of the Father.

As we abide in His Word, our faith deepens, resulting in greater trust in the Lord and a stronger prayer life. The Bible says, "Faith cometh by hearing, and hearing by the word of God" (Rom. 10:17).

George Mueller, a man of great faith, had a ministry with orphans in England in the 1800s. He never told anyone his needs, but through his prayers, he received several million dollars to support this work.

In his quiet time it was his habit to pray first, and then read the Word. One day he reversed the order, reading the Word first and then praying. From then on he sensed new power in his prayer life. He said, "The vigor of our spiritual life will be in exact proportion to the place held by the Word in our life and thoughts."

When we are in fellowship with the Lord and controlled by His Word as it abides in us, He promises to answer our prayers.

JUNE 20

*Now the God of peace, that brought again from the dead our Lord
Jesus . . . make you perfect in every good work to do his will, work-
ing in you that which is well-pleasing in his sight, through Jesus
Christ; to whom be glory for ever and ever (Heb. 13:20–21).*

n the above Scripture, we learn a great deal about our God. He
is the **God of peace.** Only God can bring peace into a troubled
heart and world. His peace is the inner peace of the heart,
regardless of circumstances. "For he is our peace" (Eph. 2:14).

He is the **God of power.** The power of God that raised Jesus from the
dead is the same power that works in our lives. Yet we struggle along in our
weakness when the almighty power of God is available. Paul wrote, "Be strong
in the Lord, and in the power of his might" (Eph. 6:10).

He is the **God of perfection.** He will make us "perfect in every good
work . . . to do his will." The phrase *make you perfect* means to make an
adjustment, such as resetting a dislocated bone. We may need an adjustment to
return to the place of doing His will. It may be painful, but He entrusts this
operation to no one else. He performs it Himself as tenderly as possible.

He is the **God of performance.** He is working in us "that which is
well-pleasing in his sight." This means doing His pleasure. He works in us,
helping us please Him, and what He calls us to do, He also enables us to do.

As a man was watching a potter at work, he asked if he could try to make
a pot. The potter let him, but he failed. Sitting behind the man, the potter put his
arms, hands, and fingers over the man's. Then the wheel began to spin. "Do
not let your fingers resist mine," cautioned the potter. As the man yielded to the
potter, he made a beautiful vessel. And as we yield our lives to the skillful touch
of the Master Potter, He can work in us that which is pleasing to Him.

What a God! A God of peace, power, perfection, performance. He is the
God to be **praised.** As we ponder His greatness, we also realize that He
lovingly cares for the individual—you and me. With the psalmist, we say, "O
come, let us worship and bow down: let us kneel before the LORD our maker"
(Ps. 95:6).

JUNE 21

For the kingdom of God is not food and drink but righteousness and peace and joy in the Holy Spirit" (Rom. 14:17 NRSV).

n this verse Paul is describing of the kingdom of God—the inner kingdom of the heart. Luke 17:21 says, "The kingdom of God is within you."

The citizens of a kingdom become subject to their king, giving him complete allegiance. Nothing is to undermine their loyalty to their king. We become citizens of God's kingdom through our personal faith in and acceptance of Jesus Christ as Savior.

His kingdom has certain characteristics. Paul said it is not a kingdom of food and drink but of righteousness. His righteousness in the inner kingdom of our lives will help us live right. It is not our own righteousness but the righteousness of Jesus Christ. "Of him are ye in Christ Jesus, who of God is made unto us wisdom, and righteousness" (1 Cor. 1:30).

God's kingdom is also one of peace. Our days may be filled with fear, frustration, and futility. But God's kingdom within gives us peace in the midst of problems, perplexities, and pressures, for He is our peace. Not only are we at peace with God through Jesus Christ but we can be at peace with others and with ourselves.

His kingdom is one of joy not dependent on our circumstances. The psalmist says that in the Lord's presence is fullness of joy.

His kingdom of righteousness, peace, and joy is produced in us by the power of the Holy Spirit.

God's kingdom must have priority in our lives. Jesus, the king of that kingdom, said, "Seek ye first the kingdom of God, and his righteousness; and all these things shall be added unto you" (Matt. 6:33). It is easy to seek the *all things* instead of the *first things* of God's kingdom of righteousness.

Who is the king of your life today? Have you abdicated the throne of your life? Have you given the Lord Jesus Christ His rightful place as king of your life? Have you crowned Him as your King of Kings and Lord of Lords? Jesus Christ cannot become your King until you give Him the throne.

It is good for me that I have been afflicted; that I might learn thy statutes (Ps. 119:71).

ave you ever attended night school? Sometimes it is more difficult to keep up with your studies, yet evening classes have enriched the lives of many who attend.

God holds some of His classes during the night hours, too. One of them is the class of *affliction*. David was one of His pupils in this night-hour class. Although David found it difficult, he experienced how profitable affliction can be. He became a better person because of it. He said, "It is good for me."

We may ask, "If God really loves me, why should this happen to me?" It isn't God's desire to punish us by sending affliction. But He wouldn't be good if He saw we needed discipline and didn't administer it. He allows it because of His deep and abiding love for us.

A loving parent will punish his child, not to show his power and authority over the child, but for the child's own good. So it is with God. Because of His great love for us, God is willing to discipline and train us. It is for our benefit.

The Bible says, "My son, don't be angry when the Lord punishes you. Don't be discouraged when he has to show you where you are wrong. For when he punishes you, it proves that he loves you. When he whips you it proves you are really his child. Let God train you, for he is doing what any loving father does for his children" (Heb. 12:5–7 LB).

One day, a shepherd was carrying a sheep in his arms. When questioned, he said he had broken the sheep's leg. This surprised the questioner. The shepherd replied, "This sheep was self-willed, ever straying from me. I broke its leg and now while the bone is healing, this sheep is learning to obey and follow me. I won't have trouble with it again."

Our affliction is good when it brings us into the arms of our Good Shepherd.

David could say his affliction was good for him. Why? Because God had been faithful in allowing it. Can we trust His faithfulness enough to say that our affliction is good?

JUNE 23

Wait on the LORD: be of good courage, and he shall strengthen thine heart: wait, I say, on the LORD (Ps. 27:14).

 ow many times a day do we become annoyed by delays? Traffic, telephone calls, unfavorable weather conditions—each delay increases our frustration. But someone has said that the stops as well as the steps of a good person are ordered of the Lord.

We miss many blessings by being in such a hurry. Often we are too busy to stop and gaze at one of God's beautiful sunsets, listen to the song of a bird, give a smile or a cheery word, offer encouragement to those who carry heartaches, or spend time with the Lord to build a strong friendship with Him.

Throughout the Bible we read of God's "lingerers," those who took time to linger in His presence, to wait on the Lord.

David was one of God's choice lingerers. He said, "One thing I have desired of the LORD, that will I seek after; that I may dwell in the house of the LORD all the days of my life, to behold the beauty of the LORD, and to inquire in his temple" (Ps. 27:4).

Moses lingered in the presence of the Lord, too. One day as he took his sheep to the backside of the desert, he saw a bush burning yet not being consumed. The burning bush was symbolic of the presence of the Lord. There in God's presence Moses was chosen for a very special mission—the deliverance of His people.

Mary of Bethany lingered at the feet of Jesus. She was aware that more important than what she could do for Jesus was what He could do for her. Jesus said she had chosen the best part.

Too often we rush into His presence, bring our needs to Him, and rush out again without waiting for Him to speak to us. We need to be quiet and listen to Him say, "Stand thou still a while, that I may shew thee the word of God" (1 Sam. 9:27).

Rich benefits come from being a lingerer. In His presence we become more and more like Him, and our trust in Him deepens. We are encouraged and strengthened to face our daily trials. We are filled with His radiance, alerting the world of something different in our lives.

God is looking for lingerers. Wait upon the Lord.

JUNE 24

The LORD shall be thy confidence (Prov. 3:26).

hile living in Denver, we experienced a devastating flood. Heavy winter snows in the mountains and heavy spring rains filled the creeks and streams to overflowing. Pouring into the South Platte river, the rushing water carried everything in its path right through the city.

One or two mobile home parks were completely swept away. Entire homes floated away. A large new cement bridge, unable to withstand the force of the water, toppled into the raging river.

Later, after several of these demolished areas were opened up again to traffic, we drove through one section where many retired couples lived and watched many who had returned to view the damage to their homes.

Discouragement etched their faces as they looked at what was left. Some homes had been destroyed completely. These people had saved for years to have security in their retirement. Yet in a few hours that which had seemed so secure was swept away.

How often we build our lives on the security of material possessions. We accumulate a large savings account, buy a home, a car, and other material things to give us a sense of security. It is wise, of course, to make plans for the future. But it is not wise to build our security on them.

Jesus said, "Lay not up for yourselves treasures upon earth, where moth and rust doth corrupt, and where thieves break through and steal: but lay up for yourselves treasures in heaven, where neither moth nor rust doth corrupt, and where thieves do not break through nor steal" (Matt. 6:19–20).

Solomon reminds us where our security must be. "The LORD shall be thy confidence." Our confidence is not to be placed in possessions, but in the person of Jesus Christ. He is our security. He will never fail.

The Bible says, "Cast not away therefore your confidence, which hath great recompence of reward. For ye have need of patience, that, after ye have done the will of God, ye might receive the promise" (Heb. 10:35–36).

As we face an unknown future, uncertain of what lies ahead, we must be careful where we place our confidence. We can either cast it away on material possessions, or we can let *Him* be our confidence. "Jesus Christ the same yesterday, and today, and for ever" (Heb. 13:8).

Thy will be done in earth, as it is in heaven (Matt. 6:10).

hen life is easy and things are going our way, it is not difficult to say, "Thy will be done." But when our lives are falling apart, we may question His will.

Often we pray the above words of Scripture without thinking. But knowing and doing the will of God is the most important part of our lives.

Jesus showed us how to live that way. His one great purpose was to do His Father's will and to glorify Him. He told His disciples, "My food (nourishment) is to do the will (pleasure) of Him Who sent Me and to accomplish and completely finish His work" (John 4:34 AMPLIFIED). He also said, "I have come down from heaven, not to do My own will and purpose; but to do the will and purpose of Him Who sent Me" (John 6:38 AMPLIFIED).

When He was facing Calvary, He prayed, "O my Father, if it be possible, let this cup pass from me" (Matt. 26:39). But His struggle ended with, "nevertheless, not my will, but thine, be done" (Luke 22:42).

The out-working of God's will on earth did not end when Christ returned to heaven. It has continued through the lives of His children for centuries. You and I have a part, too. His will should be our great desire. God has expressed in His written Word His will for our everyday living. To know His will, we must read His Word.

Sometimes our will agrees perfectly with His. There is no struggle. But often there is conflict before we can exchange our will for His.

When we realize that He loves us and His will is always the best for us, we can pray with the psalmist, "I delight to do thy will, O my God" (Ps. 40:8).

Paul wrote, "Don't let the world around you squeeze you into its own mold, but let God remold your minds from within, so that you may prove in practice that the plan of God for you is good, meets all his demands and moves toward the goal of true maturity" (Rom. 12:2 PHILLIPS).

Someone has said that there can be no success out of the will of God, and there can be no failure within the will of God.

Thou wilt shew me the path of life: in thy presence is fullness of joy;
at thy right hand there are pleasures for evermore (Ps. 16:11).

avid's life was filled with many difficulties. Often he was
uncertain of the path he should take. But he knew the One who
knew the way. He wrote, "I will bless the Lord who counsels
me; he gives me wisdom in the night. He tells me what to do"
(v. 7 LB).

God was his personal Guide. "Thou wilt shew me the path of life." His
confidence was in his heavenly Guide who would reveal His way step by step.

He said, "*Thou* wilt." His thoughts went to his Guide. "I am always
thinking of the Lord; and because He is so near, I never need to stumble or to
fall" (v. 8 LB).

Jesus came to this earth to become the path of life for us. He said, "I am
the way, the truth, and the life: no man cometh unto the Father, but by me"
(John 14:6). The highway that led from earth to heaven was costly. It cost the
Lord Jesus His life on the cross.

The psalmist said, "*Shew* me the path of life." Our Heavenly Father
promises to lead us. In Psalms 32:8 we read, "I will instruct thee and teach
thee in the way which thou shalt go: I will guide thee with mine eye."

The presence of our Guide also gives day-by-day joy in our walk through
life. Joy is confidence that our heavenly Father is in control of our lives, and joy
comes from living in His presence. "In *thy presence* is fullness of joy."

In John 15 Jesus gives us a key to that joy. He says, "I have told you this
so that you will be filled with my joy. Yes, your cup of joy will overflow!"
(v. 11 LB). Nehemiah wrote, "The joy of the LORD is your strength" (Neh.
8:10).

In Him are pleasures forevermore. Pleasure is something that gives delight
and satisfaction. And His pleasures are long lasting. This psalm can be titled
"God-satisfied." At God's right hand we find complete satisfaction.

The Lord will return one of these days to take us home. Then we will be
in His presence forevermore. There our souls will be completely satisfied. There
our joy will continue forever. "Even so, come, Lord Jesus" (Rev. 22:20).

JUNE 27

For the LORD God is a sun and shield: the LORD will give grace and glory: no good thing will he withhold from them that walk uprightly. O LORD of hosts, blessed is the man that trusteth in thee (Ps. 84:11–12).

ow incredible it is to take off in a plane on a dismal, cloudy day and suddenly break through the clouds into the brilliant sunshine.

Often that is our experience in our daily walk. We are enveloped in dark clouds of trouble. Suddenly, the light of God's presence bursts upon us. The dark clouds are still there, but He has lifted us above them, encircling us with the warmth of His loving presence.

We may not see our way ahead, but we need not fear. We can move forward with the assurance that the Lord has become the light for our way and will light every step ahead of us as we take it.

In times of danger, the Lord is our shield, protecting and shielding us from the strong onslaughts of our enemy. In Genesis 15:1 the Lord says, "Fear not, Abram: I am thy shield." He who protected Abram is our shield, too. We couldn't be safer. Not one thing can come into our lives unless He allows it. It must come through Him to us. What have we to fear with the Lord as our sun to light our way and our shield to ward off danger?

The psalmist also said that the Lord would give grace and glory. Grace is unmerited, undeserved favor. It is God's gift for our inner life, giving us inner peace. It takes us through the pressures of life. God told Paul, "My grace is sufficient for thee" (2 Cor. 12:9).

Glory is the outward expression of inner reality. God's glory is all that God is. He gives us the privilege of expressing its reality in our daily walk. His grace and glory are fulfilled in Jesus Christ, who lives within us.

Today's verse continues, "No good thing will he withhold from them that walk uprightly." God's evaluation of good may not be the same as ours. If something is withheld from us, we can know that God has decided it would not be good for us.

This promise is for those who walk uprightly—those whose daily conduct is genuine. Let us then "walk (lead a life) worthy of the [divine] calling to which you have been called—with behavior that is a credit to the summons to God's service" (Eph. 4:1 AMPLIFIED).

For we walk by faith, not by sight (2 Cor. 5:7).

any times I have said, "If only I could see the way ahead. If I could know what step to take next." But God does not promise that we will be able to see the path ahead. Ours is to be a walk of faith, walking where we cannot see the way.

The Amplified Bible says, "For we walk by faith [that is, we regulate our lives and conduct ourselves by our conviction or belief respecting man's relationship to God and divine things, with trust and holy fervor; thus, we walk] not by sight or appearance."

What is faith? Webster defines it as "allegiance or duty to a person; belief and trust in and loyalty to God." Faith is having complete confidence in God. It is the certainty that what we hope for is waiting for us, even though we cannot see how. Faith obeys God's Word even when we don't understand what is happening.

One time my sister and her little son came to visit. My husband and I took them for a ride into the mountains. As we started up the first steep incline, her little boy looked up and saw the road winding up the mountain ahead of him. His eyes got big, and he said to my husband, "Uncle Clarke, I don't think you can make it." However, as Uncle Clarke stepped on the gas, the car steadily moved up the steep grade, and soon we were at the top. My husband had faith in what the car could do and trusted it to take us up the steep road to the top.

Perhaps in your walk of faith today, you have a steep mountain ahead of you. As far as you can see, it is insurmountable. Humanly speaking, there is no solution. God is in the moving business—His specialty, mountains. Faith trusts Him to move them.

Some mountains are steeper than others, some are higher, but they are all *His* mountains. We possess them by faith. Prayer is the key and faith turns the key. You can look beyond and above your mountain to God, who is in control.

Someone has said, "Faith is to trust God so absolutely that you are more willing to believe the impossibilities than to doubt."

JUNE 29

Blessed are the poor in spirit: for theirs is the kingdom of heaven (Matt. 5:3).

esus came to bring a new standard of living. It is a life that brings lasting happiness, a life that is lived above the circumstances.

Jesus said, "Blessed are the poor in spirit." He is speaking of a blessedness that brings this happiness. The poor in spirit are happy. But it is not the happiness the world gives. It is not the happiness that comes from outer circumstances. This happiness gives inner contentment no matter what happens.

The poor in spirit are the humble who acknowledge their need and cry for help. Aware of their helplessness and inadequacy, they have to admit they are nothing in the presence of God. They cannot justify themselves before Him or cope with life.

Jesus sets a standard of humbleness. The Phillips paraphrase of this verse reads, "How happy are the humble-minded, for the kingdom of Heaven is theirs!" To be poor in spirit means to empty our lives of self to give room to God. It is admitting our inadequacy and accepting Christ's all-sufficiency. We come to God, lifting empty hands to Him. As poet Martha Snell Nicholson wrote, "God could not pour His riches into hands already full!"

Our greatest danger is feeling we have no need, that we are self-sufficient. The world emphasizes self-reliance, self-expression, self-confidence. But these are not God's standards. In Revelation, God rebuked the self-sufficient Laodiceans because they said, "I am rich, and increased with goods, and have need of nothing." They didn't know that they were "wretched, and miserable, and poor, and blind, and naked" (Rev. 3:17). They felt no need of anything from God.

The poor in spirit are happy because they have been given the kingdom of heaven. Only Christ can give us this happiness. He said, "I am come that they might have life, and that they might have it more abundantly" (John 10:10).

A person may have all the world can offer and not be happy, for happiness comes through a right relationship with Jesus Christ, recognizing our spiritual bankruptcy and committing ourselves to Him.

In Christ, there is a happiness that is real. "Christ is all, and in all" (Col. 3:11). In Him we have contentment and fulfillment and true happiness.

He leadeth me beside the still waters (Ps. 23:2).

ave you ever wished someone could guide you in the right way for you to go? We have such a leader in our Good Shepherd, the Lord Jesus Christ. John wrote of Him, "He calleth his own sheep by name, and leadeth them out" (John 10:3).

David tells us that our Good Shepherd leads us beside the still waters. Can you picture a quiet, restful place beside a refreshing pool? The Good Shepherd takes us to the clear, cold water that will satisfy our thirst.

The word *still* in this verse could be translated *stilled.* Sheep are frightened of running water. They seem to sense that they could be in danger of drowning if their wool became saturated with water. When they come to a rushing stream, their fear often keeps them from drinking.

About 70 percent of a sheep's body is composed of water, so water is essential to its health. When sheep become thirsty, they need to have their water replenished. For this reason the shepherd leads them daily to a watering place. He takes a few stones and makes a quiet pool of water for them to drink from.

Our Good Shepherd knows that we need to drink of the Water of Life regularly or we will become spiritually dehydrated. He leads us to His stilled water so that we may be spiritually refreshed. Jesus said, "If any man thirst, let him come unto me, and drink" (John 7:37). He is our pool of still water.

You may be saying, "But the circumstances in my life are not beside still waters." Perhaps God is allowing your circumstances to give you a thirst for Him. You may have been trying to satisfy your thirst at the pool of fame, fortune, education, possessions, society, entertainment, or pleasures. But only Jesus, the Water of Life, can quench your thirst and satisfy you fully. Only as you drink from the pool of the One who is real and genuine will you be refreshed.

Are you thirsty today? Do you need to be refreshed? Let the Good Shepherd lead you to His pool of stilled water. Drink deeply. He satisfies.

The Bible says, "Let Him that is athirst come. And whosoever will, let him take of the water of life freely" (Rev. 22:17).

JULY 1

Lord, what wilt thou have me to do? (Acts 9:6).

Saul, an enemy of Jesus Christ, was on his way to Damascus to seek out Christians to imprison. Suddenly, he had a personal encounter with Jesus, and the direction of his life changed. Immediately, he recognized the lordship of Jesus Christ over his life. He said, *"Lord,* what wilt thou have me to do?" A *yielded heart* indicates a life totally committed to the Lord.

"What wilt thou have me to do?" was evidence of a *listening ear.* He was ready to listen to the Lord's Word to him. Our ears need to be tuned in to God's message.

"Wilt thou" shows that Saul's (now Paul's) *will* was committed to God. Often we seek our will instead of God's. The will seems to be the most difficult to give to Him.

"Have me indicates that Paul made a personal commitment of his *body* to God. His life was filled with service for His Lord's glory.

A young lady wanted to commit her life to the Lord, but two things held her back. First, she was an accomplished pianist and didn't want to give up her career. And second, she was afraid God would send her to India as a missionary.

When she went to see her pastor, he asked her to read Acts 10:14: "Peter said, Not so, Lord." The pastor reminded her that if Jesus was Peter's Lord, Peter had no right to say, "Not so."

The pastor wrote the words, *Not so Lord,* on a sheet of paper, then left her alone for a time of prayer, during which she was to cross out either *Not so* or *Lord,* according to her decision. When he returned, she had crossed out, *Not so.* She decided to let Jesus be the Lord of her life.

What has been your answer to God, "Not so," or "Lord"?

Have you committed your heart, ears, will, body, and service to Him?

JULY 2

And Jacob was left alone (Gen. 32:24).

acob was a schemer, a conniver. He directed his own life. His plans did not revolve around God. But there came a time when he had to decide who would control his life—Jacob or God?

Through his scheming, Jacob had enraged his brother and had to flee for his life. After a number of years, God told Jacob to return to his home. As he approached, he learned that his brother was coming to meet him. He was frightened. Would Esau carry out his threat to kill him?

In desperation, Jacob prayed to God then made plans as if he needed to help God. To protect his family, he sent them across the River Jabbok.

This left him all alone that night, alone with his thoughts, memories, and fear of the future. He was alone by divine appointment. Jacob, not Esau, was the real problem. God had to get Jacob alone to make him face himself.

While alone, a man, very likely the Lord in human form, appeared and wrestled with him. After Jacob had wrestled all night, with divine power God suddenly touched Jacob's thigh, rendering him completely powerless. He couldn't struggle anymore but clung to God, saying, "I will not let thee go, except thou bless me" (v. 26). He was finally willing to let God take control.

Then Jacob the schemer, became Israel, the prince whom God commands. God said, "For as a prince hast thou power with God and with men, and hast prevailed" (v. 28).

Perhaps you have been trying to run your own life. You make your own plans and then ask God to bless them instead of asking God what He wants. In a lonely "night" experience He gets your complete attention. Perhaps your prayer has been, "Lord, change the other person" when you need to pray, "Lord change me."

Are you willing to let God break you? Only in your weakness can you be strong. Your strength will then be His strength. God says, "My power shows up best in weak people." To that Paul replied, "Now I am glad to boast about how weak I am; I am glad to be a living demonstration of Christ's power, instead of showing off my own power and abilities" (2 Cor. 12:9 LB).

May we be willing to be broken.

JULY 3

"Don't be afraid," the prophet answered. "Those who are with us are more than those who are with them" (2 Kings 6:16 NIV).

 he king of Syria was waging war on Israel, but his secret plans of attack were leaking out to the enemy. God was revealing them to Elisha. The king's schemes were nothing against a man who had an open line of communication to God.

When the king learned what was happening, he sent his army to capture Elisha. As Elisha's servant went outside one morning, he saw the king's army surrounding their city. Filled with fear, he rushed back into the house, crying, "Oh, my lord, what shall we do?" (v. 15 NIV). What could the two of them do against an entire army? There was no way out.

Elisha prayed and asked God to open the eyes of the servant. When God opened the servant's spiritual eyes, he could see what his physical eyes could not. "Behold, the mountain was full of horses and chariots of fire round about Elisha" (v. 17). God had put an invisible host around them for protection.

Elisha walked by faith. He trusted God. He knew that all the reinforcements of heaven stand ready to protect those who are committed to His care.

Today you may be in the midst of a heated battle with no way out. You, too, confess that you are frightened. But God says, "Don't be afraid . . . those who are with us are more than those who are with them." God has conscripted the army of heaven to move into your battle zone to fight for you. As you turn your physical eyes away from the conflict and look through your spiritual eyes, you can see His battle-ready troops. "For he shall give his angels charge over thee, to keep thee in all thy ways (Ps. 91:11).

You need not feel guilty about your fear. It is a natural reaction. Looking through our physical eyes fills our hearts with fear. But what do you do with your fear? The psalmist said, "What time I am afraid, I will trust in thee" (Ps. 56:3).

God encourages us, "Be strong and courageous; be not afraid nor dismayed . . . with us is the LORD our God to help us and to fight our battles" (2 Chron. 32:7–8).

Today are you looking at the battle with your physical eyes or your spiritual eyes?

JULY 4

Daniel determined in his heart that he would not defile himself by [eating his portion of] the king's rich and dainty food or with the wine which he drank (Dan. 1:8 AMPLIFIED).

hen Daniel was a teenager, King Nebuchadnezzar besieged Jerusalem. Daniel and three of his friends were taken to Babylon as hostages. They, along with other young men, were selected to serve the king. During the three-year training course, they were to be fed from the king's table and drink his wine.

Daniel had a choice. It would have been easy to conform to the customs of this new land. But Daniel knew the food and wine had been offered to the Babylonian gods first, and he couldn't partake of them. God had said that they must not put any other gods before Him. Daniel had two choices. He could compromise, or he could stand true to God. But having lived his life in obedience to God's Word, Daniel knew he could not compromise. He would let nothing hinder his relationship with God.

Purposing in his heart to stand true to God and His principles, Daniel asked permission for his friends and him to be put on a special diet. God rewarded them for their loyalty. At the end of ten days, their appearance surpassed that of the other young men. God honored them, giving them favor with the king.

I remember a time when my husband and I had to make a choice. My husband had started working for a new company. The annual company picnic was to be on Sunday, starting about the time of our church service.

What should we do? It was our habit to attend church. We did not want to offend the owner and his wife. They were friends and members of our church. Yet we knew that we must not compromise our loyalty to God. After praying about it, we decided to go to church first then go to the picnic. When we arrived, the owner's wife said, "You went to church, didn't you?" "Yes," we replied. Then she said, "We shouldn't have this picnic at a time that might keep anyone from church." The next year the picnic was scheduled for a Saturday. God had honored our choice.

Are you determined to live a life pleasing to God? On what principles do you make your choices? Principles from God's Word or from the world? The Lord says, "Them that honour me, I will honour" (1 Sam. 2:30).

When Daniel learned that the decree had been published, he went home to his upstairs room where the windows opened toward Jerusalem. Three times a day he got down on his knees and prayed, giving thanks to his God, just as he had done before (Dan. 6:10 NIV).

D aniel was a man of great influence in Babylon. But trouble began when the king decided to appoint him to a top leadership position.

Other officials in the kingdom became jealous and looked for ways to depose him. However, they could find no fault with him, nothing about which they could complain to the king. What a testimony Daniel had!

They soon realized that if they brought any charge against him, it would have to be something related to his faith in God. So they asked the king to sign a decree that no one could ask a request of any god or man except the king for thirty days. The penalty? Being cast into a den of lions. The king signed the law, not realizing what was behind it.

How would Daniel react? Early in his life, he had purposed to be loyal to God. He had become a man of prayer, a man who walked with God. Habitually, he would go to his place of prayer, next to his open window facing Jerusalem, looking toward the Temple in his homeland. His soul was open to God. Three times a day he knelt there, talking to God.

Prayer was not an emergency measure. It was an expression of his faith. His life, a consistent life of prayer, would not change now.

How effective and consistent is your prayer life? Is your prayer window open to God? Is it in regular use? Sometimes the winds of adversity, busyness, ambition, or personal desires may blow our prayer window shut. Do not let it remain closed.

An effective, consistent prayer life is costly. It costs time, strength, love, and tears. But the cost of neglecting prayer is far greater. David promised God, "My voice shalt thou hear in the morning, O LORD; in the morning will I direct my prayer unto thee, and will look up" (Ps. 5:3).

"O Daniel, servant of the Living God, was your God, whom you worship continually, able to deliver you from the lions?"
(Dan. 6:20 LB).

O ccasionally, God gives an examination to test our commitment to Him. This was happening to Daniel. He was facing another test. How would he pass it?

Daniel had no choice. He would not compromise his faith in God. The king had signed a decree that for thirty days no one could pray to anyone except the king. But Daniel continued his regular habit of praying three times a day.

The king had no choice, either. He was upset when he learned the underlying motive of the law. Being very close to Daniel, he spent most of the day trying to revoke the law but was unsuccessful. The king knew the power of Daniel's God. He said, "May your God, whom you worship continually, deliver you" (v. 16 LB). Then Daniel was thrown into the den of lions.

That night, Daniel was aware of the presence of a God more powerful than a den of lions. He trusted God, knowing that not one lion could touch him unless God permitted it. How his heart must have filled with praise as the angel of the Lord shut the lions' mouths.

Early the next morning, the king hurried to the den and called to Daniel. Would he answer? Was he alive? To the king's joy, Daniel called back, "My God has sent his angel . . . to shut the lions' mouths so that they can't touch me" (v. 22 LB).

God had delivered him. Why? Because he believed God (v. 23 LB). God honored his faith.

Daniel's life had a great effect upon the king. He saw God do the impossible—deliver a man from a den of lions. As a result, the king sent a proclamation throughout the land, "that everyone shall tremble and fear before the God of Daniel in every part of my kingdom. For his God is the living, unchanging God whose kingdom shall never be destroyed and whose power shall never end" (v. 25 LB). Daniel proved to a pagan world that the living God is a strong deliverer.

As we walk with God, people are watching our lives. Many will only know the God they see living in us. You can influence your world for God. Chuck Colson once said, "Do not limit what God can do through one person totally committed to Jesus Christ."

JULY 7

And let them be for lights in the firmament of the heaven to give light upon the earth: and it was so (Gen. 1:15).

t the time of creation, God said, "Let there be lights in the firmament of the heaven to divide the day from the night" (v. 14). He continued, "And let them be for lights in the firmament of the heaven to give light upon the earth: and it was so" (v. 15).

Centuries later, Jesus said, "I am the light of the world: he that followeth me shall not walk in darkness, but shall have the light of life" (John 8:12).

One day Jesus said to His disciples, "Ye are the light of the world. A city that is set on an hill cannot be hid" (Matt. 5:14).

I recall the beauty of the sanctuary of a large city church I used to attend. The loveliness was enhanced by beautiful stained glass windows. As the last rays of the late afternoon sun streamed in through the windows, they took on the colors of the rainbow—reds, blues, and yellows radiating a special splendor. Just as the windows reflected the beauty of the sun, we are to reflect the beauty of the Light of the World, Jesus Christ, through the windows of our lives.

God placed the lights in the firmament to give light upon the earth. We, too, have been placed in a darkened world of sin to shine for Him.

A doctor received a call one night to visit a very sick child who lived in the country. It was a dark, snowy night and the roads were slippery. The doctor telephoned the first farmer along the road, asking him to put a light out so he could see it. He was to call the next farmer and so on until each farmer had a light outside to guide the doctor on his way. The doctor drove through the snow, with a light always ahead to guide him. Each farmer had a part in saving that child's life.

Are you a light for Christ in today's dark world, guiding someone to Him? God will place us where we can shine. It may not be the place of our choosing, but it will be His. God's part is to place us where He wants us; our part is to shine. The Bible says, "Now are ye light in the Lord: walk as children of light" (Eph. 5:8).

JULY 8

Cast thy burden upon the Lord, and he shall sustain thee: he shall never suffer the righteous to be moved (Ps. 55:22).

avid was experiencing despair. Friends had failed him. Family had rejected him. He said, "Oh that I had wings like a dove! for then would I fly away, and be at rest" (v. 6). He felt that if he could just get away from his trouble he would find a place of quiet and peace. "I would hasten my escape from the windy storm and tempest" (v. 8).

However, he recognized that his answer would come from God, not just a quiet place. He said, "I will call upon God; and the Lord shall save me. Evening, and morning, and at noon, will I pray, and cry aloud: and he shall hear my voice" (vv. 16–17). Prayer put him in touch with God, Who had the answer.

Can you identify with David? How often have you said, "If only I could get away from it all"? But that isn't our answer. The answer is, "Cast your burden on the Lord [releasing the weight of it] and He will sustain you" (AMPLIFIED). Too often we try to carry our burdens ourselves. We add today's burdens to yesterday's and then tomorrow's load. The weight is almost too much. We feel crushed beneath them.

Instead of carrying them, we are to cast them on Him. In the Hebrew, the word for *burden* has the meaning of *a portion assigned to them*. We are to cast back on Him that which He has placed on us. "Casting all your care on him; for he careth for you" (1 Peter 5:7).

The Lord Jesus understands what it means to carry burdens, for He carried a burden greater than we could possibly comprehend. He endured the punishment for all the sins of the world. Now our great Burden Bearer wants to carry the burden of our cares, and He doesn't impose a weight limit.

Are you overburdened today? The Lord Jesus says, "Come to Me, all you who labor and are heavy-laden and overburdened, and I will cause you to rest—I will ease and relieve and refresh your souls" (Matt. 11:28 AMPLIFIED).

Don't hold back one burden. Cast every one on Him. He is willing and able to bear them all.

His invitation is personal: Cast *your* burdens upon Me and I will sustain *you.*

My prayer for you is that you will overflow more and more with love for others, and at the same time keep on growing in spiritual knowledge and insight (Phil. 1:9 LB).

 couple was ecstatic when they learned that a little girl was available for adoption. They redecorated a room to be hers and furnished it with everything she could want. They bought toys and filled her closet with clothes.

When they went to pick her up, they opened their arms wide and said to her, "You are our own little girl now. You are coming home with us." They told her about everything waiting for her at home. The little girl didn't seem very excited, so they said, "Is there something else you want?" She said, "All I want is someone to love me."

The world is filled with people who want someone to love them. Paul prayed that the Philippians would be characterized by a love that overflowed to others.

The love Paul wrote about is God's love. "For God is love" (1 John 4:8). It is *agape* —love that is the very nature of God. It is a giving love. God demonstrated His love when He gave His Son. "For God so loved the world, that he *gave* his only begotten Son, that whosoever believeth in him should not perish, but have everlasting life" (John 3:16, emphasis mine).

God depends on His children to channel His love to others. Paul prayed that the Philippians' love would grow and keep on growing until it overflowed into other lives. In effect he was praying that they would love like God loves.

We are living in a hurting world today. What a ministry we can have to those who are lonely, who feel neglected, who are begging for someone to love them. *Agape* reaches out to include everyone. God can love even the unlovely through you if you'll let Him.

There are people who have everything they could ask for materially, but they desperately need someone to love them. Some build around themselves walls of self-pity and bitterness. Yet, behind these self-imposed walls, they are still reaching out for love.

God gives us the privilege of sharing *agape*, the love of God overflowing from our lives into theirs.

"The Lord make you to increase and abound in love one toward another, and toward all men" (1 Thess. 3:12).

JULY 10

And this is my prayer: that your love may abound more and more in knowledge and depth of insight, so that you may be able to discern what is best and may be pure and blameless until the day of Christ (Phil. 1:9–10 NIV).

ove is one of the most convincing expressions of the reality of the Christian faith. Jesus said, "Your strong love for each other will prove to the world that you are my disciples" (John 13:35 LB).

When you invite Jesus Christ into your heart, the Holy Spirit implants God's love there. This seed of divine love begins to grow as it is nourished by the Word of God. "As newborn babes, desire the sincere milk of the word, that ye may grow thereby" (1 Peter 2:2).

Paul prayed that the Philippians might mature in their Christian walk. He prayed that they would not only be filled to overflowing with love but that it would be a discerning love.

Through the Word of God, we develop a deep-rooted knowledge of God and His love. Then we need insight to apply this knowledge to our life situations. Discerning love is sensitive to God and to others. It responds to others with God's love.

Paul prayed that they might mature in discernment in order to choose what is God's best. "So that you may surely learn to sense what is vital, and approve and prize what is excellent and of real value" (v. 10 AMPLIFIED). So much emphasis is put on materialism today that we need discernment to choose that which has eternal value. Controlled by His love, we will do what is vital and important.

Discerning love results in a pure and blameless life. The word *pure* is sometimes translated, *sincere,* without impurity. It comes from a word meaning *without wax.* In Paul's day, when some merchants found cracks in the pottery they were to sell, they filled the cracks with wax to cover the imperfections. The pottery could be tested by holding it up to the sun to see if it was filled with wax. Honest merchants would advertise their flawless pottery with a sign saying, Without Wax.

Are our lives pure and blameless? Are they free from imperfections? Could God put a without-wax sign over our lives, indicating that they are pure and sincere?

May our lives produce the character qualities that will attract others to the Christ they see in us. Such lives bring glory to God.

*Do not store up for yourselves treasures on earth, where moth and
rust destroy, and where thieves break in and steal. But store up
for yourselves treasures in heaven, where moth and rust do
not destroy, and where thieves do not break in and steal (Matt.
6:19–20 NIV).*

hat is your dearest treasure? What means everything to you?
Jesus commands us to store treasures in heaven, not on earth.
He is not talking about acquiring treasures but where we
store them. There is nothing wrong necessarily with possessing
treasures, but it is wrong to let them possess you.

Treasures stored on earth are not secure. They can be destroyed by moths
and rust or stolen by thieves. Earthly treasures are never beyond the risk of loss.

Treasures laid up in heaven are never lost. As we invest our lives for God,
we are storing up treasures in heaven. Heavenly treasures include such things as
making a phone call or writing a letter of encouragement, strengthening one
another, visiting the sick, sharing Jesus Christ with someone, praying for others,
giving financially to God's work. How sad to invest our lives in things that only
last during our lifetime. Deposits we make in heaven draw large dividends.

In Luke 12:15, we read, "A man's life consisteth not in the abundance
of the things which he possesseth." While a clergyman was visiting a very
wealthy man, the man took him outside to view his land. He nodded in one
direction. "All of those oil wells are mine," he said. In the opposite direction,
he indicated the vast fields of grain that were his. In another direction he pointed
to all of his cattle grazing. In the last direction he showed the forests that
belonged to him. "I came here penniless," he said, "and now see how rich I
am." The clergyman stood quietly for a moment and then pointed upward.
"How much do you own up there?"

Jesus said, "Where your treasure is, there will your heart be also" (Matt.
6:21). If your treasure is in heaven, that is where your heart will be. Before
missionary Jim Elliott was martyred, he said, "He is no fool who gives what he
cannot keep to gain what he cannot lose."

If you lost everything and only had Jesus left, would you be satisfied?
Would I? I have pondered that question, and I believe I can honestly say that
Jesus satisfies me completely. He is my dearest treasure on earth and will be my
dearest treasure someday in heaven. I have found Him to be not only real but
adequate.

JULY 12

And after you have suffered a little while, the God of all grace—
Who imparts all blessing and favor—Who has called you to His
[own] eternal glory in Christ Jesus, will Himself complete and make
you what you ought to be, establish you and ground you securely,
and strengthen (and settle) you (1 Peter 5:10 AMPLIFIED).

We are living in a trouble-filled world. Most people are experiencing problems that seem insurmountable. They are being tried almost to the limit of endurance.

We need not be surprised when suffering comes. It is inevitable. But in our trouble we have a source of help—the God of all grace. "Let us therefore come boldly unto the throne of grace, that we may obtain mercy, and find grace to help in time of need" (Heb. 4:16). Suffering is part of the process of maturing.

God uses suffering to **perfect** us. The word used here means adjusting and restoring or mending, as mending of nets. It is God Himself who does this mending in our lives. He wants to complete us, making us what we ought to be in Christ Jesus.

God will **establish** us through suffering. He gives us the firmness to stand unshaken in our faith. "For we have become fellows with Christ, the Messiah, and share in all He has for us, if only we hold our first newborn confidence and original assured expectation [in virtue of which we are believers] firm and unshaken to the end" (Heb. 3:14 AMPLIFIED). Rains may beat upon us, the winds of adversity may blow against us, but nothing can move us.

He will **strengthen** us in suffering. "The LORD is the strength of my life" (Ps. 27:1). He **settles** us on the firm foundation of Jesus Christ. We can stand firm in our faith. Job, a model of suffering, learned through his suffering the adequacy of God in his life. He said, "Though he slay me, yet will I trust in him" (Job 13:15).

It has been said that the old Damascus blade was so tempered by heating, cooling, and hammering that it would not break even if the point were bent back to the hilt. God uses suffering to temper our lives, to perfect and strengthen us so that we will not break under the pressures and tensions of our lives. In our suffering we discover the inexhaustible sufficiency of God.

*Remember how the LORD your God led you all the way in the desert
. . . to humble you and to test you in order to know what was in
your heart, whether or not you would keep his commands (Deut.
8:2 NIV).*

od doesn't waste time. He uses the experiences in our lives to mature us, to make us the people He wants us to be. Often our problem is that we want maturity today. We don't want to wait for the process.

As the children of Israel were coming to the end of their wilderness journey, Moses called them together for a time of retrospection. During their travels, the Israelites had murmured and complained as they faced the vicissitudes of the desert. They rebelled against God's leading, yet He did not forsake them. He led them all the way. Someone has said, "If we cannot see the wisdom of His hand in our affliction, we can trust the love of His heart."

Perhaps you are in a desert experience today. God, in His loving patience, is working His plan in your life. You may not understand, but He knows His purpose.

God had to empty the Israelites of their pride and self-sufficiency so that they would recognize their dependence on Him. In our desert, God often takes away our human resources to teach us to draw upon His All-sufficiency. The Bible says, "Not that we are in any way confident of our own resources—our ability comes from God" (2 Cor. 3:5 PHILLIPS). Our attitude of pride must be changed into humility.

Moses reminded the Israelites that God knew what was in their hearts—the murmurings, complaining, and criticalness. Sometimes we, too, forget that "the LORD looketh on the heart" (1 Sam. 16:7). God sees such sins as anger, bitterness, jealousy, and criticalness, and He brings them to light so that we might confess them, asking for cleansing and forgiveness.

God tested the Israelites to see if they would keep His commandments. Do you check His Word to see if you are obedient? The Bible says, "Man shall not live by bread alone, but by every word that proceedeth out of the mouth of God" (Matt. 4:4).

You may not understand your desert experience. But God won't waste it. Look for the lessons He wants you to learn. He will use them in your maturing process. "I am confident of this very thing, that He who began a good work in you will perfect it until the day of Christ Jesus" (Phil. 1:6 NASB).

JULY 14

And Noah builded an altar unto the Lord (Gen. 8:20).

he flood had ceased! The earth had dried up! In God's perfect timing he ordered Noah and his family to come out of the safety of the ark. What must Noah have felt as he looked at the devastation all around him? They had no food. They had no home. He would have to rebuild and replenish the earth. What a gigantic undertaking. Where should he begin?

Noah knew. There was no question in his mind. Noah had a close relationship with God. In Genesis 6:9 we read that "Noah walked with God." As he looked about, he could have thought, "The first thing we must do is rebuild. Then we will take time to praise and worship God." But not Noah. As he realized anew what God had spared them from, his heart was filled with love and worship. The first thing he did was to build an altar. There he offered a sacrifice of praise and worship to God.

What about your life and mine? Does worship have first place in our lives, or do we only give God the time left over? Someone has said, "God doesn't want our spare time but our precious time."

John 12:2-3 gives another example of worship. "They made [Jesus] a supper; and Martha served: but Lazarus was one of them that sat at the table with him. Then took Mary a pound of ointment of spikenard, very costly, and anointed the feet of Jesus, and wiped his feet with her hair: and the house was filled with the odour of the ointment."

Here we see three phases of Christian life: Martha's service, Lazarus's fellowship, and Mary's worship. All three are important, but only three words tell of Martha's service; thirteen words describe Lazarus' fellowship, and thirty-five words portray Mary's worship. Does this not indicate the place worship should have in our lives?

"Let us worship and bow down: let us kneel before the Lord our maker" (Ps. 95:6). "Exalt ye the Lord our God, and worship at his footstool; for he is holy" (Ps. 99:5). "Give unto the Lord the glory due unto his name; worship the Lord in the beauty of holiness" (Ps. 29:2).

Take time today to meditate on these Scriptures and let worship have priority in your life as it did in Noah's. Ask God to show you what worship means and then prepare your heart to experience the delight that comes in worshiping Him.

No one will be able to stand up against you all the days of your life. As I was with Moses, so I will be with you; I will never leave you nor forsake you (Josh. 1:5 NIV).

oshua had been challenged! His challenger, God! God commissioned him to lead the children of Israel into the Promised Land. Joshua had been chosen to assume the responsibility of leadership in the place of Moses, one of the greatest leaders of all time. Joshua received his marching orders from God. "Arise, go over this Jordan, thou, and all this people, unto the land which I do give to them, even to the children of Israel" (v. 2).

Joshua knew that the task was beyond his natural ability. He realized the seriousness of being their leader. Fear gripped his heart. How could he handle such a responsibility? It seemed an insurmountable task. The Jordan River was at flood stage. He had been in the land before to survey it and knew the strength of the enemy. But he could move forward, standing firm on God's promise, "As I was with Moses, so I will be with thee" (v. 5).

Understanding Joshua's feelings of fear and inadequacy, God said, "Be strong and courageous, because you will lead these people to inherit the land I swore to their forefathers to give them" (v. 6 NIV). Having God with him, Joshua was a majority.

Courage is firmly facing difficulties and obstacles, knowing God has promised to be with you. Joshua could move into the land with strength and courage, focusing not on the obstacles but on God, who is completely trustworthy.

God may have placed you in a place of leadership or responsibility as a parent, in your church, in business, or in school. You may be fearful, but your feeling of inadequacy may be your greatest strength. You will have to depend on the Lord. You, too, can stand firm on God's promise, "As I was with Moses, so I will be with you." God won't ask you to do anything he can't do. "Faithful is he that calleth you, who also will do it" (1 Thess. 5:24).

Your seeming inability will not hinder Him. All He wants is your availability.

JULY 16

You need only to be strong and courageous, and to obey . . . every law Moses gave you, for if you are careful to obey every one of them you will be successful (Josh. 1:7 LB).

he children of Israel were ready to move in and possess the Promised Land. They had wandered long enough and were ready to settle down and live a life of peace and rest in the land. But, before they could do that, the enemy must be subdued. The giants in the land must be conquered.

For the second time, God told Joshua, "Be strong and courageous." God knew there would be times when he wouldn't understand what was happening. There would be times when he would have to stand alone.

God gave him a key to success—obedience. Joshua's life must be regulated by God's Word. His success would come as he consistently walked in obedience to God. He must not turn to the right or to the left. The walk that pleases God is the walk of obedience.

Joshua moved forward with the assurance that as he faithfully adhered to God's Word, they could conquer the enemy and possess the land. God has given us, too, a land to possess—a life of victory in Christ Jesus. It is a life that gives joy instead of sorrow, peace instead of anxiety, quietness instead of frustration, strength instead of weakness.

Victory in Christ is our promised possession, but we have to possess it. It has to *become* ours. Our key to success, also, is obedience to God's Word. The Bible tells us how to develop a spiritually successful life in Christ. It gives us the ability to make wise decisions for every situation we face in life.

Sometimes, we take a casual attitude toward His commands. We only obey the ones we want to. One year, I read the Bible through, hunting for all the commands that pertained to me and rating my obedience to them. It was not my most pleasant year. How well do you obey His commands?

Living in obedience to His Word will affect all our activities. "That thou mayest observe to do according to all that is written therein" (v. 8). Our actions in our home, neighborhood, work, and community will all be governed by God's principles.

Let us be strong and courageous and obedient.

JULY 17

This book of the law shall not depart out of thy mouth; but thou shalt meditate therein day and night, that thou mayest observe to do according to all that is written therein: for then thou shalt make thy way prosperous, and then thou shalt have good success (Josh. 1:8).

od is always a God of encouragement and reassurance. He promised Joshua success on his mission, but this promise was conditional on obedience to the Word of God.

In order to obey God's Word, Joshua had to know it and meditate on it. Meditation on God's Word is important in attaining success in whatever God calls us to do. Joshua's conversation was to be filled with the Word of God. "Constantly remind the people about these laws, and you yourself must think about them every day and every night so that you will be sure to obey all of them. For only then will you succeed" (v. 8 LB).

God was reminding Joshua that meditating on God's Word would give him God's direction in successfully leading the people into the land.

There is a life of rest in Christ for you and me to enter into also. "Let us then be eager to know this rest for ourselves" (Heb. 4:11 PHILLIPS). God gives us the same formula for achieving this spiritual rest—walking in obedience to God's Word. In order to obey God's Word, we must not only read it but meditate upon it.

Through meditation, the words we read in Scripture become spiritual food for our souls. We reflect and ponder on God's truths until they become established in our hearts and minds. We are then led from meditating on His Word to meditating on God Himself. "My meditation of him shall be sweet" (Ps. 104:34).

As we reflect on God's Word, we will become more acquainted with His mind and His will. The more we fill our minds with His Word, the more we will begin to think His thoughts. God's truths take root and grow in our lives, keeping us spiritually alive and fresh and eager to be obedient.

Are you taking time to meditate on God and His Word? We will never attain spiritual maturity without it. Jeremiah wrote, "Thy words were found, and I did eat them; and thy word was unto me the joy and rejoicing of mine heart: for I am called by thy name, O LORD God of hosts" (Jer. 15:16).

It has been said that we only know as much Scripture as we put into practice.

JULY 18

Have not I commanded thee? Be strong and of a good courage; be not afraid, neither be thou dismayed: for the LORD thy God is with thee whithersoever thou goest (Josh. 1:9).

e strong and courageous! This is the third reminder God has given Joshua. This time Joshua is assured of the presence of the Promiser Himself. "The LORD thy God is with thee whithersoever thou goest." The Lord would be his constant Companion.

More important than Joshua's campaign plans was God's presence. God was real to Joshua. He knew that since the Lord had promised to be with him, he had nothing to fear. He and the Living God could do it together. Psalm 32:8 gives this encouraging promise of God's guidance. "I will instruct thee and teach thee in the way which thou shalt go: I will guide thee with mine eye." This is what God promised to do for Joshua—and for us.

God has promised us a life of victory and rest—not a passive life but a life of confidently moving forward, daily resting in the Lord whatever our experiences. You may be saying, "Life is not like that for me. It is filled with disappointments, hurts, and loneliness. Where is my victory? Where is my rest?"

Our victory and rest is in Jesus Christ. "Thanks be unto God, which giveth us the victory through our Lord Jesus Christ" (1 Cor. 15:57). He reveals Himself and what He can do for us in His Word.

We can stand firm not just on His promise but on the Promiser. The Bible says, "Yes, be bold and strong! Banish fear and doubt! For remember, the Lord your God is with you wherever you go" (Josh. 1:9 LB).

There is a painting that depicts a ship being tossed about by a tempestuous sea. It appears that the crew will be unable to weather the storm. Close by is a larger ship riding the turbulent waves. Its mast is flying a number of signal flags, conveying the message: I will not abandon you.

Perhaps today you wonder if your Heavenly Father has abandoned you. The storm is raging and you are almost sinking. For you, today, God flies His signal flags with the message, "I will not abandon you."

Jesus promised, "Lo, I am with you alway, even unto the end of the world. Amen" (Matt. 28:20).

JULY 19

*Let the beauty of the LORD our God be upon us: and establish thou
the work of our hands upon us; yea, the work of our hands establish
thou it (Ps. 90:17)*

 ne day, with great excitement, I learned that the daughter of a
friend was to compete in the Miss America Pageant. Years
before, my friend had given me her daughter's picture and asked
me to pray for her. I had been faithfully praying for her, and as
we watched the final competition, how excited we were when she won the title.

This beautiful young woman has a warm personality, but more
importantly, she has the inner beauty of a personal relationship with Jesus
Christ. Her heart's desire is to radiate the person of Christ wherever she goes.
The beauty of the life and character of our Lord is certainly upon her. In Psalm
96:9 we read, "O worship the LORD in the beauty of holiness." *Holiness*
means separation. Wearing the beauty of the holiness of the Lord requires
separation from those things that are unlike God.

Paul often speaks of putting on the things that are like Jesus and putting off
the things that are unlike Him. He wrote, "Put them all aside: anger, wrath,
malice, slander, and abusive speech from your mouth. Do not lie to one
another, since you laid aside the old self with its evil practices, and have put on
the new self who is being renewed to a true knowledge according to the image
of the One who created him" (Col. 3:8—10 NASB).

It is so easy to set our own standards, thinking that our actions determine
our inner beauty. But our attitudes, motives, priorities, and reactions can hinder
the beauty of His holiness from shining forth.

Who ever heard of the beauty of a bad temper or gossip? Is there beauty
in jealousy, criticism or resentment?

Are the words we speak the words of a holy life? We sing, "Let the
Beauty of Jesus Be Seen in Me." But do we reflect His inner beauty wherever
we go, whatever we do or say? Someone has said that we can only radiate
what is inside.

After the Earl of Chesterton met Fenelon, Archbishop of Cambrai, he said,
"If I stayed another day in his presence, I would have had to become a
Christian, his spirit was so pure, so attractive, so beautiful." Could that be said
of us?

Men ought always to pray, and not to faint (Luke 18:1).

rayer is the most vital part of a Christian's life and ministry. God says we ought to pray. Prayer prepares us for our work. Prayer is our work. We must keep our communication lines with God strong. This means we must know well the One to whom we pray, who He is, and what He can do for us. The Bible says, "Be still, and know that I am God" (Ps. 46:10). The better we know Him, the stronger will be our faith.

Another version emphasizes persevering in prayer: Jesus told his disciples a parable to show them that "they should always pray and not give up" (NIV). Prayer should be a habit.

Rubenstein, the great musician, once said, "If I omit practice one day, I notice it; if two days, my friends notice it; if three days, the public notices it." Usually prayer needs more practice than proof.

We are to pray always at all times, under all circumstances, in our prosperity, and in our adversity. We are not only to pray in our regular quiet time but all during the day—when driving our car, making beds, jogging, as often as possible throughout the day.

But our enemy hates a strong prayer life in Christians. His most effective tool against us is discouragement. God reminds us of this and counters with His own word of encouragement: We are "not to faint." Phillips paraphrases it "never to lose heart."

We must not give up praying. "Continue in prayer, and watch in the same with thanksgiving" (Col. 4:2). We may be weary while praying but not of praying. "Be earnest and unwearied . . . in your prayer [life], being [both] alert and intent in [your praying] with thanksgiving" (AMPLIFIED).

In a gospel meeting in the western United States, an elderly man was converted. Another elderly man stepped forward, and with tears in his eyes, related that fifty years before, a group of twenty-five young people (of which he was one) had agreed to pray for this man every day until he became a Christian. He said, "I am the only one of the twenty-five still living to see our prayers answered."

We are to continue to pray and not become discouraged. As long as there are people who do not know Jesus as Saviour, we must keep on praying.

Do not be anxious for your life, as to what you shall eat, or what you shall drink; nor for your body, as to what you shall put on. Is not life more than food, and the body more than clothing? (Matt. 6:25 NASB).

n our age of anxiety it is easy to become so caught up in the pressures of providing our material needs that we become anxious and worried. Worry is more than concern. It has been said that "worry is the interest we pay on trouble before it comes due."

This verse does not mean we should neglect our basic needs. But the problem comes when we become so involved in accumulating material things that stress and tension develop.

Jesus was talking about the futility of anxiety over what we eat, drink, or wear. When we worry, we are not trusting God to take care of us.

Jesus used the illustration of birds and lilies. "Look at the birds of the air; they do not sow or reap or store away in barns, and yet your heavenly Father feeds them. Are you not much more valuable than they?" (v. 26 NIV). Birds are not idle. They forage for food, yet they are not anxious.

Since God created you in His image, you are special to Him. If Jesus was willing to die on the cross for your sin, doesn't that mean you have great worth? Through faith we can trust God with the everyday affairs of life, as well.

Jesus also called attention to the lilies. "And why do you worry about clothes? See how the lilies of the field grow. They do not labor or spin (v. 28 NIV). They grow where they are placed. They do not strive to provide for themselves.

Jesus said, "If that is how God clothes the grass of the field, which is here today and tomorrow is thrown into the fire, will he not much more clothe you, O you of little faith?" (v. 30 NIV).

The life of faith is free from anxiety. Our faith gives us confidence that God will take care of us. The cure for anxiety is trust in the Lord. "You can throw the whole weight of your anxieties upon him, for you are his personal concern" (1 Peter 5:7 PHILLIPS).

You are in the hands of the Living God. Your part is to give Him your anxieties; His part is to give you His peace.

JULY 22

But seek ye first the kingdom of God, and his righteousness; and all these things shall be added unto you (Matt. 6:33).

hortly after I became a Christian, I was told I should make a priority list. I struggled over it. I knew the Lord should be at the top. My family and church should be next. But in what order should everything else come. Finally, I realized I was to put Christ as the center of my life instead of at the top of a list. Then I fitted every area of my life around Him.

The Lord removed some areas from my life but added others. Some areas decreased, others increased. With Him at the center, He is in touch with every area, controlling everything.

Sports have always had a special place in my life. I am glad He is in control of that area, for I might let it get out of balance. Not long ago he removed another area from my life. There was nothing wrong with it, but He said it was time for it to go.

Jesus was talking about priorities when He said, "But seek ye first. . . ." Seeking is a continuing action. The continuing priority of our lives should be God's kingdom and His righteousness. It must be put above and before everything else. All the other things are to be added—they are not to be first.

I have a friend whose husband was sales manager of a large firm. During the year, he would bring all of his salesmen in for a meeting, and there would be several social events as well. As my friend went with her husband, she prayed for opportunities to further God's kingdom and righteousness.

The salesmen and their wives were aware that there was something different about her. Often they would confide their hurts and problems, and she would share her answer to life. Many of them came to a personal relationship with Christ because the Lord was the priority of her life.

With Him ruling over His kingdom, everything we do, every place we go, every decision, habit, and pleasure is to be under His direction. Is He first in your life? Are you seeking continually for opportunities to share His kingdom and His righteousness "that in all things he might have the preeminence"? (Col. 1:18).

JULY 23

So don't be anxious about tomorrow. God will take care of your tomorrow too. Live one day at a time (Matt. 6:34 LB).

omeone has said, "What I have to do tomorrow has made a wreck of me today." After talking to His disciples about living free from anxiety, Jesus gave a prescription for such a worry-free life. If we make God's kingdom and His righteousness our priority, we can be free from anxiety, for we can trust God to provide all of our needs. He assumes this responsibility for us.

Our trust in Him is a moment-by-moment trust. Yesterday is gone, never to return. We are to forget its care, sorrow, and mistakes. It is in God's hands. Tomorrow is also in God's hands, so we are not to be anxious about tomorrow's problems, heartaches, and frustrations, either.

Today is the only time we have, so "live one day at a time." All of the tomorrows of our lives pass by God before they can reach us. Our problem is that we add all of tomorrow's cares onto today's load, and it is more than God intended us to carry. Each day is one for us to use or lose.

God doesn't provide our needs ahead of time but meets today's needs today. Jesus told us to pray, "Give us this day our daily bread" (Matt. 6:11). When His kingdom is a priority in our lives, we can trust God to provide our needs day by day.

When God sent manna as food for the Israelites on their journey through the wilderness, they were to gather it fresh each morning, just enough for that day. In the same way, we are to feed on God's Word and spend time in prayer daily. "Each morning I will look to you in heaven and lay my requests before you, praying earnestly" (Ps. 5:3 LB).

We must learn to live one day at a time. As we do, we discover His grace is sufficient for that day. "As thy days, so shall thy strength be" (Deut. 33:25).

The antidote for fear is faith; the cure for anxiety is trust in the Lord.

Behold, I am with thee, and will keep thee in all places whither thou goest, and will bring thee again into this land; for I will not leave thee, until I have done that which I have spoken to thee of (Gen. 28:15).

acob's name means schemer, and he lived up to his name. He worked to get what he wanted by trickery.

As a result of his own scheming against his brother Esau, he had to flee from home. As he plodded along, alone for the first time in his life, he was lonely and weary. With an open field as his bed and a stone for his pillow, soon he was fast asleep.

That night, Jacob had an unusual experience with God. In a dream, he saw a ladder stretching from heaven to earth, with a procession of angels descending and ascending. The ladder stretched right down to the fugitive Jacob, and right up to God. It was God's communication system between Himself and Jacob.

At the top of the ladder stood the Lord, saying, "I am with you and will watch over you wherever you go" (v. 15 NIV). God had not cast Jacob off, schemer though he was.

When Jacob awakened out of his sleep he was aware that even in that lonely place, God was with him. Far from home and family, God's presence was with him. He said, "Surely the LORD is in this place, and I was not aware of it" (v. 16 NIV).

God draws close to us in our troubled times, our dark nights alone—our heartache, discouragement, loneliness, or failure. Sometimes our vision becomes so clouded with our difficulties that we lose sight of God. We think if we were in a different place or circumstance, our problems would be solved. Yet the Lord is with us wherever we are, whatever our situation. There is no place where we can go that He is not already there. He reminds us, "I am with thee in this place."

He also promises us His protection, "I will keep thee." We need not worry when His presence is with us. He assures us that He will never leave us. "Lo, I am with you alway, even unto the end of the world. Amen." (Matt. 28:20).

We can relax and rest in the assurance of His unfailing presence during the night times of our lives. He transforms this place of ours from the ordinary into the extraordinary. Someone has said, "The greatest sorrows and afflictions may become the gateway to fresh revelations of God."

JULY 25

I am the vine, ye are the branches (John 15:5).

hen Jesus wanted to teach the importance of His relationship with believers, He used the illustration of the vine and the branches. Jesus said, "I am the vine, ye are the branches." The word used for *I* is *ego*, and it is an emphatic word. "I am the True Vine. No one else is." He is the genuine vine. He is real. As the vine is the source of life for the branch, so is Christ the Source of our spiritual life.

The vine and branches together make one fruit-bearing system. God's fruit is not borne on the vine but on the branches. As the life of the vine flows into the branches, so the life and power of Christ flows into each branch, producing God's fruit. The life of Christ is manifest or expressed on the branches.

The fruit is the natural outgrowth of the vine. Apart from the vine, the branch has no life of itself. Apart from the vine, the branch cannot bear fruit.

We have been chosen for spiritual fruitbearing. "Ye have not chosen me, but I have chosen you, and ordained you, that ye should go and bring forth fruit" (v. 16). The fruit is borne on our branches, but the fruit is His.

The fruit that Jesus is referring to is Christlikeness. It is the character of Jesus reproduced in us. Galatians 5:22-23 says, "When the Holy Spirit controls our lives he will produce this kind of fruit in us: love, joy, peace, patience, kindness, goodness, faithfulness, gentleness and self-control" (LB).

This does not come instantly. It is a gradual growth, the work of a lifetime. "We all, with unveiled face, beholding the glory of the Lord, are being changed into his likeness from one degree of glory to another" (2 Cor. 3:18 RSV).

God *expects* to see fruit in our lives. That is His purpose for us. Why? We are living in a world that is looking for reality. The Lord wants our lives to be an example to the world that He is real.

The Bible says, "Be a pattern for them in your love, your faith, and your clean thoughts" (1 Tim. 4:12 LB).

JULY 26

I am the vine, ye are the branches: He that abideth in me, and I in him, the same bringeth forth much fruit: for without me ye can do nothing (John 15:5).

esus is the Vine. We are the branches. Abiding is the requirement for fruitbearing. Jesus said, "Abide in me, and I in you. As the branch cannot bear fruit of itself, except it abide in the vine; no more can ye, except ye abide in me" (v. 4).

Jesus didn't say, "Abide with me" but "Abide in me." To abide means to live, dwell, or be at home in. It is living in the realization that Christ is in us, and we are in Him—an intimate relationship. It means to live lovingly and obediently close to Him.

When we abide in Him and He in us, we will bear fruit. We won't have to struggle. It will be natural for us because we are a part of the Vine whose nature is to produce fruit.

However, there are branches that do not bear fruit. Since the purpose of the branch is to bear fruit, those that do not are removed. Jesus said, "Every branch in me that beareth not fruit he taketh away" (v. 2).

God's purpose is to have a productive harvest of fruit. But to produce more fruit requires pruning. This process, though not pleasant, is necessary. "Every branch that beareth fruit, he purgeth it, that it may bring forth more fruit" (v. 2).

When you feel the pruning knife applied to your life, remember it will help you produce more fruit. We can trust the pruning process to our heavenly Father, for He will only prune the right amount in the right place.

When I had my own home, I grew beautiful roses. But I soon learned that the secret of beautiful roses was pruning them drastically. This same process is true in our lives.

God desires a maximum harvest of fruit from our lives—much fruit. This requires a close abiding in Him, and He in us. "He that abideth in me, and I in Him, the same bringeth forth much fruit" (v. 5). As we abide in Him, he becomes our sufficiency. "Without me, ye can do nothing," said Jesus (v. 5).

Some people are content to live on the fringe of their relationship with Him. But I want to live so close that I don't miss even one of His whispers to me. I often pray, "Lord, do you have a vacancy a little closer to You? If so, I want to move in."

The Bible says, "Herein is my Father glorified, that ye bear much fruit; so shall ye be my disciples" (v. 8).

JULY 27

Paul, a servant of Jesus Christ, called to be an apostle, separated unto the gospel of God. (Rom. 1:1).

The first time I went to Washington, D.C., I was impressed with the official residences and offices of the ambassadors representing their countries in our nation.

When these ambassadors are appointed, they are given credentials with authority for them to act on behalf of their country. Their own interests, opinions, and ambitions must be put aside. The decisions they make must be in the best interest of their country. Their whole life must be given over completely to fulfilling their mission.

Paul was called to be an apostle. He was commissioned with the authority to represent the Lord. Jesus said, "He is a chosen vessel unto me, to bear my name" (Acts 9:15). Paul's special mission was proclaiming the gospel and representing the heavenly kingdom on earth.

As an apostle, he had to put aside his desires, interests, and opinions. His wholehearted loyalty belonged to God, who had commissioned him. He recognized himself as the purchased possession of his Master, the Lord Jesus Christ.

We, too, have a special commission: "Go ye into all the world, and preach the gospel to every creature" (Mark 16:15). The Bible calls us ambassadors. "We are Christ's ambassadors. God is using us to speak to you: we beg you, as though Christ himself were here pleading with you, receive the love he offers you—be reconciled to God" (2 Cor. 5:20 LB).

An ambassador is the highest ranking representative of his country. As God's ambassadors, we are representing the heavenly country on earth. The Lord has a right to use us the way He desires, for we are His blood-bought ambassadors. "Ye are not your own . . . ye are bought with a price: therefore glorify God in your body, and in your spirit, which are God's" (1 Cor. 6:19–20). It cost Him His life to redeem us.

One day, in a home where she was visiting, Frances Ridley Havergal saw a painting of the crucifixion. Underneath were the words, *This I did for thee.* She was so impressed with this that later she wrote this thought in a hymn: "I gave my life for thee; what hast thou given for me?"

When we realize all that He has done for us, how can we do less than give Him our best? How well do we represent Him?

And the angel of the Lord spake unto Philip, saying, Arise, and go toward the south unto the way that goeth down from Jerusalem unto Gaza, which is desert (Acts 8:26).

Great things had been happening in Samaria where Philip was preaching. Then one day God told him to leave Samaria and go to the Gaza desert.

Go to the desert? Leave Samaria when so much was happening there? Surely, the logical thing would be to stay where so much activity was going on for God. Who could be reached for God out in the desert? But Philip was sensitive to the leading of the Holy Spirit. When he was asked to go, he obeyed immediately.

God had a purpose in taking him there. An Ethiopian official with a seeking heart would be passing down that road. As Philip came near, he heard the man reading from the fifty-third chapter of Isaiah. God told Philip to go near the chariot, and when Philip obeyed, he was able to point the man to Christ.

Every individual is important to God. He will even call a person away from a crowd to reach one needy person out in the desert. Philip was God's person in God's place by God's appointment at God's time.

Today there are many people with deep spiritual needs. God may divinely appoint us to meet them—perhaps in some unexpected place. How important it is that we be tuned in so we can hear the Holy Spirit say, "Arise and go." Even in a desert place we may find a seeking heart with whom we are to share Christ.

Once, after I had flown to a convention to speak, the airline went on strike, and I was rerouted for my trip home, scheduled to leave before the convention was over. I should have been thankful for any reservation, but I said I could not leave early. I was finally put on a different plane at a later time.

Between Tulsa and Kansas City I discovered why I was on that plane. There was one empty seat—beside me. The hostess sat down and began asking me questions about my work, which gave me an opening to talk about the Lord. I discovered she had a hungry heart; she was seeking reality. What a privilege to share with her how to get to heaven. I was thankful that I had been obedient to God's command to arise and return home by way of Tulsa and Kansas City.

God's way is always the right way.

The name of the LORD is a strong tower: the righteous runneth into it, and is safe (Prov. 18:10).

ishermen on the coast of Cornwall found that they could not make an adequate income from fishing, so they supplemented it by growing flowers, such as narcissus, daffodils, and anemones, for which their country is famous.

One of the fishermen had a small shack on the sheltered side of the cove in which he stored his gardening tools and fishing tackle. One day, while some friends were visiting, he said, "Come, I have something to show you."

For some time he had noticed a tiny wren fluttering around the shack. He discovered a small hole in the window where a piece of glass had been broken out. Inside were traces of the bird and he soon found its nesting place.

A huge ball of string, which he used to tie up his flowers, was hanging from the ceiling. He said to one of his friends, "Put your finger in the hole in the middle of the ball. You will discover the bird's secret." There, in the safety of the ball of string was a soft little nest with five baby birds in it.

Hidden from the stormy coast, out of the view of people, secure in the protection of the ball of string, the baby birds found safety.

When we see a storm approaching, we hurry to reach home or a place of safety before it breaks. Storms may break upon our lives in various ways: disappointment in a person in whom we had great confidence, the loneliness of feeling we have been deserted, criticism which seems unjustified.

Where do you run in times of storms? To a person or to God? In the midst of storms, our loving God has provided a place of safety for us. "The name of the LORD is a strong tower." His Name represents His character, who He is. The Bible says, "Some trust in chariots, and some in horses: but we will remember the name of the LORD our God (Ps. 20:7).

The Lord Jesus Christ is our strong tower. In Him we are secure. "The righteous runneth into it, and is safe."

Our safety in Him is in the present tense: *is* safe. We can be confident that He will lead us safely step by step.

JULY 30

That in every thing ye are enriched by him, in all utterance, and in all knowledge (1 Cor. 1:5).

 ou and I, as children of God, are "called to be saints" (v. 2), set apart for Jesus' pleasure and use.

As Paul wrote to the saints in Corinth, he thanked God for the grace they had through Jesus Christ and for the great source of riches they had in Him.

They were enriched both in all utterance and in all knowledge. Utterance literally means "outerance," the ability to speak out the knowledge you have within.

Their lives were enriched by being a "voice of utterance" for God. They had personal knowledge of Jesus Christ. They could speak because they had something to say.

We, too, have been enriched by a voice of utterance entrusted to us. When we receive something special or when something beautiful has happened to us, we want to share it with someone. What more wonderful privilege could we have than sharing what Jesus means to us?

Not only do we have a message to proclaim, but we have a life to live. God's greatest demonstration of the power of the Gospel is a life revealing His presence within.

Unsearchable riches are ours through Jesus Christ, but we must appropriate them and use them. Today, are you a voice of utterance, not only by what you say, but by your life? Are you sharing with others the personal knowledge you have of Jesus?

We are not all given the same voice of utterance. Many share verbally, others through distribution of literature or a ministry of prayer. What is your voice of utterance?

The Bible says, "He has enriched your whole life. He has helped you speak out for him and has given you a full understanding of the truth" (1 Cor. 1:5 LB). Won't you speak out today?

JULY 31

*Bless the LORD, O my soul: and all that is within me, bless his holy
name. Bless the LORD, O my soul, and forget not all his benefits
(Ps. 103:1–2).*

n this psalm, David immediately carries us into a spirit of praise.
He begins, "Bless the LORD" or give grateful praise to Him.
Often we come to God, asking Him to bless us, but here the
psalmist reminds us that we are to bless God—the Supreme
Object of our praise.

David was occupied with God Himself—"Bless the LORD." God was
real to him. In Psalm 34:3 he says, "O magnify the LORD with me, and let us
exalt his name together." Sometimes, we become so occupied *for* Him that we
neglect being occupied *with* Him.

David praised God not with just his lips, but with his entire personality:
"all that is within me" (v. 1). He blessed the Lord with every part of his
being, including his affections, his thoughts, his mind.

Not only was God the object of his praise, but God's blessings were the
subject of it. "Bless—affectionately, gratefully praise—the Lord, O my soul,
and forget not [one of] all His benefits" (v. 2 AMPLIFIED). It is so easy to take
for granted all the blessings God has given us. As we meditate on God
Himself—who He is—suddenly, we begin to thank Him for all He has done
for us and our hearts overflow in thanksgivng and praise.

In the rest of the psalm David enumerates all the wonderful things God
has done for him. We, too, need to take time to count our blessings. Often,
instead of counting our blessings, we count our trials, defeats, and failures. But if
we list our blessings, we may be surprised how long the list is. As we meditate
on His many expressions of love and goodness to us, how can we help but
overflow with praise?

As the psalm concludes, we are lifted close to the heart of God. There is a
great crescendo of praise as David cries, "Bless the Lord, ye his angels [v. 20]
. . . ye his hosts [v. 21] . . . all his works [v. 22]." And again the final
resounding chord of this great symphony of praise is "Bless the LORD, O my
soul" (v. 22).

AUGUST 1

Thus did Noah; according to all that God commanded him, so did he (Gen. 6:22).

od saw the wickedness of the human race in Noah's day and said He would destroy it by a flood. But He instructed Noah to build an ark for the safety of Noah's family. These instructions must have seemed strange because the earth had only been watered by a mist up until this time.

Yet Noah's faith responded in obedience to God's directions even though he probably didn't understand. Noah pleased God.

His obedience was not partial but complete; he did "according to all that God commanded him." He didn't pick and choose what he wanted to obey.

Throughout the Bible we read of others who were obedient to God. Peter was one. In the early days of the church, Peter and other apostles were imprisoned because of their boldness in preaching the Gospel. But the angel of the Lord opened the prison doors at night, releasing them. The next morning, they returned to the temple again, preaching about Jesus Christ. When the high priest discovered them there, he said, "We gave you strict orders not to teach in this name." Then Peter and the other apostles replied, "We must obey God rather than men!" (Acts 5:28–29 NIV).

Samuel said, "To obey is better than sacrifice (1 Sam. 15:22). And Jesus gives us the best example of obedience: "Being found in fashion as a man, he humbled himself, and became obedient unto death, even the death of the cross"(Phil. 2:8).

God is looking for obedience from us today. We may tell Him we love Him, we may give to His work, we may even try to serve Him in our own way, but God wants us to do "according to *all* he commands." He doesn't ask obedience from us just to show His authority. He sees the end from the beginning in our lives and desires to do nothing less than His very best for us.

Obedience is the language of faith. It is doing what God says without always knowing why. Obedience is one of the hardest lessons to learn, and partial obedience is disobedience. What is God asking you to do today? Will you obey?

AUGUST 2

For God hath not given us the spirit of fear; but of power, and of love, and of a sound mind (2 Tim. 1:7).

od does not want us to be afraid. Yet many people in our society live lives full of fear. You may be experiencing fear today. It is a natural feeling. Some people's temperaments are more susceptible to fear than others. But God does not want us to be obsessed with fear.

Timothy was evidently a fearful young man who could easily become discouraged and defeated. While Paul, his spiritual father, was in prison, he wrote Timothy a letter of encouragement. He said, "For God hath not given us the spirit of fear; but of power, and of love, and of a sound mind."

Paul reminded Timothy that God would provide for his needs. He shared three keys for overcoming fear—power, love, and a sound mind (or self-control). Through this threefold balance, inner peace is also available for us today.

First, God gives us a spirit of power. Jesus said, "Ye shall receive power, after that the Holy Spirit is come upon you" (Acts 1:8). The Holy Spirit empowers us to overcome all our fears. He gives us power to live, to resist temptations, to endure. No problem is too great. His power is always available. The Spirit of God's power holds us steady during the traumatic times of life.

Second, God gives us a spirit of love. Human love is not sufficient. "Herein [in Christ] is our love made perfect. . . . There is no fear in love; but perfect love casteth out fear (1 John 4:17–18). God's love can calm our fears.

Third, God gives us a spirit of a sound mind. God's Holy Spirit gives wisdom for the decisions we have to make. Paul wrote, "Don't let the world around you squeeze you into its own mold, but let God remold your minds from within" (Romans 12:2 PHILLIPS).

I have to confess that many times my first reaction to a problem is fear, but I have learned the importance of going to God's Word. My confused thinking clears as His Holy Spirit controls my mind. His perfect love casts out my fear and gives me His peace, but I must first let go of my own power and appropriate His.

Filled with His power, calmed by His love, and controlled by His Holy Spirit, we can trust and not be afraid.

AUGUST 3

I will climb my watchtower now, and wait to see what answer God will give to my complaint (Hab. 2:1 LB).

hy haven't You answered my prayer?" "How long before You are going to do something?" "Why don't You judge the sin so rampant on every hand?" In his perplexity, Habakkuk asked God these questions, but God was silent. How often have you and I asked these same questions? We have prayed, but no answer came. God was silent to our prayers.

Habakkuk knew where to go with his perplexities. He went into his watchtower. There he could draw near to God and share what was on his heart. Alone there, he became quiet enough to hear God speak to him.

There God broke His silence and assured Habakkuk that He was working but in a way Habakkuk couldn't see or understand. God was going to send in the Chaldeans, a ruthless enemy, to carry out His judgments. Now Habakkuk was more perplexed than ever.

In his watchtower, Habakkuk committed his problem to God. He learned that God was in control, but he must watch and wait. God would fulfill His purposes in His own way and time.

In the meantime, Habakkuk learned to live by faith. In God's presence, he came to the place where he could praise God for who He is and not for what He could do for him. He said, "Yet I will rejoice in the LORD" (Hab. 3:18).

You may be perplexed today with what God is doing in your life. You may have problems you can't cope with. You wonder if God really cares. You ask, "Lord, why don't You answer?" "How long before You do something?" God does understand. He knows your problem, and you can trust Him not to make a mistake.

In the meantime, we have the same privilege Habakkuk had. We can take our questions into our watchtower. There, alone with God, we can commit them to Him—take our hands off and let God take over. He already entered the answer in His heavenly Computer, and it will come in His perfect way and time.

As we spend time in our watchtower with God, waiting and watching, we can trust Him. He is in control. And getting to know God in a more intimate way is all that really matters. Be still and know that He is God.

AUGUST 4

"You are the salt of the earth; but if the salt has become tasteless, how will it be made salty again? It is good for nothing anymore, except to be thrown out and trampled under foot by men" (Matt. 5:13 NASB)

n the portion of Matthew we call the Beatitudes, Jesus describes the qualifications of a Christian. After giving this picture of a Christian, Jesus makes a practical application of their influence in the world. He says, "You are the salt of the earth; you are the light of the world" (vv. 13, 14 NASB).

Salt is an ordinary commodity, yet necessary. It is usually on the table for every meal. We use it in our cooking. Often a cook will taste the food being prepared and discover it needs a little more salt.

Salt's essential qualities are to purify, preserve, and season food. Jesus said that we are the salt with which the earth is to be salted. As Christians we are to be to the world what salt is to food.

We are in a world that has forsaken many of its moral standards. Our function in the world is to have a purifying effect. This means we must not isolate ourselves from our world, but have contact with it.

As a seasoning agent, salt brings out the best in food. Do we bring out the best in a person? I have a friend who is very conscious of her language when she is with me, although I never mention it to her. The Bible says, "Let your speech always be with grace, seasoned, as it were, with salt, so that you may know how you should respond to each person" (Col. 4:6 NASB). The presence of Christians in the world has a part in producing a better society.

Although salt adds flavor to food, it remains obscure. We don't say, "This is tasty salt." It enhances the flavor of the food. We are the salt, but our responsibility is to enhance the presence of God on the earth.

Jesus warns that salt may lost its savor, becoming tasteless and useless. We must not let the impurities of the world infiltrate our lives until we lose our effectiveness.

Another important quality of salt is that it creates a thirst. As salt, are we creating a thirst in the world? One day I sat by a woman at a luncheon who told me that she didn't know any non-Christians. How is the world going to know about Jesus Christ if we don't make contact with it?

Are you creating a thirst for Christ in the lives of those in *your* world? Ask God to put you with those who do not have a thirst for Christ and use you to create that thirst.

Remember: Jesus said, "*You* are the salt of the earth."

Let your light so shine before men, that they may see your good works, and glorify your Father which is in heaven (Matt. 5:16).

s a mechanic was searching for the trouble in a car he was repairing, his assistant stood by with a powerful flashlight. Distracted for a moment, the assistant inadvertently turned off the light. The mechanic looked up and said, "Shine your light. What are you here for anyway?"

We have been chosen by Jesus Himself to shine for Him here on earth. That's what we're here for. Jesus said, "Ye are the light of the world" (Matt. 5:14). What a privilege!

We are living in a dark world, a world that needs light, for light dispels darkness. Jesus said, "You are the world's light—a city on a hill, glowing in the night for all to see" (v. 14 LB). God wants us to have a part in dispelling darkness by radiating the light of Jesus, the Light of the World. What a choice place God has given us—lightholders to radiate Christ's light!

But before we can be the light of the world, letting His light shine through us, the Lord Jesus must be the Light shining in us. The Bible says, "In him was life; and the life was the light of men" (John 1:4). Because of our personal relationship with Him, Christ the Light shines in and through us.

About to return from a trip to France, a man brought his wife a beautiful match box. It was supposed to glow in the dark, but it didn't. They were disappointed. Then they noticed some lettering on the box in French. It said, "If you want me to shine at night, keep me in the light during the day." If we are to shine for Jesus in a dark world, we must spend time in His presence regularly being recharged.

When oil and kerosene lamps were used for light, the wicks had to be cleaned often to keep the lamps burning brightly. The wicks of our lives must also be cleaned often if we are to shine brightly for Jesus. Such things as fretting, indifference, worry, or bad habits can dim our lights. Only as our wicks are clean, can we brightly reflect His light.

"Arise, my people! Let your light shine for all the nations to see! For the glory of the Lord is streaming from you" (Isa. 60:1 LB).

AUGUST 6

Therefore whosoever heareth these sayings of mine, and doeth them, I will liken him unto a wise man, which built his house upon a rock . . . and every one that heareth these sayings of mine, and doeth them not, shall be likened unto a foolish man which built his house upon the sand (Matt. 7:24,26).

esus often used stories to explain abstract truth. In today's Scripture, he tells a story about two builders, one wise and one foolish. Each builder built a house that was similar in outward appearance.

Then one day a storm struck. The fury of the storm lashed against both houses. The rains descended, the floods came, and the wind blew. One house withstood the raging storm; the other collapsed.

What was the difference? The foolish man had been satisfied with a shelter. He gave no consideration to the foundation. The wise man knew the importance of a solid foundation. The difference in the houses had not been detected before. It took the storm to reveal it.

But Jesus was talking about more than houses. He was talking about lives. Our lives are built on either rock foundation or on sand. Eventually, our lives will experience a storm. It may be a hurting heart, discouragement, or a crushing defeat. The Bible promises "a place of refuge . . . from storm and from rain" (Isa. 4:6).

Floods may seem to almost drown us—floods of temptation, cheating, alcoholism, or drugs. The Bible promises, "When thou passest through the waters, I will be with thee; and through the rivers, they shall not overflow thee" (Isa. 43:2).

Winds of adversity, distress, or sorrow may howl against us. The Bible says that "[Jesus] arose, and rebuked the wind, and said unto the sea, Peace, be still. And the wind ceased, and there was a great calm" (Mark 4:39).

The one who hears God's Word but takes no heed is like the man with the sand foundation. During the storm his house crashes. Only those whose lives are built on the Rock foundation will weather the storm. The Bible says, "That Rock was Christ" (1 Cor. 10:4). Those who hear and obey the Word of Christ have built their house on the Rock.

The Rock foundation of Christ Jesus provides security in the most tempestuous storm. Christ is the Rock who will carry us through the storm of judgment and take us to our home in heaven.

Be sure your life is built on the foundation that never fails, the Rock Christ Jesus.

AUGUST 7

If I regard iniquity in my heart, the Lord will not hear me
(Ps. 66:18).

in unconfessed and unforgiven hinders prayer. David said, "He would not have listened if I had not confessed my sins" (LB). In order to have an effective prayer life, we must let the Holy Spirit reveal our unconfessed sin. The Bible says, "And when he has come he will convince the world of its sin, and of the availability of God's goodness, and of deliverance from judgment" (John 16:8 LB).

We often blame God for unanswered prayer, but He is not to blame. Unconfessed sin may have put a barrier between us and God. "Behold, the LORD's hand is not shortened, that it cannot save; neither his ear heavy, that it cannot hear: but your iniquities have separated between you and your God, and your sins have hid his face from you, that he will not hear" (Isa. 59:1–2).

But we can be forgiven. "If we confess our sins, he is faithful and just to forgive us our sins, and to cleanse us from all unrighteousness" (1 John 1:9).

God is faithful. He will be true to His promises. He is just. He will act consistently with His Word. The cleansing agent is Christ's blood. "The blood of Jesus his Son cleanses us from every sin" (1 John 1:7 LB). His blood cleansed us at the time we received Christ as Savior, and it remains available for cleansing throughout our life.

For seven years, my sister had to be on a dialysis machine three times a week. One kidney had been removed and the other had quit functioning. This was the only way for her blood to be purified.

The blood of Christ is the only thing can purify us from sin. As we honestly confess our sin, the blood cleanses us and God forgives. Even more wonderful, God forgets, and we are restored to fellowship. Our prayer line is restored.

Are there hindrances in our lives that keep our prayers from reaching the throne of God? Let us take time to let the Holy Spirit search our lives and reveal anything which may be hindering our prayers and making us powerless. Take time today to confess them and receive God's cleansing and forgiveness.

AUGUST 8

*Shew me thy ways, O LORD; teach me thy paths. Lead me in thy
truth, and teach me: for thou art the God of my salvation; on thee
do I wait all the day (Ps. 25:4–5).*

ife is full of the unknown. We need guidance from One who
knows the way; otherwise we may get lost among the maze.
David wanted to know God's will. He knew there was no
one better to ask than the One who had planned his way for
him. He said, "You chart the path ahead of me" (Ps. 139:3 LB).

We cannot know His way without divine assistance. When we come to a
point of decision and find no clear direction, we cry out to our unfailing Guide,
and He replies, "This is the way, walk ye in it" (Isa. 30:21).

The psalmist desired to know and obey the truth. The Bible says, "Thy
word is truth" (John 17:17). The Word of God will never lead us contrary to
the will of God.

David not only asked to be *shown* the way but to be taught God's ways:
"Teach me thy paths." David wanted to be taught how to walk God's paths.
We, too, need to be taught His way, for in our walk through life there are many
obstacles—paths too crooked to maneuver, mountains too steep to climb, rivers
too deep to wade through.

At one such time David cried, "Wherever I am, though far away at the
ends of the earth, I will cry to you for help. When my heart is faint and
overwhelmed, lead me to the mighty, towering Rock of safety" (Ps. 61:2 LB).
The Lord promises, "I will instruct you . . . and guide you along the best
pathway for your life" (Ps. 32:8 LB).

One time, a man was about to cross a busy street when the little girl
beside him looked up, slipped her hand in his, and said, "Will you take me
across the street to the other side?" He led her through the busy traffic safely to
the other side. What joy it gave him, knowing the little girl would trust him.

We have to cross streets of difficulty, of trouble, of the unknown. Not
only will our heavenly Guide show us the way, but we can slip our hand into
His All-powerful hand and let Him lead us through our traumatic situations. We
need not be afraid. We will never lose our way when we walk hand in hand
with God.

But be holy now in everything you do, just as the Lord is holy, who invited you to be his child. He himself has said, "You must be holy, for I am holy" (1 Peter 1:15–16 LB).

 e often equate holiness with certain types of dress or certain mannerisms. But holiness is conforming to God's character. It has been defined as "a heart of love for God expressed in our character, conversation, and conduct. It is Christ enthroned in our life, expressed in our living, speaking, and being." Holiness is Christlikeness.

Christlikeness is a winsome quality—the holy calm of Christ mirrored in our face; the holy quietness of Christ manifest in our voice; the holy gentleness of Christ expressed in our manner; the holy fragrance of Christ emanating from our whole life.

The holy calm of Christ is mirrored in our face. How interesting it is to study faces. The face can be a reflector of our innermost being. It registers such expressions as joy, anger, fear, and pain. The presence of Christ will reflect the holy calm of Christ in our face. "Let the beauty of the LORD our God be upon us" (Ps. 90:17).

The holy quietness of Christ manifests itself in our voice. The Bible says, "Your beauty should not be dependent on an elaborate coiffure, or on the wearing of jewelry or fine clothes, but on the inner personality—the unfading loveliness of a calm and gentle spirit, a thing very precious in the eyes of God" (1 Peter 3:3–4 PHILLIPS).

The holy gentleness of Christ expresses itself in our manner. This gentleness comes from a life controlled by the Holy Spirit. As we turn our lives over to Him, the Holy Spirit reproduces His life in ours, conforming us to the image of Jesus Christ. He becomes our patience, our graciousness, our kindness, our peace. He produces His gentleness in our manner.

The holy fragrance of Christ emanates from the whole life. Mary's alabaster box had to be broken before its perfume filled the house. So, too, our lives have to be broken—of self, desires, ambitions, goals—before the fragrance of His presence can emanate to those around us.

"As far as God is concerned there is a sweet, wholesome fragrance in our lives. It is the fragrance of Christ within us " (2 Cor. 2:15 LB).

The Son of man came not to be ministered unto, but to minister, and to give his life a ransom for many (Matt. 20:28).

ne day, the mother of James and John came to Jesus, requesting that her two sons might sit on His immediate right and left in His kingdom. Jesus told her it would not be His responsibility to make such an appointment. Jesus taught His disciples that the true measure of greatness was not prominence, position, or power, but a spirit of humility.

He said, "Whoever wishes to be great among you must be your servant . . . just as the Son of man came not to be waited on but to serve" (vv. 26, 28 AMPLIFIED).

Jesus is the best example of a servant, One who ministers to others. Paul said that He "made himself of no reputation, and took upon him the form of a servant, and was made in the likeness of men: and being found in fashion as a man, he humbled himself, and became obedient unto death, even the death of the cross" (Phil. 2:7–8).

When we consider His willingness to give up the glories of heaven and submit Himself to the ignominious death of the cross, doesn't it motivate us to follow His example as a humble servant? This is our purpose for living—to serve Him.

In Birmingham, Alabama, on top of Red Mountain stands a huge iron figure of Vulcan, the Roman god of fire. It symbolizes the industrial wealth of that great city and its booming steel industry.

At the foot of the mountain in the center of a parkway is a life-size statue of a little man on his knees in prayer, head bowed, one hand lifted up to God. It is the statue of Brother Bryan. Around the corner is the church where he was pastor for a half century. When he died, the city mourned. Flags flew at half mast. Businesses closed. A holiday was declared to observe his funeral. For years, he ministered to the needs of the people on the streets of Birmingham. Although he had no prominent position and few earthly possessions, he had humbly served the people, ministering there for Jesus Christ.

The Vulcan statue, symbolizing the wealth and success of that city, will one day be gone. The life of Brother Bryan will stand throughout all eternity.

A truly humble person is one disciplined to the will of God. "Not my will, but thine be done."

AUGUST 11

And this is the confidence that we have in him, that, if we ask any thing according to his will, he heareth us: and if we know that he hear us, whatsoever we ask, we know that we have the petitions that we desired of him (1 John 5:14–15).

re you praying to know God's will in a special situation? It may be for God's place of service for you, the college you should attend, a mate for life. The above Scripture assures us that we can know the mind and will of God. We often think of prayer as asking for what we want, but it really is asking God for what He wants.

John knew that prayer works. He had confidence that God hears and answers prayer. Confidence means boldness or assurance. Our confidence is not in our prayers but in the Lord. And we can be certain that if we ask in accordance with His will, He will hear our prayer.

In Psalm 40:8 we read, "I delight to do thy will, O my God." We need not fear His will, for His will is good. Often, we think of God's will as something we won't want to do. But Paul wrote, "Do not conform any longer to the pattern of this world, but be transformed by the renewing of your mind. Then you will be able to test and approve what God's will is—his good, pleasing and perfect will" (Rom. 12:2 NIV).

How can we know God's will? We need to know His Word, for His will is never contrary to His Word. Jesus said, "If ye abide in me, and my words abide in you, ye shall ask what ye will, and it shall be done unto you" (John 15:7).

Having His Word abide in us does not mean just turning to Scripture in emergencies. It means reading it regularly. It means applying it to our life situations and obeying it.

There are times when we seem to have no direction from God about which option to take. Then, we have the Holy Spirit's promise that He will pray our request aright before the throne of our Father. "We don't even know what we should pray, nor how to pray as we should but the Holy Spirit prays for us with such feeling that it cannot be expressed in words" (Rom. 8:26 LB).

Knowing that the Holy Spirit will know God's will even if we don't, gives us confidence that God hears and will answer our prayer.

Kneeprints before footprints.

AUGUST 12

*But as we were allowed of God to be put in trust with the gospel,
even so we speak (1 Thess. 2:4).*

ne day, a young mother came to me with a darling little one on each hand and said, "How can I have a ministry for the Lord?" Looking at the children I said, "They are your ministry for now." As we visited, what joy it gave her to know that she had a ministry—her children. Some who cannot be out in active ministry have a tremendous prayer ministry at home.

Someone said to missionary William Carey, "I understand you are a cobbler." "No," he replied, "I am in full-time Christian service. I cobble shoes to earn my living."

Our ministry should glorify God, not people. "We speak; not as pleasing men, but God, which trieth our hearts" (v. 4).

Our ministry should be one of tenderness and compassion. Paul wrote, "We were gentle among you, even as a nurse cherisheth her children" (v. 7).

One day, I discovered that a group I was working with was doing something wrong. Instead of writing to scold them, I planned a trip to visit them without telling them why I had come. As we met, I shared the right way of doing things. Later, they came to me and said, "We have been doing something wrong. We will change." I never told them that that was the reason I was there. I could have upset them, but God gave me a tactful, loving way of handling it.

Paul was pleased that the Word of God was working in the Thessalonians' lives. That was his ministry. "Thank we God without ceasing, because, when ye received the word of God which ye heard of us, ye received it not as the word of men, but as it is in truth, the word of God, which effectually worketh also in you that believe" (v. 13).

Paul realized that everything he had to endure would be worth it all when he stood before the Lord. These believers would be his crown of rejoicing.

We, too, will know it is worth it all when we see Jesus, knowing we have ministered for Him. "What is our hope or happiness or our victor's wreath of exultant triumph when we stand in the presence of our Lord Jesus at His coming? Are not you? For you are [indeed] our glory and our joy!" (vv. 19–20 AMPLIFIED).

AUGUST 13

And he led them forth by the right way, that they might go to a city of habitation (Ps. 107:7).

ave you ever been lost? I recall being lost in a desolate area of South Dakota one night. Realizing we were on the wrong road, we turned around and started back. When we came to a fork in the road, we didn't know which path to take. We were getting desperate, for our gas supply was low. We used a compass, but it didn't help. We called upon our heavenly Guide. The road we took proved to be the right one, and soon we were back in an inhabited area.

In this psalm, we read of some homeless travelers wandering through the wilderness. They were hungry, thirsty, and almost fainting. Can you picture them struggling across the burning sand of the desert with the sun beating down upon them? They could not find their way.

But these discouraged, disheartened travelers knew what to do. "They cried out to the LORD in their trouble" (v. 6 NASB). Their cry must have been weak, but the Lord hears even the faintest cry, and He heard theirs. Not only did He hear, but He answered. "He delivered them out of their distresses."

There was only one right way and one Person who knew it, and He led His weary ones out of the wilderness to a home where they were refreshed and satisfied.

Many people today wander from place to place, seeking a place of fulfillment, security, peace, and joy. This may describe your experience. In the desert you cannot put down roots for stability and security. God is waiting for your cry for help.

When you call to Him, He is ready to be your Guide, leading you out the right way, never the wrong way. God promises, "I will bring the blind by a way that they knew not; I will lead them in paths that they have not known: I will make darkness light before them, and crooked things straight" (Isa. 42:16).

Our Guide satisfies our lives completely. "He satisfieth the longing soul, and filleth the hungry soul with goodness" (v. 9). No wonder the psalmist said, "Oh that men would praise the LORD for his goodness, and for his wonderful works to the children of men!" (v. 8).

AUGUST 14

Keep and protect me, O God, for in You I have found refuge, and in You do I put my trust and hide myself. (Ps. 16:1 AMPLIFIED)

God-satisfied! This is the title Dr. Graham Scroggie gave to this psalm. Through the experiences of David's life, he learned that only in the Lord could he be satisfied. In companionship with God, David learned that he could trust Him. He experienced His keeping and protecting power. But David's satisfaction did not come from what God did for him—it was in God Himself. "I say to the Lord, You are my Lord; I have no god beside or beyond You" (v. 2 AMPLIFIED).

David continued, "The Lord is the portion of mine inheritance and of my cup: thou maintainest my lot" (v. 5 AMPLIFIED). Portion means an allotment or share. The Lord Jesus Christ is the portion of our inheritance. He is our all.

A wealthy Roman had a faithful slave named Marcellus and a son who brought him much sorrow. When he died, it was discovered that the Roman's will left everything to his slave; however, his son was given the privilege of choosing one thing as his inheritance. The son said, "I'll take Marcellus." By taking him, he had all. When we take Jesus as our portion, we have all that He can be to us.

He is our satisfactory counselor. "I will bless the Lord who counsels me; he gives me wisdom in the night. He tells me what to do" (v. 7 TLB). How often we seek counsel from people, forgetting that the Lord knows all things and can give the counsel we need. He never makes a mistake.

He is our source of perfect security. "I have set the Lord always before me: because he is at my right hand, I shall not be moved" (v. 8). With God before us, we are never moved out of the place of His will for us. No storm can shake us.

David saw beyond his present position and knew that one day he would have fullness of joy. "Thou wilt show me the path of life: in thy presence is fullness of joy; at thy right hand are pleasures forevermore" (v. 11). One day we, too, will be in His presence. There will be no sorrow, no loneliness, no weariness. We will know fullness of joy.

As we wait for that day, we can enjoy His companionship today. God knows and loves us as no one else does. He can do for us what no one else can. No wonder He completely satisfies!

What is that in thine hand? (Ex. 4:2).

hen Richard Baxter lay dying, his friends, sympathizing with him in his pain, tried to comfort him by speaking of the good he had achieved by means of his writings. Baxter shook his head. "No," he said, "I was but the pen in God's hand. What praise is due to a pen?"

When Saladin saw the sword with which Richard Couer de Leon had fought so bravely, he marveled that so common a blade should have wrought such mighty deeds. "It was not the sword," replied one of the English officers. "It was the arm of Richard."

When Paganini appeared for the first time at the Royal Opera House in Paris, the aristocracy of France gathered to hear him. In his own peculiar manner, he came onto the stage amidst the breathless silence of the expectant throng. As he commenced to tune his violin, a string snapped. The audience tittered. Commencing again, a second string broke, and a moment later a third one broke. The people stared in consternation. Paganini paused for a second, and then, giving one of his grim smiles, he lifted his instrument, and from that single string, drew music that seemed divine.

Only a pen—but a pen in the hand of a poet! Only a common sword— but a sword in the hand of Richard! Only a damaged violin—but a violin in the hand of a master!

Moses learned what God could do with an insignificant shepherd's rod. Moses had been giving God one excuse after another why he should not be the leader of the Israelites. But God was determined to show Moses what He could do with him. He said, "What is that in thine hand?" Moses said "A rod." Just a shepherd's rod—but in the hand of Moses, it was to become a rod of power, the rod of God. It was symbolic of the power available to Moses as he led the Israelites across the desert to the Promised Land.

Today, God may be asking you, "What is that in your hand?" You may say, "Nothing." But God sees what you have, and He can use it. It can become God's rod of power, mightier than the vastest army, as you commit it to Him. The Bible says, "Faithful is he that calleth you, who also will do it" (1 Thess. 5:24).

AUGUST 16

Whatsoever ye do in word or deed, do all in the name of the Lord Jesus, giving thanks to God and the Father by him . . . and whatsoever ye do, do it heartily, as to the Lord, and not unto men (Col. 3:17, 23).

 o the Hebrews, a person's name was very important. If you touched his name, you touched him. The name of Jesus Christ is important to Christians, for it represents the One who is most important to us.

In the merchandising field, certain brand names represent quality. Many products, after being tested and proved superior, receive a "stamp of approval." For Christians, there is a name that is above all names—the name of Jesus. "God also hath highly exalted him, and given him a name which is above every name" (Phil. 2:9).

Paul reminds us that as God's representatives, we are to say and do everything in His name. "Whatever you do or say, let it be as a representative of the Lord Jesus" (v. 17 LB). To do everything in His name means to do it in His will, for His glory, by His power.

Sometimes we separate the secular from the spiritual in our lives. However, the Bible teaches that everything we do and say in every area of our lives is to be done in His name.

When we truly love the Lord, we will have the **right spirit.** We will do everything enthusiastically as unto the Lord. We will put our whole being into it. We will be sold on what we do. "Whatever may be your task, work at it heartily (from the soul)" (Col. 3:23 AMPLIFIED).

We must have the **right motive.** "Work at it . . . as [something done] for the Lord and not for men" (v. 23 AMPLIFIED). Our motivation should be to please the Lord.

Then we are assured of the **right reward**: 'Knowing (with all certainty) that it is from the Lord [and not from men] that you will receive the inheritance which is your (real) reward. [The One Whom] you are actually serving [is] the Lord Christ, the Messiah" (v. 24 AMPLIFIED).

When a secretary writes a letter for her employer, she doesn't sign her name but his. Are you able to sign the name of Jesus Christ over all your words and deeds, saying, "I am doing this in His name and for His glory?" "Whatever ye do in word or deed, do all in the name of the Lord Jesus."

"For ye serve the Lord Christ" (v. 24).

AUGUST 17

If you [really] love Me you will keep (obey) My commands (John 14:15 AMPLIFIED).

ow easily we say we love the Lord, but love goes beyond the words of the lips to the devotion of the heart. It is a test of our discipleship.

How do we prove our love genuine? By **obedience.** Our love is measured not by our feelings, nor by what we say, but by our willing obedience to His Word. Jesus didn't say, "If you love Me you will *have to* keep My commands, but "If you love me, You *will.*" And we must know His commands if we are to obey them. We can find them in His Word.

Love is not just an emotion. Love desires in every way to please the object of that love. As we submit ourselves to His Word, we will have a greater desire to please Him. "Now the God of peace . . . make you perfect in every good work to do his will, working in you that which is wellpleasing in his sight, through Jesus Christ" (Heb. 13:20–21).

Our loving obedience brings **revelation.** The Lord Jesus says, "The person who has My commands and keeps them is the one who [really] loves Me. . . . I will let Myself be clearly seen by him and make Myself real to him" (John 14:21 AMPLIFIED). The Lord Jesus will reveal Himself more completely to the obedient one, the one who really loves Him. The more the Lord reveals Himself to us, the more real He becomes.

And as loving, obedient children who are getting to know him better, we are assured of **His abiding presence.** What a privilege! His presence within. Fellowship with Him. Jesus said, "If a person [really] loves Me, he will keep My word—obey My teaching; and My Father will love him, and We will come to him and make Our home (abode, special dwelling place) with him" (John 14:23 AMPLIFIED). If we love the Lord with all our heart and walk in obedience to His will, we will live in special, close fellowship in His presence.

"Whom having not seen, ye love; in whom, though now ye see him not, yet believing, ye rejoice with joy unspeakable and full of glory" (1 Peter 1:8).

AUGUST 18

The whole Bible was given to us by inspiration from God and is use-
ful to teach us what is true and to make us realize what is wrong in
our lives; it straightens us out and helps us do what is right. It is
God's way of making us well prepared at every point, fully
equipped to do good to everyone (2 Tim. 3:16–17 LB).

oday we are hearing much about cholesterol-free and high-fiber diets. They are important for our physical well-being, but God's Word is the proper diet for our spiritual well-being. All of the Bible is "God-breathed" (NIV). It gives us the very mind and purpose of God.

The Bible is a storehouse of God's essential truths and practical help for our daily walk. Shortly after I became a Christian, I took a class in the doctrines of the Bible. It was one of the most helpful things I ever did, for it gave me a strong foundation for my belief and behavior.

The Bible "makes us realize what is wrong in our lives." It reproves us and convicts us. It is like a mirror in which we see ourselves as we are and learn what we need to correct in our lives.

The Bible "straightens us out." Just as a plumb line is a standard for a straight line, His Word is a standard by which we can set and reset our lives to please God.

The Bible "helps us to do that which is right." It gives the training and discipline necessary for a well-rounded, well-balanced Christian life.

The Bible equips us for our God-given task. "The scriptures are the comprehensive equipment of the man of God, and fit him fully for all branches of his work" (v. 17 PHILLIPS).

What is your purpose in reading the Bible? Do you do it just as your Christian duty or because you want to know God's instructions for your life? If we are to be strengthened spiritually, we must know what the Bible says, appropriate it in our everyday living, and obey it.

Some books are for information, others are for our inspiration, but the Bible is for our transformation. A young man was asked once which translation he preferred. He quickly replied, "The translation in my Aunt Mary's life." May His Word be translated into our minds and hearts, changing us into the people He wants us to be. May our prayer be, "Order my steps in thy word" (Ps. 119:133).

AUGUST 19

But it is good for me to draw near to God: I have put my trust in the Lord GOD, that I may declare all thy works (Ps. 73:28).

ne day, a father and his young son were riding along a dark road. The little fellow snuggled up close to his father. Thinking the boy wanted to ask a favor, the father said, "Out with it, what do you want?" "Nothing, Father," the boy replied. "I just wanted to be near you." Those few words delighted the father's heart, and the bond of love between them became more precious.

The psalmist Asaph wanted to get close to God. He had reviewed his past and had faced the future, but now in the present he wanted to draw near to God. That's all that mattered, having an intimate relationship with God and being assured of His presence as he faced the uncertainties of life.

How do we keep close to God? We read His Word regularly, seeking His mind and will to guide our lives. We pray frequently, telling Him our concerns and listening to His counsel. And we obey Him consistently, wanting to please Him in everything.

As we draw near to God, we learn to trust Him. We can say, "I have put my trust in the Lord God, that I may declare all thy works." To trust, as a verb, means "to commit to the care of another with assurance," and as a noun means, "confidential reliance on the integrity, veracity, and justice of another."

To put our trust in God means to commit to the Lord God our needs, problems, and burdens. As we put Him at the center of our lives, we can lean all our weight, our entire person, on Him.

Are you perplexed and frustrated in the midst of feverish activities? Is your mind confused? We each need to make the decision Asaph did: "I get as close to him as I can! I have chosen him and I will tell everyone about the wonderful ways he rescues me" (LB).

Living close to Him, we experience joy, peace, and satisfaction. Close to Him, we find comfort in times of heartache, strength to face problems, and peace for the pressures of life. "The LORD is good, a strong hold in the day of trouble; and he knoweth them that trust in him" (Nah. 1:7).

Perhaps today, you need to draw closer to Him.

AUGUST 20

Walk in wisdom toward them that are without, redeeming the time (Col. 4:5).

nce when I was admitted to the hospital, I asked God to give me the roommate of His choosing. I soon discovered that the lovely woman who shared the room with me had little interest in spiritual things. She was not against God; she just seemed to ignore Him.

One day she began sharing some of her heartaches. Suddenly she said, "What kind of a doctor is yours?" When I told her he was a surgeon, she looked disappointed. "Oh, he isn't a general practitioner? I wish I could have him for my doctor. He is so sympathetic and kind."

That gave me my opening. "My doctor is a fine Christian," I said. This lonely woman began to share with me some of her deep hurts. Her life had been very difficult. When I told her about how God had sustained me in some of the sorrows and tragedy in my life, she became very quiet and I could see tears in her eyes. The next morning, she went home, but before she left, I had another opportunity to talk to her about the Lord. She asked me to come and visit her, which I did, ministering to her spiritual needs.

God opened the way for me to talk to her about Christ but only after she had seen something different in the life of a doctor who knew Jesus Christ personally—one who was walking in wisdom toward those who don't know Him.

Walking refers to our daily conduct and behavior. Our neighbors and coworkers may be influenced more by what they see in our lives than by what we say.

How do we walk in wisdom? Jesus Christ is our wisdom. "But of him are ye in Christ Jesus, who of God is made unto us wisdom, and righteousness, and sanctification, and redemption" (1 Cor. 1:30). Walking in wisdom means to depend on Christ to help us use tact and discretion, being consistent in both our talk and our walk.

Paul said, "Look carefully then how you walk! . . . making the very most of the time—buying up each opportunity—because the days are evil" (Eph. 5:15–16 AMPLIFIED). How many opportunities there are to share Jesus Christ in our needy world today. May we not miss one.

AUGUST 21

The LORD is my light and my salvation; whom shall I fear? The LORD is the strength of my life; of whom shall I be afraid? (Ps. 27:1).

 ear is a natural emotion, one that is very real. All of us have experienced fear at some time in our lives. Fear grips your heart when the phone rings in the middle of the night. Fear terrorizes you when the doctor mentions the word *cancer*. Fear paralyzes you the first time you stand before a microphone. Fear can control our lives.

David knew fear. He had experienced attacks from his enemies on every side, but he wrote these confident words: "The LORD is my light and my salvation—whom shall I fear? The LORD is the stronghold of my life—of whom shall I be afraid? (NIV). He is our light, our deliverance, our defense. David did not say the Lord *gives* light, deliverance, and defense but He *is* all of these.

David said, "He is my light." Jesus said, "I am the light of the world: he that followeth me shall not walk in darkness, but shall have the light of life" (John 8:12). I need not fear, for He will bring light into my dark places. I never walk alone. I never need to be afraid.

The first time I went to Carlsbad Caverns in New Mexico, when we descended to the very bottom of the cavern, they turned off all the lights. We could almost feel the darkness. It was frightening. Suddenly, one little light was turned on. That light dispelled the darkness.

Sometimes the darkness of a problem brings fear. But when we invite Jesus, the Light of the World, into our problem, He dispels our darkness. The Light of Life leads us to His answer.

David said, "He is my salvation." The word for salvation conveys the thought of deliverance. As my salvation, He will deliver me in time of trouble. "I sought the LORD, and he heard me, and delivered me from all my fears" (Ps. 34:4).

David said, "He is my strength." *Strength* is sometimes translated *defense*. We need never fear for He is our defense. "My defense is of God, which saveth the upright in heart" (Ps. 7:10).

Regardless of what we're facing today, we can say with Isaiah, "I will trust and not be afraid" (Isa. 12:2).

AUGUST 22

And when he putteth forth his own sheep, he goeth before them,
and the sheep follow him: for they know his voice (John 10:4).

n eastern lands a shepherd and his sheep share a close intimacy.
No flock is without a shepherd. The shepherd knows each of his
sheep by name, and he lovingly and continually watches over
them, providing for their every need. He stands between the
sheep and any danger that arises. Each sheep receives his personal care. They
learn the security of following the shepherd and being completely dependent
upon him. No wonder they follow him!

The shepherd puts forth his sheep early in the day. Because they trust their
shepherd, they follow him. They have learned that the shepherd knows where
the best pastures are. He will never lead them on a wrong path.

David knew that the Lord was his shepherd. He said, "The Lord is *my*
shepherd" (Ps. 23:1). Because the Lord was his shepherd, he rested in the fact
that he would lack nothing. Even though his life was filled with turmoil, he was
not fearful, for he had the assurance of the constant presence of his shepherd:
"For thou art with me" (v. 4).

This illustrates our personal relationship with Jesus Christ, our Good
Shepherd. "We are his people, and the sheep of his pasture" (Ps. 100:3).
Our Good Shepherd has a special path planned for each of His sheep. He
knows our path, charting it for us as we go through life. Just as the Eastern
shepherds lead their sheep forth each day, our Good Shepherd puts us forth day
by day. Although our path is unknown to us, He knows it perfectly and He
leads us step by step. He knows where to lead for provisions and for protection.

Our path may not be one of our choosing. We may be perfectly content
where we are, but He may move us out of our comfort zone on to a path of
turmoil, frustration, or pain. But He has already prepared it for us, because He
never makes a mistake.

When I was a small child, I lived in Michigan. The doctor told my father
that because of a health problem, he must move to the West. He made a trip to
Colorado, where he made all the arrangements for a job and a place to live.
When he returned, he took us to the place he had prepared for us.

We may not understand the way God leads, but we trustingly follow
Him. Someone has said, "The footprint of the obedient sheep is always found
in the larger footprints of the Shepherd."

Not that we are sufficient of ourselves to think any thing as of ourselves; but our sufficiency is of God (2 Cor. 3:5).

ne day, a young homemaker said to me, "How can I know God in the real way you seem to?" Another day, a young man said, "I am searching for the answer to life." As people turn to us for spiritual help, we realize that we are not sufficient of ourselves for the task, but our sufficiency is of God.

In his letter to the Corinthians, Paul wrote of his ability to go through persecution and come out triumphant. Though he recognized his *human* inadequacy, for every trial he knew he had adequate resources that could only come from God. Paul knew he could draw on his great Source—God Himself. In place of his human insufficiency, he claimed God's sufficiency.

God has entrusted us with an important task, the task of sharing the Gospel of Jesus Christ. "As we were allowed of God to be put in trust with the gospel, even so we speak; not as pleasing men, but God, which trieth our hearts" (1 Thess. 2:4).

Regardless of our natural ability or our inability, our sufficiency is in the Lord, our All-sufficient One. Paul had learned that in Christ, we can do all things. He wrote, "I have strength for all things in Christ Who empowers me— I am ready for anything and equal to anything through Him Who infuses inner strength into me, [that is, I am self-sufficient in Christ's sufficiency]" (Phil. 4:13 AMPLIFIED).

In 2 Corinthians 2:16 Paul asks, "Who is sufficient for these things?" God's answer comes in chapter 12, "My grace is sufficient for thee: for my strength is made perfect in weakness" (2 Cor. 12:9). God's strength is only sufficient when we recognize our weakness and appropriate the power of God.

We may feel insecure. We may feel inferior. We may feel unworthy. But we can lift our hearts in overflowing praise, for Jesus Christ is our confidence. What a change it makes in a life when we know He is our All-sufficient One.

Meditate on these thoughts: I can be confident in Christ, and I can do all He asks of me because He is my All-sufficient One. Praise Him!

AUGUST 24

A voice came from the cloud, saying, "This is my Son, whom I have chosen; listen to him." When the voice had spoken, they found that Jesus was alone (Luke 9:35–36 NIV).

 recall one time driving with several women through an extremely heavy rainstorm. The rain was coming down in torrents. One of the women in the car became so frightened, we could hardly calm her. That is often the natural reaction to our stormclouds in life.

Clouds of unrest, strife, and trouble hang over the world today. In the midst of all the turmoil, we never know when we will be entering some cloud that will bring a feeling of uncertainty.

One day, Jesus took Peter, John, and James up to a mountain to pray. As He was praying, He was transfigured before their eyes. Two men, Moses and Elijah, appeared and were talking with Jesus. In his impulsive way, Peter suggested building three shelters to celebrate the occasion, one for Jesus, one for Moses, and one for Elijah.

Suddenly, a cloud appeared and overshadowed them. "They feared as they entered into the cloud. And there came a voice came out of the cloud, saying, This is my beloved Son: hear him. And when the voice was past, Jesus was found alone" (vv. 34–36).

Today, you may have entered a cloud. Your cloud may be a cloud of sorrow, disillusionment, trouble. Fear may fill your heart. Just as God told the disciples to listen to Jesus, we, too, need to become quiet. He says, "Listen to Me." Then we will become aware that Jesus is there in the cloud with us. We can hear His comforting words, "I will never leave thee, nor forsake thee" (Heb. 13:5) and "Let not your heart be troubled, neither let it be afraid" (John 14:27). God knows that clouds can draw us closer to Him. We will be alone with Jesus in our cloud. His presence will be real to us.

We can learn some precious lessons in our cloud. We learn that Jesus draws very close to us at such times; not one thing can touch us that hasn't come through Him first. We learn to trust Him, to depend completely on Him. And we learn that whatever He allows to come into our life, He allows because He loves us.

"Blessed is the man that trusteth in the LORD, and whose hope the LORD is" (Jer. 17:7).

Abraham believed God, and it was imputed unto him for righteous-ness: and he was called the Friend of God (James 2:23)

s we read of Abraham, we are impressed with the familiarity and intimacy of the relationship which existed between him and God. Three times in the Bible, he is spoken of as a friend of God.

I like this definition of a friend: A friend is one who comes in when everyone else goes out.

We cannot merit friendship with our heavenly Father, but we become friends of God through Jesus Christ. And how does our friendship with God develop?

Our friendship develops as we genuinely **love** Him. The Bible says, "We love him, because he first loved us" (1 John 4:19). Because of our heavenly Father's great love for us, we can never do too much for Him. No cost is too great.

Jesus said to Peter, "Lovest thou me more than these?" (John 21:15). What would we have answered if Jesus had asked us that question? What might the word *these* have referred to in our lives? Does He see something in our lives that we love more than Him?

Our friendship develops as we learn to **trust** Him. One day, I was discussing something with a friend who replied, "I trust you." In our friendship, God desires our trust. Are you willing to trust Him with your insurmountable problems? Do you trust Him when He puts you on hold and you have to wait for His answer? David said, "Those who know your name will trust in you" (Ps. 9:10 NIV).

And our friendship develops as we make every effort to **please** Him. Paul said, "You already know how to please God in your daily living, for you know the commands we gave you from the Lord Jesus himself . . . live more and more closely to that ideal" (1 Thess. 4:1–2 LB).

Are you giving Him the friendship He longs for through your love, trust, and efforts to please Him? May He be able to say that we are His friends.

To many people Jesus is nothing at all. To some people Jesus is something. But to how many people is Jesus everything?

Blessed is the man whom thou choosest, and causest to approach unto thee, that he may dwell in thy courts: we shall be satisfied with the goodness of thy house, even of thy holy temple (Ps. 65:4).

re there times in your life when you feel no one appreciates you or seems to need you? At such times remember there is Someone who loves you with a unique love, Someone to whom you are very special—God Himself.

We are special, for God has chosen us for Himself. The Bible says that those God has chosen are blessed. It cost Christ a great price to choose us for His own; but because He loved us, He willingly paid it. "God showed his great love for us by sending Christ to die for us while we were still sinners" (Rom. 5:8 LB). How much He must love and care for us! No wonder we are so special to Him when He invested His whole life in us. In 1 Peter 2:9 we read, "You have been chosen by God himself—you are . . . holy and pure, you are God's very own—all this so that you may show to others how God called you out of the darkness into his wonderful light" (LB). That gives purpose to our living.

God has chosen us to live with Him. What a privilege that He will make our lives His home. Can you imagine a God who is mighty, holy, and powerful, not only willing but desiring to live in us? He has chosen us for that purpose.

God has chosen us to be satisfied with Him and His goodness. Many seek satisfaction in material possessions, but these things are only transitory. "We shall be satisfied with the goodness of thy house." There is only one source of complete satisfaction—the Lord Jesus. "For he satisfieth the longing soul, and filleth the hungry soul with goodness" (Ps. 107:9).

A young artist who spent all his time in a studio of a great painter in Rome had such talent that his friends urged him to move to his own study. They predicted he would win fame and become wealthy. "No," he replied, "I have found the master. I want to paint like Raphael. In order to do that I must be near him so I can study his method and listen to his instructions and catch his spirit. I have no other ambition but to be like him."

God has chosen us that we might be like Him.

AUGUST 27

As you sent me into the world, I have sent them into the world
(John 17:18 NIV).

 s God's Sent One, sent on a special mission to redeem humankind, Jesus prays to the Father for His disciples, not just the ones who were with Him then but all believers down through the ages, whom He is now sending into the world to carry on His mission.

As His "sent ones," we need to be totally committed to our task. Paul said, "This one thing I do . . . I press toward the mark for the prize of the high calling of God in Christ Jesus" (Phil. 3:13–14). And commitment leads to involvement in the work He has sent us to do.

A missionary in India was invited to have dinner with three naval officers. During their conversation, one of the officers remarked, "Why don't missionaries stay at home and mind their own business?" The missionary replied, "Suppose you were ordered to take your battleship to Constantinople tomorrow, would you choose whether to obey or not?" The officer answered, "If we are ordered to go, we must go, even if every ship is sunk and every sailor killed."

"Quite right," said the missionary. "I have orders from the divine government, "Go ye into all the world, and preach the gospel to every creature" (Mark 16:15).

Our marching orders come from God Himself. His Son obeyed orders and came to earth to die for sinners. In turn, Jesus gave orders to His disciples and all believers who would follow after Him—share the good news!

God has never revoked His commission to evangelize, and the task has not yet been completed. It has been said, "A missionary does not necessarily go outside of his country, his state, or even his community. A true missionary needs only to go outside of himself."

Each day, we need to remember that Christ has sent us forth and given us work to do. Our time for serving Him may be short. Jesus sounded a note of urgency when He said, "All of us must quickly carry out the tasks assigned us by the one who sent me, for there is little time left before the night falls and all work comes to an end" (John 9:4 LB).

You may choose how you will spend your life, but choose wisely. You spend it only once.

AUGUST 28

Simon's mother-in-law was in bed with a fever, and they told Jesus about her (Mark 1:30 NIV).

 eter's mother-in-law was very ill. The disciples, aware of her illness, knew that Jesus could heal her. But Jesus was a busy person. Everywhere He went, He ministered to crowds of people. The disciples might have wondered if they should interrupt Him now with this need.

But they knew that the need of one individual was important to Jesus. Immediately Jesus left the crowd to minister to her. "And he came and took her by the hand, and lifted her up; and immediately the fever left her" (Mark 1:31).

One day as He went into the city of Nain, He saw a funeral procession. It was the son of a widow. "And when the Lord saw her, he had compassion on her, and said unto her, Weep not. And he came and touched the bier: and they that bare him stood still. And he said, Young man, I say unto thee, Arise. And he that was dead sat up, and began to speak" (Luke 7:13–15).

Wherever Jesus went He healed the lame and the blind. His heart was moved with compassion for them, and He was never too busy to stop and minister to someone with a need. Today His heart is still filled with compassion for those with needs.

Are we watching for ways to comfort others, or are we insensitive to the needs of those around us? Do we take time to show God's love by sending a card or making a phone call, or do we let such opportunities slip by?

One time I asked someone I had met a short time before if she were hurting. She said, "How did you know?" I replied, "I saw the hurt in your eyes."

One day a dear friend of mine told me she had had foot surgery. I failed to show much interest in it or tell her I was sorry. I heard her but I didn't really listen. The next time I saw her I discovered she had been hurt by my indifference. I have asked the Lord to make me more loving and caring, for compassion expresses itself in active involvement in the hurts and heartaches.

The Bible says, "Therefore, as God's chosen people, holy and dearly loved, clothe yourselves with compassion, kindness, humility, gentleness and patience" (Col. 3:12 NIV). It also says, "Here are my directions. Pray much for others; plead for God's mercy upon them; give thanks for all he is going to do for them" (1 Tim. 2:1 LB).

And the people murmured against Moses, saying, What shall we drink? (Ex. 15:24).

In some desert areas of our country we find an occasional oasis with a few trees, a limited water supply, and a filling station. As Moses led the children of Israel through the wilderness, there were few trees and no filling stations. It was a rigorous march.

They had not gone far when they began to complain to Moses and Aaron. Their murmuring had begun while they were in Egypt, but now they were out of Egypt, and they were still complaining.

After traveling three days without water, they approached Marah and were delighted to find water there. However, to their disappointment, the water was bitter. They began to murmur. When Moses cried to God for help, God showed him a tree that could purify the water. Moses put the tree in the water, and the people hesitantly took a drink. To their delight, the water was sweet. God had answered prayer. All along their wilderness journey, they constantly complained. Yet, in answer to Moses' prayers, God always met their needs.

God may have scheduled a wilderness journey for your life. You may be at Marah with its bitter waters. Plans for your life have been shattered. Your heart is crushed with sorrow. A disappointment has come. Perhaps you have begun to murmur. Bitterness has crept into your life. It is easy to be sweet when everything is going your way. But when things are difficult, we often murmur and complain. Paul's life was filled with hardships, yet he said, "I have learned, in whatsoever state I am, therewith to be content" (Phil. 4:11).

God can use your bitter waters as a proving ground to test you or as a training ground to make you stronger. The Lord Jesus sweetens the bitter waters of our lives. He will give victory. The Lord told James, "Blessed is a man who perseveres under trial; for once he has been approved, he will receive the crown of life, which the Lord has promised to those who love Him" (James 1:12 NASB).

When you're tempted to murmur and complain, rejoice instead. "Consider it all joy, my brethren, when you encounter various trials, knowing that the testing of your faith produces endurance" (James 1:2–3 NASB).

A heart full of praise has no room for complaining.

AUGUST 30

And Stephen, full of faith and power, did great wonders and miracles among the people (Acts 6:8).

tephen was a man chosen by God for a special place of service in the early church. The disciples were so busy giving out the Word of God and praying that they appointed another group of men to take care of the widows' needs. Stephen was one of the appointees, and we are impressed with one word used to describe him—the word *full*. Some people are full of themselves, but not Stephen.

Stephen was first of all *full* of *faith*. He knew the Word of God, for "Faith cometh by hearing, and hearing by the word of God" (Rom. 10:17).

Stephen was *full* of *grace*. Grace is charm and winsomeness. Christ Himself was full of grace. "The Word became flesh and made his dwelling among us . . . full of grace and truth" (John 1:14 NIV). The grace of Jesus was reflected in His voice and on His face. We, too, need to be winsome with His winsomeness.

Stephen was also *full* of *power*. He did not try to perform his duties in his own strength; he was full of the power of God, and served in His power.

He was also *full* of *wisdom*. He needed God-given wisdom in his work. He was a man with practical common sense.

Stephen was full of faith, grace, power, and wisdom because he was *full* of the *Holy Spirit*. That's why God could use him.

But even the most godly Christians can have enemies. And Stephen's enemies eventually stoned him to death. As he was being stoned, his face shone as the face of an angel. A young man stood by, watching, who would never be able to forget the angelic face of Stephen. Saul, later named Paul, became a Christian and eventually one of the greatest missionaries ever known. He had seen a man full of faith, grace, power, and wisdom—filled with God's Holy Spirit.

What is your life filled with, self or the Holy Spirit? You may never know the impact your life has on the life of someone else.

"Be filled up with God himself" (Eph. 3:19 LB).

AUGUST 31

I will love thee, O LORD, my strength (Ps. 18:1).

his psalm reveals the psalmist David's intimate relationship with his God. In each of the first three verses, David calls him Lord. He begins, "I will love thee, O LORD, my strength." God delights to have us come humbly, not asking for our needs at first, but taking time to say, "I love you." When was the last time you paused to say, "Dear Lord, I love you"?

When we love someone dearly and we know they love us, we have complete trust in that person. David spoke of "The LORD . . . in whom I will trust" (v. 2), and he enumerated some reasons why he trusted God.

He said, "The LORD is my rock." A rock foundation is a strong one. We could not have a stronger foundation for our lives than Jesus Christ.

"The LORD is . . . my fortress." A fortress is a place of shelter and safety. With crime so rampant in our world today, how thankful we can be that we have a fortress, the Lord Jesus, as our place of safety.

"The LORD is . . . my deliverer." He has power to deliver us from the enemy of our souls.

"The LORD is . . . my strength." He does not just *give* strength, He *is* strength, *my* strength.

"The LORD is . . . my buckler"—a shield protecting us from the enemy.

The LORD is . . . the horn of my salvation." Salvation means deliverance. It is interesting that the word *horn* and *shone* are the same Hebrew word. When David spoke of the Lord as the horn of his salvation, he recognized that the Lord was the light or glory of his salvation.

"The LORD is . . . my high tower"—a place of safety above the trials of earth.

In the first verse, David declares his love for God: "I will love him," who strengthens me. In verse two, he voices his trust in God: "I will trust him," who protects me. In verse three, he expresses his confidence in God: "I will call upon Him," who will save me.

He is worthy to be praised. Pause now and praise Him.

SEPTEMBER 1

Come to Me, all you who labor and are heavy-laden and overburdened, and I will cause you to rest—I will ease and relieve and refresh your souls (Matt. 11:28 AMPLIFIED).

n the midst of today's restless world Jesus invites the overburdened and weary, "Come unto me." To those carrying burdens of heartaches, bitterness, rejection, guilt, or loneliness, He says to come and find rest. To those who are frustrated and overburdened with responsibilities, He offers rest if we'll just come to Him. If you fall into any of those categories, you may claim His promised rest.

Jesus invites you to experience the **reality of relationship.** This is the rest we receive through a personal relationship with Jesus. "But as many as received him, to them gave he power to become the sons of God, even to them that believe on his name" (John 1:12).

Through our relationship with Him, we experience the **reality of release.** We aren't guaranteed freedom from burdens, but we experience His rest as we release them to Him.

As we release our burdens to Him, we experience the **reality of rest** in our daily living. This is not rest *from* activity, but rest *in* activity. We can have this rest even when we are physically exhausted. It is rest in our souls that takes us through times of tragedy, devastation, and storms in our lives.

Jesus said, "Take my yoke upon you, and learn of me" (Matt. 11:29). In Palestine, after the ox was measured, the wooden yoke was roughed out. Then it was adjusted to fit the ox perfectly. Jesus' yoke is the will of the Father. When we take His yoke, we are yoked with Jesus to do God's will. His yoke is easy. The Greek word means well-fitting. Jesus said, "Wear my yoke—for it fits perfectly—and let me teach you; for I am gentle and humble, and you shall find rest for your souls; for I give you only light burdens" (v. 29 LB). His burdens are light, for He carries the heavy end of them. We experience the reality of rest when we submit to being yoked to Jesus as Lord of our lives.

Are you restless, or are you resting in the Lord Jesus Christ? Through your personal relationship with Christ, you can release each day to Him and experience the reality of His rest. Jesus alone can give your soul rest.

"Rest in the Lord, and wait patiently for him" (Ps. 37:7).

SEPTEMBER 2

You know that it was not with perishable things such as silver or gold that you were redeemed from the empty way of life handed down to you from your forefathers, but with the precious blood of Christ, a lamb without blemish or defect (1 Peter 1:18–19 NIV).

nce a father and his little boy decided to make a wooden boat together. After selecting the design, they spent hours crafting it. When they had finished, the beautiful boat was the child's dearest treasure. They attached a long cord so the little boy could sail it on the lake and still control it. But one day, he accidentally dropped the cord, and his treasured boat floated out of his sight. He was heartbroken.

Weeks later, the little boy saw his boat for sale in a toy shop window. He went in and told the shop owner that it was his boat, showing him a special identifying mark on it. The shop owner had bought it from a man who had found it, but he said, "I will sell it back to you for the price I paid for it."

The little boy worked hard to save enough money to buy it back, then returned to the toy shop. As the owner put the boat into his arms, the little boy hugged it tightly and said, "Little boat, you are twice mine now. First, I made you, and now I have bought you back."

To believers, God says, "You are twice mine. First, I created you. Now I have bought you back."

Our redemption was costly. It cost Jesus His very life. He died on the cross to redeem the whole world from sin. Paul said, "We have redemption through his blood" (Eph. 1:7), and when John saw Jesus one day, he said, "Behold the Lamb of God, which taketh away the sin of the world" (John 1:29).

Sin is disobedience and unbelief. It is going our way instead of God's. To be redeemed means to be set free from the penalty of sin by the payment of a ransom. The purchase price of Jesus' shed blood releases us from our old life of sin. By accepting Christ as our personal Savior, we become one of God's redeemed children. The Bible says, "What? know ye not that your body is the temple of the Holy Ghost which is in you, which ye have of God, and ye are not your own? For ye are bought with a price: therefore glorify God in your body, and in your spirit, which are God's" (1 Cor. 6:19–20).

May we glorify our Redeemer today.

SEPTEMBER 3

Don't be concerned about the outward beauty that depends on jew-
elry, or beautiful clothes, or hair arrangement. Be beautiful inside,
in your hearts, with the lasting charm of a gentle and quiet spirit
which is so precious to God (1 Peter 3:3–4 LB).

ost women have a natural desire to be as attractive as possible. The billion-dollar cosmetic industry confirms the fact that women make every effort to beautify themselves.

We are to be good representatives of Jesus Christ in the world today. This includes our entire person, who and what we are as well as what we say and do. Some people, in their eagerness to please the Lord and glorify Him, have concentrated on their spiritual development and overlooked the care of their physical being. We must not neglect the outward person. We must keep ourselves looking lovely on the outside, too, for that is what people see first.

However, the outer appearance is not the criterion for real beauty. Have you not met people who were beautiful outwardly, but you soon discovered it was only on the surface? They lacked the real beauty within. The outer attractiveness is not sufficient. We must pay attention to beautifying the inner life, which Peter says, "is so precious to God."

More important is the transformation of the hidden person of the heart. In 1 Samuel 16:7 we read, "Man looketh on the outward appearance, but the LORD looketh on the heart." We must spend time developing our inner loveliness.

True beauty is Jesus Christ revealed in our lives. The psalmist said, "They looked to Him, and were radiant" (Ps. 34:5 AMPLIFIED). The Holy Spirit develops inner qualities of beauty, such as a gentle and quiet spirit. This does not mean a weak spirit. Sometimes we need great strength to remain quiet. But we are not to complain, argue, nag, or be domineering. A quiet spirit reacts calmly when the pressures come. This quiet restfulness comes from God.

As the years pass, our natural beauty begins to fade. Wrinkles come, the hair is streaked with gray, our energy diminishes. But our inner loveliness remains through the years. In the Song of Solomon we read that "He is altogether lovely." Altogether means complete, whole, and permanent. Christ is completely and permanently lovely. His loveliness, radiance, and beauty in our lives never fades.

Let the beauty of Jesus be seen in me.

SEPTEMBER 4

Fear thou not; for I am with thee: be not dismayed; for I am thy
God: I will strengthen thee; yea, I will help thee; yea, I will uphold
thee with the right hand of my righteousness (Isa. 41:10).

any of us fear being alone. I face this fear often. But over and over throughout Scripture, God has spoken two words to comfort and cheer our troubled hearts: Fear not. Immediately you may think, "Don't be fearful in my situation?" But then God tells us why: "For I am with you." We are assured of the presence of Almighty God. He doesn't say, "I have been with you," or "I will be with you," but "I *am* with you." This means today in your present circumstances. God is always the God of the present.

Fear comes when we focus on our problems instead of Him. But God says, "Fear not [there is nothing to fear], for *I* am with you" (AMPLIFIED). Experiencing His presence within, we have not one thing to fear. He knows our problems better than we do, and He also knows the solution. When we realize who He is, the God who created and maintains the universe, why should we fear?

Then God makes three promises. The first one is **I will strengthen thee.** In our weakness, He gives us His strength. The Bible says, "As thy days, so shall thy strength be" (Deut. 33:25). Have you reached the end of your strength? God promises *He* will be our strength. He will enable us to go on.

Then He has promised **I will help thee.** Where do you need help today—at home, at work, at church, in your neighborhood? Whatever your need, He has promised help. His help never comes too early or too late but always on time.

His third promise is **I will uphold thee with the right hand of my righteousness.** His right hand symbolizes His power. His powerful right hand assures victory. It may not always be the way we expect, but He promises victory in His perfect way and time.

And He goes with us everywhere. David responded to this promise by saying, "Even when walking through the dark valley of death I will not be afraid, for you are close beside me, guarding, guiding all the way" (Ps. 23:4 LB).

We never have to face any situation alone.

SEPTEMBER 5

[The Bereans] were more noble than those in Thessalonica, in that they received the word with all readiness of mind, and searched the scriptures daily, whether those things were so (Acts 17:11).

he most important book in the world is the Bible. What would it be like not to have a copy? Most of us have several. But how much has the Bible become a part of us?

The Bible is the Word of God filled with messages for each of us. It encourages us, rebukes us, and reveals to us the message of salvation through Jesus Christ.

The Berean Christians were eager to know God's Word. With all readiness of mind, they received the Word of God that Paul and Silas shared with them. They were open-minded, teachable. But they weren't satisfied just to listen. "They . . . studied the scriptures every day to see if what they were now being told were true" (PHILLIPS). They did not necessarily disbelieve Paul, but they were eager to know these truths for themselves. They studied God's Word regularly—day by day. "As a result, many of them believed" (v. 12 LB).

We receive spiritual encouragement as we listen to others share God's Word through books, tapes, seminars, or messages at conferences. God uses these things to strengthen our spiritual life. However, it is important for us to daily read and study God's Word for ourselves to know what it says and appropriate it for our own lives.

We need to approach the Bible, as the Bereans did, with an open mind and teachable spirit. As the voice of God speaks to us through His Word, we need to give full attention to what He says.

Because there is a great deal of false teaching in the world today, we need to be sure we are not led astray. We need to read God's Word to be sure we know what it says.

As we take time to reflect on what we read, we will receive new insights. Our hearts will be open to the working of the Holy Spirit, and we will gradually become the person God desires us to be. As our lives are changed within, those around us will notice.

Spending time with God in His Word is a choice that can become a habit that in turn can become a glorious life-style.

SEPTEMBER 6

O God, thou art my God; early will I seek thee: my soul thirsteth for thee, my flesh longeth for thee in a dry and thirsty land, where no water is (Ps. 63:1).

eople are searching everywhere for things that will satisfy. Some hunger for position, some for power. Others hunger for pleasure, love, or acceptance. But nothing seems to fill them up. They pack their lives full of activity to avoid feeling the emptiness of their lives.

David was in the wilderness—a dry and thirsty land where there was no water. At this time he was probably running from his son, Absalom. Very likely, he was lonely and discouraged. But he knew where to go in his wilderness experience. He went into God's presence, saying, "O God, thou art my God." He approached God with confidence because God was personal to him. He could say, "Thou art *my* God." What greater words can be said?

Then David continued, "Early will I seek thee." He eagerly sought God Himself. He loved God and longed to be with Him. "My soul longeth, yea, even fainteth for the courts of the LORD: my heart and my flesh crieth out for the living God" (Ps. 84:2). David had claimed God's promise to reveal Himself to those who would earnestly seek Him. "If . . . thou shalt seek the LORD thy God, thou shalt find him, if thou seek him with all thy heart and with all thy soul" (Deut. 4:29). He sought the Lord with a longing and thirst as intense as the thirst of a traveler in a dry and thirsty land, and God satisfied his longing.

Is there a desire in your heart for God? Are you seeking after Him? Or have you let your life become so packed with activity that you have pushed God out without even realizing it? To be satisfied and fulfilled you need to seek Him and spend time with Him. He is longing for sweet fellowship with us. What we need is a fresh glimpse of God.

A Thai man once came to a mission station, and the missionaries asked why he had come. "Are you looking for medicine?" When he said no, the missionaries persisted. "What are you looking for, then?" they asked. He replied, "I am looking for God."

"As the hart [deer] panteth after the water brooks, so panteth my soul after thee, O God. My soul thirsteth for God, for the living God" (Ps. 42:1–2).

In a dry land a thirsty soul needs a satisfying God.

SEPTEMBER 7

Since then, you have been raised with Christ, set [our] hearts on things above, where Christ is seated at the right hand of God (Col. 3:1 NIV).

 hen I lived in Denver, we would often spend a few days at our mountain cabin. It was quiet—no phone, no mail—a wonderful place to relax and rest. As we watched the fleecy white clouds drifting across the blue sky, we could see the mountains in the background. We seemed to be living in the heavens. Living above the rush of city life, our focus in life would change. When we returned to the city, we could view our circumstances in proper perspective.

As believers, we are identified with Christ in His resurrection life. In union with Him, we are living at a new altitude. We have been raised to live a new life in the heavens. Paul wrote that God "hath raised us up together, and made us sit together in heavenly places in Christ Jesus" (Eph. 2:6).

Seated with Christ in the heavens, we receive power for living in newness of life on earth. As citizens of heaven, we are to "set our hearts on things above," which gives us new direction in life. We become occupied with Jesus. Our heart is set on the things that concern Him—His interests, His purposes, His will. Yet, we are not to be so heavenly minded that it distorts our earthly walk.

We are to seek the answers for our problems in the heavens from Him. Earthly answers, earthly solutions, are not sufficient. We are to seek our strength, wisdom, and patience in the heavens from Him. The answers to our needs are all in Him. And above all, we are to seek *Him*.

Though we are seated in the heavens, we must not stay there. Jesus commissioned us to go out to the people in the marketplace. He showed concern for the condition of the people who came to Him. "What pity he felt for the crowds that came, because their problems were so great and they didn't know what to do or where to go for help. They were like sheep without a shepherd" (Matt. 9:36 LB). Then He challenged his disciples. "The harvest is so great, and the workers are so few" he said. "So pray to the one in charge of the harvesting, and ask him to recruit more workers for his harvest fields" (Matt. 9:37–38 LB).

What is your response?

SEPTEMBER 8

Christ in you, the hope of glory (Col. 1:27).

n the world today, many are without hope because they are without God. Worldwide tensions and problems add to their feeling of hopelessness, which often leads to despair. Hope is one of our greatest needs.

Our hope is our confidence in the person of Jesus Christ, our hope of glory, who lives within those who have committed their lives to Him. It is not enough that He came, lived, died, and rose from the dead. He is our hope in coping with life in today's world.

The hope we have in Christ is a living hope. "In his great mercy he has given us new birth into a living hope through the resurrection of Jesus Christ from the dead" (1 Peter 1:3 NIV). This hope removes all fear, for He is our All-sufficiency. If He is a living reality in our heart, He will be a living reality in our experiences. Our hope is in Him, not in our circumstances and their outcome.

Our hope is an anchor. "We have this hope as an anchor for the soul, firm and secure (Heb. 6:19 NIV). An anchor holds us steady through the storms, for it keeps us from drifting and gives us security.

This hope gives us joy. "We rejoice in the hope of the glory of God" (Rom. 5:2 NIV). It is an overflowing hope. "May the God of hope fill you with all joy and peace as you trust in him, so that you may overflow with hope by the power of the Holy Spirit" (Rom. 15:13 NIV).

Our confident hope in God is strengthened by the Word of God. "Everything that was written in the past was written to teach us, so that through endurance and the encouragement of the Scriptures we might have hope" (Rom. 15:4 NIV).

Hope grows with the expectation of Christ's return. We are "looking for that blessed hope, and the glorious appearing of the great God and our Saviour Jesus Christ" (Titus 2:13). And our hope of His return affects our behavior. "Every man that hath this hope in him purifieth himself, even as he is pure" (1 John 3:3).

Our eternal hope is also our hope for today.

SEPTEMBER 9

I am come that they might have life, and that they might have it more abundantly (John 10:10).

 esus came to give us not only eternal life, but life in abundance. The Greek word means overflowing all around the edges. Abundant life is possible because of Christ's death and resurrection, and it can be a reality because of the indwelling of the Holy Spirit.

The Holy Spirit makes the abundant life of Christ real to us in our everyday situations. We will speak as He would speak, we will walk as He would walk, we will do as He would do, we will go where He would go, we will react to situations as He would react. His motives will be ours. And the abundance of His life provides power to overcome such attitudes as hatred, jealousy, selfishness, and criticalness.

In the abundant life Jesus Christ's All-sufficiency permeates every area of our conduct. Paul wrote, "For to me to live is Christ" (Phil. 1:21), and his goal was: "That I may know him, and the power of his resurrection, and the fellowship of his sufferings, being made conformable unto his death" (Phil. 3:10).

Christ's resources are always available. We will have an abundance of His wisdom, patience, and joy as we need it. And the abundance of His life will overflow our lives, blessing others. "I came that they may have and enjoy life, and have it in abundance—to the full, till it overflows" (AMPLIFIED).

You may not feel like you have abundant life today. You may feel discouraged. You may be saying, "I have tried and failed over and over again. I am ready to give up." Remember, none of us have attained the ultimate of this life. We are in a lifetime process with ups and downs.

When we fail, we can ask the Lord for forgiveness. He lifts us up and puts us back on His path again. God is grading us on our heart attitude and effort, not on our attainment.

We cannot have the abundant life in our own strength. We depend totally on Christ. "For in him we live, and move, and have our being" (Acts 17:28).

Beloved, now are we the sons of God, and it doth not yet appear what we shall be: but we know that, when he shall appear, we shall be like him; for we shall see him as he is (1 John 3:2).

esus is coming again! God's Word assures us of this. John wrote, *"when* he shall appear" not *if.* He was confident because of an experience the disciples had at the end of Jesus' earthly stay.

After His resurrection, Jesus remained on earth for forty days. Then one day, He took His disciples out toward Bethany. After giving them a final message, He "was taken up; and a cloud received him out of their sight" (Acts 1:9).

The disciples watched the sky intently as He ascended. Then two men dressed in white stood beside them and said, "Men of Galilee . . . why do you stand here looking into the sky? This same Jesus, who has been taken from you into heaven, will come back in the same way you have seen him go into heaven" (Acts 1:11 NIV).

With anticipation of Christ's return John probably remembers the words of those men at Christ's ascension as he writes to those he calls beloved, those who are the privileged, the children of God. John assures God's children of a better future. Even though we don't know exactly what it will be like, we know life will be infinitely better when He comes again.

Paul describes the future of the children of God this way: "For I consider that the sufferings of this present time (this present life) are not worth being compared with the glory that is about to be revealed to us and in us and for us and conferred on us! For (even the whole) creation (all nature) waits expectantly and longs earnestly for God's sons to be made known—waits for the revealing, the disclosing of their sonship" (Rom. 8:18–19 AMPLIFIED).

Christ *is* going to return, and when he does, "We shall be like him; for we shall see him as he is." As we gaze on Him in all His perfection, we will have perfect bodies, we will no longer be controlled by sin and bad habits, and we will experience no more sorrow or sickness.

"We shall all be changed, in a moment, in the twinkling of an eye, at the last trump: for the trumpet shall sound, and the dead shall be raised incorruptible, and we shall be changed" (1 Cor. 15:51–52).

We have something wonderful to look forward to. What a day that will be!

I know that God is first in your life—you have not withheld even your beloved son from me (Gen. 22:12 LB).

braham experienced one of the most severe tests a person ever faced. One day God appeared to him and said, "Take now thy son, thine only son Isaac, whom thou lovest, and . . . offer him there for a burnt offering upon one of the mountains which I will tell thee of" (v. 2).

Abraham couldn't understand what God was doing. God had promised him that Isaac would be the seed of a new nation. But now God commanded him to sacrifice his son. He must choose either to obey God or disobey. It was as if God were saying, "Abraham, who is most important in your life—Isaac or me?"

Abraham obeyed God. What a demonstration of faith! Since God had promised that Isaac would be the seed of His chosen people, Abraham believed that even though Isaac would die, God would bring him back to life again.

Just as Abraham was about to sacrifice his son to God, an angel of the Lord stopped him. And a lamb appeared in the thicket nearby for him to sacrifice. It was not really Isaac that God wanted, it was Abraham's heart. God must have no rivals; He must have first place. When God is first, everything else falls into its rightful place. Abraham had passed his test successfully.

But sometimes God shares the priority spot in our lives. We put Him first plus our families, plus our possessions, or plus our service. But we will not know the true lordship of Jesus in our lives until we let Him be first and sacrifice those pluses, yield them to Him, and let Him put them in their rightful place. When He is on the throne of our lives, all that we have and all that we are will be in the place Jesus wants them to be.

Paul sums up our sacrifice this way: "I am crucified with Christ: nevertheless I live; yet not I, but Christ liveth in me: and the life which I now live in the flesh I live by the faith of the Son of God, who loved me, and gave himself for me" (Gal. 2:20).

SEPTEMBER 12

Casting all your care upon him; for he careth for you
(1Peter 5:7).

ften as I sit in an airport, I study the faces of people. The majority have careworn faces, evidence of troubled hearts. All classes of people are victims of care and worry. No one is exempt from its devastating effects. Some of you may say, "I can't take any more." Others may look at someone else and say, "I couldn't take what they are going through."

In Exodus 2, we read of the children of Israel, who were in bondage as slaves in Egypt. When they could take no more, they cried out to God, and He was there to deliver them. "And the children of Israel sighed by reason of the bondage, and they cried, and their cry came up unto God . . . And God heard . . . and God remembered . . . and God looked . . . and God had respect unto them" (vv. 23–25). He cared.

We live in such a mixed-up world that it is easy to fret. Yet no matter how much we worry, it never accomplishes anything. And if our hearts are filled with worry, we have lost touch with God. We say as Martha did, "Dost thou not care?" (Luke 10:40).

Peter says that He does care. God's heart beats with love for you. And He has provided a cure for worry. God asks us to *cast* our cares on Him today. We must release them to Him and never take them up again. We are to cast *all* our cares on Him—not just the easy ones but the heart-crushing ones as well.

A story is told of a man carrying a heavy burden on his back, who was offered a ride. The driver said, "Put your bundle in the back of the wagon." "Oh, sir, you are kind enough to give me a ride. I couldn't ask you to carry my burden, too."

How like that we are. Yet God gives rest in exchange for our anxieties the moment we hand them over to Him. Instantly, it becomes a matter of honor for Him to do what is best for us. We need only trust Him.

Trust and prayer lessen care!

SEPTEMBER 13

*And in the morning, rising up a great while before day, he went out,
and departed into a solitary place, and there prayed (Mark 1:35).*

he Lord Jesus made prayer a prominent part of His earthly
ministry. The early morning hours found Him in some solitary
place alone, praying to His heavenly Father. Sometimes, He
spent a whole night in prayer. With so many demands upon
Him there was little time to relax. But He never neglected communion with His
Father.

One morning, after a very busy day, Jesus had slipped out alone to His
place of prayer. That time with His Father must have been very special. I
wonder if they discussed His work yet to be accomplished as well as His
schedule for that day.

But His disciples knew where to find Him, and they came to tell Him that
the crowds again were seeking Him. "Everyone is looking for you!" they said
(v. 37 NIV). He replied, "Let us go into the next towns, that I may preach
there also: for therefore came I forth" (v. 38). The "next towns" were part of
God's purpose for Him. The people there were waiting for Him to preach the
gospel, too.

There are many "next towns" for us to reach today. Each of us has a
plan from God, and we can say, "Therefore came I forth." Our next town may
be a phone call. It may be a letter we need to write. It may be prayer for
someone God has put upon our heart.

During a Billy Graham crusade, a young woman went forward and
received Christ, but she said, "I don't even know what made me come
tonight." Her counselor said, "Someone has been praying for you." The young
woman couldn't think of anyone who would be praying for her, but a few days
later a neighbor brought her a pie and welcomed her to her new neighborhood.
As they began to visit, she told her neighbor of her conversion. The neighbor
burst into tears. "When you moved here, God put you on my heart," she said.
"I have been praying for you."

God says, "But thou, when thou prayest, enter into thy closet, and when
thou hast shut thy door, pray to thy Father which is in secret; and thy Father
which seeth in secret shall reward thee openly" (Matt. 6:6).

Are you praying for your "next towns," or are you living the barrenness
of a busy life?

SEPTEMBER 14

Order my steps in thy word (Ps. 119:133).

n today's world many voices compete for our attention. As we listen, we are confused. Who is right? The psalmist asked for God's direction. He asked God to order his steps. To *order* is to command or instruct, usually backed by authority.

The Bible is the voice of authority from God. "Thy word is truth" (John 17:17). It gives us guidance so that we can know and do His will. It tells us what will please Him. It reveals the truth about the One who said, "I am . . . the truth" (John 14:6).

Some people read only their favorite portions, but Paul said, "The whole Bible was given to us by inspiration from God and is useful to teach us what is true and to make us realize what is wrong in our lives; it straightens us out and helps us do what is right. It is God's way of making us well prepared at every point, fully equipped to do good to everyone" (2 Tim. 3:16–17 LB).

I make a habit of reading the Bible through over and over again. I do not bind myself to a schedule of having to read a certain number of chapters a day, but I read from Genesis through Revelation. I do not understand all of it, but each time I read it, the Holy Spirit reveals more to me.

Beyond reading it, we get nourishment from assimilating it. "O how love I thy law! it is my meditation all the day" (Ps. 119:97). Meditating on His Word helps us grow more and more like Jesus Christ.

I knew a Christian man with only one leg, little education, and few material possessions. Although he couldn't read, he had such a desire to read the Bible that he asked God to help him. With almost no help from anyone except the Holy Spirit as his Teacher, he did learn to read God's Word. What a challenge for those of us who had been reading most our lives to hear this dear man read God's Word with such appreciation.

What does God's Word mean to you? Is it your Guidebook for daily living? Only when we put a Scripture into practice can we say we know it.

In this [union and communion with Him] love is brought to completion and attains perfection with us (1 John 4:17 AMPLIFIED).

aul paints a picture of a love-filled life in 1 Corinthians 13. It is the picture of Jesus Christ's inner character. He is the Original, but He desires many reprints.

"This love of which I speak is slow to lose patience" (1 Cor. 13:4 PHILLIPS). In the rush of life today, we see little patience exhibited. We are impatient if an appointment is delayed, impatient to be waited on in a shop, impatient with our families. Genuine love, however, is slow to lose its patience. Even though treated unjustly, it doesn't strike back. It refuses to be resentful even though it may have reason. Peter writes of Jesus, our example, "Who, when he was reviled, reviled not again" (1 Peter 2:23).

"Love is kind" (v. 4 NIV). The Phillips paraphrase reads, "It looks for a way of being constructive." This is not just being kind to those who are kind to us. It is being kind to those who are unkind. This love is quick to return good for evil—being kind to someone who has wronged us. It does not retaliate. Love not only takes the wrong but shows kindness to the person responsible.

"Love never is envious nor boils over with jealousy" (v. 4 AMPLIFIED). Love does not begrudge another what they have or what they are doing. It rejoices in their success and advance. It is not possessive. Love is content with God's will.

Love "is neither anxious to impress nor does it cherish inflated ideas of its own importance" (v. 4 PHILLIPS). It does not parade or display self. It doesn't boast or brag. If self is prominent, love is lacking. Love is not arrogant or proud, but humble. Love cannot coexist with a superiority complex.

Love "does not pursue selfish advantage" (v. 5 PHILLIPS). Such love is self-forgetful. It is not rude but courteous. It lives to serve others.

Love "does not demand its own way" (v. 5 LB) or seek its own rights. Love has good manners. It is always thinking of what is best for others.

And love is more important than knowledge. "While knowledge may make a man look big, it is only love that can make him grow to his full stature" (1 Cor. 8:1 PHILLIPS).

Make love your goal.

SEPTEMBER 16

We know how dearly God loves us, and we feel this warm love ev-
erywhere within us because God has given us the Holy Spirit to fill
our hearts with his love" (Rom. 5:5 LB).

he Lord wants to reproduce His love in your life and mine. Let
us consider more characteristics of that love.

Love "is not touchy" (1 Cor. 13:5 PHILLIPS). Love is
not irritable, bad-tempered, resentful, or sensitive. A woman
apologized to a friend for something at which her friend could have taken
offense. The friend just laughed it off. "I am honest," she said. "I never pick up
things that don't belong to me—not even slights."

Love "does not keep account of evil or gloat over the wickedness of other
people" (v. 5 PHILLIPS). Love doesn't keep a record of wrongs done against it
but will keep a record of kindnesses. It is never glad when others fail.

"On the contrary, it is glad with all good men when truth prevails"
(v. 5 PHILLIPS). Love will look for and be delighted with what it sees of good in
others. It does not expose weaknesses of other people.

Love "knows no limit to its endurance" (v. 7 PHILLIPS). Love endures
patiently. It bears its load to the limit. It bears slights and wrongs—even from
friends and relatives—without retaliation.

Love knows "no end to its trust" (v. 7 PHILLIPS). Love is not suspicious
but believes the best in people as long as it can. It always looks for good.

Love knows "no fading of its hope" (v. 7 PHILLIPS). Love never despairs
of anyone. The Lord Jesus never gives up on anyone.

Love "can outlast anything" (v. 7 PHILLIPS). When all else is gone, love
endures to the very end. Love is permanent, for God is love.

Does this type of love seem impossible? Can anyone live that way all the
time? There was One of whom this love-filled life was completely true: Jesus
Christ Himself.

Perhaps you are saying, "If only this were true of me. But I am impatient.
I say things I am later sorry for. Can I love as Paul has described? Can it be real
in my life?"

We cannot do it in our own strength. It is not the result of our own effort.
We can only love in this way by submitting to the work of the Spirit of God in
us. "The fruit of the Spirit is love" (Gal. 5:22).

SEPTEMBER 17

Now set your heart and your soul to seek the Lord your God; arise therefore, and build (1 Chron. 22:19).

he great desire of David's heart was to build the temple for God. But to his disappointment, that privilege was given to his son, Solomon. David could have become embittered over this, but instead he cooperated fully in the construction plans.

Then he gave these encouraging words to his son. "Set your mind and heart to seek—inquire of and require as your vital necessity—the Lord your God. Arise and build the sanctuary of the Lord God . . . to the name and renown of the Lord" (v. 19 AMPLIFIED).

How important this reminder is to us today when there seems to be so much to do that the Lord is crowded out of our daily schedule. David reminded Solomon that before he started the construction of the temple he must seek the Lord for whom the temple was to be built. We, too, must be careful not to crowd the Lord out of our schedule. We are not to seek programs, methods, or plans first, but we are to seek *Him* first. "Blessed are they that keep his testimonies, and that seek him with the whole heart" (Ps. 119:2).

We seek Him in His Word. We seek Him in prayer. We seek Him in our circumstances. Seeking Him is important if we are to serve Him effectively. Our relationship with Him must have top priority. "That in all things he might have the preeminence" (Col. 1:18).

When Leonardo da Vinci finished his famous painting, *The Last Supper,* he invited friends in to view it. As they looked at it, their ohs and ahs gratified him. All were enamored by the wonderful lace tablecloth of the painting. They talked of nothing else. Suddenly, he dipped his brush in his paint and wiped out the lacework. They looked at him in surprise, and he said, "Look at the face of the Master." They had almost missed the glory of the painting by looking at the lacework instead of the face of Jesus. "Seek the Lord and his strength, seek his face continually" (1 Chron. 16:11).

Before we can *arise and build,* we must look beyond the lacework of our service and gaze on the face of our Lord Jesus Christ.

Be strong and of a good courage . . . and the LORD, he it is that doth go before thee; he will be with thee, he will not fail thee, neither forsake thee: fear not, neither be dismayed (Deut. 31:7–8).

hile in London, I watched the changing of the guard at Buckingham Palace. What a display of pomp and pageantry! As the guards being relieved of duty marched away, new ones took their places, united in their purpose of protecting the royal family. Each had a place of service, and each accepted personal responsibility in his place.

You and I have been chosen of God to assume a place of responsibility for Him. "Ye have not chosen me, but I have chosen you, and ordained you, that ye should go and bring forth fruit, and that your fruit should remain" (John 15:16).

Our place of service may not be the one of our choosing. Your God-chosen place of service may be on the plains of Kansas, and you would rather it be in the bustling city of Denver. You may be confined at home caring for your husband's parents, and you would prefer being active in your church. You may be weary and discouraged. But God-chosen people can expect God-given help for them in their God-chosen place.

God has promised His **power.** "Be strong and of a good courage." We can claim God's strength for our place of service. Though weary from the care of a loved one or exhausted from our business, as we switch onto His power, He will give the strength we need.

God promises His **presence.** "The Lord, he it is that doth go before thee." God is the Lord of our tomorrows; He goes *before* us. An uncertain future need not cause fear. Not only does He go before us, but He accompanies us step by step.

He has also promised His **trustworthiness.** "He will not fail thee, neither forsake thee." He has never broken one of His promises, so we can trust Him in the constant changing of the guard in our lives. While serving in one place, we may be suddenly moved. Just when we get used to one situation, another pops up. Regardless, the Lord says, "Fear not, neither be dismayed." We should not fear what we *can't* see, and we should not be dismayed at what we *do* see.

God promises, "I will be with thee."

SEPTEMBER 19

He that goeth forth and weepeth, bearing precious seed, shall
doubtless come again with rejoicing, bringing his sheaves with him
(Ps. 126:6).

ne time a man was a guest in the home of the great missionary statesman, Dr. A. B. Simpson. Early one morning, the guest decided to take a walk. As he passed the study door, he saw Dr. Simpson seated at his desk. He started to greet him but paused as he saw that Dr. Simpson was reading the Bible.

When Dr. Simpson finished reading, he began to pray. Silently watching, the guest saw him pull the world globe toward him and begin revolving it, praying aloud for the lost multitudes of the world, country by country. Suddenly he put his arms around the globe, drew it to himself, and wept over it until the whole world was wet with his tears of compassion. The visitor said, "I felt I was standing on holy ground. All I could think of was, 'They that sow in tears shall reap in joy.'"

Before each of us today lies a field to be sown. There are millions in the world today without hope, for they do not know God. Before there can be a harvest, the seed has to be sown. Then it must be nourished, watered, and cultivated. Then comes the harvest. We are to go forth sowing the precious seed, the Word of God because "faith cometh by hearing, and hearing by the word of God" (Rom. 10:17).

But in the above Scripture, the sower went forth weeping. Seed doesn't grow well in dry ground. Do tears of compassion well up from our hearts for those with whom we sow the Word?

And we sow, we shall reap. "He . . . shall doubtless come again with rejoicing, bringing his sheaves with him." The amount of reaping depends upon the amount of sowing. "He which soweth sparingly shall reap also sparingly; and he which soweth bountifully shall reap also bountifully" (2 Cor. 9:6).

There will come a day when we will stand before God. He will expect an accounting from each of us. Will we stand before Him empty-handed, or will we have an abundant harvest to lay at His feet?

SEPTEMBER 20

By faith Abraham, when he was called to go out into a place which
he should after receive for an inheritance, obeyed; and he went out,
not knowing whither he went (Heb. 11:8).

Faith is taking God at His Word, following the Lord without any reservations. Faith is going forth with God, not knowing where He will lead.

Abraham is a classic example of a person who walked by faith. One day, God appeared to him and said, "Leave your own country behind you, and your own people, and go to the land I will guide you to" (Gen. 12:1 LB). Imagine Sarah's surprise when Abraham came home and said, "We are going to move." "Where?" "I don't know." "When?" "Right away." "Why?" "God told me to." Abraham didn't know any details, but he was ready to answer God's call. Along with God's call came His promise to bless Abraham and make of him a great nation. God doesn't always give His reasons, but He does give His promise.

Faith is linked with obedience. "By faith Abraham, when he was called . . . obeyed." Faith is traveling with God under sealed orders. Abraham was willing to follow God's will for him. He didn't know where it would take him, but he committed himself to it. He believed his call from God, and that was enough. He trusted the unknown to God. Uncertainties meant little to Abraham, for he was committed to the God of certainty.

God's will for us may be a call to the unknown. All God wants is our willingness to go. He may not tell us where we are going or what He wants us to do. Our part is to respond in obedience; His part is to lead us in the path of His will.

In Romans 12:2 we discover that God's will is good, acceptable, and perfect. We can trust Him to plan what is best for us. Faith involves committing ourselves to God before we discover His plan. Like Abraham, is our response, "I went out, not knowing where I was to go"?

When we walk by faith with God through the unknown, God has the liberty of showing us that only He could have worked things out so well. Paul wrote, "I know whom I have believed, and am persuaded that he is able to keep that which I have committed unto him against that day" (2 Tim. 1:12).

SEPTEMBER 21

Coming, as unto a living stone, disallowed indeed of men, but chosen of God, and precious, ye also, as lively stones, are built up a spiritual house (1 Peter 2:4–5).

eter here paints a picture of a spiritual house with the Lord Jesus Christ, the "Living Stone" as the chief cornerstone. A Living Stone—this is a paradox, for stones are mineral and not alive. Yet Jesus Christ, the Living Stone, is the very bedrock of that which is real and genuine. Stone symbolizes invincible strength, His permanent stability.

As the Living Stone, He was chosen to come to earth to become the Chief Cornerstone in the building He was erecting, "Jesus Christ himself being the chief corner stone" (Eph. 2:20). In order to be the world's Redeemer, He had to give His life on the cross. Then, triumphantly, He who was dead came forth a Living Savior, alive forevermore, a Living Person who is loving and caring. No wonder He is precious to God.

The Living Bible says, "Come to Christ, who is the living Foundation of Rock upon which God builds; though men have spurned him, he is very precious to God who has chosen him above all others" (1 Peter 2:4 LB).

In our relationship to the Lord, we, as believers, also become lively or living stones. We have His life, His nature: "that [by his promises] ye might be partakers of the divine nature" (2 Peter 1:4). We have His stability, His love, His warmth of compassion. "In whom all the building fitly framed together groweth unto an holy temple in the Lord: in whom ye also are builded together for an habitation of God through the Spirit" (Eph. 2:21–22). God, through the power of the Holy Spirit, can produce in our lives a rocklike stability and a warm, genuine reality.

When our lives are anchored on this firm Foundation of Rock, we can face the uncertainties of our times. We will remain steadfast, no matter how severe the storm. He is precious to us as we cling to His stability in the rough times of our lives.

We can say with David, "He only is my rock and my salvation; he is my defence; I shall not be greatly moved" (Ps. 62:2).

SEPTEMBER 22

When I heard this, I sat down and cried. In fact, I refused to eat for several days, for I spent the time in prayer to the God of heaven (Neh. 1:4 LB).

ehemiah was in a key position. He was cupbearer to the king. It was a place of great influence, requiring a person who was trustworthy. Nehemiah had gained the respect and friendship of the king.

One day a group of men returned from a trip to Jerusalem. When Nehemiah inquired about the city, he received a discouraging report. The walls around the city had been broken down, leaving it unprotected. The news greatly disturbed Nehemiah.

He recognized the dangerous plight of his fellow countrymen. He could have said "I am sorry for them; I wish I could help, but I have an important position in the court of the king and I can't leave." But not Nehemiah. Instead, he wept, mourned, fasted, and prayed. When the well-being of his people was at stake, how could he do anything but mourn? How could he enjoy the ease of the palace when they were suffering? As he fasted and prayed, he felt God's call to return and rebuild the walls. Nehemiah's life challenges us to serve the Lord, reaching the full potential of God's plan for our lives. His personal heart concern for the people led him to personal involvement.

William Carey, a London cobbler, also had a heart concern. He longed to go as a missionary to those who did not know Christ. While working in his cobbler's shop, he made a globe of leather on which he drew all the continents and islands of the world. He gathered all the information he could about the people of these lands. With his arms around the globe and tears trickling down his cheeks, he would say, "And they are all heathen." Eventually God opened the door for him to take the gospel to the people of India.

God's same message of redemption needs to go out to the many people of our world today. Are your arms outstretched around your city or your neighborhood? Many still do not know Jesus Christ. Do you care enough to become involved?

WANTED: MODERN NEHEMIAHS.

SEPTEMBER 23

*Let thine ear now be attentive, and thine eyes open, that thou may-
est hear the prayer of thy servant, which I pray before thee now,
day and night, for the children of Israel thy servants (Neh. 1:6).*

 ehemiah had a heart for God. He didn't wait to pray until an
emergency arose; prayer was the habit of his life. He kept in
such close touch with the Living God that when there was a
need in Jerusalem, God could burden Nehemiah's heart even
though he was miles away. God's work of rebuilding the walls of Jerusalem
began in the heart of one person on his knees.

Nehemiah knew he faced an impossible task unless God intervened on his
behalf. Nehemiah needed permission from an unbelieving king to return to
Jerusalem to do God's work. He did not depend on the king in Shushan but on
the Almighty God in heaven whose specialty is the impossible. The Bible says,
"The king's heart is in the hand of the LORD, as the rivers of water: he [God]
turneth it whithersoever he will" (Prov. 21:1).

Nehemiah knew he must not rush into the presence of the king. First, he
spent time in the presence of the King of Kings. In an earnest prayer he
recognized God's greatness and confessed the sins of his people. He claimed
God's promise, believing that God would answer. He made a specific request:
"Please help me now as I go in and ask the king for a great favor—put it into
his heart to be kind to me" (v. 11 LB).

For four months, he talked to no one but God. Then one day, the king
asked Nehemiah what was troubling him. At this crucial moment Nehemiah
knew his case was in higher hands: "Then I prayed to the God of heaven, and I
answered the king" (2:4 NIV). When we are in touch with God, we can lift
our hearts quickly and have God's ready answer.

He told the king his concern about his homeland. As a result, the king
agreed to let him return to Jerusalem and provided all the supplies Nehemiah
would need, even protection for the journey.

God needs Nehemiahs today who are willing to help rebuild broken-
down spiritual walls in the lives of family members, friends, neighbors, people
living about us, perhaps even broken walls in our own lives.

J. Hudson Taylor, missionary to China, said, "It is possible to move
people to God through prayer alone." What greater privilege can we have?

SEPTEMBER 24

Come, and let us build up the wall of Jerusalem, that we be no more a reproach (Neh. 2:17).

he secret to the effectiveness of Nehemiah's ministry for God was the priority he gave God in his life. When Nehemiah arrived in Jerusalem, he spent three days alone in prayer. He wanted to be sure of God's plan of action, so he remained quiet and listened to God. "Neither told I any man what my God had put in my heart to do at Jerusalem" (v. 12). God could use him, for Nehemiah first took time to listen. Often, when we begin a new undertaking for the Lord, we rush into it hurriedly, not taking time to wait for God to reveal His plan.

Later, Nehemiah took a few men with him on an inspection tour of the ruined walls, surveying the extent of the work needed. Then he issued a challenge for the people to *join him* in the work. He said, "Let *us* build up the wall of Jerusalem," and they rallied to his call. People usually follow a person they know is in touch with God.

Nehemiah organized the work, assigning a particular section of the wall to each group and giving them the responsibility of completing it. "So they strengthened their hands for this good work" (v. 18). The work of rebuilding the wall began as they all took their own sections as their responsibility.

Today, God is looking for working partners—those who are willing to obey and follow His directions—in building the walls of His Kingdom. He will assign the rebuilding of a section of the wall to each one of us. He assigns the walls of our own homes to each of us. Some have responsibility for walls in the business world and in the neighborhood. Some work behind the scene. The walls of others will be in public view. Wherever our assignment, we can say with Nehemiah, "I told them of the hand of my God which was good upon me" (v. 18).

Partnership with God will cost compassion, prayer, and time; but it will pay big dividends in eternity.

SEPTEMBER 25

They perceived that this work was wrought of our God (Neh. 6:16).

o sooner had Nehemiah and his workers begun rebuilding the wall than opposition began. Satan and his emissaries launched an all-out drive to hinder the work. A small group of men began to ridicule. They questioned the ability of Nehemiah's men, intimating that they were weak and the task impossible. The ridicule didn't disturb Nehemiah. His confidence was in God.

In spite of the opposition, the workers continued their labor. What were the secrets to their steadfast determination? First, they were committed to the task. "The people worked with *all* their heart" (4:6 NIV). Second, they were committed to prayer. "We prayed to our God" (v. 9 NIV). They knew that only the power of prayer could overcome the enemy. Third, they were committed to safeguarding the project. They "posted a guard day and night to meet this threat" (v. 9 NIV). They carefully prepared for the opposition of the enemy.

Not only did they have opposition from without, but soon dissension grew within their ranks. They had become physically exhausted, and discouragement gripped them. They had taken their eyes off the Lord. All they could see was the *rubbish* about them. It hindered their work. Nehemiah reminded them that their confidence must be in the Lord. "Remember the Lord, who is great and awesome" (v. 14 NIV).

As they diligently worked, watched, prayed, and followed God-given instructions, they finished the work. And even their enemies confessed that "this work was wrought of God" (v. 16).

Today, you may be facing opposition in some area of your life. Opposition is inevitable to those who love the Lord and live according to His will. It may come from family, friends, or neighbors. It may come in the form of ridicule or discouragement. You may be ready to give up.

Your *rubbish* may not be the same as Nehemiah faced. Yours may be difficult people to work with, unpleasant conditions, complacency of those who should carry the responsibility with you. Focus your eyes on the Lord. Your confidence and strength must be in Him. As you commit yourself and your obstacles to Him in prayer, God promises a power that prevails, a strength that overcomes.

"Be strong in the Lord, and in the power of his might" (Eph. 6:10).

SEPTEMBER 26

And he said unto them, Cast the net on the right side of the ship, and ye shall find. They cast therefore, and now they were not able to draw it for the multitude of fishes (John 21:6).

he disciples were confused and troubled as they stood on the shore of the Sea of Galilee. Their hope of Jesus setting up a Kingdom had been shattered. He had died. Their love for fishing must have tugged at their hearts again. This was all they had left to do.

Impulsively, Peter said, "I'm going out to fish," and the others replied, "We'll go with you" (v. 3 NIV). Quickly they got into a boat, pushed off from shore, and eagerly cast their net. No fish. Again and again they cast their net. No fish. Hour after hour passed and still no fish.

They were experienced fishermen. They had fished at the best time—night. They knew all the techniques. But they failed. No wonder. Jesus had not sent them back to their old occupation. They had gone out on their own, and all they had was an empty net. Jesus had told them that without Him they could do nothing.

But there is always a morning after a night of failure. When morning came, the risen Jesus stood on shore. When He questioned them about their fishing, they had to confess failure. Jesus didn't ask them why they had gone back to fishing. He didn't rebuke them. He told them to cast their net on the right side of the boat. The result—multitudes of fish.

The side of the boat didn't make the difference. But self-effort brings empty nets. Only the supernatural power of the resurrected Christ could fill their net.

You, too, may have been "fishing" and failed. You may be fishing on the side of self-effort, but Jesus says, "Cast the net on the right side." The right side is the side of reading His Word, praying, submitting to Him, obeying Him. When we obey Him, we can accomplish what we could not alone. The resurrection power of Christ fills our nets with "fish" of satisfaction and fulfillment.

This is what Paul speaks of when he says, "I am crucified with Christ: nevertheless I live; yet not I, but Christ liveth in me: and the life which I now live in the flesh I live by the faith of the Son of God, who loved me and gave himself for me" (Gal. 2:20).

SEPTEMBER 27

When they had finished eating [breakfast], Jesus said to Simon
Peter, "Simon son of John, do you truly love me more than
these?" "Yes, Lord," he said, "you know that I love you." Jesus
said, "Feed my lambs" (John 21:15 NIV).

an you imagine being served breakfast by the Lord, a breakfast
which He also had cooked? Jesus did that for His disciples. He
knew they were hungry after a night of fishing.

After breakfast, Jesus turned to Peter and said, "Do you truly love me
more than these?" Before Jesus' crucifixion, Peter had boasted that even though
all others forsook Jesus, he would remain true to Him. Soon after that, he
denied Jesus three times. Now, Jesus faced him with his commitment. "Do you
truly love me more than the other disciples, more than your boat, your fish,
your fishing nets, more than anyone or anything?"

When Peter said that he did, Jesus recommissioned him. He changed
Peter's role from a fisherman to a shepherd of His flock. Jesus said, "Feed my
lambs."

When Jesus asks us the question, "Do you truly love me more than
these?" what is our answer? Do we love anyone or anything more than Him?

The dynamic for our service is our love for Him—not our education, our
ability, not even our passion for souls. When we are motivated by love for
Him, everything else will be right.

This love will manifest itself as we assume our role of shepherding His
flock. Jesus was concerned for His flock. The Bible says, "When he saw the
multitudes, he was moved with compassion on them, because they fainted, and
were scattered abroad, as sheep having no shepherd" (Matt. 9:36). He trusts
us to be shepherds to the multitudes of sheep.

The Bible says, "The love of Christ controls us" (2 Cor. 5:14 NASB).
When His love controls us, we no longer live for ourselves but for Christ. And
when He asks us to show our love by feeding His sheep, we will willingly say,
"Yes, Lord!"

Hudson Taylor was once introduced as a great missionary because he
loved the Chinese. "No," Taylor replied, "Not because I love the Chinese, but
because I love God."

"And hope does not disappoint us, because God has poured out his love
into our hearts by the Holy Spirit, whom he has given us" (Rom. 5:5 NIV).

SEPTEMBER 28

Evening, morning and noon I cry out in distress, and he hears my voice (Ps. 55:17 NIV).

rayer is talking with God. It should have a very vital part in our spiritual life. Our relationship with Jesus Christ provides the **reality** of prayer. Prayer is real because we are talking with a God who is réal. The best way to learn the reality of prayer is to pray. We do not need to understand everything about prayer, but we need to pray. We do not need to use pious phrases, nor talk in a formal way. We can talk with God as friend to Friend.

David knew God in a personal, intimate way. Because God was real to him, his prayers to God were real. His prayers were filled with praise to his heavenly Father. In Psalm 63:7 he said, "Because thou hast been my help, therefore in the shadow of thy wings will I rejoice."

David's life was also filled with distress, but he learned that prayer could change his attitude and sometimes his circumstances. In his time of distress, he knew where to go for help. He said, "I cry out in distress." He prayed **regularly,** morning, noon, and night.

And then God promises His **response** to our prayers. God heard and answered David's prayers. He said, "When I called, you answered me; you made me bold and stouthearted" (Ps. 138:3 NIV).

We need not follow the exact pattern of David, praying three times a day, but a regular habit of prayer is important. My usual prayer time is early in the morning, but some of my sweetest times of prayer have been in the afternoon or evening. We can go to God in prayer when we are happy, when we are in distress, when we are unsure which direction to take, when we are afraid, when we are tired, when we are lonely. He is always there, listening, caring, and ready to help.

Prayer is the access to all that God is and all that He wants us to have. Are we taking advantage of all He makes available to us?

We can become no greater than our prayer life!

SEPTEMBER 29

Thou wilt keep him in perfect peace, whose mind is stayed on thee: because he trusteth in thee (Isa. 26:3)

 n the midst of our confusion, pressure, frustration, and stress, God promises us peace. Even if your life is shattered, He offers you His *perfect* peace. Perfect peace allows no room for worry. His peace is a calm quietness to face the stress of life.

Peace is not something we can achieve on our own. It is God's gift to us, and He maintains and preserves it for us. "Thou wilt *keep* him in perfect peace."

His promised peace comes to us today in the person of Jesus Christ. Knowing the storms and trials of life His followers would face after He left this earth, Jesus promised, "Peace I leave with you, my peace I give unto you: not as the world giveth, give I unto you. Let not your heart be troubled, neither let it be afraid" (John 14:27).

The peace that Jesus offers is a peace beyond understanding that can give us stability in the trying times of life. "The peace of God, which passeth all understanding, shall keep your hearts and minds through Christ Jesus" (Phil. 4:7). Only God can give us this kind of peace, and no one and nothing can take it away. It is a God-given and God-appropriated peace in our lives.

God gives His perfect peace to those whose minds are stayed or resting on Him. Peace of heart and mind comes to those who fix their minds steadfastly on God and trust Him for the outcome, no matter how circumstances may look at the moment.

We experience God's perfect peace as we lean on Him—not only on His promises—but on the Lord Himself. The psalmist said, "The Lord is my strength and my [impenetrable] shield; my heart trusts, relies on, and confidently leans on Him, and I am helped; therefore my heart greatly rejoices, and with my song will I praise Him" (Ps. 28:7 AMPLIFIED).

Every believer can experience God's perfect peace. With our minds stayed on the Lord, trusting Him, we can rest in the peace of God.

Jesus said, "These things I have spoken unto you, that in me ye might have peace. In the world ye shall have tribulation: but be of good cheer; I have overcome the world" (John 16:33).

Don't worry! God will never run out of resources.

SEPTEMBER 30

O give thanks unto the LORD; call upon his name: make known his deeds among the people. Sing unto him . . . talk ye of all his wondrous works (Ps. 105:1–2).

hankfulness is a gift we give to God. "O *give* thanks unto the LORD." All we have is a gift from Him. The Bible says, "Every good gift and every perfect gift is from above, and cometh down from the Father of lights, with whom is no variableness, neither shadow of turning" (James 1:17). Yet how easy it is to accept what He gives, forgetting to show appreciation.

What is special to you that you want to share with others? When your heart overflows with thanksgiving for what He has done for you, you will want to "make known his deeds among the people." You will be eager to share Him.

Thanksgiving will overflow from our hearts in song, and our singing will be beautiful. Do you know why? Because we are singing to Him. To our ears, our singing may sound off-key. But He hears the music of our heart and it is melodious. Do you hold a concert of song for Him each day? If not, try it.

Not only will we be eager to sing, but we will be eager to talk to others about Jesus Christ. "Talk ye of all his wondrous works"(v. 2). There is much we can share about Him—His marvelous gift of eternal life, His daily provisions for our daily needs, His protection over us. I am enthusiastic as I watch sports events, but that enthusiasm cannot begin to compare with my enthusiasm when I talk about the Lord Jesus Christ.

Throughout Scripture, worship and praise take priority. Many of the psalms are filled with praise to the Lord. David wrote so beautifully: "The one thing I want from God, the thing I seek most of all, is the privilege of meditating in his Temple, living in his presence every day of my life, delighting in his incomparable perfections and glory. There I'll be when troubles come. He will hide me. He will set me on a high rock out of reach of all my enemies. Then I will bring him sacrifices and sing his praises with much joy" (Ps. 27:4–6 LB).

Psalm 50:23 says, "Whoso offereth praise glorifieth me." May our lives be filled with praise to the glory of God.

OCTOBER 1

Yes, furthermore I count everything as loss compared to the posses-
sion of the priceless privilege—the overwhelming preciousness,
the surpassing worth and supreme advantage—of knowing Christ
Jesus my Lord, and of progressively becoming more deeply and inti-
mately acquainted with Him, of perceiving and recognizing and un-
derstanding Him more fully and clearly (Phil. 3:8 AMPLIFIED).

ew life! New values! New assets! This describes Paul's transformed life after he became a Christian. In the past, Paul had possessed assets that he believed gave him acceptance with God—his family heritage, his educational background, his religious achievements. Now he was a new person in Christ, and he had a new standard to live by, conformity to the person of Jesus Christ. Things he had once thought important, were worthless when compared with the new life he had in Christ Jesus. He had a new perspective, a new focus.

His desire now was that Christ become a greater reality to him. He recognized that Christ far surpassed all that he had considered important. Jesus Christ was real to him.

As we take time to reevaluate the assets in our lives, what place do we give our talents, possessions, and time in relation to the place we give the Lord? Can we say as Paul did, "But what things were gain to me, those I counted loss for Christ (v. 7). "I count all things but loss . . . that I may win Christ" (v. 8).

One evening, a father called his young daughter to him when he came home and asked her to bring him her strand of pearls. She hesitated. Those pearls, though imitation, were her dearest treasure, and her father knew that. Again, he asked her to bring them to him.

Because she loved her father dearly, she obeyed, and reluctantly dropped them into his hand. He reached into his pocket and brought out a beautifully wrapped package and handed it to her. Opening the package, she saw a lovely strand of real pearls. Overcome with joy, she realized she had almost missed the real pearls her father had for her because she was satisfied with the imitation.

Sometimes we can be satisfied with the imitation and miss the reality of the Pearl of Great Price, the Lord Jesus. Do we count everything as loss in our lives when compared with what we have in Christ? Are we rejoicing in the priceless privilege of knowing the preciousness of His life within?

May our supreme goal be *that we may know Him.*

That I may know him, and the power of his resurrection, and the fellowship of his sufferings, being made comformable unto his death (Phil. 3:10).

aul was a goal setter. He had one supreme life goal—to know Jesus Christ intimately. When he met Jesus on the Damascus road and committed his life to Him as Savior and Lord, his life was transformed. From that time on, there was no question what he wanted out of life. His one burning desire was to know the Lord Jesus.

The Greek word Paul uses for *know* here, means knowing by experience. Paul wanted to know the reality of Christ in his daily life situations. The more time we spend with people, the better we get to know them. Our friendship grows. This is also true in our relationship with Christ. He said, "Take my yoke upon you, and learn of me" (Matt. 11:29).

We become better acquainted with Him as we read His Word. Jesus said, "Search the scriptures . . . they are they which testify of me" (John 5:39). Also, we get to know Him better as we talk with Him in prayer. "Be still, and know that I am God" (Ps. 46:10). The more intimately we know Him, the deeper our trust in Him will be. We will be confident that no problem is too great for Him.

I remember a day when I was thankful I knew Him intimately and could trust Him. My life fell apart. Our doctor informed us that my husband had Hodgkins disease. Our future was not bright. They did not have the treatment then that they do today. Tears came to our eyes as we left the office. Suddenly, we were aware of a peace from the God we had learned to trust.

Through those rugged years, many times I said, "Lord, I can't go on another day." Often it seemed that He picked me up in His loving arms and carried me through the day when I thought I could not make it.

Because I had given God priority time in Bible reading and prayer, He had become my dearest friend. I had learned to trust Him to carry us through the deep waters of our life. And He did. Every believer can know the reality of Christ within.

That I may know Him: **The person—Jesus Christ.**

OCTOBER 3

That I may know him, and the power of his resurrection
(Phil. 3:10).

aul's desire was to really know Jesus Christ. And the first characteristic of Christ that he wants to experience in his life is the power of Christ's resurrection.

Power—what a dynamic word! Resurrection power! When Christ lives in us, we have the same power operating in us that raised Christ from the dead. Incredible! Paul wanted all believers to know "what is the exceeding greatness of his power . . . which he wrought in Christ, when he raised him from the dead" (Eph. 1:19–20).

Paul wanted to experience that dynamic reality, "the power outflowing from His resurrection [which it exerts over believers]" (Phil. 3:10 AMPLIFIED). He wanted that power to flow through his life so that things beyond his power could be accomplished for the Lord.

This same resurrection power operates in our lives today through our relationship with Christ. Jesus said, "All power is given unto me in heaven and in earth" (Matt. 28:18). Paul called Christ "the power of God" (1 Cor. 1:24). Through our union with Jesus Christ, we have sufficient power to meet every problem we are facing. You may think your problem has no *human* solution, and perhaps it doesn't, but isn't the power that raised Christ from the dead powerful enough to work out your need?

When temptations come, when habits have a grip on us, when our daily schedule overpowers us, we can know the reality of His power at work in every area of our lives, accomplishing what we cannot possibly do in our own power. He is only waiting for us to say, "I give up, Lord. I give it all to you."

In the midst of all our pressures, tensions, and frustrations, we can experience a quiet, confident trust as we rest in what He does for us. "Be strong in the Lord, and in the power of his might" (Eph. 6:10).

When God said, "My power shows up best in weak people," Paul said, "Now I am glad to boast about how weak I am; I am glad to be a living demonstration of Christ's power, instead of showing off my own power and abilities" (2 Cor. 12:9 LB).

That I may know Him: **His power—Resurrection power.**

OCTOBER 4

That I may know him . . . and the fellowship of his sufferings (Phil. 3:10).

Christian leader was asked what he considered the qualifications for a Christian worker. He replied, "Bent knees, wet eyes, and a broken heart." Paul realized that if he were to really know Christ, he must experience the burden Christ carried on his heart for a lost world.

The Lord suffered as He wept over Jerusalem. "He beheld the city, and wept over it" (Luke 19:41). He had *seeing eyes* and a *weeping heart*. His heart was broken every time he saw people in need. "What pity he felt for the crowds that came, because their problems were so great and they didn't know what to do or where to turn for help" (Matt. 9:39 LB).

Paul's *passion* was to share Jesus' deep heart concern for the spiritual destiny of people. Today Jesus is looking for those who will have seeing eyes and weeping hearts for a dying world. This is how we enter into some of His sufferings. Do we see the world today as He sees it? Do we love the world as He loves it?

One time after boarding a small commuter plane and taxiing out, instead of taking off we returned to the gate. One engine was not working. While they repaired the plane, I invited a young woman passenger to have breakfast with me. The day before, she had made her first flight, and she was frightened. I told her that I flew often and that this was a reliable airline.

When she asked me my occupation, I said, "The lives of many women today are falling apart. I have a wonderful answer for them." She said, "You are describing my life. My life has fallen apart, and I don't know where to turn for help." After two hours of sharing Jesus Christ with her, we both knew why our plane had been delayed.

Every day, we are in touch with people whose lives are falling apart. Are we spiritually sensitive to their cries for help? The Bible says, "Is it nothing to you, all ye that pass by?" (Lam. 1:12).

Do the lost mean something to you? Or do you pass by without noticing?

That I may know Him: **Passion—The fellowship of His sufferings.**

OCTOBER 5

That I may know him . . . being made conformable unto his death (Phil. 3:10).

aul's consuming passion was to know Christ in all His fullness, even His death. Paul said, "That I may so share His sufferings as to be continually transformed [in spirit into His likeness even] to His death" (AMPLIFIED).

Paul's love for the Lord was so deep that he was willing to die to all his own his desires, interests, and plans—his very self—in order that he might experience Christ living in him. He said, "For to me to live is Christ" (Phil. 1:21).

Being made conformable means to bring into the same form as something else. This is the same word translated *conformed* in Romans 8:29. The Amplified Bible paraphrases it this way: "to be molded into the image of His Son [and share inwardly His likeness]."

When we become one of God's children, He begins the work of making us Christlike. We die to self. We die to our ambitions and plans. We begin to walk in the newness of life we have in Christ. "Look upon your old sin nature as dead and unresponsive to sin, and instead be alive to God, alert to him, through Jesus Christ our Lord" (Rom. 6:11 LB).

We cannot do this ourselves. The Holy Spirit must mold us into the likeness of Jesus Christ. The Bible says, "When the Holy Spirit controls our lives he will produce this kind of fruit in us: love, joy, peace, patience, kindness, goodness, faithfulness, gentleness and self-control" (Gal. 5:22–23 LB).

The great sixteenth-century Scottish reformer, John Knox, knew the importance of dying to self in order to share in God's burden for the lost. He said that when he cried to God, "Give me Scotland or I'll die," the Lord replied, "Die, and I will give you Scotland." John Knox died to his desires and wishes, and God gave him many souls in Scotland who turned to Christ.

Only as we are made conformable to His death will we walk in the victorious resurrection life of Christ and share God's deep concern for lost humanity, including our family and friends.

That I may know Him: **Christlikeness.**

OCTOBER 6

*The effectual fervent prayer of a righteous man availeth much
(James 5:16).*

 ave you ever observed a camel's knees, how calloused they are?
James, the writer of the book of James in the Bible, was said to
have had knees like a camel because he spent so much time on
his knees in prayer.

Whether this is true or not, at least James knew the reality of a life spent in
much prayer. His life showed the results. As we read through the Bible, we
recognize that many of the people God used drew their spiritual strength from
their prayer life.

What God has done in the past, He can do today. The privilege of prayer
is ours. He needs those who will pray for His work in the world today. James
says that the prayers of a righteous person are dynamic, powerful. The righteous
are those in a right relationship with Jesus Christ, those who demonstrate their
faith in their actions and words.

We all have our own circle of family and friends for whom we are
concerned. Through our prayers, they can be reached for Jesus. Through our
prayers, the world can be moved to God.

Years ago, while I was praying, God burdened me to pray for a particular
part of the world. I did not know where it was except that it was in the Orient. I
prayed regularly for it, asking God to reach the people of that area with the
Gospel. Later, I read of a Christian couple who went to Nepal in the interest of
their professions but also with a deep concern for the spiritual welfare of the
people. There was a picture of Nepal, and I recognized it as the country I had
been praying for.

Through the years, I have continued to pray for Nepal. Recently, I read
that at the time I had begun to pray for that country there were about ten or
fifteen Christians. Recent statistics indicate that there are now about forty
thousand.

As you read the following Scripture, fill in your name. "The earnest
(heartfelt, continued) prayer of _____ makes tremendous power
available—dynamic in its working" (AMPLIFIED).

God's power is released through prayer. Don't give up praying!

OCTOBER 7

Not by might, nor by power, but by my spirit, saith the LORD of hosts (Zech. 4:6)

 once read of a mountain that was an obstruction on a mission field in South America, and the missionaries began to pray for its removal. They had faith to believe God would do it. One day as they looked out, they saw earth-moving equipment removing the mountain. The government needed the dirt for a project somewhere else.

In today's passage of Scripture, Zerubbabel, heir to the throne of Judah, had been sent back from captivity to restore the temple. But he had to face a mountain of opposition to the completion of the work. God sent the prophet Zechariah to Zerubbabel to tell him that his mountain, the opposition, would be removed and the work completed.

Zechariah said, "Not by might [not by the resources of Zerubbabel's human accomplishment], nor by power [accomplishment of the task by Zerubbabel's human power], but by my spirit, saith the LORD of hosts." Eventually the work was completed, not by Zerubbabel's power but by the power of the Spirit of God.

God has put each of us in the place of His choosing. He has a purpose for our being there. Early in my Christian life, I was very active in service for the Lord. I learned all the latest methods. I developed plans and programs that were effective. I appeared successful.

But eventually, I became restless. I knew something was wrong. God showed me that although I had committed my life to Him, I had held back part of it. I was serving Him in my own power. God didn't want *my* programs, plans, or methods. He didn't want *my* ability. He wanted those programs and abilities to be His. What a change it made when I committed my life totally to Him. I learned my service was not by might or power but by my God's Spirit.

All of us encounter mountains in our way, hindrances in achieving the purpose God has for our lives. Your mountain may be exhaustion from your household duties. It may be an impossible boss or a habit you are trying to break. God reminds us, "You can't do it in your own strength, but I can do it for you by My Spirit."

Paul said, "I can do all things through Christ which strengtheneth me" (Phil. 4:13).

OCTOBER 8

Fear not, Abram: I am thy shield, and thy exceeding great reward
(Gen. 15:1).

ear not!" These were God's words of **reassurance** to Abram, precisely what he needed to hear. Having defeated four kings and rescued his nephew Lot from captivity, he had made enemies, and he didn't know when they might retaliate. Abram had reason to be afraid. But God said, "Fear not!"

Circumstances come into our lives that fill our hearts with fear. Regardless of what the circumstances are, God says to us, "Fear thou not; for I am with thee . . . I will strengthen thee . . . I will help thee" (Isa. 41:10). "Fear not . . . thou art mine" (Isa. 43:1).

God promised to be Abram's **refuge,** his protection: "I am thy shield." No shield could be safer for Abram, for it was God Himself. David said, "But thou, O LORD, art a shield for me; my glory, and the lifter up of mine head" (Ps. 3:3).

In our times of fear, we, too, are promised His protection. The shield of faith is Jesus Christ: "Looking unto Jesus the author and finisher of our faith" (Heb. 12:2). With Jesus as our shield, we experience safety and security. No dart of the enemy can penetrate the shield that covers the weakest believer in Christ. We must be sure to carry our shield at all times.

God also promised to be Abram's **reward.** I am "thy exceeding great reward." God says, "Abram, I myself, will be your reward." No wonder Abram need not fear.

God is our reward, too. What greater reward could we have? He is our portion, exactly what we need. "My flesh and my heart faileth: but God is the strength of my heart, and my portion for ever" (Ps. 73:26). He who fills heaven and earth can satisfy us with Himself.

You may be fearful in the midst of your circumstances today. God is saying to you, "Fear not. I am *your* shield and exceeding great reward."

Remember, no shield is safer. No reward is greater. God protects without and satisfies within.

OCTOBER 9

Grow in grace, and in the knowledge of our Lord and Saviour Jesus Christ. To him be glory both now and for ever. Amen (2 Peter 3:18).

fter encouraging his friends to remain steadfast in their trials (v. 17), Peter spurs them on in their Christian growth. The believer's goal is to become more like Jesus Christ, "until we all attain to the unity of the faith, and of the knowledge of the Son of God, to a mature man, to the measure of the stature which belongs to the fulness of Christ" (Eph. 4:13 NASB).

All that Jesus is, we can become. "Speaking the truth in love, we are to grow up in all aspects into Him . . . even Christ" (v. 15 NASB). He becomes the center of our life.

Growth into His likeness requires spending time in His Word. "As newborn babes, desire the sincere milk of the word, that ye may grow thereby" (1 Peter 2:2). As we spend time in His Word, we become more like Him.

Growing in grace might be illustrated in this way. We look at a flower in all its beauty and realize that God designed it. As it begins to grow, its roots go down into the soil. As it grows downward, it also begins to grow upward. A strong root system is necessary to have a strong plant.

So it is with our lives. God has a design for our lives. Although each of us is different, different in shape, height, and color, our design is to be conformed into the image of the Lord Jesus.

The process of growing in grace is the work of the Holy Spirit developing the fruit of the Spirit in our lives. Growth in knowledge will give us a deeper insight into God's design for our life and how our lives fit into God's greater design. Paul said, "Keep on growing in spiritual knowledge and insight" (Phil. 1:9).

May our lives show a continual growth in grace and knowledge, making us more Christlike.

OCTOBER 10

Make a joyful noise unto the LORD, all ye lands. Serve the LORD with gladness: come before his presence with singing (Ps. 100:1–2).

 sn't this an exciting way to begin a psalm? "Make a joyful noise unto the LORD, all ye lands." The original word for *noise* signifies a glad shout given by loyal subjects to their king at his appearance. Can you visualize a joyful group of God's people lifting their voices in the praise that overflows from thankful hearts? From all the nations of the world, God's family unites its voice in glad shouts of praise to God.

Sometimes a choir will separate, going into different parts of the sanctuary to sing antiphonally. One group will sing from one section, another group from another section, echoing back and forth. Then they will unite their voices in one great crescendo of praise. God has put His people in various parts of the world to sing His praises in all lands, a type of antiphonal anthem of gratitude and adoration.

With singing hearts we fellowship with Him. With glad hearts we serve Him. "Serve the LORD with gladness: come before his presence with singing" (v. 2).

Whatever our responsibilities are, we can serve Him joyfully. We can say, "I am doing my laundry for you, Lord." "I am typing these letters for you, Lord." "I am studying for you, Lord." Everything we do can be an act of worship for our King.

Our service for Him overflows from our gratitude. "Know ye that the Lord he is God: it is he that hath made us, and not we ourselves" (v. 3). We belong to the Creator of universe! What security we have in knowing that we belong to the God who is in control. God made us and redeemed us from our sin through His Son's death on the cross. If we have gratefully accepted His gift of salvation, we simply need to let God be God in our lives and let Him do His work through us.

We never need fear any task He gives us to do, "for the Lord is always good. He is always loving and kind, and his faithfulness goes on and on to each succeeding generation" (v. 5 LB).

Sing praises to the Lord and serve Him with gladness!

OCTOBER 11

Know ye that the LORD he is God: it is he that hath made us, and not we ourselves; we are his people, and the sheep of his pasture . . . be thankful unto him (Ps. 100:3–4).

he Lord is God. He is Jehovah. He is the faithful Covenant-keeping God. Jehovah of the Old Testament is Jesus of the New Testament. "Know ye that the LORD he is God." Are we letting God be God in our lives? Is the Lord in control? Since we belong to Him, He has a right to direct our lives.

Our Lord is our Creator. He made us. We had no part in it. He made us His way for a special purpose. No one else is made just like we are. We are special to Him.

We are the sheep of His pasture. What a comforting thought! How tenderly a shepherd takes care of his sheep. So is our Good Shepherd. He is dedicated to providing for our needs and protecting us from harm. He leads us to green pastures and still waters. He leads us in the paths of His choosing. He lovingly restores our hurting hearts. We have nothing to fear for He is with us constantly.

The psalmist tells us to "enter into his gates with thanksgiving, and into his courts with praise" (v. 4). The gates of His courts are open to us. These gates open to His love, His mercy, His care. They open into His presence.

As we enter His gates, we are to remember to "be thankful unto him, and bless his name" (v. 4). We are to have thank-filled and praise-filled lives throughout the entire year, not just on Thanksgiving Day. Sometimes we become so concerned about tomorrow that we fail to be thankful today.

We are not just to be thankful for the pleasant, easy things but everything. "In every thing give thanks: for this is the will of God in Christ Jesus concerning you" (1 Thess. 5:18).

God's considers praise the ultimate gift from His children. "Whoso offereth praise glorifieth me" (Ps. 50:23).

Praise comes from a heart that is satisfied with the Lord. A satisfied customer is one of the greatest assets a business firm can have. Does the Lord see us as satisfied customers?

"Giving thanks always for all things unto God and the Father in the name of our Lord Jesus Christ" (Eph. 5:20).

OCTOBER 12

There was a famine in the land: and Abram went down into Egypt to sojourn there; for the famine was grievous in the land (Gen. 12:10).

ave there been times in your life when you followed what you thought was God's will, yet things didn't go as expected? Perhaps your circumstances became worse. You wondered if you were wrong in thinking it was God's will for you.

The Bible tells us of people who have experienced this. Abraham was called by God to leave his home in Ur of Chaldees and go to Canaan. After his arrival, there was a terrible famine. No rain fell, crops burned up, pastureland became dry and brown, and food supplies diminished.

Abraham was a stranger in a strange land. His resources dwindled. Had he mistaken God's call? Could he have been wrong in coming to Canaan? We do not read that he received any divine direction, but he went down to Egypt. Realizing the seriousness of the famine, he began to fear for his future and that of his family.

Abraham's mistake was in trying to work out his own plans instead of turning his need over to God. Overwhelmed by the famine, he forgot that no problem is too difficult for God to solve.

How do we react when our circumstances seem to contradict the guidance we received from God? God sometimes permits such experiences to deepen and strengthen our spiritual lives. He may allow trials to remind us that the only real peace we can have is in Him. Otherwise we may mistake the peace of our circumstances for the peace of God.

In times of panic and pressure, we may try to take things into our own hands. But we need to wait until He moves us. Even though we do not understand, He knows the reason for our trouble, and He is fitting it into His plan for our good and His glory. We need to wait on God for His directions and then obey them. We can say to God, "You brought me here. Here I will stay until you clearly show me what to do."

Someone has said, "It is better to walk in the dark with God than to walk alone by sight."

In God's will there is perfect peace, not fear.

OCTOBER 13

If you are pleased with me, teach me your ways so I may know you and continue to find favor with you (Ex. 33:13 NIV).

Many people who believe in God would have to confess that they do not know Him in a close, personal way.

When Jesus walked on earth, people knew Him on different levels. The crowds knew Him on a casual basis. They heard Him speak, saw what He did, and talked with Him. The disciples knew Him on a more intimate basis. Peter, James, and John were even closer in their relationship to Him, and John seemed to have a special place of fellowship with Christ. Someone has said that "Jesus doesn't have favorites; He has intimates."

Knowledge of God often comes through tough experiences. They draw us closer to Him and give us a desire to know Him better. This was true of Moses. Difficult experiences deepened his knowledge of God and stirred up a burning desire to be an *intimate* of God's.

Disappointed with the children of Israel, a disillusioned Moses turned to God and said, "Teach me your ways so I may know you." The word used for *know* here means to experience, to understand. Moses wanted more than head knowledge *about* God. He longed to draw closer. The Bible says, "The LORD spake unto Moses face to face, as a man speaketh unto his friend" (v. 11).

Is your desire to be one of God's intimates? His intimates walk in close fellowship with Him. His intimates desire to please Him. His intimates obey His wishes.

Jesus came to reveal God to us, to show us what God is like. He said, "Anyone who has seen me has seen the Father" (John 14:9 NIV). As we spend time in the Word we get to know God better.

A little boy was playing in his yard with some of his friends, and one boy boasted, "My dad knows the mayor." "That's nothing," said another boy. "My dad knows the governor." The third boy said, "That's nothing. My dad knows God."

May each of us have that reputation—that we know God, that we are His intimates.

OCTOBER 14

I will bring the blind by a way that they knew not; I will lead them in paths that they have not known: I will make darkness light before them, and crooked things straight. These things will I do unto them, and not forsake them (Isa. 42:16).

As we walk through life, we may come to a place where we cannot see our way ahead. It is dark before us. We are just like a blind person who cannot see the way.

It is amazing to watch seeing-eye dogs lead blind people. They move when the dog moves and stop when the dog stops. They move in the direction the dog moves. The dog has been trained, and the person learns to trust the dog.

I developed an appreciation of this kind of trust when I was experiencing some excruciating pain in my face. It was a very cold winter day with several inches of snow on the ground and high winds. As I left a meeting to go home, the piercing, cold wind hit me, and I screamed from the intensified pain in my face.

Some of my friends took a large, warm scarf and wrapped my head so completely that I couldn't see even a step ahead. Then they said, "Just trust us." One on each side, they led the way. I couldn't see anything. It was scary. But they kept saying, "Trust us. We can see. We will lead you home safely." I began to relax. I trusted them, and soon I was safely home. I learned in a new way what Proverbs 3:5–6 means: "Trust in the Lord with all thine heart; and lean not unto thine own understanding. In all thy ways acknowledge him, and he shall direct thy paths."

He promised, "I will make darkness light before them." He can do this for us because Jesus Himself is the Light of the World.

Someone has said, "I do not know what is around the next turn in this winding trail of life, but I know this: whatever is around the corner, I shall have my hand in Another's hand. And if I feel even a little disturbed, I shall move my finger around in the palm of that hand till I find that scar, and then I shall know that Jesus Christ, who was wounded for my sins, is not going to leave me no matter what corner I go around on the winding road of life."

OCTOBER 15

We have this treasure in jars of clay to show that this all-surpassing power is from God and not from us (2 Cor. 4:7 NIV).

ars of clay have no great value in themselves. But God chose us, jars of clay, to hold His precious Treasure, the glorious Gospel in the person of Jesus Christ.

God's Treasure in our weak bodies demonstrates that the power is not ours but God's. "To those whom God has called . . . Christ [is] the power of God and the wisdom of God (1 Cor. 1:24 NIV).

Paul's life was not easy. He encountered trials and persecution beyond measure. He had every right to give up. But he said, "We do not lose heart" (2 Cor. 4:1 NIV). He could face every situation with a power beyond himself.

The Christian is not immune from the pressures of today's complex world. But the apostle Paul, who experienced much suffering and persecution, encourages us, "We are pressed on every side by troubles, but not crushed and broken" (v. 8 LB). Our pressures at home, in our workplace, and at school need not crush us, for we have the precious Treasure, the power of God within, that is greater than the pressures from without.

"We are perplexed because we don't know why things happen as they do, but we don't give up and quit" (v. 8 LB). In our limited understanding, we may not know what decision to make or where to turn, but the power of God within keeps us going.

We are "persecuted, but not forsaken" (v. 9). There may be attacks on our reputation. There may be misunderstandings. But God always understands and never forsakes us.

"We may be knocked down, but we are never knocked out!" (v. 9 PHILLIPS). Our trouble may be stronger than we think we can withstand, but the surpassing greatness of His power within lifts us up and sets us on our way again.

Today you may be pressured, perplexed, knocked down, but within your weak jar of clay, you are carrying God's Treasure, Jesus Christ. He can strengthen you so that you are not crushed, you are not knocked out, and knowing you are not forsaken, you won't give up.

"Thanks be unto God, which always causeth us to triumph in Christ" (2 Cor. 2:14). We triumph not through the strength of the vessel but through the power of God dwelling in the vessel.

OCTOBER 16

Again, I tell you that if two of you on earth agree about anything you ask for, it will be done for you by my Father in heaven. For where two or three come together in my name, there am I with them (Matt. 18:19–20 NIV).

o you have a dear friend with whom you enjoy doing things, one who reacts to things the same way you do, who always seems to agree with you? Do you have such a friend with whom you can pray as a prayer partner?

When we agree with even one or two other believers in prayer, God hears our requests as a beautiful symphony with intricate harmonies, no jarring noises. "Again I tell you, if two of you on earth agree (harmonize together, together make a symphony) about—anything and everything—whatever they shall ask, it will come to pass and be done for them by My Father in heaven" (v. 19 AMPLIFIED).

As we agree in prayer, we must remember to agree with God's answer, not ours. Sometimes, we say God hasn't answered our prayer, but we haven't prayed in agreement with Him. We must also pray in the will of God, in the name of Jesus, and in the power of the Spirit.

Partnership in prayer means **power** in prayer. "Whatever . . . they shall ask will . . . be done for them by My Father in heaven." But hindrances such as an unforgiving spirit, bitterness, or anger can cause a power shortage. The psalmist said, "If I had cherished sin in my heart, the Lord would not have listened" (Ps. 66:18 NIV).

Partnership in prayer means His promised **presence.** What could be a sweeter experience than getting together with one or two prayer partners, knowing the reality of Jesus is in our midst as we pray? "For wherever two or three are gathered (drawn together as My followers) in . . . My Name, there I AM in the midst of them" (v. 20 AMPLIFIED).

Sometimes we need assurance of His presence more than the specific answers we're praying for. Once a little boy ran away from home, but when he returned the next day, lonely, cold, and hungry, he didn't look first to see if there was any food on the table. He just ran into his mother's arms. So it is with us. We need *Him* more than the things He gives us.

Get together with someone today and pray.

OCTOBER 17

The LORD is the portion of mine inheritance and of my cup: thou maintainest my lot (Ps. 16:5).

Often, someone will say, "I must get my priorities in order." David had his priorities right when he said, "The LORD is the portion of mine inheritance."

A portion is an allotment to a person—his or her share. The Lord is our allotted portion. "The Lord himself is my inheritance, my prize. He is my food and drink, my highest joy!" (v. 5 LB). We could say, "I have no prize or treasure that I value more highly than the Lord." The Lord is our confidence, our nourishment, our joy.

Paul experienced this when he wrote, "I count everything as loss compared to the . . . overwhelming preciousness . . . of knowing Christ Jesus my Lord" (Phil. 3:8 AMPLIFIED).

Many people today make their portion their home, family, friends, car, wealth, or fame. But our portion is the Lord. In Him, we have a security that material possessions could never provide. He puts us in touch with His inexhaustible supply of resources, sufficient for every need.

He is our portion in times of discouragement, when we are dissatisfied with life. We can appropriate His joy instead of feeling sorry for ourselves. The psalm reads, "He is . . . my highest joy!" (Ps. 16:5 LB).

He is our spiritual food and drink. He satisfies completely, regardless of our circumstances. The last few months my sister lived, she spent in the hospital as the result of a massive heart attack. Most of the time she was in intensive care. But one day, she showed a little improvement, and they moved her into a private room. A young friend of ours asked if he could go with me to see her. He had a beautiful voice, so I asked him to sing to her. He sang, "I'd Rather Have Jesus than Anything."

Later that evening, she became much worse, and they had to take her to a special cardiac unit. The doctors told us they had little hope that she would live through the night. Her son stood on one side of her bed and I on the other, reading Scripture and praying. About midnight, she suddenly opened her eyes and said, "I'd rather have Jesus than anything." What a comfort those words were to her and to us.

Our priorities are in order when we can say, "I'd rather have Jesus than anything!"

OCTOBER 18

Therefore being justified by faith, we have peace with God through our Lord Jesus Christ (Rom. 5:1).

f you were to take a survey, asking people what they desire more than anything else in the world, many would say, "Peace." Paul tells us that we can have peace. God used the death and resurrection of Jesus Christ to provide justification for the ungodly.

Through an act of disobedience, Adam and Eve broke their relationship with God, and sin passed on to the whole human race. "All have sinned, and come short of the glory of God" (Rom. 3:23). As sinners, we were at enmity with God. As sinners, we stand guilty before God.

But in a great demonstration of love, Jesus willingly became our substitute, dying on the cross to take the punishment for our sins. "While we were yet sinners, Christ died for us" (Rom. 5:8).

When we receive Christ as personal Savior, we are forgiven and cleansed of our sins. "He hath made him to be sin for us, who knew no sin; that we might be made the righteousness of God in him (2 Cor. 5:21).

We are justified by faith in Christ. Justified means just as if I had never sinned. God sees us then as righteous and perfect in the Son of God, and He can write over our life—"Not guilty." Our enmity with God is over. We are no longer alienated but reconciled to God.

But Jesus also rose from the dead that we might have His life within. "He died for all so that all who live—having received eternal life from him—might live no longer for themselves, to please themselves, but to spend their lives pleasing Christ who died and rose again for them" (2 Cor. 5:15 LB).

We are at peace with God when a new life has begun within. "When someone becomes a Christian he becomes a brand new person inside. He is not the same any more. A new life has begun!" (2 Cor. 5:17 LB).

Peace with God is the ultimate goal. Faith makes that peace a reality. Are you at peace *with* God? If so, the peace *of* God is available for your daily walk.

OCTOBER 19

Let us arise, and go up to Bethel; and I will make there an altar unto God, who answered me in the day of my distress, and was with me in the way which I went (Gen. 35:3).

ost of us have had the experience of being away from home too long and saying, "I can't wait to get home." In today's Scripture we see Jacob going home at last. Thirty years earlier, Jacob had fled from home because of his brother's anger. It was at Bethel that Jacob met God personally. On his first night away from home, God promised Jacob that He would bring him back to Bethel, and now God was ready to keep His promise.

When Jacob left home, he lived by his self-made plans, giving little thought to God's plan for him. Now God was leading Jacob back to Bethel. But true to his scheming character, Jacob began making his own plans for his return. On his way back, in a memorable personal encounter, God broke Jacob's will. For the first time, the schemer became willing to go God's way.

It had taken Jacob a long time to learn God's lessons. As we read through these accounts, we might wonder, "Jacob, how long will you go your own way?" But through a spiritual change, he finally let God be in control.

In reflecting back on his life, Jacob realized that God had always been close enough to hear his cry. He speaks of "God, who answered me in the day of my distess." God was always in calling distance and was waiting for Jacob to cry out to Him for help. He did not forsake Jacob. He was always there waiting. Jacob said He "was with me in the way which I went."

Why didn't God write Jacob off as a failure? Jacob's God (and ours) isn't like that. He is patient. He loves us through all our failures and mistakes. His love is steadfast and unchanging. He promises, "I will never leave thee, nor forsake thee" (Heb. 13:5).

Does He seem far away today? Have you lost the sweetness of His presence? Return to your Bethel, your place of communion with Him. Say with the psalmist, "The nearness of God is my good; I have made the Lord God my refuge" (Ps. 73:28 NASB).

OCTOBER 20

I delight to do thy will, O my God: yea, thy law is within my heart (Ps. 40:8).

n this psalm, David is not writing of himself. He is presenting Jesus Christ, the Messiah, the one who came into the world and went to the cross because it was the Father's will.

Throughout His life on earth, the Lord Jesus had one great purpose, doing His Father's will. He delighted in it—"who for the joy that was set before him endured the cross" (Heb. 12:2). He died to give us a reason for living. "God . . . purposes in his sovereign will that all human history shall be consummated in Christ, that everything that exists in Heaven or earth shall find its perfection and fulfillment in him" (Eph. 1:9–10 PHILLIPS).

Jesus said to His disciples, "My food (nourishment) is to do the will (pleasure) of Him Who sent Me and to accomplish and completely finish His work" (John 4:34 AMPLIFIED). He also said, "I have come down from Heaven, not to do what I want, but to do the will of him who sent me" (John 6:38 PHILLIPS).

The climax came in a great struggle in the Garden of Gethsemane. "He . . . fell on his face, and prayed . . . O my Father, if it be possible, let this cup pass from me: nevertheless not as I will, but as thou wilt" (Matt. 26:39).

There had been no self-seeking, no self-pleasing spirit in His life. He always brought pleasure to His Father. Now, He had completed His purpose on earth. Through His death and resurrection, He provided a way for humankind to become a part of God's family. It has been said, "Though His sufferings were exceedingly bitter, yet the fruit of them was exceedingly sweet."

Just as Jesus delighted to do the will of His Father, so can we. Because we know Him, His will can be our delight—not because it is easy but because we have placed our lives in His hand to do what He desires. He sees the end result and knows how to fit today's circumstances into His completed plan for us. "I love to do God's will so far as my new nature is concerned" (Rom. 7:22 LB).

The secret of a life pleasing to God is losing our self-will in the delightfulness of the will of God.

OCTOBER 21

As ye have therefore received Christ Jesus the Lord, so walk ye in him: rooted and built up in him, and stablished in the faith, as ye have been taught, abounding therein with thanksgiving (Col. 2:6–7).

aul wanted the Colossian Christians to know how to keep on for the Lord Jesus Christ. They had received Him by faith, so they were to walk with Him by faith. "We walk by faith, not by sight" (2 Cor. 5:7). To walk by faith means to let our faith determine our conduct and strengthen us in our daily tasks. The Living Bible reads, "Just as you trusted Christ to save you, trust him, too, for each day's problems; live in vital union with him" (Col. 2:6 LB).

The Lord is our walking partner. We can walk in confidence, knowing that nothing will come into our lives that He cannot handle. As we give each day to Him and let Him lead us through the day, not one problem will be too much for Him. We can exchange our weakness for His strength. His strong hand will keep us from stumbling.

To walk by faith, we must send our roots deep. "Let your roots grow down into him and draw up nourishment from him" (v. 7 LB). With this stability we will not be shaken or uprooted when storms strike. The psalmist said, "He is like a tree planted by streams of water, which yields its fruit in season and whose leaf does not wither" (Ps. 1:3 NIV).

To walk by faith, we must be "built up in him." The Lord Jesus Christ is not only our Builder, He is our foundation. "For other foundation can no man lay than that is laid, which is Jesus Christ" (1 Cor. 3:11). Built on Him, our lives become a strong superstructure.

To walk by faith, we must become "established in the faith." We are to be continually strengthened in the faith, steadfast. "Become strong and vigorous in the truth you were taught" (Col. 2:7 LB). Our faith becomes stronger as we spend time in God's Word. "Faith cometh by hearing, and hearing by the word of God" (Rom. 10:17).

A walk of faith results in thanksgiving. When we realize that all we have and do is through Christ, our hearts will overflow with thanksgiving. True joy comes from a close walk with Him.

As we walk by faith, rooted in Him, built up in Him, firmly established in Him, He becomes our all in all.

OCTOBER 22

And it came to pass, when Moses held up his hand, that Israel prevailed: and when he let down his hand, Amalek prevailed (Ex. 17:11).

s Israel faced their enemies the Amalekites in battle, Moses selected Joshua to lead and told him, "Choose us out men, and go out, fight with Amalek: tomorrow I will stand on the top of the hill with the rod of God in mine hand" (v. 9).

The battle would be fought in two realms. Joshua would fight the physical battle on the plain; Moses would fight the spiritual battle on the mountain above. Aaron and Hur accompanied Moses to the top of the mountain, and Moses took his stand at the top of the hill, the place of prayer, where the real work would be done.

With him, Moses took the rod of God, the symbol of his authority and power with God. As long as Moses held up the rod, Israel was winning. When his arms became weary and he lowered the rod, the Amalekites began to triumph. Finally, his arms became so weak, he could not hold them up. Then Aaron and Hur held up his arms so that "his hands were steady until the going down of the sun" (v. 12). Joshua and his army won the battle, but victory really came from the hillside—the place of prayer.

You may be in a battle today with your family, with your co-workers, even with yourself. You may feel you are losing. But God doesn't lose battles. "The battle is not yours, but God's" (2 Chron. 20:15). Battles are lost or won on the battlefield of prayer.

Years ago, Wilbur Chapman became pastor of a prestigious church in Philadelphia. After his first sermon, a man in the congregation told him, "You are too young for this church, but I will help you all I can." The next Sunday, he and two others went into a side room and prayed for the pastor. The next Sunday, there were ten. Eventually, the number praying for the pastor on Sunday mornings was over two hundred. During the first three years of his pastorate, over eleven hundred people came to know Christ.

Whatever tough assignment you face today, God may take you out of the battle or He may give you victory in it. But He always wins! "Thanks be unto God, which always causeth us to triumph in Christ" (2 Cor. 2:14).

OCTOBER 23

But [God] led His own people forth like sheep and guided them
[with a shepherd's care] like a flock in the wilderness. And He led
them on safely and in confident trust, so that they feared not; but the
sea overwhelmed their enemies (Ps. 78:52–53 AMPLIFIED).

n a bus depot I noticed a poster advertising a particular bus line. It said, "What a difference the guide makes." I paused and thought, *Thank you, Lord, that I have a Guide who will lead me through life.*

A guide or leader is one who goes before, leading us along. Christ Jesus is our Leader. The writer of Hebrews writes about "looking unto Jesus the author and finisher of our faith" (Heb. 12:2). God says, "I am the LORD thy God which . . . leadeth thee by the way that thou shouldest go" (Isa. 48:17).

As God led the Israelites out of Egypt, He performed many miracles. The way ahead was unknown. There were no well-marked highways, no supermarkets, no restaurants. Soon after they started on their way, Pharaoh sent his army after them. Hemmed in by the mountains around them, the Red Sea before them, and their enemies behind them, the Israelites had every reason to fear. But God did a miracle. "He divided the sea and led them through; he made the water stand firm like a wall" (Ps. 78:13 NIV).

That is the God who leads us. David said, "He leadeth me beside the still waters" (Ps. 23:2). Our Guide knows when to lead us from life's pressures and 'tensions to a place beside the still waters—waters of rest for our body and rest for our soul.

Our Leader is also our Safekeeper. We can say, "I will fear no evil: for thou art with me" (Ps. 23:4). During World War II, one day when General Eisenhower was with his troops, he noticed a young soldier who looked depressed. "How are you feeling?" Eisenhower asked. "General, I'm nervous," the soldier said. "I was wounded two months ago, and I just got out of the hospital."

"You and I make a good pair then," replied General Eisenhower, "I'm nervous too. Maybe if we walk together, we will be good for each other." The young man's spirits lifted. "Oh, sir," he said, "I'm not nervous anymore." He felt secure for he had someone to walk with him.

Because our Guide is walking with us, we are safe. We need not fear.

OCTOBER 24

So I have looked upon You in the sanctuary to see Your power and Your glory (Ps. 63:2 AMPLIFIED).

avid was in the wilderness, fleeing from his enemies when he prayed this prayer. In that lonely place, he cried out, "O God, you are my God, earnestly I seek you" (Ps. 63:1 NIV). In the wilderness he kept a close relationship with God.

David's thoughts wandered back to his experiences with God in the sanctuary. There he had worshiped God. There he had seen the power and glory of God displayed in the Shekinah glory. But David knew that God wasn't confined to the sanctuary. God could reveal Himself in all His power and glory anytime, anywhere.

Do you feel like you are in a barren wilderness? Perhaps your wilderness is a child's rebellion, a financial crisis, a job lost, a frustrating schedule, or a dream shattered.

We must not be satisfied to reminisce about our past experiences with God. We need a fresh glimpse of God and His glory—the manifestation of His attributes—so that we can display it to the world. Only when we allow Him to give us something new will we have something to share with others.

In the sanctuary of God's presence, we see His power available for today's needs. We need His power when we feel we are falling apart. We need His power when we face insurmountable problems. Only God's power is great enough to meet our need. Paul prayed for the believers in Ephesus that they would "begin to understand how incredibly great his power is to help those who believe him" (Eph. 1:19 LB).

In the sanctuary of God's presence, we also see His glory—His character, the very essence of who He is. God came to earth in the person of His Son, Jesus Christ, to reveal His glory to us. Once we have seen His glory, we can reveal it to others. "God, who first ordered light to shine in darkness, has flooded our hearts with his light. We now can enlighten men only because we can give them knowledge of the glory of God, as we see it in the face of Jesus Christ" (2 Cor. 4:6 PHILLIPS).

May we reflect God's might and glory in our wilderness.

OCTOBER 25

In the multitude of my (anxious) thoughts within me, Your comforts cheer and delight my soul! (Ps. 94:19 AMPLIFIED).

orry is fretting about something beyond our control. It is paying interest on trouble before the interest comes due. Ironically, a worrier is never happy unless he is perfectly, horribly miserable.

Some people see calamity in everything and worry about it. They count their *troubles* one by one instead of their blessings.

The psalmist was perplexed as he looked at the evil conditions surrounding him. He could have worried, but instead, he turned to God. He said, "Blessed—happy, fortunate [to be envied]—is the man whom You discipline and instruct, O Lord, and teach out of Your law; that You may give him power to hold himself calm in the days of adversity" (Ps. 94:12–13 AMPLIFIED).

Regardless of what kind of trouble the psalmist was experiencing, he turned to his heavenly Father for help. He recognized that God had a purpose in these trials. Through them, the psalmist learned God's power to calm him in the midst of adversity. God comforted his heart and mind.

You may be perplexed or disappointed today. Your mind may be filled with anxious thoughts. You may be worried. No matter what you are facing, you can be sure that God can and will do for you what He did for the psalmist.

In our anxious moments, the Great Comforter of our souls, Jesus Christ, enters into our trouble and lovingly says, "I will not leave you comfortless: I will come to you" (John 14:18). We can rest in the God of all comfort. "Casting the whole of your care—all your anxieties, all your worries, all your concerns, once and for all—on Him; for He cares for you affectionately, and cares about you watchfully" (1 Peter 5:7 AMPLIFIED).

God may not always give us relief from our situation, but He can change our anxious thoughts into peaceful ones. "He maketh the storm a calm, so that the waves thereof are still. Then are they glad because they be quiet; so he bringeth them unto their desired haven" (Ps. 107:29–30).

May we allow God to comfort and cheer us today!

OCTOBER 26

But Abraham stood yet before the Lord. And Abraham drew near
(Gen. 18:22—23).

robably Abraham's greatest honor was being called "the Friend of God" (James 2:23). Because of their close relationship, God delighted to have a friend like Abraham with whom He could share His thoughts and plans.

One day, three people came to visit Abraham. One of them was the Lord. As the Lord started to leave, He said, "Shall I hide from Abraham that thing which I do?" (Gen. 18:17).

He did not keep it a secret but shared with Abraham His plan to destroy the wicked city of Sodom. Immediately, Abraham showed concern for his nephew Lot and Lot's family living there. Abraham stood in the presence of God, faithfully interceding not only for his relatives but also for Sodom. As a result of his concern and prayer, Lot and his family were spared.

Today we have the privilege of interceding for our needy world, our neighbors, friends, and loved ones. As we stand before the Lord, we can draw near, interceding on their behalf. Intercession is "speaking to God from a burdened heart for a world on its way to a Christless eternity."

One day, I heard on a newscast that a well-known dance band leader in my city had been critically injured in a car accident. Although I did not know him personally, I felt constrained to pray for him. I dropped to my knees and asked God to spare his life until someone could talk to him about Jesus Christ.

Several years later, I heard of his conversion. He dedicated his musical ability to writing Christian music. Whenever I hear his beautiful song, "I've Found a Friend," I thank God that Barclay Allen came to know that Friend, Jesus Christ, personally.

I wonder how many times I may have missed God-given opportunities to pray for someone because I have not been listening to His voice. "He that goeth forth and weepeth, bearing precious seed, shall doubtless come again with rejoicing, bringing his sheaves with him" (Ps. 126:6).

Are you standing before the Lord as an intercessor?

OCTOBER 27

Call upon me in the day of trouble: I will deliver thee, and thou shalt glorify me (Ps. 50:15).

e are not exempt from trouble just because we are Christians, but Jesus says: "In the world ye shall have tribulation: but be of good cheer; I have overcome the world" (John 16:33).

When trouble strikes—*pray*. God has promised that if we bring our troubles to Him, He shall deliver us. We are as near to God as a call. Whether our trouble is great or small, God never panics. Not one is too big, for He is All-powerful; not one is too small for He is All-loving. He cares about your trouble today.

David's life was full of trouble, yet God delivered him. David wrote, "God is our refuge and strength [mighty and impenetrable to temptation], a very present and well-proved help in trouble" (Ps. 46:1 AMPLIFIED). Sometimes deliverance comes just as we asked. Sometimes God delivers us in a different way and at a different time. But He always does what is best for us.

One evening while in Basel, Switzerland, I went out for dinner, and it was dark when I returned to the home where I was staying. There were two doorbells at the entrance. I rang one, but there was no answer. I rang the other. No answer. I pounded on the door. No answer. Alone on the street in a strange country, I began to panic. I could not speak German. I had no German money. I didn't know where to find a telephone.

But I did have a special telephone line reaching to heaven. I put in a call to my heavenly Father and was directed to pound the door again. This time I pounded so hard I almost shook the door off its hinges. My hostess finally heard and came to the door. I later learned that a blown fuse had silenced the doorbells, but I joyfully thanked my heavenly Father for delivering me from my trouble.

Our troubles have a purpose. Paul said, "Our light and momentary troubles are achieving for us an eternal glory that far outweighs them all. So we fix our eyes not on what is seen, but on what is unseen. For what is seen is temporary, but what is unseen is eternal" (2 Cor. 4:17–18 NIV).

By the mercies of God . . . present your bodies a living and holy sacrifice, acceptable to God, which is your spiritual service of worship . . . prove what the will of God is, that which is good and acceptable and perfect (Rom. 12:1–2 NASB).

any people are searching for God's will for their lives. A young woman reading a love letter prays, "Dear Lord, is he the right one to be my mate? I must be sure." A man sitting at his office desk prays, "Show me the right decision for this business deal." A mother on her knees prays, "Father dear, give me wisdom in handling my teenager's rebellion." A young man reading his Bible prays, "Lord, I must know your will for my life. I am willing to serve wherever you want me, but I must know where."

Today's Scripture implies that learning God's good, acceptable, and perfect will begins with our total commitment to Him. "Present your bodies a living sacrifice." We put our bodies at His disposal, giving Him our whole person.

When we present our bodies as a living sacrifice, we make Jesus Christ the Lord of every part of our lives. We turn all rights over to Him and give Him the key to every room of our lives. God has a right to control us, for He purchased us with the life-blood of Jesus Christ. "You were not redeemed with perishable things like silver or gold . . . but with precious blood, as of a lamb unblemished and spotless, the blood of Christ" (1 Peter 1:18–19 NASB).

To present our bodies as a living sacrifice is an act of spiritual worship, yet it also includes our service. We sing, "Take my life and let it be consecrated, Lord, to Thee," but do we realize what that commitment means? It means we give Him our best, our all.

A mother in India had two children, both of whom she loved dearly. One was sickly and the other healthy. She believed her heathen god demanded a sacrifice from her, so she decided to give her most treasured possession, her healthy child, to her god. When asked why she didn't give the sickly child, she replied, "Do you think I would give anything but my best to my god?"

Are you giving Him your best?

Do not be conformed to this world, but be transformed by the renewing of your mind, that you may prove what the will of God is, that which is good and acceptable and perfect (Rom. 12:2 NASB).

he world around us is making a constant impact on our lives. In our struggle with peer pressure we are not to conform to the lifestyle of the world. "Don't let the world around you squeeze you into its own mold, but let God remold your minds from within, so that you may prove in practice that the plan of God for you is good, meets all his demands and moves toward the goal of true maturity" (PHILLIPS).

Transformed means changed in form or character. The metamorphosis of a caterpillar to a butterfly is an example of such a transformation. The changed being cannot be recognized as the same.

This inner change shows outwardly as the Holy Spirit controls the body and mind. "All of us who are Christians have no veils on our faces, but reflect like mirrors the glory of the Lord. We are transfigured in ever-increasing splendor into his own image, and the transformation comes from the Lord who is the Spirit" (2 Cor. 3:18 PHILLIPS). After we present our bodies to Him as a living sacrifice, He renews our minds and transforms our inner beings to make us like Jesus Christ.

During the reign of Queen Victoria, the Penjab province of India came under British control. The young maharajah, who was just a boy, sent the queen a gift, the beautiful Kohnoor diamond. When the prince became a young man, he visited the queen, and after paying honor to her asked to see the diamond. The queen ordered it brought by armed guard.

The maharajah took the beautiful diamond, walked over, and knelt at the feet of the queen, saying, "Your Majesty, I gave you the jewel when I was young. Now, I want to present it in my strength, with my heart, affection, and gratitude, realizing now what I am doing."

Have you presented your body to the Lord with all the dedication, love, and adoration of your heart? If you never have, today is your opportunity.

OCTOBER 30

Hereby we do know that we know him, if we keep his command-
ments (1 John 2:3).

n Washington, D.C., the United States Bureau of Standards
maintains the precise standards for weight and length measurements. All measurements are based on these standards. In the
Bible God maintains His Bureau of Standards by which we
measure various aspects our lives.

The first measurement is **obedience.** Obedience is one of the most
important areas of our Christian lives. Keeping His commandments proves that
we know God. The word *know* in this verse means to come to know Him and
to continue to know Him. Obeying His Word also perfects His love in us.
"Whoso keepeth his word, in him verily is the love of God perfected" (v. 5).

The commandments mentioned here are not the Ten Commandments,
but the teachings of Christ. Jesus said, "Why call ye me, Lord, Lord, and do not
the things which I say?" (Luke 6:46). An obedient heart proves the reality of
our faith.

The next measurement is our **walk.** Jesus Christ is our pattern for daily
conduct. "He that saith he abideth in him ought himself also so to walk, even as
he walked" (v. 6). Again, it is more than saying we are walking with Him. If
we truly are, we will have the rhythm of His step, the companionship of His
company, and the direction of His life. The walk in complete dependence on
God is the walk that pleases Him. Paul said, "As ye have therefore received
Christ Jesus the Lord, so walk ye in him" (Col. 2:6). How did Jesus walk? He
walked in unbroken fellowship and complete dependence on His Father in
heaven.

The third measurement is **love.** "He that loveth his brother abideth in the
light, and there is none occasion of stumbling in him" (v. 10). Brotherly love
proves that we are abiding in the light. Jesus said, "A new command I give you:
Love one another. As I have loved you, so you must love one another" (John
13:34 NIV).

Obeying, walking, loving—how do you measure up?

You can only be as useful to Him as you are consecrated.

OCTOBER 31

*And one of them, when he saw that he was healed, turned back,
and with a loud voice glorified God, and fell down on his face at his
feet, giving him thanks" (Luke 17:15–16).*

en lepers met Jesus as He entered a village in Galilee. "Jesus,
Master, have mercy on us," they called (v. 13). Very likely
they were despondent, deploring their loathsome condition.
Their future was not bright.

As they saw Jesus approaching, hope sprang into their hearts. Undoubtedly they had heard of His miracles. They knew no one could heal them but
Him. But because they were lepers, they had to keep their distance. They cried
out, "Master, have mercy on us."

Perhaps they expected a miracle to happen right then. But Jesus said, "Go
shew yourselves unto the priests" (v. 14). According to law, a person
cleansed of leprosy had to show himself to the priest before returning home.

By this command, Jesus was putting them to a test. If they believed Him,
they would obey Him. They did believe and obeyed. As they went, they could
feel something happening. What joy must have been theirs as they realized that
they were healed. After going to the priest, they were eager to return to their
families and tell the good news.

Suddenly, one of them stopped. He remembered the One who had
healed him. Quickly, he returned to Jesus in joy and gratitude "and with a loud
voice glorified God, and fell down at his feet, giving him thanks." He realized
that God was there in the person of Jesus Christ, and he fell at His feet and
worshiped Him.

Jesus said to him, "Were there not ten cleansed? but where are the
nine?" (v. 17). Perhaps there was a touch of sadness of Jesus' voice. The nine
had gone their own way—happy, but forgetful and unthankful. They had
focused on what He had done for them, not on the One who had performed
the miracle. To the grateful one Jesus said, "Arise, go thy way: thy faith hath
made thee whole" (v. 19).

We may say, "How ungrateful the others were." But how many times,
we, too, fail to thank Him for what He has done. We are often quick to ask and
slow to thank.

God appreciates those who come into His presence with thankful,
worshipful hearts. "Thank God at all times for everything, in the name of our
Lord Jesus Christ" (Eph. 5:20 PHILLIPS).

NOVEMBER 1

I urge, then, first of all, that requests, prayers, intercession and thanksgiving be made for everyone—for kings and all those in authority, that we may live peaceful and quiet lives in all godliness and holiness. This is good, and pleases God our Savior, who wants all men to be saved and to come to a knowledge of the truth (1 Tim. 2:1–4 NIV).

ur world is in a desperate condition—family tensions, increasing crime, political unrest, environmental dangers. We are shocked at what we hear and see. People need Jesus Christ, and God wants Christians to pray.

Paul encourages us to pray for everyone. Why? So that we may live peaceful, quiet lives and so that we may please God "who wants all men to be saved" (v. 4 NIV).

Praying for everyone means praying specifically for those who are the closest to us—our family and neighbors. Praying for everyone means praying specifically for those in authority—kings and government leaders in our city, state, nation, and the entire world. Praying for everyone means praying specifically for pastors, church leaders, missionaries, Sunday school teachers, and those in Christian ministries. Paul said, "Pray for us, too, that God may open a door for our message, so that we may proclaim the mystery of Christ, for which I am in chains" (Col. 4:3 NIV). And Jesus told us to pray specifically for those who share His good news of salvation through Jesus Christ. "Pray ye therefore the Lord of the harvest, that he will send forth labourers into his harvest" (Matt. 9:38).

We pray specifically because people have specific needs. Many around us are desperate. They need someone who will pray specifically for them in their particular situation. We have the right to take the needs of others (as well as our own needs) into the presence of God. Specific prayer receives specific answers.

Are you praying for those close to you? Are you praying for government and spiritual leaders? We can make a great impact on the world through specific prayer. If we examine our prayer lists, we may discover areas we have been neglecting.

God says, "If my people, which are called by my name, shall humble themselves, and pray, and seek my face, and turn from their wicked ways; then will I hear from heaven, and will forgive their sin, and will heal their land" (2 Chron. 7:14).

NOVEMBER 2

He shall deliver the needy when he crieth (Ps. 72:12).

he needy are God's special concern, and who is not in need? You may have a burden too heavy to carry, you may have reached the end of your resources, you may have exhausted your physical strength, or you may have a broken heart. You are ready to give up. You can't see your way ahead. You can't even see your next step. You are the perfect candidate for His help. You are that special one He has promised to deliver. God specializes in delivering helpless people.

The psalmist wrote, "I am poor and needy; yet the Lord thinketh upon me: thou art my help and my deliverer; make no tarrying, O my God" (Ps. 40:17). God has promised to meet our needs when we cry to Him. Someone has said, "Need alone is the begetter of despair. But need with crying is the birthplace of prayer."

In times of helplessness and distress, our first impulse is to worry. He does not say He will deliver the needy when they fret and worry and scheme but rather *when they cry.* When needs arise, God says, "Call upon me in the day of trouble: I will deliver thee, and thou shalt glorify me" (Ps. 50:15).

One night, the disciples were in deep need. They were crossing the Sea of Galilee when a severe storm swept across the sea. The wind blew strong, tossing their boat about until the disciples knew they would drown.

But Jesus slept soundly during the storm. When the disciples awakened Him, accusing Him of not caring about them, Jesus simply stood and rebuked the wind and said to the sea, "Peace, be still!" Even in their cry of doubt, Jesus delivered them.

Are you one of his needy children? When you cry, He will deliver you. He may deliver you from your storm, or He may deliver you in it. The Bible says, "The eyes of the LORD are upon the righteous, and his ears are open unto their cry" (Ps. 34:15).

NOVEMBER 3

Shine out among them like beacon lights, holding out to them the Word of Life" (Phil. 2:15–16 LB).

ne of my choice memories is a special Christmas Eve service at my church. In the darkened sanctuary one large candle burned brightly, representing Jesus Christ, the Light of the World, and each person who came received a smaller candle. One person lighted his candle from the large one, and then from candle to candle, the light spread until the packed church glowed with light. Then, we were asked to hold our lighted candles aloft.

At the end of the service, we extinguished our candles, but I became aware of the responsibility of keeping the Light of the World shining in a world so desperately in need of spiritual light. Jesus said, "I am the light of the world" (John 8:12). And John wrote of Christ, "In him was life; and the life was the light of men" (John 1:4).

God has placed each one of us in a special place in this dark world to shine for Him. Jesus is the original Light. We are His reflected light. When He indwells us, *His* Light shines forth. We are the container; He is the Light. His light in our lives transforms us. The Light of the World, Jesus Christ, shines out in all we do and say.

However, sometimes our light flickers or even goes out. One time at a consecration service I attended, each person had a small flashlight. Standing in a circle around the room, we turned on our flashlights while the challenge was being given. As my finger tired, I couldn't hold the button on, and the light flickered off and on instead of shining in a steady ray of light.

This is true of our lives sometimes, too. When we try to keep the light on in our lives by our own power, it flickers or goes out. Only the Holy Spirit keeps the Light of the World shining steadily in our lives. He will make us a light in whatever dark place God puts us.

May Christ's light shine steadily through us today.

NOVEMBER 4

You chart the path ahead of me, and tell me where to stop and rest.
Every moment, you know where I am (Ps. 139:3 LB).

od had a special custom-designed plan for David's life. David said to God, "You chart the path ahead of me." In fact, David's life was designed for him before birth: "You saw me before I was born and scheduled each day of my life before I began to breathe. Every day was recorded in your Book!" (v. 16 LB).

God tells us that He has such a plan for each of us. " 'I know the plans that I have for you,' declares the Lord, 'plans for welfare and not for calamity to give you a future and a hope' " (Jer. 29:11 NASB).

God is omniscient. David said, "You have examined my heart and know everything about me" (Ps. 139:1 LB). He knows things about us that we do not even know. Because He knows us through and through, He plans the very best for us. We can trust Him not to make a mistake.

He knows our every moment, even our sitting and standing (v. 2). Can you imagine the great God of the Universe being interested in where we sit or stand? He is.

"When far away you know my every thought" (v. 2 LB). There are times when I wish He didn't know some of the thoughts that creep into my mind. But He sees the critical thought, the unloving thought, the proud thought. He knows our most personal secrets.

God is also interested in our physical well-being. "You . . . tell me where to stop and rest" (v. 3 LB).

"Every moment, you know where I am" (v. 3 LB). He knows the obstacles on our way, the mountains we have to climb, the dark valleys we must go through. He knows when we are lonely and discouraged. He is with us from the beginning of our Christian walk to the end.

"You know what I am going to say before I even say it" (v. 4 LB). Sometimes we may think, "Then, Lord, why didn't you keep me from saying it?"

"You both precede and follow me, and place your hand of blessing on my head" (v. 5 LB). How encouraging to know that His presence surrounds us.

"This is too glorious, too wonderful to believe!" (v. 6 LB). Yet it is true. God is wonderfully, gloriously real!

NOVEMBER 5

If I ride the morning winds to the farthest oceans, even
there your hand will guide me, your strength will support me
(Ps. 139:9–10 LB).

hile Brother Lawrence, a sixteenth-century monk, was walking in the forest one winter day, he stopped beneath a tree which had shed its foliage. He thought about how the tree, which now seemed dead, would return to life in the spring with beautiful new green leaves.

"God must be here," he said. This awareness of God's presence never left him. God's presence was always real to Brother Lawrence. He was as deeply impressed with the sense of God's presence when preparing food for his fellow monks as when he was kneeling before the sacraments.

David, too, sensed God around him everywhere. He said, "I can never be lost to your Spirit! I can never get away from my God! If I go up to heaven, you are there; if I go down to the place of the dead, you are there . . . If I try to hide in the darkness, the night becomes light around me. For even darkness cannot hide from God" (vv. 7–12 LB).

Have there been times when you have tried to run away from God? You can't. He is in all places at all times. He knows where we are each moment of the day. Wherever we go, God goes with us. Even though we may be in the depths of despair, He never leaves us. Even though we fly to the uttermost part of the earth to get away from our problems, He is there with us. We can face our situations with Him honestly and openly. Oh, the overwhelming joy and peace to know that God is *always* with us.

Where are you today? What circumstances do you find yourself in? Wherever you are, *even there* God is with you.

With David we can say, "How precious it is, Lord, to realize that you are thinking about me constantly! I can't even count how many times a day your thoughts turn towards me. And when I waken in the morning, you are still thinking of me!" (Ps. 139:17–18 LB).

NOVEMBER 6

Jesus increased in wisdom and stature, and in favour with God and man (Luke 2:52).

esus lived a well-balanced life. As He grew up, He matured in every way.

Jesus matured mentally. When He went to the Temple at twelve years of age, the doctors of the law questioned Him, and they were astonished at His wise answers. After He had grown to manhood, people said, "Never man spake like this man" (John 7:46).

We are to mature mentally, too, for a well-balanced life. Paul wrote, "Let this mind be in you, which was also in Christ Jesus" (Phil. 2:5). We need to fill our minds with His Word and meditate on Him. "Be ye transformed by the renewing of your mind" (Rom. 12:2). We would also do well to read some good books on various subjects for balance, perhaps setting a goal of one every month or every three months.

Jesus matured physically. "He increased in stature." We, too, should mature physically. Our bodies are not our own but His. We are responsible for taking care of them for Him. It takes discipline, but we must keep physically fit, for the way we feel physically affects the other areas of our lives, even the spiritual.

Jesus also matured spiritually. God confirmed His favor upon Jesus when He said, "This is my beloved Son, in whom I am well pleased" (Matt. 3:17). We, too, need to mature spiritually—in our relationship with God. Our ambition should be to please Him in all we do. "Continue to learn more and more of the life that pleases God" (1 Thess. 4:1 PHILLIPS). Is He pleased with what we do? see? think? say?

Are we developing a well-balanced life? Jesus is the perfect example of well-balanced maturity. The writer of Hebrews exhorts, "Let us go on unto perfection" (Heb. 6:1). Perfection means maturity—the goal of our growth. To mature means to become more and more the person God has planned for us to be.

May our prayer be that of John the Baptist, who said, "He must increase, but I must decrease" (John 3:30).

NOVEMBER 7

Epaphras . . . a real servant of Christ Jesus . . . works hard for you even here, for he prays constantly and earnestly for you, that you may become mature Christians, and may fulfill God's will for you (Col. 4:12 PHILLIPS).

ffectiveness in serving Jesus Christ depends on our prayer life. Epaphras was known for his effective prayers. He prayed **regularly.** Paul told the Colossian Christians, "Epaphras . . . prays constantly for you." Epaphras himself followed the admonition Paul gave in the second verse of this chapter when he said, "Always maintain the habit of prayer" (PHILLIPS).

Epaphras prayed **earnestly** for them because he carried them on his heart. He cared deeply for the Colossian Christians and took the responsibility of prayer seriously. Paul wrote, "From my own observation I can tell you that he has a real passion for your welfare" (v. 13 PHILLIPS). Epaphras believed God would accomplish His purpose in their lives as they matured in Him.

He prayed for **spiritual needs.** Often we pray for the physical and material needs of people we know but overlook the spiritual. Yet Epaphras prayed, "That you may become mature Christians and may fulfill God's will for you." He was concerned that they would stand perfect and complete in the will of God.

What about you? Are you maintaining a habit of prayer? We are only as strong as our prayer life.

Have you asked God to give you the prayer list He wants you to follow? Have you been praying for some of the countries that are now experiencing a spiritual awakening? It is so exciting to see God work in areas we have been praying for!

And what a challenge we have to intercede for others in the building of His Kingdom. Jesus prayed, "Thy will be done in earth, as it is in heaven" (Matt. 6:10). Through prayer, we have a part in fulfilling His will on earth. Prayer is fundamental to the work of God, not incidental. It is a command, not an option. Jesus said, "*When* you pray, not *if* you pray." Prayer is *the* work.

God said, "I sought for a man among them, that should make up the hedge, and stand in the gap before me for the land, that I should not destroy it: but I found none"(Ezek. 22:30).

Will you stand in the gap today?

NOVEMBER 8

Thou hast been a shelter for me, and a strong tower from the enemy (Ps. 61:3).

e often smile as we watch children cling to an old worn-out blanket, refusing to go to bed without it. Yet I wonder how many of us have a security blanket we cling to—a home, car, bank account, insurance policy, home alarm system, or even another person.

David had a security blanket. He faced many dangers, but the Lord was the security blanket he could always trust. The Lord was David's shelter and strong tower. David asked God to take him to His place of security. "Lead me to the rock that is higher than I" (v. 2). That High Rock is none other than Jesus Christ (1 Cor. 10:4). Christ became David's Rock, his Refuge, his Strong Tower.

David didn't go to his strong tower only in an emergency or when there was no other place to go. In this constant day-by-day abiding place he felt secure, no matter what happened. God is not our last resort but our continual resort. The psalmist cried out to God, "Be thou my strong habitation, whereunto I may continually resort . . . thou art my rock, and my fortress" (Ps. 71:3). God is our constant place of security.

I had to learn that the Lord alone must be my security blanket. I had a busy schedule of speaking and conducting meetings for the Lord. I trusted God, but I had a security blanket—my husband. People didn't realize that because I was timid and shy I leaned heavily on my husband's support.

Then my husband died. My security blanket was gone. What would I do without him? I had to learn that my security must be in the Lord and Him alone. My security must not be in the Lord plus anything or anyone else. "The LORD is my rock" (Ps. 18:2).

Do you have a security blanket? Is it the Lord plus something or someone else? God may not remove whatever else you are leaning on, the way He did mine, but He will take you through some experience to test you. You, too, will have to learn that your security must be in the Lord Jesus Christ and Him alone.

"O LORD my God, in thee do I put my trust" (Ps. 7:1).

NOVEMBER 9

While they communed together and reasoned, Jesus himself drew near, and went with them (Luke 24:15).

On resurrection afternoon two disciples returned home on the Emmaus road, discussing the perplexing events that had taken place in Jerusalem. They didn't understand.

When Jesus joined them on the road and asked them what they were talking about, they didn't recognize Him. They were surprised that anyone didn't know about the earth-shaking events that had happened that day. During their walk together, Jesus comforted them with an explanation from the Scriptures. They invited Him to go home with them, and as they ate together, the disciples recognized Him. But just as suddenly as He appeared, He vanished.

If you reflect upon the past year, you may recall many times that Jesus drew near to you in your time of need. Through your relationship with Him, He constantly indwells your life, but there are times when He comes near in a special way.

Each of us walks our own unique road. Your road may be the road of success or failure, happiness or sorrow, fame or disappointment. I received word recently that a friend of mine is now walking the cancer road. Jesus Himself has drawn near to her and is walking that road with her. He knows the road you are walking, too. Whatever our need, He walks with us as the God of that road.

We may be apprehensive, confused, frustrated, but He draws near, revealing Himself in new ways. As our great High Priest (Heb. 4:14), He feels with us and understands as no one else can. As the God of the Impossible (Luke 1:37) He gives hope where we thought there was none. As the God of Peace (Eph. 2:14) he calms our hearts. Today your life may be falling apart, but God walking beside you can put your life together again. "I will fear no evil; for thou art with me" (Ps. 23:4).

As we approach a new year, we can be sure that He will draw near and go through it with us day by day, need by need. Regardless of what problems we may face, we have confidence because He will draw near and walk with us, comforting our hearts.

He says, "I am with you alway, even unto the end of the world. Amen" (Matt. 28:20).

NOVEMBER 10

Wait on the LORD: be of good courage, and he shall strengthen thine heart: wait, I say, on the LORD (Ps. 27:14).

Rain for forty days! Some people can't stand rain for one day. I enjoy rain, but I am not sure how I would react to forty days of it—especially in an ark full of animals.

When at last the rain stopped, Noah sent a raven out to learn the condition of the earth. The raven didn't return, but Noah *waited* to hear from the Lord.

Later, he sent a dove out several times. Each time, he discovered that the earth was drying up, but still he *waited*. No word from the Lord. When he removed the covering and looked out, he saw that the earth was dry, but still he waited for God to speak. In my impulsive way, I would probably have left the ark. But not Noah. He was still *waiting*, not willing to move until God directed.

Finally, the day came when God said, "Go forth of the ark" (Gen. 8:16). God's *when* is as important as His *what*, and Noah respected God's timing. Waiting is difficult for most of us, but God puts us in many situations where we have to wait on Him.

And we are to wait patiently. "Rest in the Lord, and wait patiently for him" (Ps. 37:7). Many people say, "Lord, give me patience, and give it to me right now." But if we are resting in the Lord, we won't be in a hurry. Resting in the Lord puts us completely in His keeping. We can lean on Him. "Be still and rest in the Lord; wait for Him, and patiently stay yourself upon Him" (Ps. 37:7 AMPLIFIED).

We must travel at the pace the Holy Spirit sets. If we don't have clear direction from the Lord, we must wait. We must not force open a closed door or even a half-closed door. Learning to wait on the Lord is practice in the patience of faith. It prepares us for the answer that is coming and affirms the sovereignty of God—His right to give whatever He wishes to whomever He pleases. We must wait as long as He keeps us on hold.

My life verse is, "My soul, wait thou only upon God; for my expectation is from him" (Ps. 62:5). Wait and expect!

NOVEMBER 11

The land, whither ye go to possess it, is . . . a land which the LORD thy God careth for: the eyes of the LORD thy God are always upon it, from the beginning of the year even unto the end of the year (Deut. 11:11–12).

he children of Israel were soon to possess the land God had promised them, "a land of hills and valleys with plenty of rain" (v. 11 LB). And God had promised to personally care for it (v. 12 LB). He said that He would *always* keep His eyes on the land from the beginning of the year even to the end.

As we entered this year, we did not know what new blessings and new problems lay ahead. But we did know that God had promised to be with us from its very beginning to its very end. "I will never leave thee, nor forsake thee" (Heb. 13:5).

We claim that promise with great expectancy in January, but the year moves on, and as needs arise and heartaches come, we shift our focus to our needs and begin to worry and fret. In our "land of hills and valleys" the way ahead is not always smooth. Ascending our hill called "trouble" we must go to our knees before God, and He lovingly pours His comfort into our problem-filled lives, promising that His eyes are always upon us in our land, even today. "The eyes of the LORD your God are continually on it" (NIV). His eyes aren't only upon us on our good days but always, continually—when our hearts are broken, when we suffer pain, when we are frustrated, when the promotion we expect goes to someone else, when we do not receive the honor we deserve, when the deal for our dream house falls through, when the medical test results are not good. His eyes are upon us and He cares.

One day when Bishop Watts was a child, he visited a lady who asked him to read a motto on her wall, the words Hagar spoke when she was unloved and rejected. Watts read, "Thou God seest me" (Gen. 16:13). "When you are older," the woman said, "people will tell you that God is watching so He can punish you when you do something wrong. I don't want you to think of it that way. Remember all your life that God loves you so much that He cannot take His eyes off you."

Remember today, God loves *you* so much that He cannot take His eyes off you.

NOVEMBER 12

They came unto the iron gate that leadeth unto the city; which opened to them of his own accord (Acts 12:10).

eter was in prison. His enemies had taken him prisoner and placed him in the innermost part of the prison to await execution. Every door and gate was securely closed behind him. There was no way of escape. But there was one door that could not be closed, the only one through which help could come. It was the door to heaven—the door of prayer. Peter's friends interceded urgently for him without ceasing.

In the meantime what was Peter doing? He was sound asleep, trusting in the Lord. If we keep our communication line with God strong, we will be ready in time of crisis. Peter was prayed up. Later he could write, "You can throw the whole weight of your anxieties upon him, for you are his personal concern" (1 Peter 5:7 PHILLIPS). The Lord was very real to him that night in prison.

Suddenly an angel roused Peter from sleep and told him to follow him. As they came to the outer iron gate, it opened and Peter walked through, a free man. Because his friends were interceding for him in prayer, Peter was miraculously delivered from prison to continue the work God had for him.

You may be in a prison—a prison of a habit, self-pity, discouragement, rebellion, bitterness, a loved one's control. You may have made every effort to escape, but an iron gate holds you back. There is no human way out. Prayer was the secret that opened the iron gate for Peter. Prayer will do the same for you. God is still on the throne. His ear is open to our prayers. He especially loves to hear His children united in earnest prayer for one another.

Prayer is more than telling God what we want Him to do for us. God wants to do something beyond what we can ask or think. When we are trusting God for His will to be accomplished, whatever it may be, God will open our iron gate, and we can walk through, joyfully expecting to continue our service for Him.

NOVEMBER 13

Most gladly therefore will I rather glory in my infirmities, that the
power of Christ may rest upon me (2 Cor. 12:9).

 thorn in the flesh. That's what Paul called his infirmity. Three times he asked that it be removed. Three times God said no. Paul could have said, "God has forgotten me," or "God hasn't answered my prayer." But he took time to listen to God, who said, "My grace is sufficient for thee: for my strength is made perfect in weakness" (v. 9). In Paul's weakness, God's grace would be sufficient and His strength would be perfected.

God's purpose was to keep Paul humble and usable. Paul says, "There was given to me a thorn in the flesh, the messenger of Satan to buffet me, lest I should be exalted above measure" (v.7).

Paul then gloried in his infirmities. I am more apt to complain about mine. But Paul recognized this as an opportunity for God to work in his life. "Most gladly therefore will I rather glory in my infirmities, that the power of Christ may rest upon me" (v. 9). God had told him, "My power shows up best in weak people" (v. 9 LB). So Paul let God demonstrate what His power could do in a life.

Paul accepted God's purpose completely. God's grace met his needs, and God's power gave him enough strength to do "all things" (Phil. 4:13). Paul took pleasure in experiencing God's sufficiency and praised Him for the circumstances that made him dependent on God.

Most of us have a thorn in our lives. God puts us in a position where we are made weak enough for Him to work in our lives. When we depend on our strength and ability, we don't give God a chance to do what He wants to do. Our thorn becomes a blessing only when we let Him use it to perfect our character.

God needs "weak" instruments through whom He can demonstrate His power. We can be those instruments. It has been said, "Great peace—great suffering; great suffering—great power; great power—great victory."

God meets our inner needs: "My grace is sufficient for you." God meets our outer needs: "My strength is made perfect in weakness." Thus, we display what God can do in a life.

Let us say with Paul, "I am glad to be a living demonstration of Christ's power, instead of showing off my own power and abilities" (v. 9 LB).

NOVEMBER 14

And when they had prayed, the place was shaken . . . and they were all filled with the Holy Ghost, and they spake the word of God with boldness (Acts 4:31).

eter and John had been imprisoned for preaching the gospel. When the officials finally released them, they told the two not to speak or teach in the name of Jesus again. Peter and John answered, "Judge for yourselves whether it is right in God's sight to obey you rather than God. For we cannot help speaking about what we have seen and heard" (v. 19–20 NIV). The officials threatened them again and let them go.

Upon their release, Peter and John hurried to tell their Christian friends. When the friends heard about the threats, they held a prayer meeting. "They lifted up their voice to God with one accord" (v. 24). They were in complete agreement as they prayed. "And when they had prayed, the place was shaken . . . and they were all filled with the Holy Ghost, and they spake the word of God with boldness." What caused such an outpouring of God's power? Prayer.

And what was the secret of their effective prayer? They acknowledged the sovereignty of God: "Lord, thou art *God. "* They recognized Him as the creator and sustainer of all things, "which hast made heaven, and earth, and the sea, and all that in them is" (v. 24). If He had power to create and sustain the universe, surely He had power to protect them.

How can we doubt that the creator and maintainer of our universe can meet our need? Too often we hurry into His presence with our problems and fail to take time to worship and adore Him for who He is and what He does.

Their prayer was also filled with the Word of God. We can claim His promises for our prayers, too. "There hath not failed one word of all his good promise" (1 Kings 8:56).

With confidence in God and His Word, they came boldly before Him with their requests. Although they reminded God of the threats against them, they did not pray for protection from their enemies but for boldness to share the gospel.

Their answer came powerfully. The place shook, they were filled with the Holy Spirit, and they spoke the Word of God with boldness.

D. L. Moody once said that every movement of God can be traced to a kneeling figure. Has the world moved toward God because you prayed?

NOVEMBER 15

We faint not; but though our outward man perish, yet the inward man is renewed day by day (2 Cor. 4:16).

ersecution and hardship filled Paul's life. Facing angry mobs, being imprisoned, beaten, and even left for dead had taken its toll on his life. Yet Paul did not faint or lose heart. He knew that although his trials were affecting him physically, God was at work. Since God could still use him, it did not matter what was happening to him. The important thing was that he was being spiritually renewed daily.

We, too, are deteriorating outwardly. We begin to slow down. We lose some of our physical stamina. We begin to feel the effects of our troubles on our life. "The outward man does indeed suffer wear and tear" (PHILLIPS).

But Paul gives us his key to endurance. "Every day the inward man receives fresh strength" (v. 16 PHILLIPS). Our outer person may be weakening, but our inner person is growing stronger. "They that wait upon the LORD shall renew their strength; they shall mount up with wings as eagles; they shall run, and not be weary; and they shall walk, and not faint" (Isa. 40:31).

We need not become discouraged, for our inner person is filled with His strength. "That is why we never give up. Though our bodies are dying, our inner strength in the Lord is growing every day" (LB). God provides sufficient strength for our daily requirements. "As thy days, so shall thy strength be" (Deut. 33:25).

As our body begins to weaken, we may think there is nothing more we can do for the Lord. But He can use us. He keeps our inner person strong for His service. There are things we can do which do not take a lot of physical energy. A Christian woman in her eighties had a wonderful telephone ministry, reaching hundreds of people for Jesus Christ over the phone. Another woman found her ministry in the newspaper, sending Christian tracts to the families of the bereaved listed in the obituary section and to parents of newborn babies.

Inner renewal and growth comes through prayer and meditation, allowing the Word of God to affect every phase of your life. Paul prayed that his fellow Christians would "be strengthened with might by his Spirit in the inner man" (Eph. 3:16).

What does it matter if we are weakening physically if we are being renewed spiritually every day?

NOVEMBER 16

For our light affliction; which is but for a moment, worketh for us a
far more exceeding and eternal weight of glory (2 Cor. 4:17).

ow often we say, "Everything is working against me!" It often
seems that trials come one right after another. Paul spoke of our
afflictions as being light, but we say, "Paul, you can't mean it. If
you only knew what I am going through, you wouldn't call my
affliction light." But most of our troubles could not compare with his. At times,
Paul was so crushed with the weight of his troubles that he despaired of his life.

Yet he could call his afflictions light for the moment because he was
looking at the ultimate goal and comparing his trials with the future glory
resulting from them. He wrote, "The sufferings of this present time are not
worthy to be compared with the glory which shall be revealed in us"(Rom.
8:18). Glory lies ahead. An eternal weight of glory beyond comprehension is
waiting for us. What are afflictions here compared with the glory of eternity?

Our present sufferings prepare us for something far beyond description.
Our trials are working for us, not against us. Every heartache, every pain, every
sorrow, and every hardship is building for us an exceeding weight of glory.

Because the difference in tone of a violin depends even more on the
quality of wood than on how it is made, a well-known violinist made his own
instruments. He wanted to select the wood himself. Instead of going to the
forest, he went to the top of the mountain. There, on a cliff exposed to the
storms, he obtained the trees from which he made his violins. He knew the
storms toughened the wood and produced a quality of grain and resiliency that
could be developed in no other way. In fact, he used only the wood from the
side of the tree facing the wind.

Our heavenly Father allows afflictions as part of our preparation for
eternity. The secret of enduring them is the direction in which we look. The
writer of Hebrews wrote that Moses "endured, as seeing him who is invisible"
(Heb. 11:27). We, too, can endure as we look away from our trials and keep
our eyes fastened on Jesus.

NOVEMBER 17

Giving thanks always for all things unto God and the Father in the name of our Lord Jesus Christ (Eph. 5:20).

ost of us do not wait for a national Thanksgiving Day to voice our thanks to God for His daily provisions for us. Day by day, we thank Him for His bountiful care.

But Paul reminds us that we are to give thanks *always,* no matter how difficult our circumstances may be. He had learned the reality of continual thanksgiving from personal experience. Although he was beaten, put in prison, and persecuted, he thanked God. He was even able to sing God's praises at midnight in jail.

Giving thanks does not depend on our circumstances or environment. Regardless of where we are, we can thank God, not just for the easy things in life, but also for the difficult ones; not just for the pleasant days, but for the dark ones as well. When our trust is in God, we can thank Him during the storms. And someday in heaven, when God reveals the purpose of our heartaches, we will know that He allowed them for our good and His glory.

The psalmist wrote, "I will bless the LORD at all times; his praise shall continually be in my mouth" (Ps. 34:1). True thanksgiving centers our mind and heart on God. It lifts us above the gift to the Giver. We express our thanks to God for Himself, not for things.

One day, a man watched his friend draw some black dots on a sheet of paper. The friend followed no recognizable pattern, and the man watching could make nothing out of the design. As the friend drew in a few lines, put in a musical cleft and added some rests, the man looking on recognized the black dots as musical notes and began humming the tune he soon recognized as "Praise God from Whom All Blessings Flow."

Sometimes we see many black dots in our lives. We cannot understand why they are there. We see no purpose for them. If we allow God to draw the black dots where He will, put in His lines of separation, and place His rests at the right places, He can produce a beautiful melody in our lives that will bring praise to His Name.

"Oh, give thanks to the Lord, for he is good; his lovingkindness continues forever" (Ps. 136:1 LB).

NOVEMBER 18

Because thou hast been my help, therefore in the shadow of thy wings will I rejoice. My soul followeth hard after thee: thy right hand upholdeth me (Ps. 63:7—8).

David was searching for God, desiring a deeper relationship with Him. He said, "O God, Thou art my God; I shall seek Thee earnestly" (v. 1 NASB).

In his search he discovered the surety of God's presence. "Thou hast been my help." God had often undertaken for him in the past. David remembered the occasions when God had helped him kill a bear, a lion, and the giant Goliath. We have the same assurance of God's presence to help us. "For God has said, 'I will never, never fail you nor forsake you.' That is why we can say without any doubt or fear, 'The Lord is my Helper and I am not afraid of anything that mere man can do to me'" (Heb. 13:5—6 LB).

David experienced God's protection. In the shadow of God's wings he was safe from all danger. "He who dwells in the secret place of the Most High shall remain stable and fixed under the shadow of the Almighty [Whose power no foe can withstand]" (Ps. 91:1 AMPLIFIED). What comfort you and I can experience hidden in the shadow of the wings of a loving God! Are you hidden safely in His shadow?

David rejoiced in that safety. One of the great lessons we learn from him is his constant praise of the Lord. He knew the secret of rejoicing in the Lord— not in the circumstances.

David found security close to God. "My whole being follows hard after You and clings closely to You" (AMPLIFIED). David learned not to take detours.

David also experienced the strength of God's power. "I follow close behind you, protected by your strong right arm" (LB). David knew what it meant to have God's strength upholding him in time of need. We can't take detours if we let *Him* hold our hand.

"[There is nothing to fear] for I am with you; do not look around you in terror and be dismayed, for I am your God. I will strengthen and harden you [to difficulties] . . . yes, I will hold you up and retain you with My victorious right hand" (Isa. 41:10 AMPLIFIED).

Have you found a deeper walk in the security, joy, and strength of the Lord?

NOVEMBER 19

Enter into his gates with thanksgiving and into his courts with praise;
be thankful unto him, and bless his name (Ps. 100:4).

 salm 100 is filled with the excitement of praise and thanksgiving to God. Praise is our attitude toward God because of who and what He is. Thanksgiving is our expression of gratitude to God for what He does for us. Recognizing that God is the Giver of every good gift and all that we have comes from Him, our hearts burst forth with thankful praise.

Both Canada and the United States set aside a special day each year as a time of expressing thanks to God for our many blessings. Canada celebrates Thanksgiving in October and the United States in November. But we don't have to wait until Thanksgiving Day to praise and thank God for all He is and all He has done for us.

As members of His family, we always have access to Him. His gates are ever open to us. As we come before Him and look into His face, our hearts are filled with adoration and love. We simply need to set aside time to be alone with Him.

"Enter into his gates with thanksgiving." How do you and I usually come into His presence? Do we come with a singing heart? Do we pause to bring the worship and praise of our hearts to Him? As we enter His gates, we are to "be thankful," and to "bless his name." He alone is worthy to be praised.

Take time to thank Him for the blessings He has given you this year. Why not make up a "thank-you" list of things you are thankful for, especially things you may not have remembered to thank Him for recently? Sometimes, we forget to thank Him for the lessons we are learning through our difficulties. As we praise Him and thank Him at all times and in everything, the minor notes of trouble in our lives modulate to major chords of triumphant victory.

"Every day will I bless thee; and I will praise thy name for ever and ever" (Ps. 145:2).

NOVEMBER 20

Oh, how love I thy law! It is my meditation all the day
(Ps. 119:97).

 n the Middle Ages there were few copies of the Bible. Sometimes a peasant would pay the price of a wagonload of hay for the privilege of reading for fifteen minutes from a Bible chained to a pulpit. Is God's Word that important to us, or is it so accessible that we take it for granted?

The Bible is the inspired Word of God. Paul wrote, "All Scripture is given by inspiration of God" (2 Tim. 3:16). God's written Word reveals Jesus Christ, the Living Word. "These are recorded so that you will believe that he is the Messiah, the Son of God, and that believing in him you will have life" (John 20:31 LB).

Before reading God's Word, pray, "Open thou mine eyes, that I may behold wondrous things out of thy law" (Ps. 119:18). The Holy Spirit will help us to understand the Scripture, giving us fresh insights into even the more familiar passages.

Once, a reporter asked Pablo Casals, one of the world's greatest cellists, how he spent his day. Casals said that first he took a walk, then he played the piano, and then he practiced the cello. After practicing more than a hour, he was ready to play the Bach suites. Each day, he played one of them. The reporter asked, "Do you not feel you know them well enough?" Casals replied, "I will never fully know them. Each time I play them, I discover something new."

So it is with the Word of God. Each time we read it, the Holy Spirit reveals something we have never seen before. One time, God gave me a new thought from a verse in Genesis. I reveled in it all week. On Sunday, I listened to a well-known evangelist on television, who said, "God gave me a new thought this week from His Word." It was the very same thought God had given me!

We need three attitudes as we approach the Bible: a humble spirit, an open mind, and an obedient life. The most difficult translation of the Bible is the one that must be translated into Christ-like living. May we act upon what we read in His Word today.

"I have inclined mine heart to perform thy statutes alway, even unto the end" (Ps. 119:112).

NOVEMBER 21

Bless the LORD, O my soul: and all that is within me, bless his holy name. Bless the LORD, O my soul, and forget not all his benefits (Ps. 103:1–2).

he beginning of this psalm immediately carries us into a spirit of praise. "Bless—affectionately, gratefully praise—the Lord, O my soul, and all that is [deepest] within me, bless His holy name!" (v. 1 AMPLIFIED). To bless means to glorify, to praise, to make holy. We are to bless the Lord and bless His holy name. His name represents His character, who He is. How often we come to God asking Him to bless us. But in this psalm, David reminds us to bless God—the object of our praise.

God was real to David and David's praise to God was personal. "Bless the LORD, O my soul." Sometimes we become so occupied *for* Him that we neglect being occupied *with* Him.

David blessed God, not just with his lips, but with His whole being—his entire personality: "all that is [deepest] within me." His praise was like a deep well springing up from the very depths of his being.

Once, as a speaker for a conference on the West Coast, I walked along the beach while the women were in discussion groups. As I walked in the rain along the deserted beach, I sang at the top of my voice, praising God with all that was within me.

God is the object of our praise, but His blessings are the subject: "Forget not [one of] all His benefits" (v. 2 AMPLIFIED). How easily we take for granted our daily blessings. As we begin to meditate on God Himself—who He is—suddenly we remember all He has done for us, and our hearts well up with thanksgiving.

The psalm closes with a great crescendo of praise. I can picture a large choir singing this magnificent hymn of worship accompanied by a majestic pipe organ. As the organ swells, the choir lifts their voices in adoration. "Bless the Lord ye his angels" (v. 20), "all ye his hosts" (v. 21), "all his works" (v. 22). The psalm climaxes as the organist pulls out all the stops and the choir sings with all that is within them, "Bless the LORD, O my soul."

Have you joined this imaginary choir? If not, join them now as you, too, bless the Lord with all that is within you.

NOVEMBER 22

The Lord is faithful and He will strengthen [you] and set you on a firm foundation and guard you from the evil [one] (2 Thess. 3:3 AMPLIFIED).

n the fall of the year when crops are being harvested, we set aside a special day of Thanksgiving to God for His faithfulness in providing for His creation. But let us not get so caught up in the celebration that we forget our faithful God who has given us all that we have. Over and over the Bible reminds us of His faithfulness to His children. We can find great strength and encouragement in remembering His faithfulness.

There are few people today whom we can depend upon, knowing that no matter what happens they will be faithful. Yet through all generations, God has been faithful. He could not be otherwise, for faithfulness is part of His character. Even our unbelief does not affect His faithfulness. "If we believe not, yet he abideth faithful: he cannot deny himself" (2 Tim. 2:13).

Friends may fail us, family may forsake us, but the Lord is faithful. Success may come, but we cannot depend on it. Reverses may come, but they cannot defeat us.

God is reliable and trustworthy because He is the Lord. We can depend on Him. He is our firm, unshakable, changeless Rock of Ages, who holds us steady through all of life's circumstances. We can expect attacks from the enemy, but our powerful foe is a defeated one. God will guard us from each attack, faithfully bringing us through to victory. "He will strengthen [you] and set you on a firm foundation."

Our faithful God is faithful to His promises. We can trust Him to do *all* that He says He will do. God has made many promises to us, but we must claim them for our needs. Yet our confidence must not be just in the promises but in our faithful Promiser.

Some days when everything is going wrong, we may doubt that God cares about us or even knows we exist. But He knows where we are and what we need. He *is* faithful.

Let us say with the psalmist, "I will sing of the mercies of the LORD for ever: with my mouth will I make known thy faithfulness to all generations" (Ps. 89:1).

NOVEMBER 23

Be careful for nothing; but in every thing by prayer and supplication with thanksgiving let your requests be made known unto God. And the peace of God, which passeth all understanding, shall keep your hearts and minds through Christ Jesus (Phil. 4:6—7).

t is easy to say, "Don't worry," but not so easy to put it into practice. When we worry, we indicate that we think our problem is too big for God to handle.

The Bible says, "Don't worry about anything" (LB). Not even one thing. This does not mean that we will not have anxieties. We will. Some things are easier to worry about than others. The important thing is what we do about our worries. We can say, "Don't worry," but that is not the solution. Worry is unnecessary, for there is a sure remedy.

What is the antidote to worry? Prayer. Rather than worrying about everything, we are to pray about everything. Peter reminds us to cast "the whole of your care—all your anxieties, all your worries, all your concerns, once and for all—on Him; for He cares for you affectionately, and cares about you watchfully" (1 Peter 5:7 AMPLIFIED).

Someone has said that there are two kinds of care mentioned in that verse. One is anxious care, the other, Almighty care. We are to roll our anxious care on Him and trust His Almighty care.

Prayer should be accompanied with thanksgiving. God's Word emphasizes the importance of "giving thanks always for all things unto God and the Father in the name of our Lord Jesus Christ" (Eph. 5:20). Do we stop and thank Him when we are going through trials? Do we thank Him for the lessons He is teaching us through them? Thanking Him for past answered prayer increases our faith to pray for present needs.

When we turn our worries into prayers, God promises peace—not peace from all our circumstances, but peace in the midst of them. "If you do this you will experience God's peace, which is far more wonderful than the human mind can understand. His peace will keep your thoughts and your hearts quiet and at rest as you trust in Christ Jesus" (Phil. 4:7 LB).

Someone has said that the peace of God is "His own calm, restful heart possessing ours and filling it with His quietness."

"Thou wilt keep him in perfect peace, whose mind is stayed on thee; because he trusteth in thee" (Isa. 26:3).

NOVEMBER 24

*Being confident of this very thing, that he which hath begun a good
work in you will perform it until the day of Jesus Christ'' (Phil. 1:6).*

od is at work in your life. Isn't it awesome to think that God is
willing to work in each one of our lives individually? God has a
completed blueprint for each of us, and only He knows what the
finished pattern will be. He doesn't reveal the complete plan to
us but leads us step by step in its development.

We are His workmanship. "It is God himself who has made us what we
are and given us new lives from Christ Jesus; and long ages ago he planned that
we should spend these lives in helping others" (Eph. 2:10 LB). It is God's
work—*He* began the good work in us.

God is willing to involve Himself in the transformation of our lives so that
we can live with Him throughout eternity. The change does not come through
our education, our ability, or our social status but through Jesus Christ. He
knows our potential and makes us over in the image of Christ. His responsibility
is to bring His plan to completion. Our part is to cooperate and follow His
directions. This takes the pressure off us. We can quit struggling. He will
accomplish His purpose.

He will *perform* it until the day of Jesus Christ—the day when He
returns. This can be translated, "He will evermore put His finishing touches to
it." In dressmaking, the finishing touches give the dress its creative beauty and
set it apart as a special creation.

God is careful to add the finishing touches needed to make us the
complete persons He wants us to be. He knows our lives need brightness and
color, so He brings joyful, pleasant experiences as finishing touches. But, usually
a dark touch brings out the beauty of the lighter colors, so He allows trials to
come into our lives. There will be times when we won't understand or know
why. There will be times when the tears will fall. But God takes a little away
here and adds a little there to complete His workmanship of making us more like
Christ, and then He will present us to His Father.

"God who began the good work within you will keep right on helping
you grow in his grace until his task within you is finally finished on that day
when Jesus Christ returns" (LB).

Let us come before his presence with thanksgiving, and make a joy-
ful noise unto him with psalms (Ps. 95:2).

e are invited to come into the presence of God, our heavenly
Father, but there is a qualification for entrance—thanksgiving. I
recognize this as an area of my life in which I am most negligent.
The psalmist tells us why we should give thanks to God.
One reason is that God is the Supreme One, the Sovereign over all the universe.
"The LORD is the great God, the great King above all gods" (v. 3 NIV). Today,
many people have made such things as materialism, education, and pleasures
their gods. But there is only one Almighty God. When we fail to recognize who
He really is, we limit Him. The psalmist was grateful that he knew the God who
controls the universe.

He writes, "In his hand are the depths of the earth, and the mountain
peaks belong to him. The sea is his, for he made it, and his hands formed the
dry land" (vv. 4–5 NIV).

Isaiah beautifully describes our awesome God: "To whom, then, will you
compare God? . . . He sits enthroned above the circle of the earth, and its
people are like grasshoppers. He stretches out the heavens like a canopy, and
spreads them out like a tent to live in . . . 'To whom will you compare me? Or
who is my equal?' says the Holy One. Lift your eyes and look to the heavens:
Who created all these? He who brings out the starry host one by one, and calls
them each by name. Because of his great power and mighty strength, not one of
them is missing. . . . Do you not know? Have you not heard? The LORD is the
everlasting God, the Creator of the ends of the earth" (Isa. 40:18, 22, 25–
26, 28 NIV).

Another reason for giving thanks is that God is a God who cares. "We
are the people of his pasture, the flock under his care" (v. 7 NIV). If He can
control the world, surely He can control our lives.

May we join the psalmist in giving thanks. "Come, let us bow down in
worship, let us kneel before the LORD our Maker; for he is our God (vv. 6–7
NIV).

Praise ye the LORD. O give thanks unto the LORD; for he is good: for his mercy endureth for ever (Ps. 106:1).

his psalm begins on a note of praise and thanks. Praise ye the Lord! O give thanks! The psalmist continues his praise. It is a personal exhortation to praise. Praise *ye!* David said, "Great is the LORD, and greatly to be praised; and his greatness is unsearchable" (Ps. 145:3).

How can we ever adequately praise the Lord? "Who can put into words and tell the mighty deeds of the Lord? Or who can show forth all the praise [that is due Him]?" (v. 2 AMPLIFIED). Have you ever said, "I am speechless!" or "It is beyond words"? This is the thought the psalmist is conveying. Our gratitude is so great, words fail to express it.

The Lord Jesus Christ Himself set the example of giving thanks to God. When He fed the five thousand, "Jesus took the loaves; and when he had **given thanks,** he distributed to the disciples, and the disciples to them that were set down; and likewise of the fishes as much as they would" (John 6:11).

One day, an elderly lady came to see President Lincoln. As she was ushered into his presence, he asked, "What can I do for you, madam?" "Mr. President," she said, "I have not come to ask a favor. I heard you are fond of cookies. I just want to give these to you in appreciation."

Tears trickled down his cheeks. For moments, he couldn't say a word. Then he said, "Your thoughtfulness has moved me greatly. Since I have become President, many people have come into my office, asking favors of me, but you are the first one to bring me an expression of your thankfulness."

We can never find words to adequately express our love and thanks to God. At this Thanksgiving season, may we take time to pause in God's presence and offer our grateful praise to Him for His faithfulness in taking care of us day by day and providing for us need by need. "Praise the LORD, O my soul, and forget not all his benefits" (Ps. 103:2 NIV).

NOVEMBER 27

Trust in the LORD, and do good; so shalt thou dwell in the land, and verily thou shalt be fed (Ps. 37:3).

ow many times have we confided in someone, thinking we could trust them, only to have our confidence betrayed later? But there is Someone we can trust. David said, "Trust in the LORD." We can always rely on the Lord, for He never betrays our confidence. He never makes a mistake.

We can go to Him at any time, for He keeps twenty-four-hour-a-day office hours. "Trust in him at all times; ye people, pour out your heart before him: God is a refuge for us" (Ps. 62:8). We can bring any need, large or small, for He has a heart of concern. He loves us. He understands us as no one else does. His advice is never wrong, for He knows His plan for us clear to the end, and He knows what is necessary to fulfill that plan.

David said, "Trust (lean on, rely on and be confident) in the Lord" (AMPLIFIED). If we are to lean hard, the One we lean on must be strong enough to support us. He is. The Creator of the universe is our strong support. Trust! Lean on! Rely! Be confident! The Lord Himself can hold us steady through any and every difficulty.

To teach us to trust Him, sometimes the Lord tests us by putting us in a situation in which we are completely helpless; there is no human solution. In such places, we have to put our trust into practice. Are you in such a place today, a place where there is nothing you can do? Lean hard on God. You already trust Him with your mind. Now you must learn to trust Him with your problems. The more you trust Him, the less worry you will have.

We can say with Isaiah, "I will trust, and not be afraid; for the LORD Jehovah is my strength and my song; he also is become my salvation" (Isa. 12:2). But when fear does come, we can also say, "What time I am afraid, I will trust in thee" (Ps. 56:3). Through an act of our will, we lean on Him and let Him change our fear to trust. "O LORD my God, in thee do I put my trust" (Ps. 7:1).

NOVEMBER 28

Delight thyself also in the LORD; and he shall give thee the desires of thine heart (Ps. 37:4).

o you have everything you desire? How often we have translated the above verse, "If you delight yourself in the Lord, He will give you whatever *you desire.*" Our desires do not always come from delighting ourselves in the Lord. We claim the promise without fulfilling the condition.

Most people have a great desire for things. We have more things today but less real contentment. Jesus said, "Life consisteth not in the abundance of the things which [a person] possesseth" (Luke 12:15). There is nothing wrong in enjoying your possessions, but they do not bring contentment.

The desires of our heart that are in the Lord cannot be taken away. David says, "Take delight in the LORD, and he will give you the desires of your heart" (NRSV). The Lord becomes the heart's delight of the Christian.

The secret is to delight in Him—not in what He does for us or gives to us. We delight in Him because He is God. We desire to spend time with Him. We want to read His Word and talk with Him in prayer. This is how He reveals His desires to us. He pours into our heart the desires He wants us to have. Then His desires will become ours. Our desires will be fulfilled as His will is fulfilled in us.

If we are not delighting in the Lord, if we do not desire time alone with Him, we need to find out what is keeping us from experiencing the joy of the Lord. "If you return to the Almighty, you will be restored. . . . Surely then you will find delight in the Almighty and will lift up your face to God" (Job 22:23, 26 NIV).

The elementary school I attended occasionally brought in art exhibits to encourage art appreciation. One painting, *The Song of the Lark,* especially appealed to me. A young gleaner stands in the field with upturned face, her monotonous work forgotten as she listens to the song of the lark. This is what delighting in the Lord is like. We pause in the midst of our everyday tasks to lift our hearts in love and praise to our lovely Lord.

When we delight in Him, our desires will harmonize with His will.

NOVEMBER 29

Commit thy way unto the LORD; trust also in him; and he shall bring it to pass (Ps. 37:5).

 e can live free from continual worry. The secret is to give God His rightful place in our lives—the place of total commitment. To commit means to hand over to someone else or let go so another can take over.

In a deliberate act of the will, we take all our possessions and our life and drop them into God's hand. We turn our hands over to show that they are completely empty; we are holding nothing back. This is the initial act of commitment. But this is just the beginning. Each morning, we turn our day and ourselves over to Him, and then as each problem or need arises, we commit it to Him. There may be several commitments of this kind throughout the day.

God will take care of them for us. He has all the resources needed for all we have committed to Him. And He meets our needs in His perfect timing. In effect He says to us, "Just trust your need to me. I will work it out for you." Giving Him our needs as they arise and keeping our hands off them gives God an opportunity to work.

The Amplified translation reads, "Commit your way to the Lord—roll . . . [each care of] your load on Him." Sometimes our load is too heavy to lift, but we can roll it upon Him. Then it is out of our reach, committed to Him. Faith leaves all in His hands. Then He works.

A pilot, lost in the clouds and fog, was not experienced in instrument landing, so the control tower prepared to bring him in by radar. He began to follow his instructions when suddenly, he remembered a tall pole which was right in the flight path. Frantically, he told the controller about it. The command came back, "You obey the instructions; we will take care of the obstructions."

You may be in a fog with clouds of trouble settling down, and you can't see your way through. Perhaps you are looking at the obstruction in your way. God says, "Obey the instructions I give (commit and trust), and I will take care of the obstructions (I'll bring it to pass)."

Someone has said, "Relinquish, rest, and leave the results with Him."

NOVEMBER 30

Rest in the LORD, and wait patiently for him: fret not (Ps. 37:7).

n this psalm, David says, "Fret not." In Philippians Paul says, "Don't worry about anything" (4:6 LB). We have discovered several guidelines for handling worry and fretting: trusting God puts us in touch with His All-sufficiency; keeping our desires and delights in line with His will ensures receiving what we desire; and committing our way to Him guarantees the best plan for our lives, His plan.

Another principle is rest. "There still exists, therefore, a full and complete rest for the people of God" (Heb. 4:9 PHILLIPS). You may say, "You mean there is rest for me in my hectic schedule?" Yes, we are promised rest, and it is for us today.

God promises His rest regardless of our situations or circumstances. David said, "Rest in the LORD." Augustine said, "Thou hast formed us for Thyself, and our hearts are restless till they find rest in Thee." Rest is available, but we have to appropriate it in our lives. "Let us then be eager to know this rest for ourselves" (Heb. 4:11 PHILLIPS).

Resting in Him includes waiting patiently for Him. Often we get impatient and take things into our own hands. But in effect God says, "Be quiet. Trust me. I know your needs better than you do. Just wait and give Me a chance to work." God works out the immediate with the ultimate in view. He is working in the light of eternity.

"Rest in the Lord; wait patiently for him to act" (LB). To rest means to be still. As we become still, we release our perplexities, doubts, and impatience. Then we wait for Him to answer. Each day we accept from Him the day He has planned for us. We can say with David, "My times are in your hands" (Ps. 31:15 NIV).

Rest in the midst of activity is the result of taking time to rest in His presence. "They that wait upon the LORD shall renew their strength; they shall mount up with wings as eagles; they shall run, and not be weary; and they shall walk, and not faint" (Isa. 40:31).

We can relax in the Lord when He is in control.

DECEMBER 1

For unto us a child is born, unto us a son is given: and the government shall be upon his shoulder: and his name shall be called Wonderful, Counsellor, The mighty God, The everlasting Father, The Prince of Peace (Isa. 9:6).

veryone is thinking about Christmas, but not everyone is thinking about the Christ of Christmas. In all our activity we can easily overlook the real joy and peace of Christmas. A common saying these days, "Jesus is the reason for the season" focuses our attention on the true meaning of Christmas.

Years before the Lord Jesus left heaven's glory to reside on earth, Isaiah prophesied Christ's advent: "A child is born." And one day a very special child *was* born. God, in the person of His Son, Jesus Christ, entered the world in human flesh. "The word was made flesh and dwelt among us" (John 1:14). The Word was a personality, the Son of God, Jesus, God manifest in the flesh—God taking on humanity.

But more than a Babe in Bethlehem, He was a Son given. "God so loved the world, that he *gave* his only begotten Son, that whosoever believeth in him should not perish but have everlasting life" (John 3:16, emphasis mine). God became man yet remained God.

Guido Reni painted his famous fresco, *The Aurora*, on the ceiling of a palace in Rome. Because the ceiling was so high, the fresco was difficult to view. After looking up for a while, viewers became dizzy and the figures became hazy. A mirror was placed near the floor so that visitors could sit down and view the reflection of this great work.

Jesus Christ is the Mirror of Deity. "He is the exact likeness of the unseen God—the visible representation of the invisible" (Col. 1:15 AMPLIFIED). Jesus came to make God visible to us.

Isaiah also said, "The government shall be upon his shoulder." At a time when evil and corruption run rampant in the world, we take courage knowing that one day Jesus will reign as King of Kings and Lord of Lords. We look forward to His return when He will bring a Kingdom of justice, righteousness, and peace.

But we need not wait for Him to reign in our hearts. We can turn the government of our lives over to Him now. Then all His titles expressed in today's verse can be real in our daily experience. Today He can be our wonderful Counselor, mighty God, everlasting Father, and Prince of Peace.

DECEMBER 2

Unto us a child is born . . . and his name shall be called Wonderful,
Counsellor (Isa. 9:6).

saiah ascribed several titles to the God-man, Jesus Christ. The first is wonderful Counselor. How often we face problems beyond our ability to solve. Jeremiah said, "I know, O LORD, that a man's life is not his own; it is not for man to direct his steps (Jer. 10:23 NIV). We need a Counselor to give wisdom, guidance, and encouragement.

Where do you go for advice? Often we turn to people, yet who is better qualified than the Lord? He is the perfect Counselor, for He is ommiscient. He knows everything. "Thou . . . knowest the hearts of all the children of men" (1 Kings 8:39). He knows our thoughts, our temperament, our motives. "Who can advise the Spirit of the Lord . . . or give him counsel? Has he ever needed anyone's advice? Did he need instruction as to what is right and best? No, for all the peoples of the world are nothing in comparison with him" (Isa. 40:13–15 LB).

He can make sense of a confused life. "All this also comes from the LORD Almighty, wonderful in counsel and magnificent in wisdom" (Isa. 28:29 NIV). He is never confused. He never makes a mistake. "In him lie hidden all the mighty, untapped treasures of wisdom and knowledge (Col. 2:3 LB).

He is a *wonderful* Counselor. The word *wonderful* conveys the meaning of supernatural. Because He knows the future, He gives His counsel in light of what He knows will happen.

He is a also Counselor who understands. "We do not have a high priest who is unable to sympathize with our weaknesses, but we have one who has been tempted in every way, just as we are—yet was without sin" (Heb. 4:15 NIV). Our wonderful Counselor always uses the Word of God. "Order my steps in thy word" (Ps. 119:133).

His counsel is always available, but we must ask for it. "If any of you lack wisdom, let him ask of God, that giveth to all men liberally . . . and it shall be given him" (James 1:5).

We would be foolish not to rely on the wisdom of our loving, omniscient God. What a Counselor!

DECEMBER 3

For unto us a child is born . . . the mighty God (Isa. 9:6).

hen the angels proclaimed the message of Jesus' birth on the hillside near Bethlehem, it was Isaiah's message proclaimed centuries before. Jesus came as a baby in Bethlehem, but He was God manifest in the flesh. "In the beginning was the Word, and the Word was with God, and the Word was God . . . and the Word was made flesh, and dwelt among us" (John 1:1, 14).

Isaiah called Jesus the mighty God. Jesus is all-powerful. He said, "All power is given unto me in heaven and in earth" (Matt. 28:20). He demonstrated His mighty power in creation. "All things were made by him; and without him was not any thing made that was made" (John 1:3). "He is before all things, and in him all things hold together" (Col. 1:17 NIV).

Jesus manifested His power throughout His earthly ministry. At His word, the winds and waves quieted, Lazarus came forth from the tomb, the lame stood up and walked, the blind began to see. Jesus—the mighty God on earth— performed many miracles by His power.

When we receive Christ into our lives, we have His great power within us. "I pray that you will begin to understand how incredibly great his power is to help those who believe him. It is that same mighty power that raised Christ from the dead" (Eph. 1:19–20 LB).

That incredible power is available for us today, empowering us to meet our struggles, "being strengthened with all power according to his glorious might so that you may have great endurance and patience" (Col. 1:11 NIV).

This power is great enough to meet any situation. One day, while my husband was working underneath our car, the car suddenly slipped off the jack, pinning him underneath. Petrified, I called out to the Lord, not knowing what to do. Automatically, I tried to lift the car, and as I did, it raised enough for him to get out. You know that I could never have lifted it in my own strength. The power of our omnipotent God took over.

Whatever your need is today, His power is available to you. Paul speaks of Christ, who "is able to do exceeding abundantly above all that we ask or think, according to the power that worketh in us" (Eph. 3:20).

DECEMBER 4

Unto us a child is born . . . the everlasting Father (Isa. 9:6).

eople are looking for security and stability today. They want something or someone they can depend on.

Isaiah described Jesus as *everlasting* Father. Jesus is everlasting, eternal. He had no beginning and will have no ending. He is equal with the Father, and He said, "I and my Father are one" (John 10:30). He is God and will always be God. He is the everlasting Father, the Father of eternity.

Humans have a beginning but will have no ending. We will live on forever, becoming a part of eternity. We will spend eternity somewhere—either with God or apart from Him. Jesus came to earth to represent God as the everlasting Father. Just as a father gives life to his child, so Jesus is the Source of everlasting life to His children. He said, "I am . . . the life" (John 14:6). John wrote, "He that hath the Son hath life; and he that hath not the Son of God hath not life" (1 John 5:12). Our spiritual birth gives us the privilege of living with Him throughout eternity.

He is our everlasting Father, for God has entrusted to Him the fatherly care of His children. We will never be without Someone to care for us. "He is like a father to us, tender and sympathetic to those who reverence him" (Ps. 103:13 LB). He says, "I have loved you with an everlasting love" (Jer. 31:3 NIV). As our everlasting Father, He provides everything we need. "My God shall supply all your need according to his riches in glory by Christ Jesus" (Phil. 4:19).

Our everlasting Father is always with us. "He hath said, I will never leave thee, nor forsake thee" (Heb. 13:5). He has promised to be our companion through life. "He said, My presence shall go with thee, and I will give thee rest" (Ex. 33:14).

Through our relationship with Jesus Christ, we have His everlasting love, provision, and presence. He is our everlasting Father today and throughout eternity. He is Someone we can depend on.

DECEMBER 5

Unto us a child is born . . . the Prince of Peace (Isa. 9:6).

oday there is much unrest in the world—in governments, in business, in homes, and in hearts—because people have rejected Jesus, the Prince of Peace.

There can be peace, for that is why Jesus came. "He is our peace" (Eph. 2:14). Christ alone gives peace, for He alone is peace. His death on the cross brought peace between God and man.

At His birth the angels sang, "Glory to God in the highest, and on earth peace, good will toward men" (Luke 2:14). Just before returning to heaven, He bequeathed peace to His disciples. "Peace I leave with you, my peace I give unto you" (John 14:27).

When we have the peace *of* God (Jesus Christ), we are at peace *with* God. "Since we have been justified through faith, we have peace with God through our Lord Jesus Christ" (Rom. 5:1 NIV).

Not only is He our peace, but He maintains peace in our hearts in times of stress. Peace can be real in our lives when our world is falling apart. His very presence becomes our constant peace regardless of our circumstances. "May the Lord of peace himself give you peace at all times and in every way" (2 Thess. 3:16 NIV). The Living Bible says, "May the Lord of peace himself give you his peace no matter what happens."

When we are looking around at all the strife in our world, not knowing what trouble will erupt next, our hearts can fill with fear. Jesus said, "The courage of many people will falter because of the fearful fate they see coming upon the earth, for the stability of the very heavens will be broken up" (Luke 21:26 LB). But we know Jesus, the Prince of Peace! What calmness, what comfort, what confidence is wrapped up in that name. We are looking up, waiting for His second coming, when He will set up His Kingdom of Peace. Jesus says, " 'Yes, I am coming soon!' Amen! Come, Lord Jesus!" (Rev. 22:20 LB).

Christ in us—peace now and peace to come.

DECEMBER 6

You also co-operate by your prayers for us—helping and laboring together with us" (2 Cor. 1:11 AMPLIFIED).

aul was often in deep trouble. He wrote, "We were under great pressure, far beyond our ability to endure, so that we despaired even of life" (v. 8 NIV). But God was in control. Paul knew his deliverance came not only because of his faith in God, but because of the prayers of his friends.

Paul recognized the importance of believers uniting in prayer for him. He said, "I beseech you, brethren, for the Lord Jesus Christ's sake, and for the love of the Spirit, that ye strive together with me in your prayers to God for me" (Rom. 15:30).

The Greek word translated *cooperate* in today's verse is translated *helping together* in the King James Version, and it is composed of the words *with, under,* and *work*. It is a picture of laborers under the burden, working together to accomplish something.

There is no substitute for prayer. Perhaps you have heard someone say, "All I can do is pray for you. I wish I could do more." Remember, prayer is the highest service we can render. The greatest people in the world today are those in contact with heaven through prayer. They don't necessarily have more time for prayer; they take the time. Someone has said, "People may spurn our appeals, reject our message, oppose our arguments, despise our person, but they are helpless against our prayers."

How little we know just what mighty things have happened as we have helped together by prayer—souls coming to know the reality of Christ, workers sent forth, physical needs met, financial help supplied, problems solved, and burdens lifted.

My own prayer life has been strengthened because I believe God has a purpose to accomplish in the lives of those for whom I pray. To have faith in prayer I must believe in the omnipotence of God. I believe that God is able to do the impossible. And He sees the completion of our prayers—beyond today to the end.

Today, are you praying *big* prayers, prayers that can change the lives of individuals, prayers that can change circumstances, prayers that can change the world? Are you expecting God to do great and mighty things?

"The earnest (heartfelt, continued) prayer of a righteous man makes tremendous power available—dynamic in its working" (James 5:16 AMPLIFIED).

DECEMBER 7

We may boldly say, The Lord is my helper, and I will not fear what man shall do unto me (Heb. 13:6).

his is our confidence—we can *boldly* say, "The Lord is my helper, and I will not fear." The word *helper* comes from the Greek words meaning to cry and to run. A helper is one ready to run at the cry of another. The Lord is a loving, concerned Helper, waiting to run to our assistance at our weakest cry to Him.

God has said, "I will never leave thee, nor forsake thee" (v. 5). This promise gives us the confidence to boldly say, "The Lord is my helper." He is waiting to help us when we cry to Him in our times of distress. The psalmist looked to the Lord for help, for he says, "I will lift up mine eyes to the hills, from whence cometh my help. My help cometh from the LORD, which made heaven and earth" (Ps. 121:1).

When we recall the many times He has helped us in the past—"Thus far the LORD has helped us" (1 Sam. 7:12 NASB)—we are encouraged to trust Him to be our Helper in the present. He *is* (present tense) our Helper. The psalmist said, "God is our refuge and strength [mighty and impenetrable to temptation], a very present and well-proved help in trouble" (Ps. 46:1 AMPLIFIED).

Asa, the king of Judah, turned to the Lord as his Helper when he was in a crisis. One day, the mighty Ethiopian army attacked Judah. King Asa called out, "LORD, it is nothing with thee to help, whether with many, or with them that have no power: help us, O LORD, our God; for we rest on thee, and in thy name we go against this multitude. O LORD, thou art our God; let not man prevail against thee" (2 Chron. 14:11).

As Asa faced such a large army, victory seemed impossible. But God was on his side. Asa could say, "The Lord is my Helper." And victory came. The Ethiopians were destroyed.

You can claim this promise for your needs today. You can say, "The Lord will not leave me, nor forsake me. He will be my Helper in my present situation. I need not fear."

Jesus said, "Lo, I am with you alway, even unto the end of the world" (Matt. 28:20).

DECEMBER 8

He staggered not at the promise of God through unbelief; but was strong in faith, giving glory to God; and being fully persuaded that, what he had promised, he was able also to perform (Rom. 4:20–21).

braham had a strong faith. The Bible gives the best definition of faith: "Faith is the substance of things hoped for, the evidence of things not seen" (Heb. 11:1). The Living Bible says, "What is faith? It is the confident assurance that something we want is going to happen. It is the certainty that what we hope for is waiting for us, even though we cannot see it up ahead."

Abraham illustrates the kind of faith God looks for. God had promised Abraham and Sarah that they would have a son even though it was a physical impossibility; they were both past child-bearing age. Humanly speaking, their case was hopeless.

But God had made a promise and Abraham took Him at His word. Abraham did not stagger at the seeming impossibility of the promise. He believed that what God promised, God would do. "He was completely sure that God was well able to do anything he promised" (Rom. 4:21 LB). Abraham's faith was not in his faith, his prayer, or even in the promises of God. His faith was strong because it was in God.

God is still looking for people who have that kind of faith—the faith that centers in the person of the Lord Jesus Christ. By faith we come into a right relationship with God: "For by grace are ye saved through faith; and that not of yourselves: it is the gift of God: not of works, lest any man should boast" (Eph. 2:8–9). And by faith we *continue* our right relationship with Him: "For we walk by faith, not by sight" (2 Cor. 5:7).

The strength or weakness of our faith is not as important as the object of our faith. With Jesus as the object, our faith is strong in Him. "Looking unto Jesus the author and finisher of our faith" (Heb. 12:2).

Our faith is in the One who died and rose from the dead for us. Paul summarized it for us when he wrote, "I have been crucified with Christ: and I myself no longer live, but Christ lives in me. And the real life I now have within this body is a result of my trusting in the Son of God, who loved me and gave himself for me" (Gal. 2:20 LB).

DECEMBER 9

They shall call his name Emmanuel, which being interpreted is, God with us (Matt. 1:23).

gain we are caught in the rush of the holiday season—working on Christmas programs in our churches, planning for Christmas vacations, writing notes on Christmas cards, wondering if we can squeeze in time to address them. We decorate our homes for the festive season and begin making fruit cakes. Soon the delicious smell of Christmas cookies and candies will permeate our kitchens. Not to be overlooked is our Christmas gift shopping. How lovingly we choose those presents to have just the right one for each person.

As Christmas approaches, our hearts are moved with the beautiful Christmas music—"O Holy Night," "O Little Town of Bethlehem," "Silent Night." Our minds turn then from the Christmas presents to the Christmas Presence—the wonderful One Whose presence came into the world as the tiny Babe of Bethlehem.

God promised the birth of the Messiah through the prophet Isaiah. "Behold, a virgin shall conceive, and bear a son, and shall call his name Immanuel" (Isa. 7:14). This is the Scripture the angel used when he told Joseph that Jesus was to be born of Mary. Immanuel (Emmanuel) means God with us.

God had a purpose in sending His Son to the earth. Jesus came that He might be God **with** us, that we might know what He is like. But this was not His ultimate purpose. "The Father sent the Son to be the Saviour of the world" (1 John 4:14). He became the Savior so that He might be God **in** us, "that Christ may dwell in your hearts by faith" (Eph. 3:17).

Jesus was God's present to the world (His gift of love). More wonderful than all the gaiety of the season, more joyful than the beautiful Christmas music, more thrilling than opening Christmas presents is the reality of **His presence** within, Emmanuel, "Christ in you, the hope of glory" (Col. 1:27).

In our Christmas busyness, may we not forget those in the world today who do not know the joy and peace of His presence. The greatest gift we can give to the Lord Jesus this year is to share the reality of His presence with others.

Emmanuel—God with you—in the person of Jesus Christ, is with you today and every day. Share the good news.

DECEMBER 10

Stand in awe, and sin not; commune with your own heart upon
your bed, and be still. Selah. (Ps. 4:4).

his verse outlines my daily plan to keep short accounts with
God. "Stand in awe." I begin my day in worship, filling my
vision with Him. I come before Him with awe-filled adoration,
but I am not afraid. I come simply as a child to a father. Yet I am
careful not to be casual.

Awe is often a missing dimension in our worship. Awe means reverence.
Standing in the presence of God, we quietly wait upon Him, considering His
greatness and hallowing His name. "O come, let us worship and bow down: let
us kneel before the LORD our maker" (Ps. 95:6). Sometimes we tend to be too
familiar, but if we realized the wonder of knowing God, we could never
approach Him in a casual way. Yet I approach Him simply as a child to her
heavenly Father.

"Sin not." Throughout the day I try to make sure that nothing hinders
my relationship with God. "Who shall ascend into the hill of the LORD? or who
shall stand in his holy place? He that hath clean hands, and a pure heart" (Ps.
24:3–4).

"Commune with your own soul and heart upon your bed and be still."
As I commune with Him at night, I check back through my day. What have I
done that has displeased Him and needs to be made right? Perhaps it is a sharp
word I have spoken. I may have exaggerated a statement. Maybe I responded in
pride to a compliment. God sees these things, too. I can't hide them from Him.

I have to confess my sins and be cleansed. "The blood of Jesus Christ . . .
cleanseth us from all sin" (1 John 1:7). Then I am free to meditate on the
Lord in "oneness" of fellowship with Him. There is a gospel hymn that begins,
"Nothing between my soul and the Saviour." When I experience that freedom,
I can thank Him for His answers to my needs and praise Him for His faithfulness
throughout the day.

So I begin and end my day worshiping and meditating on Jesus Christ my
Lord. The psalmist concludes with "Selah [pause and calmly think of that]!"
(Ps. 4:4 AMPLIFIED).

DECEMBER 11

And seekest thou great things for thyself? seek them not (Jer. 45:5).

t this time of year, I always go on a searching expedition. It takes me among crowds of people in many shopping malls. I know most of you go on this same kind of expedition. I am seeking for Christmas gifts for those for whom I want to express my love.

The Bible tells of Baruch who went on a seeking expedition of a different kind. Apparently, he was seeking great things for himself, not for the glory of God. God could see that his motive was wrong. Baruch had become victim of a consuming desire for great things.

Many people today are on searching expeditions to bring fulfillment into their lives. They are seeking great things for themselves—a new home in a more prestigious neighborhood, a top position in business, success in their career, achievement in the political, sports, or entertainment fields.

God says, "Seek them not." Why? The problem is not seeking great things but seeking them for self rather than for God's glory. True greatness comes through living for the glory of God, not through position, place, or people.

Even in Christian activities, some people seek great things for themselves. They may desire to be the president or chairman of a group for the honor and prestige it would bring. The Lord says, "Seekest thou great things for thyself? seek them not."

Another man in the Bible sought great things. Lot, Abraham's nephew, had accumulated so many cattle that there was not enough grazing land for both his and Abraham's herds. Abraham gave Lot first choice of the land. He could either go to the right or to the left. Lot looked at the well-watered plains of the Jordan Valley and selfishly chose the best—the greatest. For a time, life went well for him. He became one of the leading city fathers. But eventually he lost all he had. He had been seeking for himself, not for God.

What are you seeking for today? Things that will give you greater honor? Or are you seeking that which will honor and bring glory to God?

Someone has said, "God knows, He loves, He cares; nothing this thought shall dim. Only the best He gives to those who leave the choice with Him."

DECEMBER 12

Jesus immediately said to them: "Take courage! It is I. Don't be afraid (Matt. 14:27 NIV).

t was the close of a busy day. The crowds had gone. Jesus had told the disciples to cross over to the other side of the lake. At last He was alone. He stayed behind to pray. What do we do after a busy day? We usually think we need extra rest. But Jesus looked forward to time alone to talk with His heavenly Father.

Suddenly a storm came up on the Sea of Galilee. These storms could be very dangerous. "The boat was by now a long way from the shore at the mercy of the waves, for the wind was dead against them" (v. 24 PHILLIPS). Did they wonder why they were in such a severe storm? Sometimes when storms come, we may think we are out of God's will, but the disciples were in His will, for Jesus Himself had sent them across the lake. Someone has said, "God's will is the safety zone for God's child."

Are the storms dead set against you today? How do you react when the storms begin to blow in your life? Do you wonder if you have missed His directions? Are you questioning why He has allowed the storm?

Just in the time of need, Jesus appeared to His disciples. At three A.M., the darkest hour of the night, He entered into the storm and came to them in their desperation.

Imagine their fright when the disciples saw someone coming toward them on the water, for they did not recognize Him. Then He spoke to them. Their fear turned to joy as they recognized His voice saying to them, "It is I. Don't be afraid." What comfort! What relief! "It is I." His *presence* was with them. "Be not afraid." His *peace* filled their hearts.

Look for Christ in your storm. He appears to us in a special way in our darkest hour, in the time of our greatest need, when the storm is dead set against us. We may cry out, "Lord, save me," and suddenly He comes close to us, saying, "Take courage! It is I. Don't be afraid." Listen to His voice today.

It has been said, "Christ is no security against storms, but He is perfect security in storms."

DECEMBER 13

But when he saw the wind boisterous, he was afraid; and beginning to sink, he cried, saying, Lord, save me (Matt. 14:30).

esterday we read of the time Jesus came walking to His disciples in the midst of a storm. Then He spoke, and immediately they knew who He was.

Then Peter, in his own impulsive way, said, "Lord, if it's you . . . tell me to come to you on the water" (v. 28 NIV). Peter had said, "*If it is you,*" but Jesus didn't rebuke him for questioning. Instead, He said "Come." Peter got out of the boat and started to walk toward Jesus. Once Peter recognized the Lord, nothing—neither the wind or the sea—could stop him.

Peter didn't have *great* faith. He had even said, "*If it is you.*" But when Jesus said, "Come," Peter took Him at His word and started toward Him. Do we have faith enough to step out into the storm when Jesus says come?

But then Peter took his eyes off Jesus and looked at the storm. His *if* had returned. He began to sink. He cried out, "Lord, save me" (v. 30). Only three short words from a desperate heart. But he knew enough to cry for help. "And immediately Jesus stretched forth his hand, and caught him" (v. 31). Jesus is always near enough to catch us before we sink in the storm.

Then Jesus pinpointed Peter's problem. Peter had turned his eyes from Jesus back to the storm. "O thou of little faith," Jesus said, "wherefore didst thou doubt?" (v. 31). Together they climbed into the boat, and the storm quieted. Then the disciples worshiped Him, saying, "Truly you are the Son of God" (v. 32 NIV).

In our storms where do we focus our eyes—on the storm or on the Lord? If we concentrate on our problems, we may begin to sink. We must instead focus on the Presence of the One who has power to control them.

The psalmist wrote, "They cry unto the LORD in their trouble, and he bringeth them out of their distresses. He maketh the storm a calm, so that the waves thereof are still" (Ps. 107:28–29).

God's power is as great in the storm as in the calm.

DECEMBER 14

Thou therefore endure hardness, as a good soldier of Jesus Christ (2 Tim. 2:3).

hen I became a Christian I was thankful that at last I had moved into a life of ease. No more problems and frustrations. You may say, "Wait. My life isn't like that. My life isn't easy. I am in a constant battle." It didn't work for me, either. I do not have an easy life. The enemy of our souls is after me, too.

When we become Christians we become soldiers in the Lord's army. We have been chosen by the Lord, "who hath chosen [us] to be a soldier" (2 Tim. 2:4). There is a battle to be fought and an enemy to be defeated.

Now under new authority, we are enlisted as soldiers in the army of the heavenly Kingdom. We must relinquish all our rights. Our loyalty belongs to the Commander-in-Chief of our army, the Lord Jesus Christ. "Know ye not that . . . ye are not your own? For ye are bought with a price: therefore glorify God in your body, and in your spirit, which are God's" (1 Cor. 6:19–20).

We receive a uniform to wear, the armor of God to protect us in battle. "Take unto you the whole armour of God, that ye may be able to withstand in the evil day, and having done all, to stand" (Eph. 6:13). Our armor, our protection, is Jesus Christ.

Our rations are the Word of God. Jeremiah said, "Thy words were found, and I did eat them; and thy word was unto me the joy and rejoicing of mine heart" (15:16).

Each morning we report to our Commanding Officer, the Lord Jesus Christ, for our marching orders. We can't say, "I'm too busy," or "I have to play tennis," or "I'm going on a vacation." We are in His service to go where He sends and do what He commands. "As Christ's soldier do not let yourself become tied up in worldly affairs, for then you cannot satisfy the one who has enlisted you in his army" (v. 4 LB).

Sometimes the training is rigorous, but as we obey our Commander, we are strengthened for the testings to come. "Endure hardness, as a good soldier of Jesus Christ."

Don't go AWOL. Instead be a soldier committed to the service of God's Kingdom.

DECEMBER 15

I am debtor both to the Greeks, and to the Barbarians; both to the wise, and to the unwise. So, as much as in me is, I am ready to preach the gospel . . . for I am not ashamed of the gospel of Christ (Rom. 1:14–16).

aul outlines here three "I ams" of Christian responsibility. First, he said, "I am debtor." If someone had asked Paul, "Who is responsible for taking the Gospel to the lost?", Paul's reply would have been "I am." He felt responsible to the civilized and to the uncivilized, to the educated and to the uneducated. Indebted to God, he paid his debt by making several missionary journeys, sharing the Gospel wherever he went, even at the risk of his life. He felt the urgency of getting the Gospel out and was willing to pour out his life for someone else.

Second, Paul said, "I am ready." He didn't say, "I can't do it" or "I'm afraid to" but "I am ready." Paul was eager to share the Gospel. He said, "So, to the fullest extent of my ability, I am ready to come also to you" (LB). Are we?

Third, Paul said, "I am not ashamed of the gospel." To be a good salesperson you have to be sold on your product. Paul was sold on the Gospel. Would he have continued his ministry after beatings and stonings if he were not sold on it? But he knew the life-changing power of the Gospel and wanted others to experience it.

Each of us, as Christians, has a debt to pay, also—a life to invest, allowing God to use it any way He desires. Can we say as Paul did, "I am debtor," "I am ready," and "I am not ashamed"? Are we as concerned for the lost as he was?

One time Babe Ruth commented about an elderly minister of the gospel, "While I have written my name on thousands of baseballs, this man has written his name on just a few simple hearts. How I envy him. I am listed as a famous home-run batter, yet beside this obscure minister, I never got to first base."

When a new drug becomes available, it is sent around the world to alleviate sickness. Our world is sick, and we have the cure for sin—the Gospel of Jesus Christ. Do we care enough about others to say, "I am ready"?

DECEMBER 16

Bring my soul out of prison, that I may praise thy name
(Ps. 142:7).

The number of people serving time behind bars is startling. But have you ever considered the vast number of prisoners serving time behind invisible prison bars?

David said, "Bring my soul out of prison." The prisons of the soul can make any of us captives. What is your prison? anger? loneliness? selfishness? alcoholism? bitterness? self-centeredness?

Whatever your soul prison may be, you can be released from it. Isaiah prophesied that the Messiah would be "opening . . . the prison to them that are bound" (Isa. 61:1). But before we can be released, we have to be honest with God and admit our bondage. Then we must have a desire to be released.

Jesus is our Liberator. He said, "The Spirit of the Lord is upon me, because he hath anointed me to preach . . . deliverance to the captives" (Luke 4:18).

There was a time when I was in the prison of unbelief. Then I heard the Gospel, believed in Jesus Christ as my Savior, and invited Him into my life. Released from my prison of unbelief and sin, I felt as though the weight of the world had been lifted from my shoulders. But I based the reality of my release on God's Word, not feelings. "As many as received him, to them gave he power to become the sons of God, even to them that believe on his name" (John 1:12).

Some people hear the Gospel but procrastinate. They think they can receive Jesus Christ later at some more convenient time. Sadly, many wait until it is too late.

Does deliverance seem impossible for you? God's Word promises that you can be delivered. "Things which are impossible with men are possible with God" (Luke 18:27). This includes your prison. There is not one thing from which God cannot deliver you. Believe it because God says it.

Accept it by faith and act upon it. Put your belief into action. Trust in the Lord to do it. Victory is possible! Move forward in the resurrection power of your Great Liberator, Jesus Christ.

"[Christ] is able to do exceeding abundantly above all that we ask or think, according to the power that worketh in us" (Eph. 3:20).

DECEMBER 17

Ye know the grace of our Lord Jesus Christ, that, though he was
rich, yet for your sakes he became poor, that ye through his poverty
might be rich (2 Cor. 8:9).

 king wanted to know the conditions under which his people
lived so that he might better understand their problems. So he
removed his kingly robes and crown and put on the clothing of
his people, traveling incognito across his kingdom. Though he
laid aside his riches, assuming the poverty of the people, his position as king did
not change.

This is a picture of what the Lord Jesus did for us. With all the wealth of
the universe at His command, He left the throne of glory to give us access to all
His riches.

"By him were all things created, that are in heaven, and that are in earth,
visible and invisible . . . all things were created by him, and for him . . . and by
him all things consist" (Col. 1:16–17). Yet, He was willing to leave all to
come to earth with God's message of love for us. He was willing to renounce all
of His riches, becoming poor that we might become rich.

Can you imagine the day in heaven when the announcement was made
that Jesus was coming to earth to redeem us? As Jesus became the Babe of
Bethlehem, can you not see the angels appearing over the fields proclaiming the
message, "Glory to God in the highest, and on earth peace, good will toward
men" (Luke 2:14)?

But it cost Him. He gave His life on the cross because of His great
personal love for each of us. "Though he was God, [he] did not demand and
cling to his rights as God, but laid aside his mighty power and glory, taking the
disguise of a slave and becoming like men. And he humbled himself even
further, going so far as actually to die a criminal's death on a cross" (Phil.
2:6–8 LB).

He died for us! That is giving. That is love. This He did for our sakes, that
we might become rich in Him. "And if [his] children, then heirs; heirs of God,
and joint-heirs with Christ" (Rom. 8:17).

When we realize that He left the glories of heaven to bring us the greatest
gift ever given—the gift of eternal life—we can only drop to our knees and
worship Him. "Thank God for his Son—his Gift too wonderful for words"
(2 Cor. 9:15 LB).

DECEMBER 18

Jacob awaked out of his sleep, and he said, Surely the LORD is in this place (Gen. 28:16).

nowing that God is an omnipresent God is a great encouragement to us. There is no place where we go that He is not already there. That means that He is right where we are now, no matter what our circumstance.

One day this truth about God became real to Jacob. Because of a family disagreement, he had to leave his home. As night descended, he was all alone, but in a dream that night God spoke to him, assuring Jacob of His presence. Jacob's inner eyes were opened, and he was filled with awe in the presence of God. "Surely the LORD is in this place," he said, "and I knew it not." His whole life was open to God.

God is everywhere. He is with us wherever we go. He draws near to us in our lonely, dark night. Trouble may be near, but God is nearer. He promises, "I am with you."

Psalm 139 beautifully portrays the omnipresence of God. "O LORD, you have examined my heart and know everything about me. You know when I sit or stand. When far away you know my every thought. You chart the path ahead of me, and tell me where to stop and rest. Every moment, you know where I am" (v. 1–3 LB).

"I can never be lost to your Spirit! I can never get away from my God! If I go up to heaven, you are there; if I go down to the place of the dead, you are there. If I ride the morning winds to the farthest oceans, even there your hand will guide me, your strength will support me" (v. 7–10 LB).

"You were there while I was being formed in utter seclusion! You saw me before I was born and scheduled each day of my life before I began to breathe" (v. 15–16 LB). How wonderful to know our lives are in the hands of this great omnipresent God!

But perhaps you are facing this Christmas season alone. Perhaps family strife or the loss of a loved one has ended some of your usual happy Christmas traditions. Even in times like these God is with you. Live in the reality of His Presence moment by moment, and He will transform the ordinary to the extraordinary.

DECEMBER 19

These things have I spoken unto you, that my joy might remain in you, and that your joy might be full (John 15:11).

 f we observe people at such places as shopping malls or restaurants, we may notice that few faces express joy. Yet joy characterizes believers. The Christian life is a life full of radiant joy.

Jesus spoke these words about joy just a short time before His crucifixion. Earlier, he had told His disciples that He was leaving His peace for them. Now He promises that His joy will remain in them. He gives us His joy. An inner joy—His joy—becomes ours.

Jesus' joy was doing the will of His Father. "I delight to do thy will, O my God" (Ps. 40:8). His joy is ours as we, too, do the will of our heavenly Father.

When Jesus said, "These things have I spoken unto you," what things was He talking about? He was referring to the teaching He had given them earlier in this chapter. He had been talking to them about the relationship of the vine and the branches. He taught that the union of the vine and branches is a vital relationship resulting in the life of the vine flowing into the branches.

Then Jesus applied this truth to our relationship with Him. In this union, we receive His life, and as we abide in Him, we will have His joy—the joy Jesus intends us to have—a consistent joy.

The Holy Spirit actually produces His joy in our lives. Joy is a part of the fruit of the Spirit. "When the Holy Spirit controls our lives he will produce this kind of fruit in us: . . . joy" (Gal. 5:22 LB). His joy cannot be taken away from us. "Your heart shall rejoice, and your joy no man taketh from you" (John 16:22).

Jesus tells His disciples that their joy is to be full. Full means complete, lacking nothing. In effect Jesus is saying, "My joy is in you, and your joy is full to overflowing."

His joy is real. How can we help but overflow with joy when we have Him in our lives. Peter wrote of Him "whom having not seen, ye love; in whom, though now ye see him not, yet believing, ye rejoice with joy unspeakable and full of glory" (1 Peter 1:8).

Joy to the world, the Lord is come!

DECEMBER 20

Acquaint now thyself with him, and be at peace: thereby good shall come unto thee (Job 22:21).

college student working in a Philadelphia post office one Christmas came across a letter addressed in a childish scrawl to Jesus. There was no place to file it but in the compartment marked *Not known.* To many people today He is "not known." Many know about Him but lack a personal knowledge of Him.

During the time of Job's sufferings, three friends came to visit him. One of them, Eliphaz, gave him some advice. "Acquaint now thyself with him, and be at peace."

To acquaint means to know thoroughly or familiarize oneself with. Eliphaz's comment literally means, "Become a companion of God." "Acquaint now yourself with Him [agree with God and show yourself to be conformed to His will]" (AMPLIFIED).

In trying times, as we submit to His will, we experience a deeper knowledge of Christ, His love, and His care. This knowledge begins with reading God's Word and prayer. You won't become acquainted with your neighbor unless you spend time with her and talk to her. Neither will you get to know God until you spend time with Him in His Word and talk to Him in prayer.

In the furnace of suffering Job came to a deeper, more intimate acquaintance with God, which brought peace. "Acquaint now yourself with Him . . . and be at peace; by that [you shall prosper and great] good shall come to you" (AMPLIFIED).

A man once visited a factory where fine china was being made. The china, before the color was burned in, was not beautiful; a drab-looking blue and a dirty-red paint had been applied. There were even touches of black, and the design was smudged in spots. But then the china was put into the furnace for the colors to be burned in. When the china was removed, the design was clear, and a bright gold color shone against the the black, the blue, and the wonderful red known as Crown Derby.

Sometimes God permits us to be placed in the furnace of affliction so that the beautiful design of His image will be reproduced in our lives. In our sorrow we often receive a fresh, deep knowledge of Him.

If we are not at peace, we are not sufficiently acquainted with God. Let God be your companion and be at peace.

DECEMBER 21

We feel this warm love everywhere within us because God has given us the Holy Spirit to fill our hearts with his love (Rom. 5:5 LB).

hristmas is a special time of expressing our love to family and friends, but the most wonderful expression of love at Christmastime is the message of love God sent us: "God has poured out his love into our hearts by the Holy Spirit, whom he has given us" (NIV).

Have you ever wondered if anyone really loved you? God does and His love is real. "God is love" (1 John 4:8). His love is personal. He loves *you* and *me*. I never get over the wonder that He loves me. Paul reminds us of "the Son of God who loved me and gave himself for me" (Gal. 2:20).

Love can melt a hardened heart. A young couple with two small children managed a halfway house for prisoners. One occupant had been in prison since he was fifteen. One day, as he sat in the lounge, one of the children climbed into his lap and hugged him, and he began to cry. Having experienced such accepting love, that prisoner later received Christ as Savior.

We cannot begin to fathom the depths of His love, but we can experience it. "[You may really come] to know—practically, through experience for yourselves—the love of Christ, which far surpasses mere knowledge (without experience)" (Eph. 3:19 AMPLIFIED).

The love of Christ is our model for our daily walk. "Walk in love, as Christ also hath loved us, and hath given himself for us" (Eph. 5:2). Love between individuals sometimes is broken. But Jesus' love is a never-ending love: "having loved his own . . . he loved them unto the end" (John 13:1).

You are the object of His love today. You may say, "I don't deserve such love." He doesn't love us because we are good or worthy of His love. He loves us because of who He is, not who we are.

The missionary's young son, who attended school in the States, was asked what he wanted most for Christmas. Glancing at the framed picture of his father, he quietly said, "I want my father to step out of the frame." In Jesus Christ, God stepped out of heaven, coming to earth that we might experience His love personally. Is His love real to you today?

DECEMBER 22

Mary said, My soul doth magnify the Lord, and my spirit hath re-
joiced in God my Saviour (Luke 1:46–47).

he above verse comes from what has been called, "The
Magnificat" of Scripture. This was Mary's song of joyful praise
when she learned she was to be the mother of Jesus the long-
awaited Messiah. Someone has called it our most beautiful
Christmas carol.

On that day when the angel Gabriel appeared to Mary with the startling
news that she would bear God's Son, Mary was overwhelmed. "How shall this
be?" she asked (v. 34). Gabriel replied, "The Holy Ghost shall come upon
thee, and the power of the Highest shall overshadow thee: therefore also that
holy thing which shall be born of thee shall be called the Son of God"
(v. 35).

Mary quietly accepted her assignment. "Behold the handmaid of the
Lord; be it unto me according to thy word," she said (v. 38). How expressive
of her humility and trust in God. She didn't question. She accepted this role on
the authority of God's Word. Do we trust God in all the affairs of our life
enough to say, "Be it unto me according to thy word" even if we don't
understand?

Eager to share her news, she hurried to see Elizabeth, a relative, who was
also expecting a baby. When Mary told her, Elizabeth said, "Blessed is she that
believed: for there shall be a performance of those things which were told her
from the Lord" (v. 45).

Realizing the magnitude of God's favor on her life, Mary burst forth into a
song of praise and worship to God from her innermost being. Her heart
overflowed in love and adoration to God. "My soul magnifies the Lord, and my
spirit rejoices in God my Savior" (v. 47 NRSV). To magnify God means to
declare His greatness. As she yielded in sweet submission to His will for her life,
her great desire was to magnify Him.

What an example she is to us today. May we take time to ponder things
in our heart as she did, to meditate on who Jesus is and how He has changed
our lives.

Let your heart burst forth in songs of praise today. "O magnify the LORD
with me, and let us exalt his name together" (Ps. 34:3).

DECEMBER 23

Speaking to yourselves in psalms and hymns and spiritual songs,
singing and making melody in your heart to the Lord (Eph. 5:19).

hristmas is a special time of singing. What happiness and joy fill our hearts as we listen to the beautiful carols. One of my most vivid memories is the time I sang in an angel choir. I have sung in choirs before and since, but this one was special. We sang, "O Come All Ye Faithful" in Latin. My innermost being was stirred as we sang, "O come let us adore Him."

Throughout the Bible, God's people were a singing people. Some sang in times of victory. It isn't difficult to sing at those times. Moses and the children of Israel sang triumphantly after they came through the Red Sea. "I will sing unto the LORD, for he hath triumphed gloriously: the horse and his rider hath he thrown into the sea" (Ex. 15:1).

Some sang in times of trouble. This is more difficult. Yet Paul and Silas sang while in prison. "About midnight Paul and Silas were praying and singing hymns of praise to God, and the prisoners were listening to them" (Acts 16:25 NASB).

Job speaks of our God "who giveth songs in the night" (Job 35:10). How often in our night time experiences, God changes our songs of sorrow into songs of praise.

The song that comes from God is not a song of happiness from outward experiences, but a song of joy from our innermost being. "*He* hath put a new song in my mouth, even praise unto our God: many shall see it, and fear, and shall trust in the LORD" (Ps. 40:3).

The Holy Spirit puts a song in our hearts when there is no song there. He gives a singing heart at all times and in all experiences—even when our world has crashed about us, when the stormclouds lower over us, when there are obstacles in our path and there is no way through. Spirit-filled and Spirit-controlled Christians have something to sing about. Even the worst circumstances cannot take away their song.

As the Holy Spirit plays on our heartstrings, a beautiful melody ascends to the heart of God.

"I will praise you, my God and King, and bless your name each day and forever" (Ps. 145:1 LB).

DECEMBER 24

Thanks be unto God for his unspeakable gift (2 Cor. 9:15).

t 2:30 Christmas morning my niece and I finished wrapping the last gift. With sighs of joyous relief we placed the pile of wrapped gifts under the tree, anticipating the scene which would soon take place there. As we looked at the waiting packages, we could say, "Mission accomplished!" It was a mission of love. We had carefully selected our gifts as an expression of our love, gifts we thought would please.

God sent His Son on a mission of love, making possible the greatest Gift the world has ever known. Paul seemed at a loss for words to adequately describe God's Love Gift. All he could say, even with the Holy Spirit directing him, was that he could not begin to express what God's Gift meant to him. Nor can we. From the outpouring of his heart filled with thanksgiving, he said, "Thanks be to God for His Gift, [precious] beyond telling—His indescribable, inexpressible, free Gift!" (AMPLIFIED).

"The gift of God is eternal life through Jesus Christ our Lord" (Rom. 6:23). And that Gift cost a great deal. Written on His price tag was, "God so loved the world, that he gave his only begotten Son" (John 3:16). Through His death and resurrection, Jesus restored man's sin-broken relationship with God. He could return home to heaven with a shout of triumph—"Mission accomplished!"

Christ made His Gift of eternal life available, but each person has to receive it personally. "As many as received him, to them gave he power to become the sons of God, even to them that believe on his name" (John 1:12).

Since I never seem to be able to thank God adequately for His Gift to me, I have a special way of expressing my thanks and love to Him at Christmas. I do something special for someone else as my Christmas gift to Jesus: give a special gift to someone, take a lonely person out for a meal, or make Christmas possible for a family that might not have much otherwise. Doing this as an expression of love to the One who "loved me and gave himself for me" has brought me great joy.

In the midst of the busyness of our Christmas season, may we take time to thank God for His unspeakable Gift to us.

DECEMBER 25

And when they were to come into the house, they saw the young child with Mary his mother, and fell down, and worshipped him: and when they had opened their treasures, they presented unto him gifts; gold, and frankincense, and myrrh (Matt. 2:11).

come let us adore Him, Christ, the Lord." Sometimes we become so busy at this Christmas season, that we forget to take time to adore Him. We forget to give Him priority in our plans.

The wisemen, called Magi, gave worship priority. One night they saw a special star, which they believed announced the birth of a new king. They took gifts with them and set out on a journey in search of him.

Reaching the end of their journey, their hearts filled with wonder as they came into the presence of Jesus, the Son of God. They fell to their knees in adoration, and after presenting their gift of worship, they presented their gifts of gold, frankincense, and myrrh.

Have we taken time this Christmas season to spend time in the presence of the One whose birthday we celebrate? Have we paused in our Christmas-packed schedule to present our gift of worship to Him? Or have all of our Christmas activities crowded Him out?

How awesome it is to worship Him. "God's Son shines out with God's glory, and all that God's Son is and does marks him as God. He regulates the universe by the mighty power of His command. He is the one who died to cleanse us and clear our record of all sin, and then sat down in highest honor before the great God of heaven" (Heb. 1:3 LB).

When we worship Him, we are filled with the glory of the Lord Himself. Out of a heart filled with worship comes our desire to present to Him the gift of our lives. Paul speaks of the Macedonians, who "first gave their own selves to the Lord" (2 Cor. 8:5).

A young lady had an aunt who gave her very lovely and valuable gifts. One Christmas the niece received a small package from her aunt. When she opened it, she was surprised to find a key. Enclosed was a note which read, "Here is the key to my house. Use it as though it were your own."

Have you presented the Lord with the key to your life? If not, this Christmas would be a perfect time to say, "Here is the key. Use my life as You will, for it is Your own."

DECEMBER 26

*The gift of God is eternal life through Jesus Christ our Lord
(Rom. 6:23).*

fter I was married, my husband and I spent Christmas Eve each
year at my brother's home. It was always exciting for he had
three children, and children have a way of making Christmas
special.

They always had a beautifully decorated Christmas tree surrounded by
piles of gifts in colorful wrappings. All evening the children eagerly looked at the
name tags to see which packages were theirs. Mike would be excited as he
brought a package to show me, shaking it, feeling it, trying to open a corner to
peek in. I would ask, "How do you know it is yours?" He would reply, "Can't
you see? My name is on it." The packages were ours Christmas Eve—our
names were on the tags. Yet they were not really ours, for we put them back
under the tree.

Christmas morning the wrappings quickly came off, and the gifts became
our personal possessions. If Nancy received a dress, we had a style show around
the tree right then. One year Karen received roller skates. In a few minutes she
was skating all around the house.

One Christmas morning as I watched the gifts being opened, the tree in
the corner faded from my view, and I could imagine God's tree. I think of the
cross as God's tree. God is the greatest Giver the world has ever known. He "so
loved the world, that he gave his only begotten Son, that whosoever believeth
in him should not perish, but have everlasting life" (John 3:16).

I could imagine gift packages under God's tree, too—gift packages of
eternal life. "The gift of God is eternal life through Jesus Christ our Lord"
(Rom. 6:23). God's love for everyone was so great that he prepared a gift
package of eternal life for everyone that would ever live.

Lovingly, He wrapped a package for you with your name on it. Many
have unwrapped their gift packages and by faith received their wonderful gift of
eternal life. Perhaps you have never received this precious gift of love waiting for
you. If you haven't, your gift is waiting. Would you not like to open it today
and receive Christ into your life? If so, please turn to the devotion for May
15th. It outlines the way to receive this gift.

Do not leave your gift unopened!

DECEMBER 27

*Whom having not seen, ye love; in whom, though now ye see him
not, yet believing, ye rejoice with joy unspeakable and full of glory"
(1 Peter 1:8).*

he meaning of Christmas began in the very heart of God. It is His
message of love for the world. No love can begin to compare
with it. "To us, the greatest demonstration of God's love for us
has been his sending his only Son into the world to give us life
through him" (1 John 4:9 PHILLIPS).

God's love for us is a sacrificial love. "The proof of God's amazing love is
this: that it was while we were sinners that Christ died for us" (Rom. 5:8
PHILLIPS).

As we personally experience His love in our lives, our hearts respond.
"We know how much God loves us because we have felt his love and because
we believe him when he tells us that he loves us dearly. God is love, and
anyone who lives in love is living with God and God is living in him. And as
we live with Christ, our love grows more perfect and complete . . . so you see,
our love for him comes as a result of his loving us first" (1 John 4:16–17,
19 LB).

His love will control us. "The very spring of our actions is the love of
Christ" (2 Cor. 5:14 PHILLIPS). It is His love loving through us—even those
we may not want to love or those difficult to love.

Our love for Him is unusual, love for Someone we have never seen, so
we need to take time to be occupied with Him. We may be occupied with our
service, or even His Word and prayer, yet not Him. How wonderful to become
occupied with the *One* we love.

When one three-year-old girl asked her mother what Christmas was, her
mother explained that it was Jesus' birthday. She said we exchange gifts at
Christmas to show our love to others. Christmas Eve the little girl placed under
the tree a package—her birthday gift to Jesus. After she was asleep, the mother,
not wanting her daughter to be disappointed, opened the package but found it
empty.

Christmas morning, the little girl was delighted to find that the package had
been opened. "What was in it?" asked the mother. "It was a box full of my
love for Jesus," was the answer. Have you taken time to give Him your gift of
love?

DECEMBER 28

*Wherefore God also hath highly exalted him, and given him a name
which is above every name: that at the name of Jesus every knee
should bow, of things in heaven, and things in earth, and things under the earth; and that every tongue should confess that Jesus Christ
is Lord, to the glory of God the Father (Phil. 2:9–11).*

ften as I sit in airports, I hear people being paged. There is no
lengthy description of the person, just their name. The name
represents the person.

The name of Jesus represents who He is, too. It is a Name
above all names, a very special Name, a precious Name.

It is a **Name of salvation.** When God was about to send His Son to
earth, He sent the angel Gabriel to Joseph saying, "She shall bring forth a son,
and thou shalt call his name JESUS: for he shall save his people from their sins"
(Matt. 1:21).

It is a **Name of honor.** No title equals the name of the Lord Jesus.
"Thou art worthy, O Lord, to receive glory and honour and power" (Rev.
4:11). No other name can compare with it.

It is a **Name of power.** Jesus said, "All power is given unto me in
heaven and in earth" (Matt. 28:18). He assured His disciples of His power.
His authority upon earth and in heaven was beyond question. Need we doubt
His power to guide and control our lives?

It is an **exalted Name.** "God also hath highly exalted him, and given
him a name which is above every name" (Phil. 2:9). When God raised Him
from the dead, He exalted Him to a place at His right hand and gave Him an
unexcelled Name.

It is a **Name we use in prayer.** "Whatsoever ye shall ask in my
name, that will I do, that the Father may be glorified in the Son" (John
14:13). The name of Jesus gives us authority to approach God in prayer.

It is a **Name to worship.** "That at the name of Jesus every knee should
bow, of things in heaven, and things in earth, and things under the earth; and
that every tongue should confess that Jesus Christ is Lord, to the glory of God
the Father" (Phil. 2:10–11). When Jesus returns to earth, everyone is going
to have to kneel and confess Jesus as Lord. But we don't have to wait. May our
lives today show the reality of Jesus Christ as Lord.

DECEMBER 29

For to me to live is Christ (Phil. 1:21).

s the year comes to a close, it is a good time to consider what you have learned about Jesus Christ this year. Have you sought Him on the pages of His Word? Has He become more real to you?

After the apostle Paul met the Lord Jesus Christ on the road to Damascus, his life was never the same. His whole life was yielded to Christ. He stated his new purpose for living when he wrote, "For me, to live is Christ—His life is in me" (AMPLIFIED).

He didn't say the Christian life was impossible because he lived in a bad environment or his circumstances weren't ideal. Even though he was in prison at the time he wrote this, he knew the reality of life centered in Christ. The Lord Jesus was the object of Paul's love and devotion, his goal was to know Him, his ambition was to please Him.

"For me to live is Christ," means that He lives in every part of our lives, filling it with His own presence. He is the center and circumference of our lives. With Christ living in us, we have His ears for hearing, His eyes for seeing, His lips for speaking, His feet for walking, His face for reflecting, His life for living. He is real and the reality of His presence radiates from our lives. Is the world getting a glimpse of Him from our lives?

You may say, "I have tried and I seem to fail so often." Remember, God sees your effort and desire, not your achievement. It takes time in His Word and prayer. It takes obedience to His Word. It takes the commitment of your life to the Holy Spirit to develop Christlikeness in you. If we fail, we can confess our weakness then continue on.

When a missionary visited a South Pacific island, he told them about Jesus. One of the natives said, "He used to live here." The missionary began to ask questions and learned that a missionary had lived there a few years before. Although the previous missionary hadn't known their language, from his life radiated the presence of the One with whom he lived in close fellowship.

If someone were to go into your neighborhood, office, or school and talk about Jesus, would people immediately think of you?

DECEMBER 30

Brothers, I do not consider myself yet to have taken hold of it. But one thing I do: Forgetting what is behind and straining toward what is ahead, I press on toward the goal to win the prize for which God has called me heavenward in Christ Jesus (Phil. 3:13–14 NIV).

enjoy watching competitive sports. What a challenge to watch each participant's look of concentration and determination. Every muscle and nerve in their bodies seems to strain as they strive to reach the goal.

Their achievement has come through years of commitment and sacrifice. They strive to do their best, to receive a top medal. What disappointment when they fail! What joy when they win!

Paul compared the Christian life to running a race. The goal to be reached is Jesus Christ: "Looking unto Jesus the author and finisher of our faith" (Heb. 12:2).

Paul had a burning desire to know Christ and to continue to know Him in a more intimate way. He said, "Yes, everything else is worthless when compared with the priceless gain of knowing Christ Jesus my Lord. I have put aside all else, counting it worth less than nothing, in order that I can have Christ" (Phil. 3:8 LB). He wanted to do nothing short of his best to achieve his goal—Jesus Christ.

Paul knew he must strip himself of everything that would hinder him in his race. He would aim straight for his goal, letting nothing distract him. We, too, are in that race. Do we have the same singleness of purpose that Paul had? Are we committed to reaching our goal—Jesus Christ?

How easy it is to live in the past. But Paul said, "Forget it." We must forget our past with its mistakes and failures. We must forget our past victories and achievements. We must press on to the prize God has ready for us at the end of the race.

Paul wrote, "Let us lay aside every weight, and the sin which doth so easily beset us, and let us run with patience the race that is set before us, looking unto Jesus the author and finisher of our faith" (Heb. 12:1–2).

Let this be our commitment. With our eyes on Jesus, may we run the race God has set before us. "I run straight to the goal with purpose in every step" (1 Cor. 9:26 LB).

DECEMBER 31

In the beginning God created the heaven and the earth (Gen. 1:1).

I n one majestic but simple statement Moses, under the inspiration of the Holy Spirit, wrote, "In the beginning God created the heaven and the earth." From this we learn two things: First, God exists. Second, He has always existed. It took One without a beginning to be present *at* the beginning of creation. In the beginning God already was. "Before the mountains were created, before the earth was formed, you are God without beginning or end" (Ps. 90:2 LB).

The Hebrew word for God in this Scripture is *Elohim. El* means strong or mighty, unlimited strength. *Elah* means to bind oneself to an oath, to make a promise. *Elohim* means One of infinite strength and power who is faithful to His Word. In the beginning *Elohim* revealed His strong creative power as the Creator of heaven and earth.

Tomorrow the door of a new year will open to us, a year of new beginnings, new goals, opportunities, challenges, privileges, and lessons for spiritual growth. The secret of experiencing personal peace and fulfillment this next year is knowing that *Elohim,* the Strong One, will accompany us through the year. He will open to us *all* the resources of heaven for *all* our needs. "My help cometh from the LORD, which made heaven and earth" (Ps. 121:2).

God will be with us not only at the beginning of the year but at the beginning of each new day. As we face difficulties, problems, and heartaches, we may feel overwhelmed. Often at such times, we turn to human resources before we turn to God. He wants us to go to Him first, knowing that He has the answer. Our *Elohim,* All-Powerful One, is able to meet every need in His perfect timing. It is as easy for Him to meet the impossible needs as the easy ones.

He who begins this next year with us will accompany us day by day to the end of it. "The eyes of the LORD thy God are always upon it, from the beginning of the year even unto the end of the year" (Deut. 11:12).